The Economics of Cities and Suburbs

William Thomas Bogart

Case Western Reserve University

Prentice Hall, Upper Saddle River, New Jersey 07458

Acquisitions Editor: Leah Jewell
Assistant Editor: Gladys Soto
Editorial Assistant: Kristen Kaiser
Marketing Manager: Patrick Lynch
Production Editor: Judith Leale
Managing Editor: Dee Josephson
Manufacturing Buyer: Diane Peirano
Manufacturing Supervisor: Arnold Vila
Manufacturing Manager: Vincent Scelta
Cover Design: Wendy Alling Judy
Cover Image: SuperStock, Inc.

Copyright © 1998 by Prentice-Hall, Inc.
A Simon & Schuster Company
Upper Saddle River, New Jersey 07458

Library of Congress Cataloging-in-Publication Data

Bogart, William T.
    The economics of cities and suburbs / William T. Bogart.
      p.   cm .
    Includes bibliographical references and index.
    ISBN 0-13-569971-1
    1. Urban economics. 2. Regional economics. 3. Metropolitan areas—Economic aspects—United States. 4. Suburbs—Economic aspects—United States. I. Title.
HT321.B66 1998
330.9173′2—dc21
                                        97-8353
                                        CIP

Prentice-Hall International (UK) Limited, London
Prentice-Hall of Australia Pty. Limited, Sydney
Prentice-Hall Canada, Inc., Toronto
Prentice-Hall Hispanoamericana, S.A., Mexico
Prentice-Hall of India Private Limited, New Delhi
Prentice-Hall of Japan, Inc., Tokyo
Simon & Schuster Asia Pte. Ltd., Singapore
Editora Prentice-Hall do Brasil, Ltda., Rio de Janeiro

Printed in the United States of America

10 9 8 7 6 5 4 3 2 1

For Mary

Contents

Preface   xiii

PART I: INTRODUCTION TO URBAN ECONOMICS

   CHAPTER 1:   What Is a City?   3

      Cities as Small Open Economies   4

      Suburbs as Small Open Economies   6

      Definitions of Cities   7

         Economic Definitions   *7*

         Political Definitions   *10*

      Why Do Cities Grow? Why Do Cities Stop Growing?   10

      Agglomeration Economies of Scale   11

      City Specialization in the United States   14

      The Size Distribution of Cities   17

      Chapter Summary   19

      Excerpt: "Masters of the Metropolis" (Randall Garrett and Lin Carter)   19

      Questions for Review and Discussion   21

      Appendix: Externalities—Problems and Opportunities   21

   CHAPTER 2:   Cities in History   25

      How Urbanized Are People?   26

      Death and Disease   27

      The Industrial Revolution   29

      Urbanization in the United States   32

      How Big Is a Big City?   32

      Chapter Summary   36

      Excerpt: *The Caves of Steel* (Isaac Asimov)   36

      Questions for Review and Discussion   38

CHAPTER 3: Market Areas and Central Place Theory 39

Implications of Space 39

Market Areas 40

The Substitution Effects of Transportation Costs 44

An Application: "Conan the Economist" 44

Strategic Interaction among Firms 45

Equilibrium Location with a Given Price 45
Equilibrium Location with Endogenous Price 46

Central Place Theory 48

Gravity Models and Market Potential 51

Firm Location and Interdependent Products 52

Chapter Summary 52

Excerpt: *The Dispossessed* (Ursula K. Le Guin) 53

Questions for Review and Discussion 54

CHAPTER 4: Location of Economic Activity 55

Location Theory with One Input Source and One Market 55

Application: Central Place Theory 58

Location Choice with Multiple Markets and Input Sources 59

Nontradable Inputs and Firm Location 61

Amenities and Urban Quality: Good Cities and Awful Cities 63

Chapter Summary 67

Excerpt: "Welcome to Slippage City" (Fred Hoyle) 68

Questions for Review and Discussion 69

PART II: AGGREGATE ANALYSIS OF METROPOLITAN AREAS

CHAPTER 5: Intermetropolitan Trade 73

Comparative Advantage 73

Preferences, Relative Size, Transport Costs, and Trading Patterns 76
Trade and Wages 78

Gains from Trade—Partial Equilibrium 80

Gains from Trade—General Equilibrium 82

Increasing Returns to Scale and Gains from Trade 84

Specific Factors of Production 85

Flexible Factor Proportions 88

Chapter Summary 93

Excerpt: "Pilgrimage to Earth" (Robert Sheckley) 93

Questions for Review and Discussion   95

Appendix: Cost Minimization and Utility Maximization   96

Cost Minimization by Firms   *96*
Utility Maximization by Households   *98*

CHAPTER 6:   Factor Abundance and Specialization   101

Trade Theorems—Hecksher-Ohlin and Factor Price Equalization   101

Factor Price Equalization   *102*

Lumpy Countries and Trade   104

Factor Lumpiness and Trade: Linear PPF   *104*
Factor Lumpiness and Trade: Nonlinear PPF   *106*

Trade Barriers and Factor Mobility   108

Nontradables   109

Economic Development—Changes in Specialization and Trade   111

Patterns of Development—The Two-Factor Case   *111*
Application: The Industrial Revolution   *112*

Further Issues: Transport Costs, Imperfect Competition,
    and Public Goods   113

Transport Costs and the Hecksher-Ohlin Model   *113*
Monopolistic Competition and the Hecksher-Ohlin Model   *114*
Public Goods and the Hecksher-Ohlin Model   *115*

Chapter Summary   115

Excerpt: *Ezekiel* 27:3–24   116

Questions for Review and Discussion   117

Appendix: Patterns of Development—The Three-Factor Case   117

CHAPTER 7:   Agglomeration and Metropolitan Growth   122

Urbanization Economies of Scale   122

Spurious Agglomeration and False Comparative Advantage   *124*
Increasing Returns to Scale and Trade: An Example   *126*

Localization Economies of Scale   127

Labor Market Pooling   *128*
Intermediate Inputs   *133*
Technological Spillovers   *134*

Countries as Collections of Cities   136

"Giant Sucking Sounds"—The Effects of NAFTA   *138*

Services versus Manufacturing   140

Chapter Summary   141

Excerpt: "The Death of the City" (Kenneth Boulding)   141

Questions for Review and Discussion   143

CHAPTER 8: Government Policy and Metropolitan Growth   144

Business Investment Decisions   144

Industrial Parks and Firm Relocation   146

Costs and Benefits of Urban Growth   147

Do Taxes Affect Business Location?   155

Taxonomy of Economic Development Policy   158
Infrastructure and Economic Development   160
Income Accounting and Constraints on Government Policy   163
Short-Run and Long-Run Effects of Policy   164

International Trade Policy and Metropolitan Growth   165

National Pollution Regulation and Local Business Activity   166

"Major League" Economic Development Policy   167

Chapter Summary   171

Excerpt: *Babbitt* (Sinclair Lewis)   172

Questions for Review and Discussion   173

PART III: INTRAMETROPOLITAN ANALYSIS

CHAPTER 9:   Clusters and Urban Form: Business Districts, Suburbs, and "Edge Cities"   177

What Do Metropolitan Areas Look Like?   177

Suburbanization: A Historical Perspective   178
When Is a Suburb a "Center"?   181

Monocentric City Model   185

Classical Land Rent   185
Factor Substitution and the Rent Gradient   187
Complications: Building Height and Land Values at the Edge of the City   189
Household Location   190
Comparative Statics: Changing Commuting Costs, Changing Income   193

Intrametropolitan Trade and Polycentric Models   195

Tradables and Nontradables   195
Specialization and Trade among Suburbs   196
An Example: Clustered Manufacturing in Cleveland   197
Edge Cities and Services   199

The Future of Urban Structure   200

The Communications Revolution and Urban Structure   202
Suburb Today, Slum Tomorrow?   203

Chapter Summary   203

Excerpt: *Gladiator-At-Law* (Frederik Pohl and C. M. Kornbluth)   204

Questions for Review and Discussion   205

Appendix: Suburban Development in a Three-Factor Model   206

CHAPTER 10: Land-Use Controls   207

Land-Use Controls: History and Institutional Background   207

Taxonomy of Land-Use Controls   210
Conflict Resolution   211

Zoning as a Trade Restriction   212

Zoning as a Response to Externalities   216

Zoning as a Collective Property Right   218

Why Is Suburban Zoning Too Restrictive?   220

Transactions Costs   220
Wealth Effect of Endowment   221
Illegitimate Preferences   221
Monopoly Control of Development   222

The Provision of Local Public Goods   223

Local Public Goods: The Tiebout Model   223
Zoning, Property Taxes, and the Tiebout Model   224

Zoning and Urban Sprawl   225

Irreversibility and Speculation   225
Agricultural Land   226

Private Zoning   227

Chapter Summary   229

Excerpt: *Utopia* (Thomas More)   230

Questions for Review and Discussion   231

**CHAPTER 11: Intrametropolitan Competition and Economic
Development Policy   232**

How Much Should a Local Government Pay?   232

Competition among Local Governments as a "Prisoner's Dilemma"   237

Central City versus Suburbs   240

Pollution and Location: The Brownfields Problem   240
Inclusionary Zoning   241
Suburban Exploitation of Central Cities   243
Demolition Costs, Downtown, and Edge City   245

Measuring and Alleviating Urban Fiscal Distress   246

Central Cities as Developing Countries   248

Chapter Summary   250

Excerpt: *The Economy of Cities* (Jane Jacobs)   251

Questions for Review and Discussion   252

CHAPTER 12: Urban Labor Markets and Poverty   254

Intrametropolitan Wage Differences   254

Manufacturing versus Services   256
Legal and Illegal Activities   258

Race and Labor Markets: "Spatial Mismatch" Hypothesis   259

Measuring Mismatch   260
Choosing Mismatch   261
The Housing Strategy, the Mobility Strategy, and the Jobs Strategy   261

Concentrated Poverty and the "Underclass"   262

Defining and Measuring the Underclass   263
Do People Move out of Poor Urban Areas?   266

Homelessness   267

How Many Homeless?   268
The Causes of Homelessness   269
Reducing Homelessness: The Role of Shelters   271

Chapter Summary   272

Excerpt: *The Condition of the Working Class in England* (Friedrich Engels)   272

Questions for Review and Discussion   274

CHAPTER 13:   Housing Markets   275

Housing: A Unique Commodity   275

Heterogeneity   276
Application: What Characteristics Are Important to People?   276
Immobility   278
Durability   278
High Expense Relative to Income   278
Large Adjustment Costs   278
Application: Adjustment Costs and the Rent Gradient   279

Hedonic Price Analysis   279

Housing Price Indices   280
Calculating Hedonic Prices   281
Application: House Prices in Brecksville and Broadview Heights, Ohio   283

Demand and Supply in the Housing Market   284

Renting versus Owning   285
Deterioration and Maintenance   288
Demand for Housing   290
Supply of Housing   290
Housing Market Equilibrium   291

Real Estate Agents   293

Filtering   294

Chapter Summary   295

Excerpt: *The Social Contract* (Robert Ardrey)   296

Questions for Review and Discussion   297

CHAPTER 14:   Housing Problems and Policies   299

Federal Housing Policy   299

Home Ownership and the Mortgage Market   300
Supply-Side Housing Policy: Public Housing   301
Demand-Side Housing Policies: Subsidies and Housing Allowances   303

Rent Control   305

Race and Housing Markets   306

Prejudice, Discrimination, and Segregation   307
Racial Segregation in Housing Markets   307
Racial Discrimination in Housing Markets: "Redlining"   309
*Racial Discrimination in Housing Markets: Steering, Price Discrimination,
    and Exclusion   312*
Racial Prejudice in Housing Markets: Neighborhood Tipping   313

Chapter Summary   316

Excerpt: *The Time Machine* (H. G. Wells)   317

Questions for Review and Discussion   318

CHAPTER 15:   Transportation   319

Commuting and Cars   319

Modal Choice   320
Congestion   321
Congestion Tolls   324
Parking   327
Highway Capacity   329
Pollution, Climate Change, and Alternative Fuels   331
Wasteful Commuting   332

Mass Transit   334

Intermodal Cost Comparisons   334
Subsidizing Transit   336
Transit Construction as Economic Development Policy   337

Chapter Summary   339

Excerpt: *City* (Clifford Simak)   339

Questions for Review and Discussion   341

Index   357

Preface

This book is a textbook for courses in urban economics and regional economics at the advanced undergraduate level. It might also be suitable for masters-level courses in urban and regional planning and public policy. The focus of the book is on the economic analysis of intermetropolitan trade and intrametropolitan structure, and it includes extensive analysis of the potential role of local governments in economic development. The analytical prerequisite is a good microeconomics background, including familiarity with indifference curves, isoquants, and factor markets. There is an extensive overlap of the material in the book and the core analytical tools taught in an international trade course, but the synthesis of the factor abundance (Hecksher-Ohlin) explanation of trade and the increasing returns to scale explanation of trade is not yet widespread in trade textbooks, and so this text should provide a challenge even to students familiar with the Hecksher-Ohlin model.

I am fascinated by cities and have had the good fortune to be exposed throughout my life to unique urban areas. I grew up outside of Washington, D.C., which is an interesting city because development in its natural downtown—the Federal Triangle—is restricted; buildings in the city are not permitted to exceed the height of the Capitol dome. I went to college in Houston, which had at least four recognizable "downtowns" as early as 1983, when I first took a course in urban economics. I did my graduate work in New Jersey, a state full of differentiated and specialized suburbs. And I now live in Cleveland, once a quintessential monocentric city but now transformed into a urban area consisting of several business centers, including recognizable "edge cities."

WHY I WROTE THIS BOOK

My goal in this book is to convey the excitement of studying cities with the aid of a set of formal tools for analyzing their economies. Textbooks for urban economics courses have traditionally been built around the monocentric model of a city. This model's essential elements are a downtown where all employment is located and a surrounding residential area, both of which are located on a featureless plain. This description of a city is far less accurate than it was even 15 years ago, as "edge cities" or "suburban downtowns" have assumed an increasingly large role in the employment picture of metropolitan areas. Empirical difficulties, though, are not by themselves sufficient reason for undertaking a different approach to teaching the material. The principal cause for my dissatisfaction with the current standard urban text is in the lack of unity in the treatment of intermetropolitan relations and intrametropolitan relations.

At least since Vernon Henderson's pathbreaking work in the 1970s, mainstream urban economists have been modeling metropolitan areas as small open economies—small countries—that specialize and trade with one another. As we teach in a course in the principles of microeconomics, these small open economies will specialize on the basis of their comparative advantages and trade with one another. These comparative advantages are, in part, based on increasing returns to scale in production, most familiar to urban economists as "agglomeration economies of scale." Mainstream international trade theorists, most notably Paul Krugman, have been emphasizing the role of agglomeration economies in determining patterns of production and trade.

What textbooks have not demonstrated is that intrametropolitan relations can be modeled on this same framework of specialization and trade. For example, bedroom suburbs export labor to downtown and import offices from downtown. They also import the services of shopping centers from commercial suburbs. Modeling the metropolitan area as a set of specialized areas trading with each other leads automatically to a polycentric model of the city. Of course, the monocentric city model remains as a special case. Taking this approach imparts an intellectual unity to the course that is very helpful. We don't develop one set of analytical techniques for intermetropolitan questions and another set for intrametropolitan questions as though there were no connection between the two. This unified approach is what gives the book its title.

Teaching urban economics as a course on trade has the advantage of emphasizing the place of urban economics in mainstream economic analysis. Comparative advantage, increasing returns to scale, and trade are at the heart of microeconomic theory. In fact, the "new" trade theory emphasizing increasing returns to scale has essentially brought international trade theory back to its roots in regional economic analysis. After all, Bertil Ohlin's 1933 book, in which he expounded the Hecksher-Ohlin model of trade, was titled *Interregional and International Trade,* and he argued in the preface that "the theory of international trade is only a part of a general localisation theory, wherein the space aspects of pricing are taken into full account." His book included extensive discussion of the theories of land rent, compensating wage differentials, and location decisions of firms, all firmly ensconced in the study of urban economics today.

The approach I take in this book removes what I consider to be an artificial division between urban economics and regional economics. After all, if urban economics is broad enough to encompass international trade, it should certainly be able to include regional economics. This approach ties in with an earlier tradition in urban economic analysis, exemplified by such authors as Walter Isard, Wilbur Thompson, and Eric Lampard, and is also consistent with the current state of theory.

THE FORMAT OF THE BOOK

I introduce the basic tools of location theory in the first part of the book (chapters 1 through 4), including agglomeration economies of scale, the principle of median location, central place theory, and the notion of resource-oriented versus market-oriented firms. Chapter 1 develops the idea of a city as a small open economy and the notion of agglomeration economies of scale; it also provides some basic terminology and facts about cities. Chapter 2 examines cities from a historical perspective, focusing on the explosive growth in the extent of urbanization and the size of cities that followed the Industrial Revolution. Chapter 3 provides a formal model of central place theory and explores the implications of including space in economic theory. Chapter 4 gives an overview of location theory that illustrates how central place theory is a special case (in that it includes only market-oriented firms and not input-oriented firms or production cost-oriented firms) of a more general theory.

In the second part of the book (chapters 5 through 8), I develop the Hecksher-Ohlin model as a model of factor-oriented firms. I also introduce models of agglomeration and market-oriented firms. This synthesis of trade theory and urban economic theory is the analytical heart of the book. Chapter 5 develops a simple general equilibrium model of an open economy and introduces the economic analysis of trade. Chapter 6 applies this model to explain patterns of urban production, trade, and development. The differences among the cities discussed in chapter 6 are all due to differential factor endowments. Here is a model of factor-oriented firms and is, therefore, a useful complement to the theory of market-oriented firms developed in chapter 3. Chapter 7 synthesizes central place theory and factor abundance trade theory, as well as formally models explanations for urban growth based on urbanization economies of scale ("big is good") and localization economies of scale ("specialized is good"). Chapter 8 uses the analytical framework developed to this point to investigate the potential role of government policy in metropolitan economic development.

The third part of the book extends the model of intermetropolitan trade to the analysis of intrametropolitan production and trade. Chapter 9 shows how a small open economy model can be used to analyze industrial clusters, commercial districts, and residential areas. The monocentric city model is developed in detail, but as a special case of this general approach. Chapter 10 examines zoning, arguably the most important exercise of local government power to determine the development of a metropolitan area. Chapter 11 considers the general role of local government policy in affecting the growth of the local economy, especially with regard to the effect of tax abatement on business location. Chapter 12 examines selected topics in urban labor markets, including the issue of concentrated poverty. Chapter 13 considers in some detail the market for housing, a unique commodity that accounts for approximately 50 percent of the land use in a typical metropolitan area. In chapter 14 I turn to selected policy issues in housing markets, with a special focus on the effects of racial prejudice and racial discrimination on the pattern of household location in a city. Chapter 15 turns to the question of transportation, especially commuters' modal choices and decisions. It concludes with an investigation of the way in which urban public transit can serve as a tool for economic development.

Some reviewers have suggested inserting chapter 15 between chapters 4 and 5. Their idea, of course, is that transportation is a vital part of trade. Aside from some specific references in chapter 15 to the monocentric city model, there is no reason that such a change in order would cause any trouble for the students. I prefer the order in the book because the material in chapter 15 is more specific and policy oriented than the material in the first six chapters. However, I have yet to teach a course using someone else's textbook without changing the order in which some material is presented, so I expect others who use my textbook to do the same.

In order to illustrate the application of economic concepts in a broader setting than that of examples and problems invented by the author, I have included excerpts from literary works—short stories, essays, novels, and even the Bible—at the ends of the chapters. A vital part of the learning process is taking the ideas learned in one situation and testing them in other situations in order to learn how useful the ideas are. These interludes illustrate and challenge important economic concepts presented in this book. I hope they will stimulate in the reader the same excitement I feel about this subject.

ACKNOWLEDGMENTS

My biggest debt of gratitude is to my wife, Mary, to whom this book is dedicated. She too is a teacher, and I have learned a lot from her.

I wouldn't have become a professor without the positive influence and example of the faculty at Rice University. Tim Cooke was the professor who introduced me to the study of cities, and I owe my initial interest in the field to his influence. I am grateful to the faculty of the economics department at Princeton University for the opportunities they gave me to learn a lot during my time as a graduate student. David Bradford, my dissertation advisor, led me to the analysis of suburbs as small open economies. Mike Fogarty, director of the Center for Regional Economic Issues at Case Western Reserve University, has always emphasized the importance of developing a critical mass of activity and has worked to develop one here in Cleveland.

Michael Harding, Jennifer Redman, and Bill Ferry provided research assistance for the book.

My students in Econ 386 during the spring semester of 1995 deserve special thanks for their patience. While deciding whether to write this book, I taught the course as if I had already written it. The enthusiasm of the students about the approach and material helped me decide to go on and write the book. I'd also like to thank the students enrolled in Econ 386 during the spring semester of 1996, who participated in the experiment of using the first draft of the book and who provided helpful feedback.

The following people reviewed all or part of the book at various stages and provided many useful suggestions. Marlon Boarnet (University of California, Irvine), Thomas Fullerton, Jr. (University of Texas, El Paso), Gaspar Garofalo (University of Akron), Abbas Grammy (California State University, Bakersfield), Simon Hakim (Temple University), Scott Houser (California State University, Fresno), Thomas Hyclak (Lehigh University), Arthur Kartmann (San Diego State University), Thomas Nechyba (Stanford University), James O'Toole (Chico State University), J. M. Pogodzinski (San Jose State University), Robert Singleton (Loyola Marymount University), Dianne Stehman (Northeast Illinois University), Timothy Sullivan (Towson State University), and Robert Wassmer (California State University, Sacramento).

I thank Leah Jewell, Judy Leale, and Kristen Kaiser at Prentice-Hall for their contributions. Marianne Hutchinson and the team at Pine Tree Composition did a great job of copyediting the manuscript and preparing it for publication.

It is a pleasure to acknowledge the many people who have helped me along the way. I also recognize that there are undoubtedly others whom I have neglected to mention and who, I hope, will forgive this lapse as reflecting upon my memory rather than their contribution. It would be wrong, though, to credit anyone but me for any mistakes of fact or interpretation in the book.

William T. Bogart

PART

I

Introduction to Urban Economics

CHAPTER

What Is a City?

1

A city is a spatial concentration of a large number of people. The fundamental characteristic of a city is its density. This density includes two related dimensions. The first, and the one that defines an urban area, is population density. The second, and the aspect we will be most concerned with, is density of economic activity.

To apprehend the extent of urban density, consider the following statistics. The population density for the entire United States in 1992 was 70 people per square mile. By contrast, the most densely populated city in the United States, New York, had a population density in 1992 of 23,671 people per square mile. The city of Cleveland, where I wrote this book, had a density of 6,526 people per square mile in 1992, even though the city's population has declined over the past 40 years. By comparison, the most densely settled European country, the Netherlands, had a population density of 958 people per square mile in 1990. Even a comparatively dispersed U.S. city—for example, Houston—has a population density of over 3,000 people per square mile, three times the density of the Netherlands.

When many people live in close contact with one another, certain results are inevitable. One result is that a city contains a greater diversity of people than is found outside its boundaries. Another is that the intensity and frequency of interactions among people are greater than would be found elsewhere. The diversity to be found in a city is not only the result of intrinsic differences among individuals, but is also the result of the added opportunities to specialize afforded by the large urban market. The intensity of interactions includes possibilities for people to affect each other outside of a formal market—in other words, externalities. Look no further than the traffic jam you were in this morning or the noise from the party down the hall in your dorm to see an externality that resulted from crowding people together. The problems (and opportunities) presented by externalities will be a recurring theme in the book, and the formal analysis of externalities is reviewed in an appendix to this chapter. The fundamental economic explanation of cities is the positive externalities that result when economic activities are located close together. The main limit to urban growth, in turn, are the negative externalities that arise from this dense pattern of activity.

CITIES AS SMALL OPEN ECONOMIES

> The distinctive feature of the great modern city is its unique pattern of relations to the world within which it is situated. . . . [T]he modern city is yet inextricably linked to, dependent upon, the society outside it; and growth in size has increased rather than diminished the force of that dependence.
>
> —OSCAR HANDLIN

The most useful way to think about cities in economic terms is as *small open economies.* This bit of jargon requires some explanation. They are "small" in the sense that they take market prices as given, and their actions do not affect market prices. They are "open" because they are not completely self-sufficient, preferring instead to trade goods and services with other open economies. This notion will be the unifying concept behind the analysis in this book. We will first consider the relations among metropolitan areas in this light. We will then move on to consider the relations among the parts of a metropolitan area using this same theoretical framework. Let us consider some data on metropolitan areas to further explore this idea of cities as small countries.

For most economic purposes, it is more useful to consider the United States as a collection of small open economies than to think of the United States as a single economy. In other words, the United States is a common market with a common currency. The countries of Europe are attempting to create the same sort of economic integration by combining their various national economies. What are the analogs to national economies within the United States? You guessed it. Cities. Lest this be misconstrued as hubris on behalf of my chosen field of study, consider the following example.

Suppose the Cleveland metropolitan area were to secede from the United States to form its own country. How big would that country be? How would it compare to better-known countries? The answer may surprise you. The Cleveland metropolitan area (CMSA—see the definition later in the chapter) in 1990 had a population of 2.86 million and a GNP of $39.4 billion (GNP is estimated as total personal income). This makes it comparable to Ireland in size of population and labor force but larger in GNP. That is to say, Cleveland has a larger economy than Ireland. (See Table 1.1 for a detailed comparison.) Cleveland is more open than the United States, as about 33 percent of its GNP is estimated to be imports and exports, as opposed to roughly 13 percent for the entire United States.

How were these calculations made? In general, trade is simply the difference between local production and local consumption. So in theory all we need to do is compare local production and local consumption in order to identify imports and exports (local consumption exceeds local production for imports, and the opposite is true for

TABLE 1.1   Cities and Countries

1990 Data	Cleveland	Ireland	San Francisco	Switzerland	Chicago	Austria
Population (million)	2.86	3.52	6.25	6.67	8.07	7.72
GNP (US$) (billion)	39.4	39.3	119.0	236.1	128.4	157.3
Labor force (million)	1.40	1.13	3.39	3.56	4.30	2.93
Exports (% of GNP)	33.8	81.3	18.6	26.9	28.6	26.1
Imports (% of GNP)	33.2	55.2	17.7	29.3	27.8	29.7
Land area (km^2)	7,569	68,890	19,189	39,770	14,676	82,730

Source: Population and income (GNP) of U.S. cities from Rand McNally 1992 *Commercial Atlas and Marketing Guide;* labor force data for U.S. cities from *State and Metropolitan Area Data Book 1991;* import and export figures for U.S. cities calculated from *City and County Data Book* (http://www.lib.virginia.edu/socsci/reis/reis.html); GNP data for countries from *Europa World Yearbook 1993;* import and export data for countries from European marketing data; land areas for countries from *CIA World Fact Book 1994* (http://www.ic.gov/).

exports). Unfortunately, detailed data about consumption and production are difficult—well, impossible—to obtain for U.S. metropolitan areas. Therefore, we must use some assumptions to compute exports and imports from the available data.[1]

Who does the country of Cleveland trade with? Other countries such as Detroit, Louisville, Toronto, Paris, Mexico City, and Jakarta. Some of these countries are within the boundaries of the United States, so trade is free and there are no currency exchange issues. Others of these countries are outside the U.S. common market.

Table 1.1 compares two other metropolitan areas in the United States, Chicago and San Francisco, with two other European countries, Austria and Switzerland. The notion that metropolitan areas are comparable to countries is clearly borne out by the evidence. The main difference is in the land areas, with the European countries between two and nine times larger than their U.S. counterparts. This comparison serves to emphasize the dense nature of the economic activity within cities.

The figures in Table 1.1 compare countries to cities that are not even among the largest in the world. The latter were chosen in order to make clear the broad applicability of the analysis. The major cities in the world have an even greater claim to consideration as countries for economic purposes. Table 1.2 shows the population of each of the world's 20 largest cities in 1991 along with its population density and projected population in 2000. Although population alone does not imply high income, the size

---

[1]Exports for the cities are estimated using industry-level aggregates and distinguish between industries that produce primarily goods and services for local consumption and industries that produce for sale to people in other cities (Isserman, 1980, calls this the "assumption method"). Imports are estimated using income accounting identities. Let Y represent income, C consumption, $(X - M)$ net exports, S savings, I investment, T taxes, and G government spending. As you know from your principles of economics courses, the identity describing income can be written in two ways: $Y = C + I + G + (X - M)$ or $Y = C + S + T$. Combining these expressions yields a formula for net exports as a function of net savings and the government budget surplus, $(X - M) = (S - I) + (T - G)$. For the purposes of the table, it was assumed that net savings equals zero. There is some evidence of this at the level of national economies (Feldstein and Horioka 1980), but no one has yet studied this issue at the metropolitan area level, so the results in Table 1.1 must be considered rough estimates.

TABLE 1.2 The 20 Largest Metropolitan Areas in the World, 1991

City and Country	1991 Population (Thousands)	Population Density (People per mi²)	2000 Population Projection (Thousands)
Tokyo-Yokohama, Japan	27,245	25,019	29,971
Mexico City, Mexico	20,899	40,037	27,872
Sao Paulo, Brazil	18,701	41,466	25,354
Seoul, South Korea	16,792	49,101	21,976
New York, U.S.	14,625	11,480	14,648
Osaka-Kobe-Kyoto, Japan	13,872	28,025	14,287
Bombay, India	12,101	127,461	15,357
Calcutta, India	11,898	56,927	14,088
Rio de Janeiro, Brazil	11,688	44,952	14,169
Buenos Aires, Argentina	11,657	21,790	12,911
Moscow, Russia	10,446	27,562	11,121
Manila, Philippines	10,156	54,024	12,846
Los Angeles, U.S.	10,130	9,126	10,714
Cairo, Egypt	10,099	97,106	12,512
Jakarta, Indonesia	9,882	130,026	12,804
Teheran, Iran	9,779	87,312	14,251
London, U.K.	9,115	10,429	8,574
Delhi, India	8,778	63,612	11,849
Paris, France	8,720	20,185	8,803
Karachi, Pakistan	8,014	42,179	11,299

Source: U.S. Bureau of the Census, U.S. Department of Commerce.

of the economy associated with a major city is in no doubt. Each of these cities has a population greater than that of Austria, with the largest having a population about equal to that of Canada.

SUBURBS AS SMALL OPEN ECONOMIES

Just as the United States can be thought of as a common market composed of many "countries" known as metropolitan areas, so too each metropolitan area can be characterized as a conglomerate of smaller open economies that specialize and trade with one another. The dominant model of the urban economy for many years was the so-called *monocentric city* model, in which all employment was assumed to be concentrated in the downtown with the remainder of the land devoted to housing. More recently, *polycentric city* models have flourished, reflecting the changes in urban structure popularly chronicled by Joel Garreau (1991). Polycentric city models allow for a variety of employment centers throughout a metropolitan area, including the historic downtown but also including suburban malls, office parks, and manufacturing centers. What these models all have in common is the prediction that different parts of the metropolitan area will specialize in certain activities and trade with other parts of the metropolitan area for other activities. For example, in a monocentric city model, the downtown is exporting jobs to the surrounding residential areas in exchange for housing provided by the residential areas. The polycentric models allow for an even richer set of exchanges, but again the basic idea is one of specialization and trade by small open economies. Some of these "suburbs" are so large and specialized in providing employment as to be indistinguishable from any reasonable definition of a "downtown." Thus, the analytical framework we develop for examining the economy of a metropolitan area as a whole will also be useful in analyzing the economic activity within a given metropolitan area. The only difference will be the scale of the economy and the precise set of goods and services in which areas specialize.

DEFINITIONS OF CITIES

We will be talking about cities, metropolitan areas, and other concepts for the remainder of the book. It is important to familiarize you with some of the ways that cities are defined for practical purposes. There are two main ways of defining a city. The first is economic and the second is political.

Economic Definitions

The U.S. Census Bureau has several statistical definitions, all of which emphasize the relative population density of a geographical region. An *urban place* is defined as a geographical region with at least 2,500 inhabitants in a relatively small area. An *urbanized area* is defined as an area with a total population of at least 50,000 consisting of at least one large central city and a surrounding area with a population density greater than 1,000 people per square mile. The Census Bureau defines the urban population as all people living in urbanized areas and also people living in urban places outside of urbanized areas. A *metropolitan statistical area (MSA)* is defined as an area containing a large population nucleus and nearby areas that are economically integrated as measured by commuting flows and population density. To put it simply, an MSA is a labor market. The nucleus is either a central city of at least 50,000 people or an urbanized area, and the nearby areas are defined as surrounding counties. Metropolitan statistical areas that are close neighbors and whose combined populations exceed one million may be collectively considered a *consolidated metropolitan statistical area (CMSA)* if they are also economically integrated. The metropolitan areas composing the CMSA are known as *primary metropolitan statistical areas (PMSAs).*

The Cleveland CMSA is shown in relation to the state of Ohio and also in relation to its components in the maps in Figure 1.1. The CMSA consists of two PMSAs: Cleveland-Lorain-Elyria, consisting of six counties; and Akron, consisting of two counties. The central cities of the PMSAs are shown. The urbanized area is also illustrated in Figure 1.2, and it should be noted that even within the metropolitan area there are large areas that are not considered urban.

The United States is predominantly urban. In 1990, 77.5 percent of the population lived in MSAs and CMSAs, 63.6 percent of the population lived in urbanized areas, and 77.2 percent of the population lived in urbanized areas plus urban places outside of urbanized areas. Although the population of the United States is over-

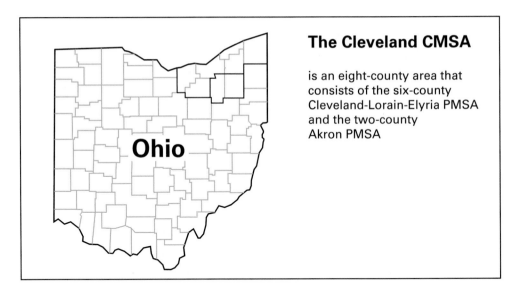

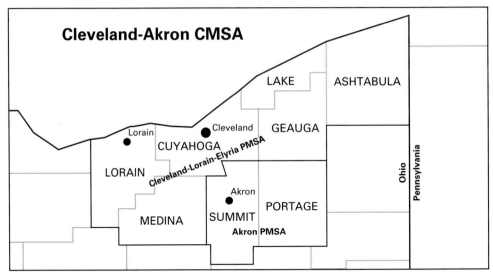

FIGURE 1.1 The Cleveland CMSA.

whelmingly urban, land use is overwhelmingly rural; only about 2 percent of the land in the 48 contiguous states is in urbanized areas and urban places, while 25 percent of the land is devoted to crops (Fischel 1985, Table 1, p. 3).

The definition of "edge city," introduced by Joel Garreau (1991, p. 6), focuses on the density of economic activity. His functional criteria for a place to be an edge city include a minimum amount of retail space (600,000 square feet) and office space (5,000,000 square feet), a larger number of jobs than residents, and a perception by people that the place is a regional destination for jobs, shopping, and entertainment. As he details in his book, these places outside the previous downtowns are now home to much of American business, and any student of cities does well to appreciate this

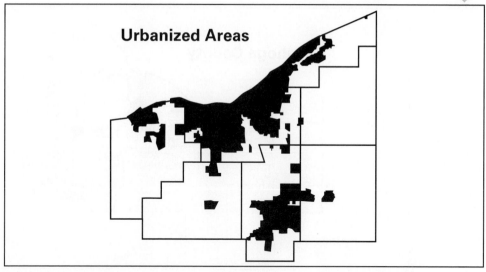

FIGURE 1.2 Urbanized Areas in Cleveland-Akron CMSA.

aspect of modern cities. More recently, Garreau compiled a list of the 40 largest job centers in the United States. Of the 40, only 22 were in downtown areas, whereas the other 18 were edge cities. The largest edge city, South Coast Metroplex/Irvine in southern California, had a total employment of 239,965, which ranked it ninth on the list, just ahead of downtown Dallas. The smallest of the 40, the Princeton/Route 1 edge city in New Jersey, had an employment of 98,484, larger than that in downtown Pittsburgh (Garreau 1994).

The Census Bureau changed its definition of a central city in a metropolitan area in 1983. Prior to 1983, the largest city was designated as the central city, and up to two additional cities could be designated as central cities if their population was at least one-third that of the largest city. The restriction on the number and the arbitrary population limit led to an undercount of the central cities within metropolitan areas. As edge cities have proliferated, without this change this problem would have gotten worse. The new definition of a central city includes (1) all cities with populations of at least 250,000 or at least 100,000 people working within the city limits, (2) all cities with populations of at least 25,000 that have employment/residence ratios of at least 0.75 and in which at least 60 percent of the resident employees work in the city, and (3) cities with populations between 15,000 and 25,000 that are at least one-third the size of the largest central city and that meet the other criteria for cities with populations of at least 25,000. Ottensmann (1996) details the increase in measured central city population as a result of this definitional change. For the MSAs that existed in both 1980 and 1990, for example, the total number of central cities increased from 423 to 509. This increase becomes even more extreme when attention is focused on the largest MSAs. The 50 largest MSAs in 1990 had a total of 203 central cities, 80 of which were newly identified by the change in definition. These new central cities accounted for 10 percent of the total central city population in these 50 MSAs, although 11 of the MSAs did not have any new central cities. The CMSAs with the largest number of new central cities are Chicago-Gary–Lake County with seven and Boston-Lawrence-

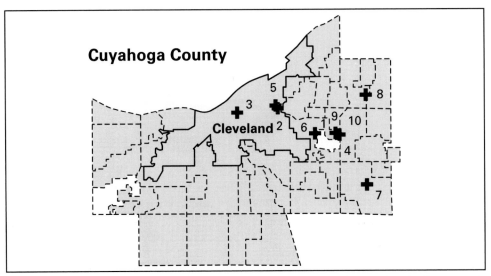

Note: The numbered crosses indicate the location of the ten busiest intersections in the county in 1995. See chapter 9, Table 9.2.

FIGURE 1.3 Political Boundaries in Cuyahoga County.

Salem with six, while the St. Louis MSA has five new central cities. The metropolitan areas where the new central cities represented at least 10 percent of the population were Phoenix MSA with 26.4 percent, Kansas City MSA with 16.1 percent, Dallas–Fort Worth CMSA with 12.4 percent, Miami–Fort Lauderdale CMSA with 11.1 percent, and Oklahoma City MSA with 11.1 percent.

Political Definitions

The second way of defining a city is political. A *municipality* is an area for which a municipal corporation provides local government services. Types of municipalities include cities, villages, townships, and boroughs. The exact rules under which municipalities form and the powers available to various types of municipality vary greatly from state to state. Although political boundaries are important, they are not the most natural way to demarcate cities for economic analysis. Unfortunately, most of the data collected on metropolitan areas use the political boundaries, so we will be constrained to use those figures much of the time. Figure 1.3 illustrates the political boundaries of the city of Cleveland and other municipalities in Cuyahoga County, Ohio.

WHY DO CITIES GROW? WHY DO CITIES STOP GROWING?

The fundamental necessity for urban growth is found in rural areas. The extent of urbanization is limited by the food surplus available to the city. The world has been as urbanized as the level of agriculture made possible throughout recorded history. The difference between current levels of urbanization and historical levels is due to the massive improvements in agricultural productivity and transportation technology aris-ing from and contributing to the Industrial Revolution.

The economic reason for the growth of cities is the existence of economies of scale, or average cost that decreases as production increases. These economies of scale can take several forms within cities. One area of increasing returns to scale is in transportation, where the fixed costs of setting up a transport system can be spread over a large number of users. Similarly, the fixed costs of creating a "market"—a spa-tial nexus for exchanging goods—can be spread over many users. In fact, the require-ment for a place to exchange goods is inexorably linked to the transportation network required to transport the goods to and from the market. Another area of increasing returns is in complementarities in production among various goods—for example, in relations among suppliers of specialized inputs. Another possibility is risk-sharing among industries whose fortunes are not perfectly correlated with each other. Finally, creativity and entrepreneurship can flourish in cities because of the intense and fre-quent interactions among their inhabitants.

One of the most important economic concepts is *comparative advantage.* A small open economy, such as a city, country, firm, or person, may specialize in the commodity that it produces at relatively lower opportunity cost than its trading part-ners. The existence of increasing returns to scale provides a rationale and an impetus for specialization and, therefore, for mutually beneficial trade. Differences in factor endowments among cities also create opportunities for mutually beneficial trade. As economic theory would predict, cities are quite specialized. Some evidence for city specialization in the United States is presented later in this chapter.

We will also consider specialization of areas within cities. For example, the down-towns of most cities have a high concentration of offices, often providing business ser-vices, while some suburbs contain housing targeted exclusively at one specific market niche. As in a metropolitan area as a whole, the desire to take advantage of increasing returns to scale and differential factor endowments creates opportunities for special-ization and trade among the regions within a metropolitan area. Because trade in some goods and services is infeasible among metropolitan areas yet feasible within a metro-politan area, the extent of specialization and the types of commodity will be different from the pattern of specialization at the metropolitan area level in interesting ways.

The limits to the growth of cities are inherent in the causes of urban growth. One limit is the extent of the market for the products the city exports. Another limit is the possible depletion of comparative advantage, because the opportunity cost of pro-ducing a product increases with larger-scale production. A third limit is the depletion of the available resources, possibly including the food surplus from agricultural areas. A final limit is congestion and other negative externalities caused by the intense human interaction implied by high population density. These negative externalities can offset the positive externalities that result from dense settlement.

AGGLOMERATION ECONOMIES OF SCALE

When the average cost of production falls as a result of the increased total output of a product, we speak of the presence of *economies of scale.* These cost savings can be *in-ternal,* that is, relating to the size of a given economic unit (firm, industry, region), or *external,* relating to the size of a group of economic units (firms in an industry, industries in a region, and so on). Economies of scale that are internal to a firm will play an important role in our analysis of the location decisions of firms, because the presence of large internal economies of scale will lead a firm to want to concentrate production at one or a few locations. If it sells its product at many locations, then the firm will be transporting its product, so it must choose where to locate relative to its markets. If it is also buying inputs from many locations, then the firm will be transporting the inputs, so it must choose where to locate relative to its sources of inputs. Much of the formal analysis in the book considers how a firm can systematically make this decision and what the implications are of its profit-maximizing decisions. Internal economies of scale are one explanation for the clustering of activity, as people move close to a large production site, which leads in turn to the relatively higher density of activity that defines a city.

Economies of scale external to a firm that are the result of spatial proximity are referred to as agglomeration economies of scale. Agglomeration economies of scale, while external to a firm, are internal to a region. The existence of agglomeration economies is fundamental to the economic explanation of urban growth. Urban economists distinguish two types of agglomeration economies: *localization economies of scale,* in which firms benefit from being near other related firms; and *urbanization economies of scale,* in which firms benefit from being located in a large city, even though the activities of those firms may be unrelated. It should never be forgotten, though, that clustering of activity also leads to congestion and other negative externalities. The interplay between advantages and disadvantages of clustering generates many of the interesting issues in urban economics. At the margin, the gains in cost savings from clustering should just equal the losses from increased congestion. The marginal benefits of clustering must exceed the marginal costs to at least some degree or else we would never observe the formation of cities. Much of the theoretical analysis in chapters 3 through 7 is concerned with examining the sources of agglomeration economies of scale, but it will be useful to introduce some of the main conclusions now.

It is important to understand that the cost savings resulting from agglomeration economies of scale benefit not only the firm involved but society as a whole, because the increase in productivity is not caused by a decrease in production elsewhere. This statement must be qualified somewhat due to the presence of agglomeration diseconomies of scale such as pollution and congestion, but the notion that clustering of economic activity is beneficial is quite well founded.

There are three sources of localization economies of scale. The first source is the benefit of labor pooling, including access to specialized labor skills for firms and access to a variety of employment opportunities for workers. The second source is the benefit from developing economies of scale in intermediate inputs for a product; this is the logic behind the development of industrial complexes. The third source is the greater ease of communication made possible by proximity to competitors, suppliers, and clients, including the ability to pass along innovations quickly.

There are three sources of urbanization economies of scale. The first is the access to a larger market, which reduces the need to transport products in order to sell them. The second is the easy access to the wide variety of specialized services that are available in larger cities but not necessarily in smaller cities. The third is the potential for cross-industry spillovers of knowledge and technology.

Economists have devoted a great deal of attention to identifying whether localization or urbanization economies are dominant in generating urban growth. Henderson (1988, chapter 5) summarizes the evidence. He finds that economies of scale in manufacturing are primarily localization. Further, he finds that industries with large localization economies of scale are ones in which cities tend to specialize. Given the negative externalities (see the appendix to this chapter for a discussion of externalities) that arise as a result of increasing urban size, this finding is not surprising. If an industry is going to cluster, it will inevitably create negative externalities. The only way for clustering to be a sustainable outcome is for the clustering to create positive spillovers that offset the negative externalities.

Some metropolitan areas have distinct areas of specialization located in close proximity. This would seem to favor the explanation that urban growth is due to urbanization economies. However, Henderson finds that different industries locate close to each other primarily because they are economizing on transport costs (for example, proximity to a scarce natural resource) rather than because of any productivity enhancement due solely to increased metropolitan size.

Although the dominant explanation for the growth of urban areas based on manufacturing is, therefore, one of localization economies of scale and specialization, we will also develop models that rely on urbanization economies of scale. This is not merely because of stubbornness and intellectual inertia but reflects the fact that manufacturing alone does not completely account for the urban economy. For example, some goods and services cannot be traded (such as climate and other amenities as well as local public schools, public safety, and other services), so that cities are prevented from completely specializing. Table 1.3 reports that even the most "specialized" of manufacturing cities (Flint, Michigan) has only 36 percent of its labor force in the industry that is the city's specialty (automobiles), and none of the other cities considered has more than 29 percent of its labor force in its specialty. Further, there are also nonmanufacturing industries whose location will need to be explained and modeled. Access to a larger market can be a draw to some firms because of the large and varied customer base that is available. It is this type of access that is definitional for urbanization economies of scale.

This focus on localization versus urbanization economies has also been restricted to the situation at a particular point in time; in other words, it is a static view. One of the advantages of spatial proximity, though, is immediate access to changes as they occur. This advantage can reinforce a city's initial cost advantage, transforming a small difference among cities at a given point in time into a large difference in the future. Henderson, Kuncoro, and Turner (1995) present evidence on U.S. cities from 1970 to 1987 consistent with this theory and emphasizing city specialization. Glaeser, Kallal, Scheinkman, and Schliefer (1992) present evidence that dynamic advantages accrue to cities that are large, regardless of the extent of specialization in the city. So there is evidence for both localization and urbanization economies in a dynamic as well as a static sense. A related implication is that it may be possible for a city to cause large changes in its future prospects with only small changes in its current conditions.

One interesting question is how to measure the size of a city for economic purposes. A natural approach is to consider population, employment, or other indicator of urban size. Clearly, the absolute levels of population and employment are important, but these can depend crucially on whether two or more near neighbors are con-

TABLE 1.3 Manufacturing Specialization of Metropolitan Areas

Industry	Metropolitan Area	Percent of Labor Force in the Industry
Auto	Flint, MI	36
	Detroit, MI	17
	Kenosha, WI	16
	Muncie, IN	13
Steel	Steubenville-Weirton, OH-WV	29
	Gary-Hammond-East Chicago, IN	26
	Johnstown, PA	13
	Gadsden, AL	11
	Pueblo, CO	8
Textiles	Greenville, NC	18
	Chattanooga, TN-GA	11
	Augusta, GA	10
Aircraft	Wichita, KS	14
	Fort Worth, TX	13
	Hartford, CT	11
	Seattle-Everett, WA	10
Petrochemicals	Beaumont-Port Arthur-Orange, TX	18
	Lake Charles, LA	12
	Galveston-Texas City, TX	11
	Baton Rouge, LA	10

Source: Henderson, 1988, Table 1.2, p. 14.

sidered as separate entities or a single city. The cases of Baltimore and Washington, D.C., or of San Francisco and Oakland are good examples. An alternative approach is to focus on density of activity. After all, cities are defined as places of dense activity, and perhaps the advantages (and disadvantages) of urban location are related more to the density of an area than to its size. Ciccone and Hall (1996) directly examine this question and find evidence that density is more important than size in determining productivity advantages. They find that the ten densest states have an average productivity per worker of $38,782 (in 1988 dollars) while the ten least-dense states have an average productivity of only $31,578—about a 25 percent difference. Of course, state density is not the same as metropolitan area density, as they realized, so they used a combination of county-level density data and state-level output data when calculating their productivity figures. Because MSAs are composed of counties, their approach is really one that focuses on metropolitan areas rather than states.

CITY SPECIALIZATION IN THE UNITED STATES

Cities differ from one another in their patterns of production. Henderson (1988, chapter 1) estimates that 50 to 60 percent of the labor force is required to produce local "nontradable" services. Thus, even an extremely specialized city could have at most

40 percent of its labor force producing its export good. There is evidence of extensive specialization in U.S. cities. Even the largest cities lack significant concentrations of employment in substantial areas, so that they are not completely self-sufficient, although most large cities have at least a small amount of employment in every industry. For example, there were 210 metropolitan areas (SMSAs) in the United States in 1970 with populations between 50,000 and 1 million. Fully 191 of these metropolitan areas had people employed in the blast-furnace and steel mill industry, but only 23 had more than 2,000 people employed in this industry. In the same year, only 7 of the 33 metropolitan areas with a population greater than 1 million had at least 10,000 people employed in the blast-furnace and steel mill industry. Other industries are illustrated in Table 1.4 and show a similar pattern.

The distribution of employment in the United States has shifted during the 1900s. Table 1.5 illustrates this shift using data from 1950 and 1990 on the fraction of the workforce employed in each of the broad industry groups defined by the Census Bureau. The largest decrease is in the percent employed in agriculture, while mining, transportation, communication, public utilities, manufacturing, and personal services also decreased as a fraction of the total employment. The industries that increased as a fraction of the workforce were concentrated in the services, the largest increase occurring in the category of professional and related services. Because so much of the country is urban, these overall totals are also a reasonable description of the aggregate shift in employment in the metropolitan areas of the country. The tendency of metropolitan areas to specialize means that each city's experience will have been slightly different over this time period. An interesting exercise is to calculate the employment mix in a city of your choice and examine the changes in this mix over time.

An interesting question is whether cities' specialization in services parallels the specialization in manufacturing identified by Henderson. Noyelle and Stanback (1984) consider the impact of the shift towards services on the production patterns and metropolitan structure in the United States. They categorize the 140 largest metropolitan areas in 1976 as belonging to one of several types, depending on their production of various goods and services. They identify four major groups of cities: diversified service (major regional and national centers with a focus on headquarters, producer services, and distribution), specialized service (headquarters for particular

TABLE 1.4 Metropolitan Area Employment in Selected Industries: 1970

Industry	210 SMSAs with Population Less than 1 Million			33 SMSAs with Population Greater than 1 Million
	Industry Employment			**Industry Employment**
	<250	**2000–5000**	**>5000**	**>10,000**
Blast furnace and steel mill	168	7	16	7
Farm machinery and equipment	185	3	3	0
Aircraft and parts	143	12	13	11
Industrial chemicals	153	4	3	1
Motor vehicles and equipment	130	16	25	13

Source: Henderson, 1988, Table 1.3, p. 16.

TABLE 1.5   United States Employment by Industry Group, 1950 and 1990

Industry Group	Percent of Employment in 1950	Percent of Employment in 1990
Agriculture, forestry, and fisheries	12.5	2.8
Mining	1.6	0.7
Construction	6.1	6.6
Manufacturing	26.0	18.6
Transportation, communication, and utilities	7.9	7.5
Wholesale and retail trade	18.6	22.3
Finance, insurance, and real estate	3.4	7.3
Business and repair services	2.3	5.1
Personal services	6.1	3.3
Entertainment, recreation	0.9	1.5
Professional and related services	8.6	24.5
Public administration	4.5	5.0
Not reported	1.5	—

Source: U.S. Bureau of the Census, *Census of Population.*

industries, government and nonprofit organizations, education), production (manufacturing, military/industrial, mining), and consumer-oriented (resort/retirement, residential). The number of cities in each group is shown in Table 1.6.

If cities specialize in service production, it must be the case that the services can be exported and imported. Knight (1973) finds that aggregate intermetropolitan trade actually decreased between 1940 and 1960 because of an increase in the fraction of the economy accounted for by services, which he claims were more difficult to trade. Noyelle and Stanback (1984) find that the specialization in services by metropolitan

TABLE 1.6   Specialization in the Service Economy: 140 MSAs in 1976

MSA Specialization	Number of MSAs	Representative Metropolitan Areas
Diversified service	39	New York, Kansas City, Salt Lake City, San Francisco
Specialized service		
Functional nodal	24	Detroit, Dayton, Allentown
Government/Nonprofit	15	Washington, DC, Albany, Sacramento
Education	5	New Haven, South Bend, Ann Arbor
Production		
Manufacturing	25	Buffalo, Flint, Chattanooga, Beaumont
Military/Industrial	13	San Diego, San Antonio, Newport News
Mining	7	Duluth, Charleston (WV)
Consumer-oriented		
Residential	3	Nassau, Anaheim, Long Branch
Resort retirement	9	Tampa, Honolulu, Las Vegas

Source: Noyelle and Stanback (1984, Tables 4.1 and 4.2).

areas mainly represents producer services rather than consumer services. This echoes Garreau (1991), who argues that improved communication technology makes many business services more tradable than they were in the past.

THE SIZE DISTRIBUTION OF CITIES

Not all cities are the same size. This obvious fact raises important questions, such as why some cities are larger than others and why the distribution of city sizes varies from country to country. Much of the next six chapters will be devoted to analyzing the sources of urban growth. Before embarking on that investigation, however, it is worth introducing some of the basic facts about urban size distributions.

The most interesting empirical regularity about city sizes is known as *Zipf's Law,* or the *rank-size rule.* This states that the population of a city multiplied by its rank in terms of population is a constant. In other words, the second largest city has one-half the population of the largest, the third largest city has one third the population of the largest, and so on. While this rule does not hold exactly, it is a good description of population distributions among cities in many countries at many points in time. Unfortunately, economic theory does not provide a convincing explanation of the reasons for this population distribution. We will see in chapter 3 one intriguing possible approach, but it remains an open research question (Bairoch 1988, p. 146; Krugman 1995).

The 1990 populations of selected U.S. cities is shown in Table 1.7, along with their populations in 1950, 1900, and 1850. This illustrates the idea that city sizes change over time, in both absolute and relative terms. The rank multiplied by the size is calculated for 1990 as well. For example, three of the largest cities in 1990 did not exist in 1850. As you can see, the smaller cities in the United States are larger than predicted by Zipf's Law.

There is a slight variation on Zipf's Law, known as *Davis's Law,* that is also interesting to explore. Suppose that 20 cities have populations of about 100,000, 40 cities have populations of about 50,000, 10 cities have populations of about 200,000, and so on. In that case, the total population in each "size" city is the same, 2 million people. Davis's Law suggests that such a relation is general. In other words, the total population in each size group of cities is the same. Table 1.8 uses data from Europe in 1800 to explore whether Davis's Law holds exactly. As the population doubles, the number of cities falls by a factor of about 2.6 (rather than 2), so that the total population in each size city falls by a factor of about 1.3. Davis's Law does not hold precisely for these data, as smaller cities have a larger total population than larger cities.

The size distribution of cities varies from country to country. Henderson (1988, chapter 10) investigates some determinants of this variation using cross-sectional data from 1976. He finds that countries with more centralized forms of government (as opposed to more federal forms of government) also tend to have a higher concentration of their populations in large cities. This tendency reflects the increased development of employment and public service provision in the national capital regions of highly centralized countries. Another finding was that countries whose cities specialized in production of resource-intensive commodities tended to be more decentralized than countries whose cities specialized in more "footloose" industries that clustered into economic centers. This "core-periphery" pattern of development is a

TABLE 1.7 Population of U.S. Cities, 1850–1990

City	Rank in 1990	1990	1950	1900	1850	1990 Rank by Population
New York, NY	1	7,322,564	7,891,957	3,437,202	696,115	7,322,564
Los Angeles, CA	2	3,485,398	1,970,358	102,479	1,610	6,970,796
Chicago, IL	3	2,783,726	3,620,962	1,698,575	29,963	8,351,178
Houston, TX	4	1,630,553	596,163	44,633	2,963	6,522,212
Philadelphia, PA	5	1,585,577	2,071,605	1,293,697	121,376	7,927,885
San Diego, CA	6	1,110,549	334,387	17,700	—	6,663,294
Detroit, MI	7	1,027,974	1,849,568	285,704	21,019	7,195,818
Dallas, TX	8	1,007,618	434,462	42,638	—	8,060,944
Phoenix, AZ	9	983,395	106,818	5,544	—	8,850,555
San Antonio, TX	10	935,933	408,442	53,321	3,488	9,359,330
Boston, MA	20	574,283	801,444	560,892	136,881	11,485,660
Cleveland, OH	24	505,616	914,808	381,768	17,034	12,134,784
Portland, OR	30	438,802	373,628	90,426	—	13,164,060
Pittsburgh, PA	40	369,879	676,806	321,616	46,601	14,795,160
Buffalo, NY	50	328,175	580,132	352,387	42,261	16,408,750
Birmingham, AL	60	265,965	326,037	38,415	—	15,957,900
Lexington, KY	70	225,366	55,534	26,369	8,159	15,775,620
Des Moines, IA	80	193,189	177,965	62,139	—	15,455,120
Huntington Beach, CA	90	181,519	5,237	—	—	16,336,710
Newport News, VA	100	171,439	42,000	—	—	17,143,900

Source: U.S. Bureau of the Census.

common one and will be investigated thoroughly in chapter 7. The idea that the size distribution of cities within a country is the item of interest is also not completely transparent in the case of small, closely integrated countries, such as the Benelux countries of Europe.

It is tempting to think that there is an "optimal" city size where the agglomeration economies would heavily outweigh the agglomeration diseconomies, and some economists have attempted to estimate it. This exercise, though, suffers from three methodological flaws. First, it is intrinsically static, in that agglomeration economies

TABLE 1.8 Davis's Law among European Cities in 1800

Size of City (in Thousands)	Number of Cities	Total Population (in Thousands)
12–24	255	3,983
24–48	88	2,728
48–96	39	2,548
96–192	14	1,832
192–384	4	1,061
384–768	1	550

Source: Bairoch, 1988, p. 146.

and diseconomies are only measured at one point in time. If the findings are to be used to prescribe policy that promotes or discourages urban growth, then they may be overtaken by events—such as technological improvements—that render them obsolescent. Second, the optimal city size can be expected to vary according to the type of industry that a city specializes in, given that not every industry is subject to the same production technology. Third, the extent of externalities will also vary from city to city depending on the unique characteristics—such as the weather—of each city.

An interesting definitional question arises when one examines the population distribution of cities within a country: What is the appropriate definition of the city? We saw earlier several alternative ways of defining a city. Each metropolitan area can be thought of as composed of smaller cities that also have economic interest. Perhaps the appropriate population distribution is of these components of metropolitan areas rather than the metropolitan areas themselves. For now, this question is left unanswered, in part because of the difficulty of acquiring data even at the metropolitan area level.

CHAPTER SUMMARY

- Cities are spatial concentrations of economic activity. They can be modeled as small open economies. As economic theory predicts, cities specialize in production and trade with other cities to obtain goods and services.

- Each metropolitan area is composed of a variety of small open economies. These include the historic downtown and bedroom suburbs and often one or more suburban business centers.

- Cities grow because the spatial clustering of production can lead to increased productivity. This can occur for three reasons: increasing returns to scale for a particular firm due to its own higher production (internal economies of scale), increasing returns to scale for a firm due to its location near closely related firms (localization economies of scale), and increasing returns to scale for a firm due to a general increase in the size of the city (urbanization economies of scale).

- The spatial clustering of production creates negative externalities, including congestion and pollution. These negative externalities provide a limiting factor on urban growth.

- Not all cities are the same size. The larger the population under consideration, the fewer the number of cities that achieve that population. An empirical regularity, the rank-size rule, is a reasonable approximation to the distribution of city sizes, although it has only limited theoretical justification.

EXCERPT: "MASTERS OF THE METROPOLIS" (RANDALL GARRETT AND LIN CARTER)

The modern city is an amazing place, but one easy to take for granted for those of us born and raised in urban settings. Much of economic analysis works to remove the mystery from everyday experiences that are otherwise hard to understand by making them comprehensible as the outcome of economic processes. It is only fair, then, to begin our study of cities by reminding ourselves of how incredible these places are. Randall Garrett and Lin Carter (1957) looked at the city as a source of science-fictional inspiration. The following edited excerpt from their story "Masters of the Metropolis" follows the wild adventures of Sam IM4 SF+ through the streets of Newark and New York.

It was in the Eighth Month of the Year 1956 that Sam IM4 SF+ strode down the surging, crowded streets of Newark, one of the many cities of its kind in the State of New Jersey. He had just left his apartment in one of the vast, soaring pylons of the city. There, living in universal accord, hundreds of families dwelt side by side in the same great tower, one of many which loomed as many as forty stories above the street.

He paused to board a *bus* which stopped at regularly-spaced intervals to take on new passengers. The bus was a streamlined self-propelled public vehicle, powered by the exploding gases of distilled petroleum, ignited in a sealed cylinder by means of an electrical spark. The energy thus obtained was applied as torque to a long metal bar known as the "drive-shaft," which turned a set of gears in a complex apparatus known as the "differential housing." These gears, in turn, caused the rear wheels to revolve about their axes, thus propelling the vehicle forward smoothly at velocities as great as eighty miles every hour!

[now Sam is in Manhattan] All about him soared the incredible towers, spires, pylons, monuments, buildings, palaces, temples, cathedrals, domes, and other breathtaking construction of the Metropolis. Through its broad streets moved the traffic of the great city. Row on row of metallic projectiles called *automobiles* passed smoothly, silently, and swiftly through the streets. Powered by the same "internal combustion engine" that powered the bus, they were marvels of mechanical genius. So common were they to the favored children of this Mechanical Age that the gaily-costumed passers-by scarcely gave them a glance, even when crossing the streets through which the autos ran.

Sam lifted his nobly-sculptured head and gazed enthralled at the towers that rose, rank upon serried rank, as far as the eye could see. Their smooth, regular sides of artificial stone literally blazed with hundreds of illuminated windows. Their lofty tops seemed to touch the very sky itself—for which reason, let me remark in passing, the inhabitants called them *Sky-Scrapers*.

Before him, in multicolored grandeur, blazed hundreds of vast advertising displays, each shining with a light that dazzled the eye of the beholder. These sign-lights were ingeniously wrought tubes of glass of no greater diameter than a common lead-pencil, but many feet in length. The tubes were curved to form the various letters and symbols which made up the great illuminated signs, and were filled with various gases under low pressure. When electrical energy of tremendous voltage was applied to electrodes at the ends of the tubes, the gas within glowed brilliantly with colored light, just as the atmosphere glows when a bolt of lightning passes through it during a thunderstorm. By filling these tubes with diverse gases, all the hues of the rainbow could be duplicated.

Sam IM4 SF+ turned his admiring gaze from the breathtaking displays and started to cross the street. By a clever contrivance of flashing signal-lamps, the flow of mechanical traffic was periodically halted, to thus allow unmounted citizens to pass from one side to the other in complete safety. Sam strode across the street as the traffic halted in strict obedience to the signal-lamps. Once on the other side, he started off through the byways of the city. On either side stretched mercantile establishments of divers sorts, selling luxuries and commodities undreamed of by earlier peoples. He strode past a theater of the age which, instead of living actors, displayed amazing dramas recorded on strips of celluloid and projected by beams of light on tremendous white surfaces within the darkened theater. Ingeniously recorded voices and sounds, cleverly synchronized to the movement of the figures on the screen, made them seem lifelike.

"Ah, the wonders of modern science!" Sam marveled anew.

Source: Takeoff! by Randall Garrett. Copyright © 1986 by Randall Garrett. Reprinted by permission of The Donning Company/Publishers.

Questions for Review and Discussion

1. Think carefully about your experiences in cities. What is an observation or experience that puzzled or fascinated you? Write it down and keep it handy as you proceed through the book. I hope you get some insight from the economic analyses presented. If I haven't addressed your issue in the book, please send it to me so that I can make up for this lack in future editions!

2. Under what conditions would cities fail to exist? Consider different combinations of the conditions you identify as present or lacking. How do the conditions determine the type of city that it is possible to observe?

3. Why aren't all cities the same size?

4. In 1969, the organizers of the Woodstock Festival ("three days of peace, love, and rock & roll") proclaimed that the 300,000 or more people at the event had created the second largest city in the state of New York. Do you agree with them? Explain briefly.

5. Calculate the employment by industry group in 1950 and 1990 for a city of your choice. Compare your results to the United States totals shown in Table 1.5. In which areas is your city different from the national averages? Can you explain the differences?

6. Read the excerpt from *Gargantua and Pantagruel* at the end of the appendix to this chapter. Do you think that the proposed solution will lead to the optimal amount of the externality-generating activity being undertaken? What do you expect will happen as a result of the judgment rendered by Seigny John?

Appendix: Externalities—Problems and Opportunities

> It was a town of red brick, or of brick that would have been red if the smoke and ashes had allowed it; but as matters stood it was a town of unnatural red and black like the painted face of a savage. It was a town of machinery and tall chimneys, out of which interminable serpents of smoke trailed themselves forever and ever, and never got uncoiled. It had a black canal in it, and a river that ran purple with ill-smelling dye, and vast piles of building full of windows where there was a rattling and a trembling all day long, and where the piston of the steam-engine worked monotonously up and down like the head of an elephant in a state of melancholy madness.
>
> —CHARLES DICKENS

Dickens's description in 1854 of the fictional city of Coketown in the novel *Hard Times* illustrates the negative externalities that can arise in cities. The smoke and ashes, water pollution, and noise and vibration are all costs imposed on people who cannot directly influence the firms' decisions. Externalities are pervasive in cities because of the dense interaction of people. Therefore, it is important to understand precisely what the problem is that they cause and also to understand potential solutions to these negative externalities.

Not all externalities are negative, though. The economic explanation of cities relies on agglomeration economies of scale, which are a positive externality. In addition to advantages in production, cultural opportunities are possible when many people live in close proximity (positive externalities in consumption) that would be difficult or impossible to maintain in a more dispersed environment. In fact, public parks as well as theaters, symphonies, and museums have been promoted as positive influences that offset the negative aspects of life in the city. Frederick Law Olmsted, the designer of New York's Central Park, said that he had created "a distinctly harmonizing and refining influence upon the most unfortunate and most lawless classes of the city—an influence favorable to courtesy, self-control, and temperance" (quoted in Levine 1988, p. 202).

A *negative externality* is defined as a cost imposed as a result of an activity on people who do not participate in the activity and who are not necessarily considered by the people participating in the activity. For example, if you snore in class, it distracts other students. However, when deciding whether to sleep, you only take into account the benefits and costs to you. The existence of a negative externality in production can be modeled by shifting the marginal cost curve to account for the costs imposed on others. This is shown in Figure A.1. A firm, in order to maximize profits, will operate at the quantity (q^e) where the marginal cost to the firm ($MC_{private}$) equals the marginal benefit. Because the firm does not take into account the external costs (such as smoke, water pollution, or vibration), it produces at a quantity greater than the one that would maximize net social welfare (q^*).

A *positive externality* in production, by contrast, would result in an equilibrium quantity of output that is too small, as you should verify.

It is possible to model negative and positive externalities in consumption through shifts in the marginal benefit (*MB*) curve analogous to those described for the marginal cost curve. An example of a negative externality in consumption is second-hand smoke from a cigarette. An example of a positive externality in consumption is the pleasure my neighbors get from looking at the flowers I've planted in my front yard. As was the case with production externalities, private actions will result in too much activity that generates negative externalities and not enough activity that generates positive externalities.

FIGURE A.1 Negative Externality in Production.

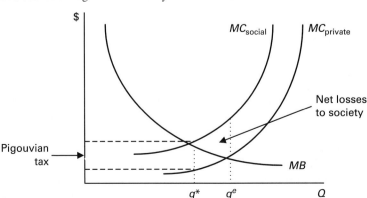

Although the discussion above considers only situations where an activity generates an externality in production or an externality in consumption, there are activities that generate externalities in both production and consumption. One example is a smokestack on a factory. The smoke from the smokestack can increase production costs for a downwind cleaner, as the cleaner might have to purchase a clothes dryer rather than use a clothesline. Further, there can be a negative externality in consumption, given that most people don't like to see or breathe smoke. It is possible, too, that an activity might generate both positive and negative externalities. Bees can pollinate flowers, but they also sting people, and the true social costs and benefits of beekeeping should reflect both possibilities.

There are several ways in which governments and private individuals can respond to the presence of externalities in order to alleviate problems of negative externalities or encourage activities that generate positive externalities. The first type of response has been the use of legal remedies of injunction and liability to respond to negative externalities. An injunction is a legal rule forbidding an activity that creates harm to someone else. A liability rule requires compensation for an activity that has damaged others. Liability and injunction rules are almost intrinsically limited to controlling negative externalities, which automatically limits their usefulness as policy. They both also have the drawback of requiring the injured party to incur the costs and uncertainty of the legal process rather than providing automatic redress of grievance.

The second type of response is direct mandates on activities that generate externalities. Air and water quality standards, for example, forbid firms from generating pollution that exceeds certain levels. Condominium associations often restrict activities likely to cause negative externalities, such as car repair on the premises. They also mandate positive activities—for example, by requiring contributions to finance a given level of lawn and garden maintenance by the association, or by restricting the colors of paint that an owner can use on the exterior of their house.

The third type of response is to force the individual or firm generating the externality to face the full costs or reap the full benefits of its actions ("internalizing" the externality). This can take the form of a tax on activities that generate negative externalities or a subsidy to activities that generate positive externalities. One of the earliest theoretical developments of this idea was due to a British economist named Arthur Pigou, and his work is recognized in the so-called "Pigouvian tax." This tax is calculated as the difference between MC_{social} and $MC_{private}$ at q^* and imposed as an excise tax (see Figure A.1). This essentially shifts the private marginal cost curve up by the amount of the tax and causes the firm to choose q^* in equilibrium.

The fourth response has been to focus on the idea that externalities arise due to the absence of clear property rights. If I owned the right to pollute as much as I wanted to, then you would know where to go if you wanted to reduce pollution. If you were willing to pay me enough, I would reduce pollution. Conversely, if you own the right to pristine air and water that I wanted to pollute, I would be forced to negotiate with you for that right. In either case, the externality is perforce internalized. If the amount that I am willing to pay when you have the property right is the same as the amount that I'm willing to accept when I have the property right, and if there are small transaction costs involved, then it is possible for private negotiations to lead to an efficient outcome. This idea was developed by Ronald Coase (1960), who emphasized the practical difficulties in implementing it. For example, if many people are affected, then the costs of negotiating could overwhelm the benefit to each individual, so that assigning property rights does not necessarily improve the situation. However, there have been examples where such trading of rights has gone on successfully and continuously. Colten and Skinner (1996, p. 50) recount the story of a chemical manufacturer in Brooklyn whose emissions damaged the laundry of people living near the plant. The company paid for the residents' laundry, and when new people purchased existing houses, they also expected the weekly payments from the company as their right. In chapter 10, we will examine local decisions over land use from the perspective of exchanging property rights.

The issue of externalities, both negative and positive, is at the core of the economic study of cities. As we have already seen, economic analysis suggests that the question of how to cause markets to operate efficiently in the presence of externalities is a difficult one. This is particularly true when allocating the benefits and costs of externalities among those affected—that is, assigning property rights. The following excerpt from *Gargantua and Pantagruel* (1546, pp. 390–391) shows that Rabelais, at least, thought that the town fool's judgment would suffice.

> The case is this: In Paris, among the cook-shops by the Petit-Châtelet, a porter was standing in front of a roast-meat stall eating his bread in the steam from the meat, and finding it, thus flavoured, very tasty. The cook let this pass, but finally, after the porter had gobbled his last crust, he seized him by the collar and demanded payment for the steam from his roast. The porter answered that he had done no damage to his meat, had taken nothing of his, and was not his debtor in any way. The steam in question was escaping outside, and so, in any case, was being lost. No one in Paris had ever heard of the smoke from a roast being sold in the streets. The cook replied that it wasn't his business to nourish porters on the steam from his meat, and swore that if he wasn't paid he'd confiscate the porter's pack-hooks. The porter drew his cudgel and prepared to defend himself. The altercation grew warm. Gaping Parisians assembled from all quarters to watch the quarrel, and, fortunately, among them was Seigny John, the town fool.
>
> When he saw him, the cook asked the porter: "Are you willing to accept the noble Seigny John's decision in our dispute?" "Yes, by the goose's blood, I am," replied the porter.
>
> Then, after hearing their arguments, Seigny John ordered the porter to take a piece of silver out of his belt; and the porter thrust an old coin of Philip's reign into his hand. Seigny John took it and put it on his left shoulder, as though to feel if it were full weight. Then he rang it on the palm of his left hand, as if to see that it was a good alloy. Next he held it close up to his right eye, as if to make sure that it was well minted. All this took place in complete silence from the gaping mob, while the cook watched in confidence, the porter in despair. Finally the fool rang the coin several times on the stall. Then, with presidential majesty, grasping his bauble as if it were a sceptre, and pulling over his head his ape's fur hood with its paper ears ridged like organ pipes, after two or three sound preliminary coughs he announced in a loud voice: "The court declares that the porter who ate his bread in the steam of a roast has civilly paid the cook with the chink of his money. The court orders that each shall retire to his eachery, without costs. The case is settled."

CHAPTER

Cities in History

2

Cities started very early and everywhere. The archaeological evidence indicates that within 1,000 years of a region's adopting agricultural methods, cities had developed within that region. A food surplus from agriculture is the most important necessity for urban growth. A population of subsistence farmers and hunters could not have cities.

Agriculture not only made cities possible, it also made them necessary. An abundance of food is a tempting target for bandits and for military activity. An area where there are increasing returns to scale not mentioned in the previous chapter is in self-defense. In other words, 100 people working together to defend one storehouse are more effective than 100 storehouses each defended by one person. The nature of storehouses is that costs go down with size within at least a certain range, because the costs increase with the area of the storehouse (quadratic), while the capacity increases with the volume (cubic). Mumford (1961, p. 44) argues that the food surplus available to cities freed up some of the population to engage in conquest of surrounding territory in addition to simply defending the existing area of settlement.

Cities in turn provided agricultural augmentation through innovation. In fact, it is possible that the first cities actually led to the development of agriculture through development of hybrid grains and domestication of animals. (The use of human waste as fertilizer also implied that the soil surrounding cities could actually be richer than soil elsewhere, according to Mumford 1961, p. 290.) These developments occurred not only as the result of local improvements but also as a result of the diffusion of innovation brought about by trade. Long-distance trade began very early, resulting in some specialization among cities from the beginnings of history. However, most goods were not traded in very large volumes, so that one of the most important items of trade was information. The one good that was traded in vast quantities was grain, in some cases—such as that of Greece and Phoenicia—permitting a higher degree of commercial specialization than would have been possible on the basis of local food production alone. However, the area of the region providing grain always greatly exceeded the area of the grain-importing region, making widespread increases in urbanization impossible for the latter. The limitations on large-scale trade implied that early cities were less specialized than modern cities.

HOW URBANIZED ARE PEOPLE?

Until the Industrial Revolution, approximately 70 to 80 percent of the population needed to be engaged in agriculture in order to produce sufficient food. This implies that the maximum fraction of the population available to live in cities of any size was only 10 or 15 percent, once nonagricultural workers living in rural areas are accounted for. The percent of the population living in cities above a minimum threshold of 5,000 in population was about 10 percent—close to the theoretical maximum—for the entire period between 1300 and 1800, as shown in Table 2.1. However, after 1800, the Industrial Revolution in Europe and America led to previously unseen levels of urbanization, and after 1900 these effects were also seen in Africa and Asia. The level of urbanization in the world is expected to increase, with projected levels of 44 percent in 2000 and 57 percent by 2025. Within two centuries, the world will have transformed from one in which only one in 11 humans lived in cities into one in which over half of all humans live in cities. Human society will have become primarily urban society.

One of the important aspects of urban life is the anonymity it entails, at least relative to life in a small rural setting. Every day we interact with many people that we do not know and might never see again. This has implications for the ways in which people behave. Thorstein Veblen (1899) hypothesized that "conspicuous leisure" was an effective way of showing prosperity in rural areas, because people knew everyone else and could observe their ability to take time off from working. In an urban setting, though, the enjoyment of leisure was not observable because of the anonymity of individuals. Thus, urban life was rife with "conspicuous consumption," where people indicated their prosperity through purchases of expensive items to impress their neighbors. We will see that urbanization and industrialization (in the sense of specialized production and trade) go hand in hand. Industrialization makes urbanization possible. Urbanization, through conspicuous consumption and other avenues, makes further industrialization necessary. The process of industrialization, by making manufactured goods more efficiently produced and thus affordable, also leads to growth in the role of services. Because many services do not display the same rate of technological progress as that in manufactured goods, it becomes both possible and necessary to increase employment in the service industries. As an example of the lack of technological progress, note that the main difference between today's college classroom and the college classroom of the 1300s is that today we are not wearing gowns and speaking Latin.

TABLE 2.1 Percentage of Population Living in Urban Areas

	1300	*1500*	*1700*	*1800*	*1900*	*1950*	*1980*
World	9.0	9.4	9.8	9.0	16.0	25.6	37.6
Africa	4.0	5.0	3.9	4.0	5.5	12.0	25.2
North and South America	8.2	8.4	11.4	12.3	28.5	47.9	63.8
Asia	10.2	10.7	10.9	9.1	9.3	14.9	25.6
Europe	9.5	9.6	10.8	10.4	30.2	42.9	64.2

Source: Adapted from Bairoch, 1988, Table 31.1, p. 495. A minimum of 5,000 is used as the criterion for an urban population.

The link between industrialization and urbanization has been recognized as far back as the work of Adam Smith in 1776. His theory of growth consisted of two parts (Stull 1986). First, the division of labor is limited by the extent of the market. So, as markets increase in size and scope, opportunities for further division of labor arise. Second, the extent of the market is limited by the division of labor. As labor becomes more specialized, it is possible to produce for a wider market.

The major change in both the level of urbanization and in the maximum size of cities came with the Industrial Revolution. Urban areas grew because of technological advances in agriculture, communications, public health, and transportation.

The increase in agricultural productivity resulting from chemical fertilizers and mechanization drastically reduced the fraction of the population needed to produce food. The development of the railroad and steamship also increased agricultural productivity by allowing agricultural areas to specialize in the product where their comparative advantage existed. This pattern of cumulative growth with increasing specialization is still going on today.

The development of the telegraph—and especially the telephone—reduced the necessity for face-to-face communication, thus making greater spatial dispersion of business possible.

Improvements in public health reduced mortality, especially from waterborne diseases, and made possible greater crowding—and, therefore, larger cities—than ever before.

The trolley and the elevator increased people's horizontal and vertical mobility, enabled cities to grow up and out. Advances in construction, especially the use of structural steel, made skyscrapers possible.

A small digression on agricultural productivity is perhaps justified here, given the importance of the ever-increasing agricultural surplus in sustaining urban growth. It is clear from Table 2.1 that preindustrial levels of urbanization varied from region to region, with Asia enjoying the highest level of urbanization. One explanation for this difference is the fact that rice is a more efficient dietary staple than wheat. First, rice provides 3600 calories per kilogram versus the 3400 calories provided by wheat. Second, a hectare planted in rice yields about 1600 kilograms using preindustrial techniques, while a hectare planted in wheat yields only about 600 kilograms. Third, it is possible in some parts of Asia to harvest two crops of rice per year. Even after accounting for the necessity to keep some of the harvest for seed, we see that rice provides three to six times more potential nourishment per hectare. This means that a given area of agricultural land can feed more people if planted in rice than in wheat, given a certain transportation technology (Bairoch 1988, p. 355).

DEATH AND DISEASE

There was both "bad news" and "good news" about dense human settlement with respect to the spread of disease. The bad news was that density led to intensive exposure to three vectors of disease transmission: direct contact with infected people, contact with feces and other human byproducts that carried disease and supported disease-bearing insects, and contact with domestic animals (including such human symbiotes as rats). The good news to civilized populations was that diseases that became endemic among "civilized" areas could be fatal to inhabitants in outlying areas, thus hastening the spread of civilization by removing the uncivilized people (McNeill 1976).

Historically, urban mortality rates exceeded those outside of urban areas, and this was not made up for by higher fertility rates, despite the fact that most migrants to urban areas were in their childbearing years. Therefore, for most of history cities could maintain their population only by constant replenishment from agricultural areas. The advent of adequate water and sewer systems were a major contributor to the increased health of city dwellers. Jonathan Swift describes, in these excerpts from the poem "A Description of a City Shower," published in 1710, the effects of a rainstorm in the days before storm sewers:

> Filth of all Hues and Odours seem to tell
> What Street they sail'd from, by their Sight and Smell.
>
> Sweepings from Butchers Stalls, Dung, Guts, and Blood,
> Drown'd Puppies, stinking Sprats, all drench'd in Mud,
> Dead Cats and Turnip-Tops come tumbling down the Flood.

Not an appealing—or healthy—picture. . . .

Detailed and accurate demographic data date only to the early 1800s for most European countries. Table 2.2 summarizes data on urban and rural infant mortality rates in several European countries, along with infant mortality rates for several cities. In the Netherlands, the urban infant mortality rate fell below the rural rate as early as the 1890s, while in Norway and Sweden the urban rate was higher until about 1930. Although not shown in Table 2.2, measures of fertility in urban areas were lower than in rural areas throughout the 1800s and 1900s.

Not only were urban dwellers having fewer children and losing more of these children in infancy, but the adults too were dying younger than their rural counterparts. Table 2.3 presents some evidence on adult life expectancy in Sweden, Japan, and the United States. All of these figures imply one conclusion: If a city were to grow during the 1800s and early 1900s, it had to induce migration from rural areas.

TABLE 2.2   Infant Mortality Rates (per thousand live births)

Years	Urban Norway	Rural Norway	Amsterdam	Netherlands	Urban Sweden	Rural Sweden
1811–1820	—	—	251	—	243	177
1831–1840	—	—	228	—	229	161
1851–1860	135	95	228	197	219	137
1871–1880	135	91	214	203	193	119
1891–1900	126	83	155	158	130	95
1911–1920	73	58	64	92	76	67
1931–1940	39	40	31	41	40	49
1951–1960	19	20	18	21	17	19

Source: Bairoch, 1988, Table 14.1, p. 230.

TABLE 2.3 Life Expectancy for Adults

Country and Years	Urban Life Expectancy	Rural Life Expectancy
Sweden (at 15 years)		
1881–1890	45.9	50.1
1891–1900	47.3	50.3
1901–1910	49.0	51.2
1911–1920	49.3	50.4
1921–1930	52.7	53.6
1931–1940	54.2	54.9
1941–1950	56.8	57.5
1950–1960	59.2	59.5
United States (at 10 years)		
1901	40.5	46.0
1910	42.0	46.4
1930	45.8	49.3
Japan (at 10 years)		
1925–1926	45.8	48.4
1935–1936	46.9	48.4

Source: Bairoch, 1988, Table 14.3, p. 235.

THE INDUSTRIAL REVOLUTION

The Industrial Revolution began in England in the 1700s and resulted in a transformation of the human race from a rural and agricultural species to an urban species. The changes wrought by the Industrial Revolution were huge and continue to the present time. We will examine the beginnings of the change here and return to various aspects of the Industrial Revolution later in the book in order to illustrate how the formal analysis can be applied.

The population in England and Wales in 1740 was approximately 6 million people, with 70 percent of the workforce employed in agriculture. This distribution of the workforce was typical of that in the previous 8,000 years, the only exceptions being small geographical areas (such as the Netherlands in the 1600s or Italy during the late Roman Republic and early Roman Empire) that were importers of food from a vast hinterland (such as Poland in the case of the Netherlands or Egypt in the case of Rome). By 1840, the population in England and Wales had grown to approximately 16 million people, but the fraction of the workforce employed in agriculture had fallen to 22 percent. Despite this drop, England was a net exporter of food during this entire period (in part due to the restrictive trade regime of the Corn Laws). Such an occurrence was unprecedented, and the scale of this transformation can only be comprehended by noting the experience in other countries. The United States, for example, reached a comparable workforce composition only in 1930, with France (1955), Italy (1968), and Spain (1975) lagging even further behind (Bairoch 1988, p. 245). By 1840, England was an extremely modern society.

Clearly, not all countries experienced the Industrial Revolution at the same time or in the same way. Even within England, not all cities had the same experience. The revolution began not in England's largest cities but in small cities that shared three characteristics. First, they had access to sources of large amounts of power, either directly through water power or indirectly through coal fields. Second, they had access to cheaper labor. Third, they enjoyed less government regulation than the larger cities of the time. Table 2.4 lists the populations of the major urban centers of England before the Industrial Revolution and in the first stages of the Industrial Revolution.

The location of manufacturing industries near sources of coal and water power was not unique to England. Pred (1966, pp. 161–162) documents the focus of U.S. manufacturing in the early 1800s along large falls in rivers rather than in the major urban areas. The mechanized cotton textile industry, for example, flourished in suburbs of Boston (Waltham), New York (Paterson, NJ), and Philadelphia (Roxborough) but not in the cities themselves. Even when coal-burning steam engines became available, limited accessibility to coal and low efficiency of the engines meant that they were initially heavily concentrated in coal-field cities. In 1840, for example, Pittsburgh's steam-powered workshops boasted a greater total capacity than all those in Boston, Baltimore, and Philadelphia combined.

The Industrial Revolution saw the rise of cities that specialized in manufacturing goods for trade. While trade has existed since cities existed, the extent of specialization was never before so large. Preindustrial cities existed on the basis of administrative, commercial, or religious reasons—all services that are intrinsically nontradable. This change to a focus on tradables also tied a city's economic prospects to the perfor-

TABLE 2.4 English Cities during the Industrial Revolution (population in thousands)

City	1700	1800	1850
London	550	860	2,320
Centers before the Industrial Revolution	119	188	426
Norwich	29	36	67
Bristol	25	61	150
Newcastle	25	33	110
Exeter	14	16	16
York	11	16	35
Colchester	8	10	12
Coventry	7	16	36
Centers during the early Industrial Revolution	47	360	1,547
Birmingham	10	71	230
Liverpool	6	76	422
Manchester	9	81	404
Leeds	7	52	185
Sheffield	8	45	141
Bradford	4	13	100
Stoke	3	22	65

Source: Bairoch, 1988, Table 15.1, p. 254.

mance of a particular industry. If the industry in which the city specialized flourished, then the city flourished. If the industry struggled, the city struggled.

Although the Industrial Revolution clearly had an impact on manufacturing productivity and structure, it would be a mistake to ascribe all (or even most) of the phenomenal growth of cities during the 1800s to employment in manufacturing. Alfred Marshall (1920, pp. 276–277) points out that the fraction of the population of England engaged in manufacturing was the same in 1901 as it had been in 1851, although the proportion working in agriculture had fallen. The part of the economy that was growing in employment share was services—government, medical, transport, and entertainment. He pointed out that the mechanical assistance in providing these services, such as the telephone and railroad, had tended to increase both the specialization and localization of service providers.

The innovations in technology that fueled and resulted from the Industrial Revolution again bring up the question of localization versus urbanization economies of scale as an explanation for urban growth. There is evidence of urbanization economies of scale in the extent of innovation and in its diffusion (Bairoch 1988, p. 336). Larger cities have greater human contact, more diverse activities that lead to cross-sector adoption of innovation, greater education and research, and less pressure to conform than rural areas; moreover, the city is the locus for trade with other cities (who in turn are innovating). The German phrase "Stadt Luft macht frei," literally "city air makes (one) free," is often used to refer to the greater latitude for individuality in an urban setting. It had an even more literal meaning during feudal times, when any serf who managed to remain within the walls of the city for a year and a day was considered free. (The law benefited urban firms by providing a source of cheap labor.)

A synthesis of the two types of agglomeration economy of scale is perhaps the most satisfactory explanation for urban growth (see Chapter 7 for a formal model that incorporates these features). Access to the larger markets and greater innovation of the city provide good reasons for firms to initially congregate and fuel initial urban growth. Localization economies of scale then provide impetus for particular industries to flourish and furnish the basis for ongoing urban growth. This growth, in turn, fuels further urbanization economies until the point is reached at which the diseconomies of size and proximity, such as congestion and pollution, outweigh the economies.

Mumford (1961, pp. 451–452) aptly summarizes both the positive and negative aspects of the ninteenth century transformation:

> Food-chains and production-chains of a complicated nature were being formed throughout the planet: ice traveled from Boston to Calcutta and tea journeyed from China to Ireland, whilst machinery and cotton goods and cutlery from Birmingham and Manchester found their way to the remotest corners of the earth. A universal postal service, fast locomotion, and almost instantaneous communication by telegraph and cable synchronized the activities of vast masses of men who had hitherto lacked the most rudimentary facilities for coordinating their tasks. This was accompanied by a steady differentiation of crafts, trades, organizations, and associations. . . .
>
>   But at the same time: forests were slaughtered, soils were mined, whole animal species were wiped out. Above all, this un-building took place in the urban environment.

TABLE 2.5   Urban Population and Share of Population in the United States, 1790–1990

Date	All Cities ≥ 2,500 Number of cities (% of U.S. Population)	Cities 25,000–249,999 Number of Cities (% of U.S. Population)	Cities ≥ 250,000 Number of Cities (% of U.S. Population)
1790	24 (5.1)	2 (1.6)	0 (0.0)
1840	131 (10.8)	11 (3.7)	1 (1.8)
1860	392 (19.8)	32 (6.7)	3 (5.2)
1890	1,348 (35.1)	113 (11.2)	11 (11.0)
1920	2,722 (51.2)	262 (16.0)	25 (19.7)
1950	4,054 (59.6)	479 (19.2)	41 (23.1)
1960	4,996 (63.1)	707 (22.5)	50 (21.9)
All cities ≥ 10,000			
1960	1,735 (50.7)	707 (22.5)	50 (21.9)
1970	2,023 (51.9)	840 (22.5)	56 (20.8)
1980	2,260 (49.6)	945 (23.2)	55 (17.7)
1990	2,425 (50.1)	1,071 (24.2)	64 (17.8)

Source: U.S. Census Bureau.

URBANIZATION IN THE UNITED STATES

The United States came into existence during the early part of the Industrial Revolution, and the increase in urbanization observed in the United States reflects that in other industrial countries during the past two hundred years. Table 2.5 illustrates the increase both in the number of cities and in the fraction of the population living in cities. What is interesting is not only the increase in the total amount of urbanization but also the changes over time in the relative distribution of the population between large (> 250,000), medium-sized (25,000–249,999), and small (< 25,000) cities.

Just as was the case in England, the pattern of growth was uneven across cities. For example, in 1860, Albany, New Haven, and Richmond were comparable in size to Pittsburgh, San Francisco, Cleveland, and Detroit. By 1910, though, the largest city in the former group (New Haven) had less than one-third of the population in the smallest city in the latter group (San Francisco) (Pred 1966, pp. 46–47). This was not the result of a decline in population—the population of both Richmond and New Haven tripled between 1860 and 1910, from about 40,000 to about 130,000 each—but instead reflected even greater population increases in the main industrial centers.

HOW BIG IS A BIG CITY?

As the overall level of urbanization has increased since the Industrial Revolution, so too has the size of large cities. As Table 2.6 shows, there has been a twenty-five-fold increase in the number of cities with a population over 100,000 since 1800. Further, there has been a steady increase in the size of the largest cities.

TABLE 2.6   Large Cities in the World

Number of Cities by Population	1300	1500	1700	1800	1900	1980
100,000–200,000	35	41	54	57	153	1,080
200,000–500,000	11	11	15	22	90	740
500,000–1,000,000	1	2	7	5	38	250
1,000,000–5,000,000	—	—	—	2	10	200
5,000,000–10,000,000	—	—	—	—	1	22
> 10,000,000	—	—	—	—	—	5
Total of over 100,000	47	54	76	86	292	2,290

Source: Adapted from Bairoch, 1988, Table 31.2, p. 502.

The growth in the number of very large cities and also in the size of the largest cities suggest that the average size of cities should also be increasing. It is, but not as dramatically as Table 2.6 might lead you to expect. Table 2.7 presents data on the average population of cities above various minimum populations. From 1300 to 1800, the average size of cities increased by only about 20 percent. After the Industrial Revolution, the pace increased; the average population in cities of more than 20,000 people reached 113,200 by 1970. Note that even though the average size of a city was between 30,800 and 113,200 in 1970, depending on the lower limit of city size, this understates the extent to which people live in large cities. For example, in Europe in 1970, only 25 percent of the urban population lived in cities of fewer than 43,000 people.

Is a big city always a big city? Anecdotally, no. In the ancient world, there is the extreme example of Rome, whose population was close to or over one million during the height of its power but had sunk to 35,000 by A.D. 1000. More recently, we can evaluate the various experiences of U.S. cities. Table 2.8 lists the ten largest cities in the United States in 1930 along with each city's rank and population (in thousands) in 1970 and 1980. What is most striking about the data in Table 2.8 is that every city except New York, Los Angeles, and Washington lost population over the 50-year period, indicating a decline not only relative to other large cities but relative to their own past experience. We will explore the issue of the changes that led to this decline in city population in chapter 9, when we consider the structure of metropolitan areas. One

TABLE 2.7   Average Population of European Cities, 1300–1970

	Cities of 2,000 or more	Cities of 5,000 or more	Cities of 20,000 or more
1300	6,600	12,900	36,500
1500	6,700	13,500	39,600
1700	7,600	15,400	51,000
1800	7,800	16,700	54,900
1900	15,400	21,200	78,900
1970	30,800	42,800	113,200

Source: Bairoch, 1988, p. 227.

TABLE 2.8 Cities in the United States, 1930–1990

	Rank 1930	Rank 1970	Rank 1980	Rank 1990	Population 1930	Population 1970	Population 1980	Population 1990
New York	1	1	1	1	6,930	7,895	7,071	7,323
Chicago	2	2	2	3	3,376	3,367	3,005	2,784
Philadelphia	3	4	4	5	1,951	1,949	1,688	1,586
Detroit	4	5	6	7	1,569	1,511	1,203	1,028
Los Angeles	5	3	3	2	1,238	2,816	2,967	3,485
Cleveland	6	10	18	24	900	751	574	506
Baltimore	7	7	10	13	805	906	787	736
Boston	8	16	20	20	781	641	563	574
Pittsburgh	9	24	30	40	670	520	424	370
Washington	10	9	15	19	487	757	638	607

Source: Census of Population and Housing.

problem with interpreting the data in Table 2.8 is that the political definition of a city is used here rather than the economic definition of a metropolitan area. This can lead us to underestimate the extent to which the leading metropolitan areas of earlier times continue to rank near the top. In fact, suburban growth can extend metropolitan areas to the point that they combine. For example, the Baltimore and Washington, D.C., MSAs recently were determined to be closely connected enough to form one CMSA. Despite the fact that the cities of Washington and Baltimore both lost population between 1980 and 1990, the CMSA had a population increase of 16.2 percent over the same time period and is the fourth largest metropolitan area in the United States.

An interesting way to see the differential growth of United States cities over the past century is to consider the case of New Orleans. During the period from 1860 to 1980, New Orleans increased steadily in population from 169,000 to about one million. During that same period, though, it fell from the fifth largest (a rank it had held since 1810) to the thirtieth largest urban area in North America. Table 2.9 shows the decade in which each of the cities passed New Orleans in size. We can see the rise of Midwestern cities during the late 1800s as well as the growth in the South and the West since the 1940s. In Columbus, Nashville, and Jacksonville, we also see the result of ongoing urban annexation policies that can lead to increased population. Nashville, which merged its government with surrounding Davidson county, is perhaps the best example in this group. Rusk (1995) argues that differences in the relative ability of cities to annex their surrounding areas play an important role in relative metropolitan area success.

A related question is the extent to which the experience of the United States generalizes to the rest of the world. A study by Jonathan Eaton and Zvi Eckstein (1994) finds that the size distribution of cities in Japan and France remained approximately constant during the twentieth century. In other words, large cities stayed large relative to small cities, although all sizes of cities increased in population. They develop a theory based on urbanization economies of scale to account for their empirical findings.

Marshall (1989) illustrates the stability of relative city sizes using data from France in 1810 and 1975 and from southern Ontario in 1871 and 1971. Twelve of the

TABLE 2.9 North American Cities That Overtook New Orleans in Size, 1860–1990

Decade	Cities
1860–1870	Chicago, Cincinnati, St. Louis
1870–1880	Pittsburgh, San Francisco
1880–1890	Buffalo, Cleveland, Minneapolis-St. Paul
1890–1900	Detroit, Milwaukee, Washington
1900–1910	Los Angeles, Montreal, Toronto
1910–1920	Kansas City
1920–1930	——
1930–1940	——
1940–1950	Houston
1950–1960	Dallas-Fort Worth, Miami, Seattle
1960–1970	Atlanta, Denver, Phoenix, San Diego, Tampa-St. Petersburg, Vancouver
1970–1980	San Jose
1980–1990	Columbus (OH), El Paso, Jacksonville, Nashville

Source: Marshall (1989, Table 2.3, p. 53) for 1860–1980; author's calculations based on U.S. census data for 1980–1990.

20 largest cities in France in 1810 are among the 20 largest in 1975, so the majority of the largest cities in the late twentieth century were already leading places while Napoleon was emperor. The total population in the largest 20 cities grew from 1.6 million to 18.5 million, so that the absolute size of the cities clearly changed while the identities of the main places did not. Looking only at the ten largest cities in 1975, we find that eight of them were among the ten largest cities in 1810. In Ontario, a similar story is told. Fourteen of the 20 largest cities in 1871 are among the 20 largest in 1971, and seven of the ten largest in 1871 are among the ten largest in 1971.

An even broader perspective in both time and space is shown in Table 2.10, which shows the population in 1300 of European cities that were large in 1800. Because of the early effects of the Industrial Revolution described in Table 2.4, the data in Table 2.10 exclude cities in the United Kingdom and the Netherlands. The evidence in Table 2.10 suggests that the urban structure at the dawn of the Industrial Revolution reflected very closely the urban structure of the Middle Ages. For example, of the 18 cities with a population of at least 100,000 in 1800, fully 13 of them (72 percent) had a population exceeding 20,000 in 1300. Almost 90 percent of the cities in 1800 were already recognizable as cities (over 2,000 population) in 1300. This does not imply a drastic shift in the urban hierarchy during that time.

One possible reconciliation of a pattern of widespread growth in city sizes with an ongoing pattern of specialization is an increase in the cost-minimizing scale of production. Bairoch (1988, p. 343) carries out some calculations that suggest that a modern city of 200,000 will support roughly ten manufacturing firms of efficient scale. This contrasts with the city of 1700, where ten manufacturing firms of efficient scale could be supported with a population of only 15,000, due to the smaller scale of operations. Interestingly, the proportion of the population of Europe living in cities of 15,000 or more in 1700 was about identical to the proportion of the population of Europe currently living in cities of more than 200,000. Thus, we have to adjust our notion of what

TABLE 2.10 Populations in 1300 of Large European Cities in 1800

Population in 1800 ↓	Number of Cities in 1800	Unknown	Less than 2,000	2,000 to 5,000	5,000 to 10,000	10,000 to 20,000	More than 20,000
20,000–50,000	127	8	5	13	29	31	41
50,000–100,000	37	2	4	7	4	6	14
> 100,000	18	—	—	3	2	—	13
Total	182	10	9	23	35	37	68

Source: Bairoch, 1988, Table 10.1, p. 154.

constitutes a "large" city to account for intertemporal differences in production technology. A widespread change in the efficient scale of production could also lead to changes in the future size of cities. For example, if manufacturing is now "leaner," then cities can be smaller, all else being equal.

CHAPTER SUMMARY

- Cities began very early in human history, and humans have been as urbanized as possible throughout history. Cities cannot exist unless there is a food surplus in the agricultural areas that can support the urban population.

- Until the Industrial Revolution, the maximum fraction of the population that could live in cities was about 15 percent, and this was roughly the percentage observed throughout the world. The Industrial Revolution resulted in huge improvements in agricultural productivity, transportation, construction techniques, and disease control. This made an increase in both the level of urbanization and the size of the largest cities possible.

- Until the 1900s, the mortality rate in cities was higher than that in rural areas and the fertility rate in cities was lower than that in rural areas. To maintain their size, cities relied on migration from rural areas.

- The United States became independent at roughly the time that the Industrial Revolution started. Until recently, there were continual increases in the level of urbanization in the United States. By 1990, about 70 percent of the population lived in urban areas.

- The evidence is ambiguous on whether the relative sizes of cities within a country remain the same over time. One reason to expect large cities to stay large is the self-reinforcing nature of urban growth—for example, the presence of urbanization economies of scale. One reason to expect small cities to grow quickly as a result of technological change is that they have lower factor prices and less dependence on the existing technology.

EXCERPT: *THE CAVES OF STEEL* (ISAAC ASIMOV)

One of the interesting lessons of history is that a big city by current standards may not be a big city by the standards of the future. By placing the current level of urbanization in historical context, you will be better able to evaluate potential future changes in cities. One fictional future is provided by Isaac Asimov (1954), who predicts that population growth will lead to ever larger cities that he terms "caves of steel." As you read the excerpt (pp. 15–17) from *The Caves of Steel,* consider which of the predicted changes has come about and whether the other ones are likely to occur during your lifetime.

The City now! New York City in which he lived and had his being. Larger than any City but Los Angeles. More populous than any but Shanghai. It was only three centuries old.

To be sure, something had existed in the same geographic area before then that had been *called* New York City. That primitive gathering of population had existed for three thousand years, not three hundred, but it hadn't been a *City.*

There were no Cities then. There were just huddles of dwelling places large and small, open to the air. These huddles (the largest barely reached ten million in population and most never reached one million) were scattered all over Earth by the thousands. By modern standards, they had been completely inefficient, economically.

Efficiency had been forced on Earth with increasing population. Two billion people, three billion, even five billion could be supported by the planet by progressive lowering of the standard of living. When the population reaches eight billion, however, semistarvation becomes too much like the real thing. A radical change had to take place in man's culture.

The radical change had been the gradual formation of the Cities over a thousand years of Earth's history. Efficiency implied bigness. Even in Medieval times that had been realized, perhaps unconsciously. Home industry gave way to factories and factories to continental industries.

Think of the inefficiency of a hundred thousand houses for a hundred thousand families as compared with a hundred-thousand-unit Section; a book-film collection in each house as compared with a Section film concentrate; independent video for each family as compared with video-piping systems.

For that matter, take the simple folly of endless duplication of kitchens and bathrooms as compared with the thoroughly efficient diners and shower rooms made possible by City culture.

City culture meant optimum distribution of food, increasing utilization of yeasts and hydroponics. New York City spread over two thousand square miles and at the last census its population was well over twenty million. There were some eight hundred Cities on Earth, average population, ten million.

Each City became a semiautonomous unit, economically all but self-sufficient. It could roof itself in, gird itself about, burrow itself under. It became a steel cave, a tremendous, self-contained cave of steel and concrete.

It could lay itself out scientifically. At the center was the enormous complex of administrative offices. In careful orientation to one another and to the whole were the large residential Sections connected and interlaced by the expressway and the local ways. Toward the outskirts were the factories, the hydroponic plants, the yeast-culture vats, the power plants. Through all the melee were the water pipes and sewage ducts, schools, prisons and shops, power lines and communication beams.

Practically none of Earth's population lived outside the Cities. Outside was the wilderness, the open sky that few men could face with anything like equanimity. To be sure, the open space was necessary. It held the water that men must have, the coal and the wood that were the ultimate raw materials for plastics and for the eternally growing yeasts. (Petroleum had long since gone, but oil-rich strains of yeast were an adequate substitute.) The land between the Cities still held the mines, and was used to a

larger extent than most men realized for growing food and grazing stock. It was inefficient, but beef, pork, and grain always found a luxury market and could be used for
export purposes.

Source: The Caves of Steel by Isaac Asimov. Copyright © 1954 by Isaac Asimov. Used by
permission of Doubleday, a division of Bantam Doubleday Dell Publishing.

Questions for Review and Discussion

1. Isaac Asimov predicts (in *The Caves of Steel*) that cities in the future will be self-
   sufficient. Do you agree with his reasoning?
2. Do you think that the current levels of urbanization will remain for the indefinite future? What would cause a major change in the extent of human urbanization?
3. What impact do you expect the World Wide Web and other communications technologies to have on the size of cities?
4. Cities grow to the point where the benefits of spatial clustering are balanced by the
   costs of spatial clustering. Is 25 million people as big as cities can get?
5. The data in Table 2.5 indicate that a declining fraction of the United States population
   lives in cities with a population over 250,000. Do you think that the fraction of the
   population living in the largest metropolitan areas has also been declining? If not,
   then how do you explain the difference in the trend in the proportion living in the
   largest cities and the proportion living in the largest metropolitan areas?

CHAPTER

Market Areas and Central Place Theory

U rban economics is defined as the study of cities. A city, in turn, is defined as a spatial agglomeration of people. Hence, the spatial location of production and consumption is inherent in all urban economic analysis. In this chapter some basic tools of spatial analysis are introduced. First, though, it is worth thinking broadly about the implications of including space in economic analysis.

The models familiar from economic principles courses do not focus on the location of economic activity. Rather, there is a vague notion of a "market" in which firms and households exchange goods and services. The fact that there needs to be a nexus for this exchange is overlooked or downplayed, despite the original meaning of "market" as signifying a place where people got together to trade.

IMPLICATIONS OF SPACE

The most obvious result of including space in economic models is that transportation costs must now be accounted for. A firm must not only incur costs to produce its outputs but must also incur costs to transport inputs to the site of production and to transport outputs to purchasers. A buyer, too, must incur transportation costs. One implication is that some sites will be relatively advantaged because of lower costs of transporting goods and services to and from them. This initial advantage can be increased if infrastructure is constructed to take advantage of this natural variation among sites. Berliant and Konishi (1994) show in a detailed model how small initial differences among sites can be reinforced by investment decisions, leading to an explanation of cities based on the necessity to transport goods to market. Their conclusions rely on the existence of increasing returns to scale in the transport network, which is not unreasonable given the large fixed costs of building a road, for example.

Because each firm and household will be located in a different place, otherwise identical firms will have different costs. Because some sites are more attractive than others, firms located in the better sites will have a cost advantage over less fortunate firms. This provides a natural distinction between *marginal firms* who earn zero economic profits in equilibrium and *inframarginal firms* who earn positive economic profits when considering the supply side of competitive product markets. Similarly, the delivered price to households will vary both by firm and by household, depending on their relative locations.

There is a slightly more subtle implication that transport costs be included. Since each firm is slightly different, the market structure of perfect competition is no longer appropriate. Rather, the heterogeneity of location implies that monopolistic competition is the appropriate market structure. We will now develop a model of monopolistic competition where the only difference among firms is their location.

MARKET AREAS

Consider the following world. The population is evenly spread out on a featureless plain. There is one homogeneous consumption good ("Thneeds") produced and sold by small identical firms ("Oncelers"). How many firms will there be, and where will they locate? This problem has a long historical lineage, reviewed by Krugman (1995, Chapter 2).

In order to answer these questions, it is necessary to introduce the concept of market area. A *market area* is defined as the area over which a firm can underprice its competitors. With apologies to Dr. Seuss ("The Tale of the Lifted Lorax"), consider the problem facing a household of choosing which among many Oncelers to buy a Thneed from. The Thneeds, made from the truffula tree, are marvelous consumption items. Each Onceler produces an identical product, but each Onceler owns a different stand of truffula trees and thus is located in a different place. In this simple model, the only difference among firms (Oncelers) is their proximity to potential customers. Let us define the *gross price* to equal the total cost to a household of purchasing a Thneed from a Onceler, including both the price charged by the Onceler and the transportation cost. If transportation costs are a constant amount per unit of travel τ, the household lives at a distance κ from the Onceler, and the price the Onceler at a given location charges is φ, then the gross price Φ is defined as: $\Phi = \varphi + \kappa\tau$.

Suppose that there are two locations, with households distributed along the line segment connecting the two locations. This situation is shown in Figure 3.1, where φ_1 represents the price charged by the Onceler at location 1, Φ_1 the gross price of a Thneed purchased from Onceler 1, φ_2 the price charged by the Onceler at location 2, and Φ_2 the gross price of a Thneed purchased from Onceler 2. The market area of Onceler 1 is the area from the origin to κ_1. At distances greater than κ_1, the gross price of Onceler 2 is lower than the gross price of Onceler 1.

Since the population is uniformly distributed by assumption, the demand facing a typical Onceler is shown in Figure 3.2. This is just the problem of a firm in a monopolistically competitive market. The profit maximizing quantity to produce, recall, is the amount where $MR = MC$. At that quantity, the price charged will be p. In Figure 3.2, the price exceeds the average cost, so the Onceler is making a profit. If the market is truly monopolistically competitive, then there are no entry barriers. In the absence of entry barriers, the existence of positive profits will encourage other Oncelers to enter the market until, in equilibrium, zero economic profits are being earned.

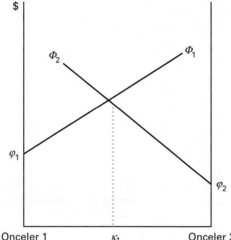

Onceler 1 κ_1 Onceler 2 **FIGURE 3.1** Gross Price

Because of the market power of the firm that results from the heterogeneity of spatial location, the firm is able to charge a price higher than marginal cost.

Of course, if there are positive profits being made, as in Figure 3.2, then there will be entry of other firms into the industry in the absence of entry barriers. The long-run equilibrium is when the marginal firm earns zero profits—in other words, when price equals average cost. This condition is illustrated in Figure 3.3. Marginal cost equals marginal revenue, so the firm is maximizing profits. Price equals average cost, so the profits equal zero. Because average cost is not minimized, the outcome is inefficient in the sense that the same total quantity could be produced at lower total cost. This finding is interpreted in principles as there being "too many firms" in equilibrium. The benefit to having this higher number of firms is the greater variety of products provided. In economic analysis that includes space, the benefit of having more firms is that people do not have to travel as far to purchase their products. We shall return to this point later in this chapter.

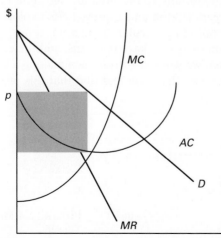

Q **FIGURE 3.2** Positive Profits

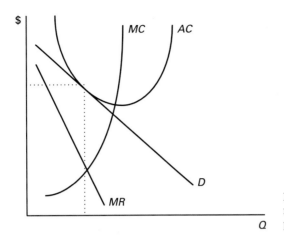

FIGURE 3.3 Long-run Equilibrium in Monopolistically Competitive Market

The diagram in Figure 3.2 does not explicitly include spatial location in the firm's decision. Consider, though, a stylized representation of the situation in Figure 3.2, drawn as Figure 3.4. The situation in Figure 3.2 looked at households located along one particular line segment. Figure 3.4 uses the idea that we can look from the Onceler along a variety of line segments—in the extreme case, completely in a circle around the Onceler's location. Figure 3.2 is thus the situation along one radius of Figure 3.4.

The situation labeled "positive profits" in Figure 3.4 is not an equilibrium if there are truly zero entry costs. A situation in which there are approximately zero profits is shown as Figure 3.5. This situation isn't exactly zero profit, because the firms serve not only the circular zero-profit market areas but also the people in between. Of course, this leaves room for entry by other firms, which in turn would alter the market areas for existing firms. If there are small positive entry costs, then a variety of close-to-zero profit configurations can be equilibria. A pattern of hexagonal market areas of zero-profit size is optimal in the sense of minimizing transport costs, but will not necessarily emerge as a market equilibrium. In the situation shown in Figure 3.5, rectangular market areas have emerged. (Eaton and Lipsey, 1976, explore the question of market area configuration in detail.) In particular, there is an "integer problem" for small geographical areas. If it is impossible to have 0.3 firms, and the equilibrium implied by the model is 2.3 firms, then we will see 2 firms each making a positive profit. Berry and Garrison (1958b) investigate this issue and find that this problem—to the

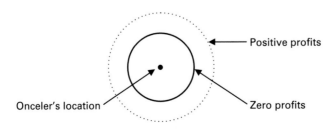

FIGURE 3.4 Market Areas for Thneeds

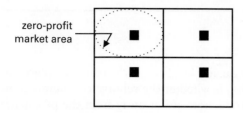

zero-profit
market area

FIGURE 3.5 Market Areas
with Small Positive Profits

extent that the persistence of economic profits is a problem—is in fact more common in small towns than in larger cities.

We can divide the costs that the firm must incur into two types—production costs and transport costs. Suppose that the average costs of production ($AC_{production}$) have the familiar U-shape and that the average transport costs ($AC_{transport}$) increase as total production increases because of the increase in the market area implied by the increase in production. A possible example is shown as Figure 3.6.

In equilibrium, identical firms earn zero profits (as shown in Figure 3.6, with price notated as p_{eq} equal to average total cost). Each household shops at the firm closest to it. (A simple extension of the model to a general equilibrium framework in which households work yields the result that each household also works at the firm closest to it.) As a result, when the quantity produced is low, transport costs (and average transport costs) are low because the demand consists entirely of households located nearby. As quantity produced increases, the average transport cost increases as the market area of the firm expands. As in the analysis of monopolistic competition familiar from principles, there are too many firms in equilibrium, since the AC curve is not minimized. Note that calculating the efficient number of firms without accounting for transport costs would understate the optimal scale of production and, therefore, overstate the efficiency cost of the equilibrium outcome. Average cost of production is minimized at a quantity of q_0, which is less than the quantity (q_1) that minimizes the average cost of production and distribution.

FIGURE 3.6 Production Costs and Transport Costs

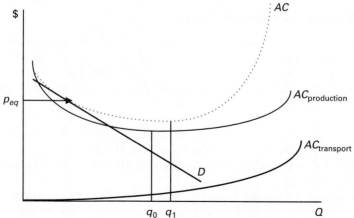

THE SUBSTITUTION EFFECTS
OF TRANSPORTATION COSTS

If a commodity that has various quality levels is produced in one place and consumed in many places, a natural question is whether the relative consumption of high to low quality will be greater at the production site or away from the production site. Consider the case of agricultural products: Do farmers keep the best produce for themselves or do they ship it elsewhere? The willingness of people to drive to rural markets suggests that farmers keep the best for themselves. On the other hand, consider rock-and-roll bands. The ones that tour nationally are presumably better than the ones whose audiences are purely local. Let us consider what light economic theory can shed on the situation, following the analysis of Gould and Segall (1969).

Suppose that the good in question is apples from the state of Washington. (An alternative commodity to consider is the services of rock bands from Seattle.) There are two quality levels, "fine" and "great," with the total production divided equally between the two quality levels. Assume that fine apples sell for $2 per pound in Washington, while great apples sell for $3 per pound. If it costs $0.50 per pound to ship either type of apple to Indiana, will the people of Indiana consume a higher percentage of great apples than the people of Washington?

The relative price of fine and great apples in Washington is 2/3 (in order to consume a fine apple you must give up 2/3 of a great apple), while the relative price in Indiana is 2.5/3.5, or 5/7. Because 5/7 is greater than 2/3, fine apples are relatively more expensive in Indiana, and we might expect people to consume relatively more great apples as a result. On the other hand, the transportation costs mean that all Washington apples are more expensive relative to other things in Indiana, so the change in consumption will depend on the relative attractiveness of substitutes for both qualities of apple. If fine apples have a lot of substitutes in Indiana while great apples do not, then the relative consumption of great apples will be higher in Indiana than in Washington, and vice versa. Economic theory is ambiguous in its predictions, so we might observe either case in practice. (Should you go to Seattle to hear the best bands or wait for the bands to visit your town?)

An Application: "Conan the Economist"

To see an example of this analysis in literature (broadly defined), consider the following conversation from *Conan the Victorious* (Jordan 1984, pp. 129–130). Conan and his comrade Hordo have joined a caravan traveling from Turan to Vendhya. Our hero is concerned about whether the merchant they are traveling with (Kang Hou) is telling them the whole truth about his activities.

"Have you looked at the goods they carry?" Conan asked quietly. "It is all carpets and velvet and tapestries. But the value of it, Hordo."

Conan had been a thief in his youth, and his eye could still gauge the price of anything worth stealing.

"'Tis mainly of the third quality, with only a little of the second. I should not think it worth carrying to Arenjun [a Turanian city], much less all the way to Vendhya."

"Distance and rarity increase value," Kang Hou said. "It is clear you are no merchant. The carpet that will barely procure a profit in Turan will bring fifty times as much in Vendhya. Do you think that the finest Vendhyan carpets go to Turan? Those grace the floors of Vendhyan nobles, yet a far greater price may be obtained by taking a carpet of the second quality to Turan than by selling one of the first quality in Vendhya."

In Kang Hou's analysis, the higher-quality goods are consumed closer to their place of production, while Conan expects the higher-quality goods to be shipped. The theoretical analysis presented earlier can help resolve this difficulty, as we can see that Conan and Kang Hou implicitly have different judgments about the availability of substitutes.

STRATEGIC INTERACTION AMONG FIRMS

The models we have considered to this point have treated each firm's decision in isolation. In practice, firms are likely to take into account the probable actions of their rivals when making decisions about location and pricing. Adding this level of complexity improves the realism of the economic models. It brings a complication, though, in addition to the basic fact that the models are more complicated. Models in which firms explicitly interact often have either no equilibrium or multiple equilibria, and the equilibria that exist are often inefficient. The economic field of "game theory" has evolved to carefully analyze strategic interactions. While we will not delve deeply into game theory here, it is important to understand the general issues that arise as a result of strategic interactions. One of the earliest analyses of the implications of strategic behavior came from Harold Hotelling (1929), and we will consider his example in the next subsection.

Equilibrium Location with a Given Price

Imagine a beach, one mile long, along which customers are evenly spaced. Two ice cream vendors sell identical ice cream cones for $1 per cone. The ice cream vendors are mobile, so they can locate anywhere along the beach, and they can change location at any time. Every person on the beach demands one ice cream cone and buys from the closest vendor. Where will the vendors locate?

To develop intuition, suppose that the vendors are located at points α and β along the beach as shown in Figure 3.7. The vendor at point α will have a market area extending from 0 to $(\alpha+\beta)/2$, as indicated by the dotted line. The vendor at point β will have a market area consisting of the rest of the beach. Is the situation drawn in Figure 3.7 an equilibrium? It is an equilibrium only if neither vendor could sell more ice cream by relocating.

FIGURE 3.7 Ice Cream Vendors on the Beach

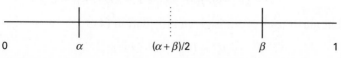

Suppose the vendor at point β moved to the left. That vendor would keep all the customers between point (α+β)/2 and 1 and also gain customers at the expense of the vendor at point α. The vendor at point α, meanwhile, has a similar incentive to move to the right. The only possible equilibrium is to have both vendors right next to each other in the middle of the beach. This equilibrium is extremely inefficient, though, in that it maximizes the total travel cost for their customers. Compare the equilibrium to a situation where the vendors are required to locate at the points 0.25 and 0.75. Their profits would be the same as in the equilibrium, but the total travel cost is lower. This illustrates the potential problems caused by strategic interactions among firms.

The Hotelling model makes some simplifying assumptions that are important. What would be the equilibrium outcome, for example, if there were three vendors? (There is no equilibrium.) What about four vendors? When you add vendors, you complicate the situation in that a move toward one rival to gain customers is simultaneously a move away from other rivals that sacrifices customers.

Another complication that is omitted from the simple model is the possibility that the vendors compete on some dimension other than travel cost. Suppose one of the vendors sells a different flavor of ice cream, for example. It should be clear that even this simple framework can be used as the basis of some intricate analysis. We will use this type of analysis later in the book to describe interactions among firms when there are agglomeration economies of scale. Using these ideas, we will also analyze interactions among local governments.

Equilibrium Location with Endogenous Price

Let us work through a more detailed and general example here that allows firms to alter their price. (This example is taken from DiPasquale and Wheaton 1996, p. 135.) We will take as given parameters the frequency with which a consumer will make a trip to purchase the good (v), the trip cost per mile (k), the marginal cost of the good to retailers (mc), the fixed cost of the retail facility (C), and the density of buyers along a line (F). We wish to solve for the equilibrium distance between stores (D), sales per store (S), and price (P). The market area for a given store charging price P extends to the distance that the gross price to the consumer is lower than that at other stores. The gross price is given by the following formula, given the notation above and the additional variables T, defined as the distance between the store and the edge of its market area, and P_0, defined as the price charged by neighboring stores.

$$P + kT = P_0 + k(D - T), \text{ so that } T = (P_0 - P + kD) / 2k \tag{1}$$

In the symmetric case $P_0 = P$, $T = D / 2$. Because each consumer is assumed to purchase one unit per trip, the total annual sales per store (S) is given by

$$S = 2TvF = vF[(P_0 - P + kD) / k] \tag{2}$$

To calculate profits, it is only necessary to multiply equation (2) by price to get total revenues, then subtract marginal costs and fixed costs. This yields equation (3).

$$\Pi = (P - mc)\{vF[(P_0 - P + kD) / k]\} - C \tag{3}$$

The price that maximizes profit is given in equation (4).

$$P^* = (P_0 + kD + mc) / 2 \tag{4}$$

Equation (4) has the following natural interpretation. The price that one store charges will be higher if its competitors charge a higher price. The price that a store will charge is also higher if transport costs are higher, because a customer is less willing to shop elsewhere. Finally, a store will charge a higher price if its wholesale costs are higher.

The difficult question is that since every store will be using equation (4) to determine its price, how do we pin down the price for the competitors? One approach is that, since the firms are identical, we expect each of them to charge an identical price in equilibrium. If we implement this assumption and substitute P^* for P_0 in equations (1), (2), and (4), we get equation (5), which gives the equilibrium price, market area, and sales volume in terms of the underlying parameters.

$$P = kD + mc; \quad T = D/2; \quad S = DvF \tag{5}$$

The price in equation (5) is higher than marginal cost as firms take advantage of the market power resulting from different locations. The extent of this market power, though, depends on the distance between stores and the transport cost. The one remaining loose end in the model is the total number of firms in a given area—in other words, D. If there is free entry into the market, then the long-run equilibrium is that profits equal zero. Thus, the distance between firms is such that the operating profits equal the fixed costs. Algebraically,

$$\Pi = (P^* - mc)vFD - C = 0 \tag{6}$$

Equation (5) gives the equilibrium price given the distance between firms, while equation (6) gives the equilibrium distance given the price. If we solve the two equations simultaneously for P^* and D, by substituting equation (5) into equation (6), then we obtain the following final solution.

$$D = (C/kvF)^{1/2}; \quad P = mc + (kC/vF)^{1/2} \tag{7}$$

Equation (7) implies that stores with high fixed costs will be spaced farther apart and will have a higher profit margin. The greater the density of buyers along a line, the closer the stores will be. The more often a consumer travels to purchase the good, the closer the stores will be. A simple application is to compare supermarkets and convenience stores. Supermarkets have larger fixed costs and sell products that are bought less frequently (such as spices) relative to convenience stores, which specialize in perishable items, such as milk.

Consider the following numerical example, summarized in Table 3.1. There are two goods, milk and paprika. The typical household purchases milk once a week but purchases paprika only once a year. In equilibrium, more stores will be selling milk than paprika, and milk will sell for less than half the price of paprika. This is true even though the wholesale price of paprika is exactly the same as the wholesale price of milk, and even though the fixed costs for a store selling paprika are no larger than those for a store selling milk.

One empirical test of the approach developed in this section is to calculate variation among industries in the radius of the region served by a single plant. This was done by Leonard Weiss, and the results are summarized in Table 3.2. Cigarettes and ice cream might be comparable in terms of per capita demand, but they have very different scale economies. Other industries can be compared in the same way.

TABLE 3.1 Market Areas and Prices: A Numerical Example

Variable	Milk	Paprika
Parameters:		
Annual trip frequency (v)	52	1
Trip cost per mile (k)	$0.40	$0.40
Wholesale price (mc)	$1.60	$1.60
Fixed costs (C)	$200,000	$200,000
Population density (F)	5000 people per mile²	5000 people per mile²
Equilibrium values:		
Distance between stores (D)	1.39	10
Annual sales per store (S)	360,555	50,000
Price (P)	$2.15	$5.60

CENTRAL PLACE THEORY

The model developed in the previous section considers only one type of product. In practice, there are many different industries, each with a different market area. Maintaining for a moment the assumption that all locations are identical, we can analyze the size distribution and firm composition of cities, given the various market areas. This model is known as "central place theory," and it has a distinguished lineage in the history of economic thought, dating back at least to the work of von Thünen in the early 1800s. Krugman (1995) gives a critical review of this literature.

TABLE 3.2 Geographic Area Served by Plants in Various Industries

Industry	Radius of Service Area
Soft drinks	68
Concrete products	144
Ice cream	158
Brick	200
Metal cans	362
Malt liquors	370
Bolts, nuts, screws, rivets, washers	467
Soap and detergents	572
Flour and grain products	682
Costume jewelry, buttons	722
Fertilizers	828
Tires and inner tubes	833
Cigarettes	1,108

Source: Weiss (1972); radius in miles is the distance that 80 percent of a plant's output was shipped.

Adam Smith, writing at the dawn of the Industrial Revolution, summarized the relationship between the nascent industrial city and its agricultural hinterland as follows (1776, Book III, Chapter 1): "The great commerce of every civilized society is that carried on between the inhabitants of the town and those of the country. It consists in the exchange of rude for manufactured produce. . . . The country supplies the town with the means of subsistence and the materials of manufacture. The town repays this supply by sending back a part of the manufactured produce to the inhabitants of the country." Central place theory extends this idea to the case where there is a hierarchy of cities as well as a distinction between urban and rural areas.

Central place theory is based on the idea that different types of firms have different market areas and that cities are composed of these firms. Consider a firm with a market area of 8,000. A city of 16,000 people will have two of these firms. Further, it will have four firms with a market area of 4,000, and so on. A city of 16,000 will export the goods and services of firms with a market area of 16,000 to cities of smaller population, and import goods and services produced by firms with market areas larger than 16,000 from larger cities. The smallest cities export to agricultural (nonurban) areas. How do agricultural regions pay for these goods and services, given that they do not have any urban goods to export in return? Quite simply, by exporting the food that all the urban areas require to maintain their population. The bottom line: Larger cities export to smaller cities, and cities of equal size do not interact. There is also the intriguing possibility that central place theory might explain the empirical finding that the rank-size rule (Zipf's Law) approximately holds, as discussed in chapter 1.

This theory provides an obvious hypothesis, that larger cities provide all the services found in smaller cities and a few more in addition. This hypothesis comes at the expense of strong assumptions, including an implicit assumption that demand for all goods and services is homogeneous throughout the population. Despite the strong assumptions, some evidence exists that central place theory is a reasonable description of the world. An extremely detailed study of places in Snohomish County, Washington, is summarized in Tables 3.3 and 3.4. The threshold population in Table 3.4 represents the population of the smallest community in which that function was found.

It is completely unsurprising to find in Table 3.3 that the larger places had more business establishments providing more functions. What is perhaps more surprising is to see that there were, on average, more establishments per function in the larger places. This accords with central place theory's predictions. For example, the theory predicts that a function with a market area of 4,000 people will only have one estab-

TABLE 3.3 Central Place Hierarchy in Snohomish County, Washington

	Hamlets	Villages	Towns
Number of places	20	9	4
Average population	417	948	2,433
Average number of establishments	6.9	54.4	149
Average number of "functions"	5.9	32.1	59.8
Average number of establishments per function	1.2	1.7	2.5

Source: B. Berry and W. Garrison (1958a).

TABLE 3.4 Number of Places Having Selected Functions

	Threshold Population	Hamlets (20)	Villages (9)	Towns (4)
Churches	265	8	9	4
Restaurants	276	6	9	4
Elementary schools	322	13	9	4
Physicians	380	0	6	4
Lawyers	528	0	5	4
Banks	610	2	7	4
Hospitals and clinics	1,159	0	1	3

Source: B. Berry and W. Garrison (1958a).

lishment in a town of 4,000 but will have four establishments in a town of 16,000. It also illustrates the idea that excess profits are less likely to obtain in larger places than in smaller places because the larger places enjoy more competition for each function.

In Table 3.4 a few of the functions are listed, along with the number of places in which each service was found. The hierarchy is clear, as some functions are ubiquitous, while others are found only in the larger places. This hierarchy was identified at the national level by Adam Smith (1776). He distinguished between four types of cities: capital, great towns, small towns, and villages. As one moves from the smaller to the larger, a greater range of commodities is found, serving a greater market area. Table 3.5 (adapted from Stull 1986) illustrates Smith's urban hierarchy.

The basic idea for central place theory assumes a static environment, in which there are a certain set of functions and a given spatial distribution of population. If either of these conditions change, then the pattern of central places can also change. For example, if economies of scale increase, increasing equilibrium market areas, then a smaller number of cities could preserve the existing urban hierarchy.

A more interesting case (analyzed in the later subsection on "Firm Location with Interdependent Demand") is when there are interfirm externalities in shopping. In the case of close substitutes, this can lead firms to locate close together in order to get access to comparison-shoppers. The "auto mall" on the outskirts of every U.S. city is testimony to the power of this force. There are also incentives for clustering in the case of firms selling complementary products. This principle is the driving force behind shopping malls, for example. The existence of either substitutes or complements provides an incentive for greater clustering of firms than our previous analysis would

TABLE 3.5 Central Place Hierarchy according to Adam Smith

Level of Hierarchy	Examples	Industries and Occupations
Capital	London	Trade, Banking, Headquarters
Great Town	Birmingham, Edinburgh	Manufacturing, Apothecary
Small Town	Kirkcaldy (Smith's birthplace)	Nailmaking, Grocer, Butcher
Village	In the Scottish Highlands	Country Carpenter or Smith

Source: Stull, 1986, Table 2, p. 303.

suggest. However, they do not contradict the idea that a hierarchy of urban areas will exist in which small urban areas import from larger urban areas. In the next chapter we will analyze the case when there are differences among firms and differences among locations. These differences will be shown to affect the simple relation among cities predicted by central place theory. In fact, central place theory is a special case of a more general location theory.

GRAVITY MODELS AND MARKET POTENTIAL

Central place theory is concerned with the relative sizes of cities and the allocation of firms to various sizes of cities. A related question is the pattern of trade among cities. As already noted, the strong prediction of central place theory is that there will be no trade among cities of similar sizes, assuming that every city produces every good. Let us relax this assumption in a small way, by allowing there to be many different cities from which a city might import any product that it does not produce. Of course, the "smaller" cities in even the simple version of central place theory above have this option already. How much will each city trade with another? Intuitively, we can pose two determinants. The first determinant is the relative size of the two cities. If one city is quite small relative to a second city, then the first city is unlikely to register as a major trading partner of the second city. The second determinant is the cost of transportation between the two cities. If two alternative sources lie at different distances from a city, then the city is likely to have a larger volume of trade with the closer source, assuming the transport cost per unit of distance is the same for the two sources. This predicted relation among cities can be expressed mathematically as follows, where T_{ij} is the volume of trade, N_i and N_j are the populations of cities i and j respectively, D_{ij} is the distance between cities i and j, and k and β are parameters.

$$T_{ij} = k \, (N_i N_j) / D^{\beta}_{ij} \tag{8}$$

This relation is similar to the gravitational attraction between two bodies of a given size and a given distance apart, and in fact equation (8) is usually referred to as the "gravity model" of trade. In physics, the coefficient on distance, β, equals 2. In general, the higher that β is, the lower the attraction between two places at a given distance. In other words, β can be thought of as summarizing transactions costs, including transportation costs. The formulation assumes that distance is the only determinant of transactions costs. Consider the case of three equidistant cities, two of which are in one country, while the third is in a second country. It is likely that transactions costs are higher between the first two cities and the third, but the basic formula does not account for this.

The simple gravity model assumes that the only difference among cities is their population. In fact, there are other dimensions of variation that a more sophisticated model might take into account. For example, the climate in one city might be different than the climate in another city, implying a pattern of demand that varies as well. Other important factors might include household income, local government tax, and spending behavior. A model that incorporates these other determinants of trade is known as calculating "market potential." The idea is that the total demand for a firm is related to the distance to its customers and that their demand might vary systematically with location. A firm will maximize profits by locating in the city with the highest market potential.

Harris (1954) constructed measures of market potential for the United States and demonstrated the correlation between it and the concentration of industry. The European commission, more recently, has found a relation between firm concentration and household income (Krugman 1995, p. 45). A recent application of this approach to economic growth in the United States is found in Carlino and Mills (1987), who apply a market potential model to explaining county growth during the 1970s. In a point that anticipates our later analysis in chapters 4 and 7, they emphasize the interdependence between firm location decisions and household location decisions. After all, a household has to work, so it will wish to locate near a firm. And a firm will want to have access to a good labor force and large market, and both of those will be found where households want to locate. Carlino and Mills find that variation in household income and climate explain much of the pattern of economic growth, while local government policies are less important.

Firm Location and Interdependent Products

The formal models developed in this chapter treated the demand for each firm's product as independent and assumed that each purchase trip involved only one item. In practice, the demand for some goods is related to the demand for other goods, and some trips involve the purchase of more than one item. How do these considerations affect the models presented earlier?

In general, accounting for the presence of complements and substitutes will change the optimal location decisions of firms. The obvious (but partially wrong) conclusion would be that firms would want to locate closer to firms that sell complementary products and farther away from firms that sell substitutes. It is unambiguously true that firms will want to locate closer to firms selling complements. In fact, this reasoning provides an explanation for both department stores and shopping centers.

The case of substitutes is more complicated, however. If the product is extremely heterogeneous or high-cost, then firms may choose to cluster to encourage consumers to search for the best price or best match to their tastes. The case of auto malls has already been mentioned, and you will find that jewelry stores in most shopping malls are located close together. On the other hand, if the product is low-cost or homogeneous, then the firm will wish to discourage search by the consumer. If a shopping mall is large enough to support two bookstores, they will usually be at opposite ends of the mall and on separate floors, if the mall has more than one story. Finally, some products that seem to be substitutes may in fact be complements. Consider the food court at a mall. If a person eats at one stand, then he or she won't eat at another. However, a person eating at one stand might eat at the mall again, and clustering all the food stands makes it easy for that person to comparison shop in anticipation of the next trip. The placement of fast-food restaurants along streets follows a similar logic.

CHAPTER SUMMARY

- Urban economics emphasizes the role of space in determining economic activity. In order for a product to be bought or sold, it must be transported from where the seller is to where the buyer is. This transportation is not free, and so there is an incentive for people to live close to others with whom they interact. Transportation costs can influence not only the location of production and consumption but also the types of goods that are produced and consumed at various locations.

- A market area is defined as the area over which a firm can underprice its competitors. The size of a market area depends on the relative production costs of firms, the cost of transportation, and the level of demand. Firms will take their competitors' location decisions into account when making their own decisions, possibly leading to outcomes that are not efficient from society's perspective although they maximize profit for the firm.

- One model of trade among cities is central place theory. Central place theory postulates a hierarchy of cities, in which the larger cities export goods and services to the smaller cities, who in turn export to agricultural areas, who export food to the larger cities.

- Another model of trade among cities is the gravity model. This theory postulates that intercity trade will depend on the distance between the cities and the relative size of the cities.

EXCERPT: *THE DISPOSSESSED* (URSULA K. LE GUIN)

The huge variety of products and services available in urban areas is a commonplace of life in modern society. This same variety could be overwhelming to someone from a different type of society. The following excerpt from Ursula K. Le Guin's novel *The Dispossessed* (1974, pp. 106–107) illustrates the confusion and horror that a visit to a commercial district—in the city of A-Io on the fictional planet of Urras—could cause to a native of a communitarian society. Enjoy your next trip to the mall!

Saio Pae had taken him "shopping" during his second week in A-Io. Though he did not consider cutting his hair—his hair, after all, was part of him—he wanted an Urrasti-style suit of clothes and pair of shoes. He had no desire to look any more foreign than he could help looking. So at his request Pae had taken him to Saemtenevia Prospect, the elegant retail street, to be fitted by a tailor and a shoemaker.

The whole experience had been so bewildering to him that he put it out of mind as soon as possible, but he had dreams about it for months afterwards, nightmares. Saemtenevia Prospect was two miles long, and it was a solid mass of people, traffic, and things: things to buy, things for sale. Coats, dresses, gowns, robes, trousers, breeches, shirts, blouses, hats, shoes, stockings, scarves, shawls, vests, capes, umbrellas, clothes to wear while sleeping, while swimming, while playing games, while at an afternoon party, while at an evening party, while at a party in the country, while traveling, while at the theater, while riding horses, gardening, receiving guests, boating, dining, hunting—all different, all in hundreds of different cuts, styles, colors, textures, materials. Perfumes, clocks, lamps, statues, cosmetics, candles, pictures, cameras, games, vases, sofas, kettles, puzzles, pillows, dolls, colanders, hassocks, jewels, carpets, toothpicks, calendars, a baby's teething rattle of platinum with a handle of rock crystal, an electrical machine to sharpen pencils, a wristwatch with diamond numerals; figurines and souvenirs and kickshaws and mementos and gewgaws and bric-a-brac, everything either useless to begin with or ornamented so as to disguise its use; acres of luxuries, acres of excrement. In the first block he had stopped to look at a shaggy, spotted coat, the central display in a glittering window of clothes and jewelry. "The coat costs 8,400 units?" he asked in disbelief, for he had recently read in a newspaper that a "living wage" was about 2,000 units a year. "Oh, yes, that's real fur, quite rare now that the animals are protected," Pae had said. "Pretty thing, isn't it? Women love furs." And they went on. After one more block he had felt utterly exhausted. He could not look any more. He wanted to hide his eyes.

And the strangest thing about the nightmare street was that none of the millions of things for sale were made there. They were only sold there. Where were the workshops, the factories, where were the farmers, the craftsmen, the miners, the weavers, the chemists, the carvers, the dyers, the designers, the machinists, where were the hands, the people who made? Out of sight, somewhere else. Behind walls. All the people in all the shops were either buyers or sellers. They had no relation to the things but that of possession.

Source: The Dispossessed by Ursula K. Le Guin. Copyright © 1974 by HarperCollins. Reprinted by permission of HarperCollins Publishers.

Questions for Review and Discussion

1. The protagonist in the excerpt from *The Dispossessed* is disturbed that the production of goods occurs in a different location from the exchange of goods. Can you enlighten him—using economic theory—as to reasons that this might occur?

2. Go to a large shopping mall. What types of stores cluster together? What types of stores are far apart? Can you use the theory developed in this chapter to explain this pattern of location?

3. Recall the discussion between Conan and Kang Hou in the section titled "Conan the Economist." What are their respective opinions on the availability of substitutes? Do you agree with Conan or Kang Hou?

4. Where is your city in the central place hierarchy? What is the next higher city? What are some of the lower cities?

5. Suppose you wanted to open a car dealership. What would you look for in a location? How would your answer differ if you wanted to open a gas station?

CHAPTER

Location of Economic Activity

4

C ities grow where firms locate. The first task in analyzing the growth of cities is, therefore, to consider the location decisions of firms in more detail than we have done to this point. In the last chapter we examined location decisions of identical firms that lie on a featureless plain. Now we will consider location decisions in a more general and more realistic setting, in which each location varies in its attractiveness to a firm. Identifying the different types of firms on the basis of the types of locations likely to attract them will also help explain the pattern of city specialization we saw in chapter 1.

This chapter begins with the simplest possible model of location: a firm with one source of inputs and one market for outputs. This model enables us to develop a taxonomy of firm types that is also useful in more general settings. One of the immediate benefits is that central place theory is shown to be a special case of urban growth resulting from firms that are all of one type. We then turn to the more general case of a firm with multiple sources of inputs and multiple markets for outputs. One of the cardinal principles of location theory is worth emphasizing from the beginning: in order for something to influence location decisions, it *must* vary across locations! No matter how important some input or other factor, if every location is identical in its supply, then that input or factor will not influence the location decision.

LOCATION THEORY WITH ONE INPUT SOURCE AND ONE MARKET

Consider the following model. A firm produces a single output, and all of this output is shipped to a marketplace M. The firm uses a single input that is transformed in fixed proportions to the output, and all of the input is obtained from a source of inputs I. The price of inputs, the price of the output, and shipping costs are determined in competitive markets. Suppose M and I are located on a line segment. The firm's problem is then to choose where on the line segment to locate in order to maximize profits.

This simple framework makes two assumptions that should be highlighted. First, the assumption of a fixed proportions transformation from the input to the output removes any possibility of factor substitution. As we will see later, the possibility of factor substitution is an important issue in explaining a city's industrial specialization. Second, the existence of a single market to ship the product to implies that a city has already formed. Thus, this simple model is incomplete as an explanation for the initial development of a city.

Two types of transport costs face the firm. The first, *procurement costs*, are the costs of shipping the input to the firm's factory. The second, *distribution costs*, are the costs of shipping the output from the factory to the market. Let w_p be the weight of the input and t_p the cost per unit distance of transporting the input (the subscript p is for procurement costs). Then $w_p * t_p$ is defined as the *monetary weight* of the input. If the factory is located at a distance x from the source of inputs I, then the procurement costs equal $w_p * t_p * x$. Similarly, the distribution costs equal $w_d * t_d * (x_m - x)$, where x_m is the distance from I to M.

The firm's profit function can be written $\Pi = TR - TC = TR -$ production costs $-$ transport costs $= TR -$ production costs $- w_p * t_p * x - w_d * t_d * (x_m - x)$. If revenues and production costs are independent of location, then maximizing profits is equivalent to minimizing transportation costs. An example is shown as Figure 4.1.

As drawn, the total transport cost is minimized by locating at I, the source of inputs. This case, where the monetary weight of the input exceeds that of the output, is known as a *weight-losing* or *input-oriented* firm. The other case, where the monetary weight of the output exceeds that of the input, is known as a *weight-gaining* or *market-oriented* firm. Note that the weights are monetary weights, which do not necessarily correspond to physical weights. Some inputs, such as eggs, are expensive to ship even if they are not particularly heavy. An example of an input-oriented firm would be an ore refinery; refined metal is only a fraction of the raw ore. An example of a market-oriented firm would be a bottling company; a high percentage of a soft drink (or beer) is water. To reduce the costs of shipping water across the country, it makes more sense to ship syrup for soft drinks and add the water at a location closer to the market. More examples are given in Table 4.2 later in the chapter.

FIGURE 4.1 Minimizing Transportation Costs

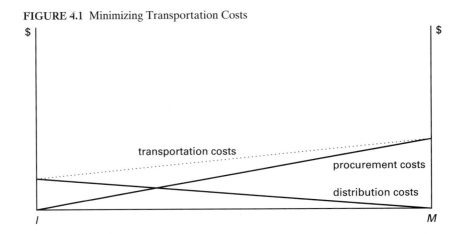

TABLE 4.1   Scale Economies in Transportation: Freight Rates in 1884

Railroad	Average Haul (Miles)	Revenue Per Ton-mile (Cents)
Chicago and Grand Trunk	73.60	2.23
Detroit, Lansing, and Northern	75.39	2.24
Detroit, Grand Haven, and Milwaukee	78.17	2.09
Flint and Pere Marquette	100.34	1.69
Chicago and West Michigan	103.33	1.15
Michigan Central	111.95	1.72
Grand Rapids and Indiana	166.83	1.50
Lake Shore and Michigan Southern	202.90	0.89

Source: Pred (1966, p. 53).

Will firms ever locate anywhere besides *I* and *M*? Examining Figure 4.1, it is clear that with linear transport costs, the only time an intermediate location is optimal is when the monetary weight of the input and the output are identical. This is unlikely, so an optimal location of either *I* or *M* is expected.

In the more general case of nonlinear transport costs, there is another reason to expect firms not to prefer an intermediate location. There are two possible sources of scale economies in transportation, meaning a decrease in the monetary weight as the distance shipped increases. The first source of scale economies is *terminal costs*, the costs of loading and unloading the inputs and outputs. Terminal costs mean that procurement costs will be greater than zero even if the firm locates at *I*, because the inputs must be moved within the town. Similarly, distribution costs are greater than zero even if the firm locates at *M*. The second source of scale economies is the possibility that average shipping rates per mile decrease with distance shipped. Table 4.1 illustrates this possibility using data on railroad freight rates from stations in Michigan in 1884.

If there are scale economies in transportation, the general transportation costs will look more like Figure 4.2 than Figure 4.1. It is clear that an intermediate location is not preferred even in the unlikely case of identical monetary weights.

FIGURE 4.2 Nonlinear Transportation Costs

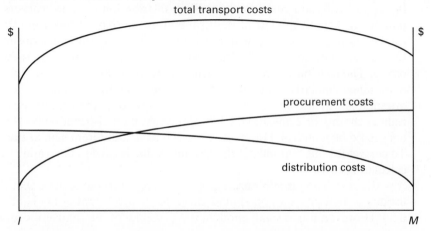

APPLICATION: CENTRAL PLACE THEORY

Central place theory, explained in chapter 3, was based on the idea that firms located so as to serve their customers. None of the analysis in that chapter mentioned the sources of the inputs for the firms. Implicitly, then, only distribution costs mattered. In the terminology introduced earlier in this chapter, this means that central place theory is a model in which all firms are market-oriented rather than input-oriented. If this is an accurate characterization of firms, central place theory can be expected to be an appropriate model of urban structure.

Consider the following formal model, developed by Paul Krugman (1991), of firm location and urban growth. The logic of the model is simple. Producers prefer to locate near large markets in order to minimize distribution costs. But markets are large precisely where other producers have already located. In that case, urban growth can be self-sustaining.

A firm is deciding where it wants to locate along the unit line segment. The firm wishes to minimize total costs, which equal production costs plus transport costs. There are assumed to be economies of scale in production to the point that the firm decides to have only one production facility. Demand at each point along the line segment is proportional to employment at that point. Two types of workers are involved: agricultural workers uniformly distributed along the line segment and urban workers concentrated in a city located at point z.

Let $t_A(x)$ equal the total distribution costs to agricultural workers if the firm locates at x, $t_U(x)$ equal the total distribution costs to urban workers, τ equal the unit shipping cost, and α the percent of the population that works in agriculture. If the firm is at x, a fraction x of the agricultural workers is located to the "left" of the firm, the average one being $x/2$ away. Similarly, a fraction $(1-x)$ is located to the "right" of the firm. Normalizing the population to one and assuming that each person demands one unit of the good, we can write the distribution costs as follows:

$$t_A(x) = \alpha\tau/2\,[x^2 + (1-x)^2]$$
$$t_U(x) = (1-\alpha)\,\tau\,|x - z|$$

Before moving on to consider the implications of this model, it is worth elaborating on the two distribution cost functions. First, distribution costs to workers involve shipping to workers to the left of the firm and to the right of the firm. The firm ships a total of αx units to the left, with the average unit being shipped a distance of $x/2$. The total distribution cost to agricultural workers to the left of the firm is thus $\alpha x(x/2)\tau$, or $\alpha\tau x^2/2$. The distribution cost to agricultural workers located to the right of the firm is determined similarly. Regarding distribution costs to workers in the city, the main question is why the absolute value of $x - z$ is used. If the firm locates 2 miles to the right of the city or 2 miles to the left of the city, then distribution costs to urban workers should be identical. However, $x - z$ will have a different sign at the two locations. To correct for this "problem," the absolute value is used to determine the distance for calculating costs.

Because $t_A(x)$ is minimized at $x = 0.5$, it is natural to assume that the city will be located at that point. (You should check for yourself that $t_A(x)$ is minimized at $x = 0.5$.) However, if α is small enough, it is possible for alternative locations to be equi-

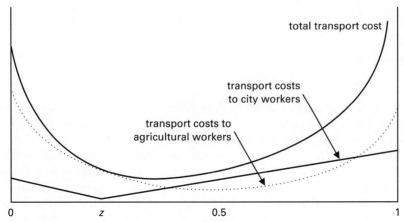

FIGURE 4.3 Location with a Large Market

libria, in the sense that it would not benefit any individual firm to locate outside the city. This is illustrated in Figure 4.3.

Two general results follow from using this type of model. First, producers will tend to group together. Second, the location of the city is indeterminate. Therefore, initial conditions and historical accidents can play a large role in determining the location of cities. We will return to this model and develop it further in chapter 7.

How do other orientations of firms affect central place theory? First, the existence of cities formed by input-oriented firms can disrupt the central place hierarchy by causing trade among cities of similar sizes or even exports from smaller to larger cities. Second, in extreme cases it is possible that the dominant city can be changed as market-oriented firms follow the now larger markets created by input-oriented firms.

One other complication should be introduced into central place theory. Suppose the demand for different products varies from place to place, as we saw in the market potential model in chapter 3. Will this disrupt the central place hierarchy? Maybe. If per capita demand for a good falls as the population of a city increases, it is possible that firms will find it optimal to locate in smaller cities and export to the few customers in larger cities who want their product. For example, if the residents of small towns demand greater amounts of handicrafts per capita than do residents of large cities, then artisans might locate in small towns. The occasional resident of a large city who desired handicrafts would then be forced to import them from the artisans in the small towns.

LOCATION CHOICE WITH MULTIPLE MARKETS AND INPUT SOURCES

Now suppose that several sources of inputs and/or markets for outputs are available. Where should the firm locate? There is a simple answer, which I will first assert and then go on to demonstrate. The answer is the *principle of median location*, which says that the optimal location divides the monetary weight into two equal halves. Let us consider an example, illustrated in Figure 4.4, to see how this principle applies.

FIGURE 4.4 Median Location Example

Consider a pizza delivery firm whose customers are located along a line segment. There are 2 customers at *A*, 10 at *B*, 7 at *C*, and 4 at *D*. Point A is one furlong west of point *B*, point *B* is 4 furlongs west of point *C*, and point *C* is three furlongs west of point *D*. Each customer wants one pizza per day, and all inputs used to produce pizza are ubiquitous. It costs $2 per round-trip furlong to transport pizza, and each pizza requires a separate trip (not everyone orders at the same time—except during the O. J. chase, which was the biggest night ever for Domino's Pizza™, surpassing even halftime at the Super Bowl).

Under these assumptions, the firm wants to locate so as to minimize transportation costs. If it locates at *A*, then total costs are $172, calculated as follows: ten pizzas are delivered 1 furlong to *B* at a cost of $20, four pizzas are delivered 5 furlongs to *C* at a cost of $40, and seven pizzas are delivered 8 furlongs to *D* at a cost of $112. Similarly, the total delivery cost equals $134 at point *B*, $142 at point *C*, and $196 at point *D*. Among these four points, point *B* is clearly the cost-minimizing location. However, it could be the case that an intermediate point is better. To see that this is not so, consider moving west from point *B*. As the firm moves west from *B*, costs of delivering to *A* decrease by $4 per furlong, but costs of delivering to *B*, *C*, and *D* increase by a total of $42 per furlong. Hence, moving west from *B* does not reduce costs. As the firm moves east from *B*, costs of delivering to *A* and *B* increase by $24 per furlong while costs of delivering to *C* and *D* decrease by $22 per furlong. Point *B* is the cost-minimizing location. It is also the median location. With a total of 23 customers, the median is customer number twelve. Counting from east to west (or west to east), that person is found at point *B*.

It is important to understand that the principle of median location applies to the monetary weight of the output, which is not necessarily the same as the median place. This can be seen in the example by noting that the median place between *A* and *D* is a point 1 furlong west of point *C*.

It is also important to realize that the median location is not necessarily the location of the median person. Consider the following modification of the example. Suppose that the cost of delivery is more expensive traveling east than traveling west. Moreover, suppose that the cost per furlong eastbound is $4 while the cost per furlong westbound is $1. In that case, the cost-minimizing location is *C*, with a total distribution cost of $74. The median person is located at *B*, but the higher transport cost eastbound makes *C* a better choice. If the firm had located at *B*, its total transportation cost would have been $226.

The principle of median location provides some immediate insights into urban growth patterns. First, it gives us a reason to expect that places that are initially larger than other places will maintain this size advantage as market-oriented firms seek the median location in order to minimize distribution costs. Second, it provides a rationale for the growth of cities that lie at transshipment points for inputs. Cities such as

Buffalo, St. Louis, and Pittsburgh in the United States and Liverpool in the United Kingdom are excellent examples of this general principle. Perhaps the best example is Koblenz, Germany, located at the confluence of two rivers—in fact the word Koblenz is derived from the Latin *confluens* (Marshall 1989, p. 13). Third, it should be emphasized that internal economies of scale are implicit in the necessity for the firm to choose one location rather than, say, building a separate factory to serve each market.

NONTRADABLE INPUTS AND FIRM LOCATION

The analysis to this point has assumed that all inputs are either ubiquitous or that they can be transported from one place to another. This has in turn implied that production costs do not vary by location, so that the location decision is simply a matter of minimizing transportation costs. However, many inputs do not fit either description. For example, the quality of local public services, such as roads and schools, can affect production costs for a firm. A good public school cannot be shipped from one place to another, though. Other nontradable inputs include energy, labor relations, climate, and agglomeration economies. These factors can cause a firm to choose a location that is different from the cost-minimizing location for transport. Table 4.2 lists characteristics that affect locational orientation of firms and provides examples of firms with their given orientation.

One explanation for the pattern of production and trade is that local production and exports reflect the tastes of the majority of firms or households in an area while imports satisfy the remainder. In that case, the pattern of production could vary considerably even if firms are *footloose*, that is, if transport costs are not an important determinant of location. This is different from saying that some firms are market-oriented; it is a statement that production will settle where demand for the product is high, even if transport costs are negligible. Justman (1994) finds just such a pattern,

TABLE 4.2 Locational Orientation of Firms

Orientation	*Relevant Characteristic*	*Example*
Transport-cost oriented	Transport costs relatively more important	
Input oriented	Inputs weigh more than outputs	Ore refining
	Inputs bulkier than outputs	Steel
	Inputs more perishable than outputs	Fruit canning
Market oriented	Outputs weigh more than inputs	Bottling
	Outputs bulkier than inputs	Auto assembly
	Outputs more perishable than inputs	Baking
Production-cost oriented	Local input costs relatively more important	
Energy	Energy-intensive production	Aluminum
Labor	Labor-intensive production	Textiles
Intermediate inputs		
Specialized inputs	Localization economies of scale	Software
Business services	Urbanization economies of scale	Corporate HQ
Amenity	Weather, recreation, taxes, etc.	R&D, tourism

using data on footloose manufacturing firms in the United States. He ascribes the results to the presence of positive externalities in information transmission. Of course, it is possible to reinterpret the results in a transportation-cost framework. All that is needed is to add an intermediate product, information, that is quite expensive to ship from place to place. If information is important and difficult to ship, then we expect to see firms cluster to take advantage of it. We will return to this explanation for urban development in chapter 7.

Even though each firm is assumed to take local conditions as given when making its location decision, the actions of firms in the aggregate can affect these conditions. For example, if a location is attractive, then the demand for land in that location will increase, and land prices will increase in turn until equilibrium is obtained. Of course, this assumes that the supply of land is approximately constant, a not unreasonable assumption in the short run at least. Market forces thus provide a natural limit to urban growth.

A succinct way of summarizing the interaction between the original characteristics of a location and the man-made changes to the location is to call the former the "first nature" of a site and the latter the "second nature" of a site. Recall from chapter 1 the explanation of urban growth as arising from economies of scale in the provision of a market and transportation system (Berliant and Konishi 1994). The first nature determines where such a system can be set up at lowest cost, given existing conditions and technology. Once a transport system is created, though, then even a change in conditions can be insufficient to alter the advantages enjoyed by existing cities. Buffalo, New York, for example, was given an impetus to grow by the fact that it is the terminus of the Erie Canal. However, the city of Buffalo did not disappear when the opening of the St. Lawrence Seaway made it possible to ship grain directly to the East Coast without going through Buffalo.

Even attractive sites that are bypassed by transportation can be unable to compete with less-attractive sites that are connected by transportation. An historical example of this is the fierce competition of towns in the western United States to be along the path of the railroad in the 1800s. A more recent example is the competition to be along the path of an interstate highway and, more important, to be near an interchange. We will return to this question of first versus second nature in the succeeding chapters; chapter 6 essentially describes urban growth on the basis of first nature (comparative advantage due to relative factor abundance), while chapter 7 complements this by modeling urban growth on the basis of second nature (urbanization economies of scale, comparative advantage because of dynamic factors such as learning-by-doing).

The implication of findings that the second nature of cities is important is that historical patterns can be preserved long after the causes for the historical patterns have disappeared. Ciccone and Hall (1996) study the productivity of U.S. regions to identify causes of differences. They find that the density of activity is important, but they also find that differences among locations that led to agglomeration in the 1800s (Eastern seaboard location, early railroad access, and so on) do not have a direct effect on productivity today. They do have an indirect effect, however, in the legacy of dense activity that they left behind. This density, according to Ciccone and Hall, leads to greater productivity, which in turn can lead to urban growth as the productivity advantages outweigh the negative externalities resulting from growth.

AMENITIES AND URBAN QUALITY: GOOD CITIES AND AWFUL CITIES

Urban areas have both amenities and disamenities. Amenities could include, for example, diverse choices, mild climate, good transportation, and good schools. Disamenities could include crime, traffic, pollution, group tensions, harsh climate, and poor government services. Population density, for example, has both a positive and a negative aspect. Density is good in that it promotes interaction and innovation, but it is bad because it fosters congestion. The noted scholar (and baseball player) Yogi Berra perhaps put it best: "No one goes to that restaurant any more—it's too crowded."

How would we decide which city is the best? the worst? There are a variety of surveys designed to answer this question from different viewpoints. A survey of corporations about the factors that influenced their site-selection decisions yielded the factors listed in Table 4.3.

The theoretical analysis earlier suggests that the relative importance of different factors should vary from firm to firm, depending on whether the firm has a transport-cost orientation or a production-cost orientation. This is one difficulty with interpreting some of the common indexes of site quality (such as those in *Fortune, Inc.,* and *Site Selection* magazines), which do not distinguish among them. A market-oriented firm, for example, will be attracted to a city that has excellent access to its customers even if lease rates are high, labor force quality is low, and so on, provided that the market access outweighs the other considerations. The only way to rank the site quality of cities would be to have a different ranking for each different orientation. One example of a study that has a tighter focus on one type of facility is Lund (1986), who focuses solely on the issues of importance to corporate R&D facilities.

The Citizens League of Greater Cleveland (1994) ranked Cleveland and 13 other metropolitan areas using indices in five categories: amenities (cultural opportunities and leisure activity), economy (economic vitality and community prosperity),

TABLE 4.3 Top Ten Site-Selection Factors

Factor	Weighted Average Score (on a Scale from 1 = Not Important to 3 = Very Important)
Low lease rates	2.81
Educated labor force	2.48
Access to major highways	2.48
Low construction costs	2.47
Access to primary consumer markets	2.41
Good energy/telecommunications	2.37
Favorable local government attitude	2.34
Low property tax rates	2.28
Low crime rate	2.26
Low corporate and business taxes	2.18

Source: Evans and Barovick 1994, Figure 1.1, p. 298.

education (educational opportunities and workforce preparedness), government (political participation and accountable leadership), and people (caring people and healthy lives). Table 4.4 lists the data used to create the index.

The strength of the index is its focus on measurable outcomes. However, its weakness is the arbitrary decision on the measures included and their division among categories. For example, is library program attendance better classified under amenities or under education? Another concern is that some of the measures are too closely related to provide independent information. For example, the median income in a region will be closely related to the college attainment because college education, on average, increases incomes significantly. Another problem is the way the findings are presented. If one city is ranked higher than another, this could reflect either a huge disparity or a slim disparity; there is no way of inferring the spread from the table. Finally, some of the indicators could be viewed either as positive or negative. Economic diversity is good in the sense that weakness in one sector won't necessarily put the entire regional economy in trouble. But economic diversity is bad if it reflects a lack of agglomeration economies of the localization type. Similarly, affordable housing is good for buyers but bad for sellers and probably reflects a lack of demand for land in the region.

Table 4.5 summarizes the results of the study. What you are likely to conclude from the data in Table 4.5 is that your opinion was correct—whatever your opinion happened to be. This illustrates the difficulty of comparing areas in this way. The Citizens League has since updated and expanded its analysis to include 25 metropolitan areas and over 100 measures of comparison—without addressing the theorical ambiguities that underly their efforts.

Perhaps the most famous of the various city-ranking indices is that produced by *Money* magazine every year. Table 4.6 lists the top 15 and bottom 15 metropolitan

TABLE 4.4   Quality of Life Index

Category	Indicators
Amenities	sporting event attendance, number of pro sporting events, game-seat availability, number of hotel rooms, number of cultural events, orchestra endowments, contributions to orchestra, library circulation rate, library program attendance, library card holders, recreational facilities, park land-to-area ratio, park acres available
Economy	median income, regional fiscal disparity, cost of living, average salary, employment growth, unemployment rate, skilled employees, research dollars level, patents granted, venture capital investment, business growth, economic diversity, commuting time, freeway accessibility, number of flights in and out, housing affordability ratio, change in housing starts, population growth trends
Education	college education attainment, spending per college student, college and university supply, minority college enrollment rate, mathematics achievement level, spending per pupil, library expenditures, high school dropout rate, preschool education enrollment
Government	financial planning strength, judicial efficiency, case disposition per judge, administration spending, ability to repay debt, debt ratio, total debt, voting rate
People	poverty rate, public assistance, teen birth rate, infant mortality rate, single-parent households, contributions to charity, donations to United Way, regional crime rate, central city crime rate, police response time, number of doctors, specialist-to-generalist practitioner ratio, health insurance cost, uninsured rate, hospital capacity, hospital occupancy rate, hospital cost, air quality, water quality, toxic releases, racial and ethnic diversity, hate crimes

Source: Citizens League of Greater Cleveland (1994).

Education Rank	Government Rank	People Rank
9	13	12
1	12	1
14	10	10
3	8	13
11	1	5
8	9	7
10	5	14
13	3	3
4	6	6
12	4	11
6	11	2
5	14	4
2	7	9
7	2	8

interesting features of the *Money* rank-
to year, as illustrated by Punta Gorda,
Louisiana. How would you interpret a
here are two explanations. First, the sys-
in the conditions in a metropolitan area
can lead to a large change in the index that *Money* uses to rank the metropolitan

TABLE 4.6 Top 15 and Bottom 15 of 300 Metropolitan Areas in 1996

Top 15 (Rank in 1995)	*Bottom 15 (Rank in 1995)*
1. Madison, WI (16)	286. Florence, SC (280)
2. Punta Gorda, FL (61)	287. Decatur, IL (258)
3. Rochester, MN (2)	288. Sioux City, IA (179)
4. Ft. Lauderdale, FL (6)	289. Augusta, GA (278)
5. Ann Arbor, MI (33)	290. Jersey City-Hudson County, NJ (294)
6. Ft. Myers-Cape Coral, FL (34)	291. Alexandria, LA (89)
7. Gainesville, FL (1)	292. Waterbury, CT (114)
8. Austin, TX (35)	293. Albany-Schenectady-Troy, NY (267)
9. Seattle, WA (4)	294. Mansfield, OH (235)
10. Lakeland, FL (41)	295. Springfield, IL (279)
11. Tampa-St. Petersburg, FL (11)	296. Lima, OH (245)
12. Orlando, FL (17)	297. Davenport, IA (290)
13. San Francisco, CA (24)	298. Peoria, IL (297)
14. Fargo, ND (30)	299. Yuba City, CA (300)
15. Naples, FL (10)	300. Rockford, IL (293)

Source: Money magazine site on the World Wide Web (http://pathfinder.com).

areas. Second, the metropolitan areas are very close in the value of the index, so even a small absolute change can lead to a large rank change. The magazine's web site offers you the capability to design your own index and see how the metropolitan areas rank; it is a feature worth exploring.

An alternative to creating an arbitrary index is to study the ways in which wages and land rents vary across metropolitan areas. If one place is less desirable to live in, then the money wages need to be higher to compensate people for living there. Of course, if firms are to pay these higher wages, the location must have productivity advantages or else those firms will be unable to compete with firms in other locations that have lower wage costs. Alternatively, firms in high-wage locations will choose production techniques that use less labor relative to other factors of production than firms in low-wage locations. Roback (1982) uses data from 98 U.S. cities to estimate the value of urban amenities. She finds that wage differences among cities are almost completely explained by amenity differences. Positive amenities include high population density and clear days. Negative amenities include crime, unemployment, pollution, snow, cloudy days, and a high population growth rate. Her findings are especially interesting because they can be used to construct an index of the overall quality of life in the different metropolitan areas in her study. Simply put, the higher the wages required to attract a worker of a given skill level, the less attractive the city. Such a wage-based index can then be compared to an index based on assumptions about the relative importance of different amenities, such as the approach taken by the Citizen's League of Cleveland described earlier in the chapter. Table 4.7 shows a comparison of Roback's ranking of metropolitan areas with a ranking developed by Liu (1976) that followed a methodology similar to that of the Citizen's League. As you can see, the differences are substantial. For example, the metropolitan area that Liu ranks as first, Seattle-Everett, is number nineteen based on its relative wages.

If there are differences in wages or amenities that make one city more attractive than another, then we would expect to see people migrating from less attractive locations to more attractive locations. Eberts and Stone (1992) present evidence that migration among metropolitan areas is quite significant—the dominant force, in fact—in determining changes in local labor supply if the time period being considered is several years long. (In any given year, the main change in labor supply comes from changes in labor force participation.) They find that differences in wages between metropolitan areas are quite persistent, which we would expect if these differences compensate for differences in productivity or amenities. Note that their finding forestalls one possible criticism of the Roback approach, namely that the wage differences she observes might change while the amenities that Liu focuses on will not. If the relative wages are stable, though, then her approach is robust. Eberts and Stone do find that differences in unemployment rates do not last for very long, suggesting that the dual migrations of people to find jobs and firms to find new sources of labor are relatively rapid.

Urban planners and government officials are prone to spend great amounts of time examining relative rankings in order to determine how to pursue the holy grail of a well-functioning metropolitan area. What is perhaps not always understood is that *every* amenity comes with a disamenity. A single-minded focus on the good side of urban amenities can lead to unrealistic expectations about the ability to eliminate the bad side of those same amenities.

TABLE 4.7   Comparison of Quality of Life Rankings of 20 Largest MSAs

Metropolitan Area	Rank Based on Wage Differences (Roback)	Rank Based on Arbitrary Weights (Liu)
Los Angeles-Long Beach	1	10
Anaheim-Santa Ana-Garden Grove	2	9
San Francisco-Oakland	3	2
Dallas	4	5
Baltimore	5	13
Nassau-Suffolk	6	—
St. Louis	7	16
Milwaukee	8	8
Boston	9	12
Minneapolis	10	4
New York	11	14
Washington, D.C.	12	3
Newark	13	11
Philadelphia	14	7
Houston	15	6
Chicago	16	18
Detroit	17	17
Cleveland	18	15
Seattle-Everett	19	1
Pittsburgh	20	19

Source: Adapted from Roback (1982, Table 6, p. 1275).

CHAPTER SUMMARY

- Profit-maximizing firms will choose a location that minimizes production costs and transport costs if their revenues are the same regardless of their location. If production costs are the same at all locations, a firm will locate so as to minimize transport costs. Input-oriented, or weight-losing, firms will locate production at the source of inputs, choosing to ship the finished product to market. Market-oriented, or weight-gaining, firms will locate production at the market, choosing to ship the inputs.

- If there is more than one market or more than one source of inputs, then firms will locate where the monetary weight of shipping in each direction is equalized. This idea, known as the principle of median location, explains both the growth of port cities and the self-perpetuating growth of large cities.

- Because production costs vary from location to location, a firm might choose its location on the basis of factors other than transportation costs. Some of the reasons that production costs could be lower in one place than in another include the presence of natural resources, relatively inexpensive labor, relatively inexpensive land, or the presence of natural amenities, such as pleasant weather.

- No site is preferable to all other sites for all types of firms and households. The features that make one location valuable for one use can make it worthless for another. Finally, no amenity comes without a corresponding disamenity.

EXCERPT: "WELCOME TO SLIPPAGE CITY" (FRED HOYLE)

A common belief is that today's cities do not function well, despite many efforts to design and implement policies targeted at making them attractive. An interesting alternative to the evidently unsuccessful strategy of designing a good city is to design a really badly operating city. In doing so, you may find that the same elements that eventually cause the failure of the city will also be the cause of whatever success the city has enjoyed. The following excerpt from a short story by Fred Hoyle (1967) about an awful city (designed by the Devil!) makes this point very clear. Any resemblance to an actual city, such as Los Angeles, for example, is strictly coincidental. . . . .

Suppose you wanted to start up a hell of a city. You'd probably put it in a lousy climate. Well, the Devil didn't make that mistake. He put his City in a beautiful place, a place with a wonderful climate. There was a plain about fifty miles wide between a chain of mountains and the sea. It was a place of nearly perpetual sunshine. Yet it was no desert, quite the reverse. What happened was that every day the air moved in and out over the sea. It came in saturated with moisture during the early morning. The water soaked into the fertile ground as a heavy dew in the morning, then during the day the warm air moved seaward to pick up a new charge of water vapor for delivery the next day.

The City itself became established near the sea. Here was a multitude of little hills and valleys, verdant and bird-filled. The houses of the first settlers fitted tastefully into the landscape. Ample water could be piped from the mountains, or even pumped from simple wells. Crops grew abundantly in the plain, aided by the beginnings of irrigation. The food was real food, not the spray-soaked rubbish that would come a hundred years later with the ultimate transmogrification of the City. At that early time, the simplest folk possessed horses, just as naturally as they possessed clothing and shelter. Later, with the march of "progress," only the children of the very rich would be able to afford horses. Later, not even the children of the very rich would have space to play in, the apparent infinity would turn out to be no infinity at all.

But the City grew only slowly in the beginning, because a great desert separated it from all large centers of population. It was a long, hazardous journey to the City, so immigrants came at first only in a trickle. At last came transportation, first the railroad. Yet the immediate effects of making access to the City much less arduous than before were more preparatory than dramatic. It was the same thing as before, but a poco a poco. More immigrants, more development, more prosperity. The railway permitted exports, at first mostly fruit, which at this stage was still of excellent quality. Prosperity and the amenities of life became added to the natural beauty of the City. Everybody who lived there was entirely convinced of the City's preeminence as a desirable place to live.

Great, far-off industrial centers took note of the City's "potential." It would be possible for well-paid executives to live cheek by jowl with the wealthy, for them to build similar homes, even for them to marry into the families of the truly wealthy. Industrial buildings could be erected more cheaply than elsewhere, in spite of the remoteness of the City, because the equable, all the year round, climate demanded very little in the way of tough, solid construction. So industry began to move in, at first in a small way of course, then poco piu mosso. It was while industrial development was thus in its early acceleration that extensive oil deposits were discovered in the vicinity of the City. Here was the first one of the Devil's jokers slipped into the pack.

A forest of derricks soon appeared on what used to be a beautiful beach. For the first time an amenity of the City had been destroyed.

Water was an obvious problem as growth continued. The natural daily air movement back and forth between land and sea was quite insufficient to provide for a vast increase in the population of the City. Water was therefore taken from the surrounding mountains, and pumped across the desert from distant rivers. Outlying communities lost their water and their lands became scrub.

There's nothing more here than the Devil's hoariest old trick, two-by-two multiplication. Get humans started on something they like, then bring in the two-by-two business, that's the standard formula. The result must always be a disaster because the multiplication can't go on indefinitely, it must blow up in your face.

In just this simple way all really big human disasters are engineered. So it was with the City. The flow of immigrants had increased like wheat grains on a chessboard, two by two, for a century or more. At first nobody minded. Quite suddenly, with the development of the automobile and the airplane, the thing blew up, the flow burst into a raging torrent. Humankind came to the City at a rate of one thousand a day. Compute it out, and you will find it amounts to one third of a million throbbing souls a year, three million or more to a decade.

Because of the naturally uneven terrain, because of the size of the City, because of the manner of its growth, transport could not be organized in any straightforward, or even rational, way. It was common for close friends to live in widely separated places. This forced a system of transportation the like of which had not been seen on the Earth before. Wide highways were driven through the heart of the City, not just one highway, but an intricate complex linking the sprawling communities of the whole urban area. They were crowded with furious, fast-moving vehicles throughout all daylight hours and through most of the night, too.

The City was perhaps the least suited of all the cities on Earth to the use of the automobile. The very air movement, in and out over the sea, which had led to the founding of the City, was now a terrible liability. The air became a stagnant pool into which the by-products of the incomplete combustion of oil gradually accumulated. The strong sunlight induced chemical reactions, resulting in a kind of tear gas. It was difficult now for anything except humans to live in this appalling atmospheric sewer.

The imposition of physical distress is only a minor aspect of the Devil's activities. The Devil is much more concerned with the induction of psychological distress. This thrilling, throbbing City of three million people provided the Devil with opportunities more varied and more rich than one could ever hope to describe in close detail.

The City was the most restless place to be found anywhere, but instead of this being thought a disadvantage, it was extolled as a virtue. People shuffled into their cars on weekends and drove hither and thither quite aimlessly. They weren't going anywhere, they were just going. They drove to the sea and were disappointed they couldn't keep on, lemming-like, on and on over the ocean.

Source: Element 79 by Fred Hoyle. Copyright © 1967 by Fred Hoyle. Reprinted by premission of the author.

Questions for Review and Discussion

1. How would you solve the problem of the declining happiness in Slippage City?
2. "Public policy designed to improve conditions in cities often results in making things worse. Therefore, we should design public policies to worsen conditions in cities so as to improve conditions." Do you agree or disagree? Explain.
3. "In a market economy, firms will choose their location to maximize profits. Therefore, the choices of firms will lead to an efficient distribution of production among locations." Do you agree or disagree? Explain.

4. "Production costs for services are less dependent on the first nature of cities than production costs for manufactured goods are. Therefore, the increasing role of services in the economy implies that historically dominant locations will no longer be as attractive, and we should see the decline of major cities as a result." Do you agree or disagree? Explain.

5. Cleveland used to advertise that it was "the best location in the nation." What is the best location in the nation? Explain.

6. "No amenity comes without a corresponding disamenity." Do you agree or disagree? Explain, using examples.

7. "The advantages or disadvantages of a location are determined by natural conditions and the state of technology. Therefore, local government policy cannot improve a city's economic prospects." Do you agree or disagree? Explain.

8. Create a quality-of-life index for college campuses. Where does your school rank?

Aggregate Analysis
of Metropolitan Areas

CHAPTER

Intermetropolitan Trade

W̲e will now develop a simple general equilibrium model of a small open economy that will be used throughout the remainder of the book. In this chapter the basic model is developed, and in chapter 6 the model is applied to studying urban specialization based on relative factor abundance. Much of the basic theory in these two chapters can also be found in an international trade textbook such as Kenen (1985).

COMPARATIVE ADVANTAGE

The focus of this book is on general equilibrium models of open economies. However, in order to review some of the important concepts, it behooves us to begin slowly, leading off with the idea of comparative advantage that will be the cornerstone of the analysis from this point on.

Consider the following simple model. There are two goods; *steel* (*S*), whose output is measured in tons, and orange juice (*OJ*), whose output is measured in hundreds of gallons. There are two cities; Cleveland and Miami. Each good requires only one input—labor—and each city has 100 hours of labor available. In Cleveland, one ton of steel can be produced per hour of labor and one hundred gallons of orange juice can be produced per hour of labor. In Miami, two tons of steel can be produced per hour of labor and six hundred gallons of orange juice can be produced per hour of labor.

Under these conditions, the opportunity cost of *OJ* in Cleveland is 1, as is the opportunity cost of *S*. In other words, producing 1 ton of *S* means forfeiting the opportunity to produce 100 gallons of *OJ*, and vice versa. In Miami, the opportunity cost of *OJ* is 1/3, while the opportunity cost of *S* is 3.

Miami can produce more *OJ* per hour of labor, so we say that Miami has an "absolute advantage" in the production of *OJ*. Miami also has an absolute advantage in the production of *S*. Since Miami is more efficient at the production of both *OJ* and *S*, it would be natural to think that there is no basis for Miami and Cleveland to enter into trade with each other. The important point with respect to trade, though, is not the existence of an absolute advantage. While Cleveland is less efficient at the production of both goods, the opportunity cost of *S* is lower in Cleveland than it is in Miami. Therefore, Cleveland has a "comparative advantage" in *S*, while Miami has a comparative advantage in *OJ*.

The relative price of *OJ* and *S* in Cleveland under autarky is 1:1 (100 gallons of *OJ* costs 1 ton of *S*), while the relative price of *OJ* and *S* in Miami under *autarky* (autarky is defined as the economy operating in isolation) is 1:3. At any relative price between 1:1 and 1:3, it would seem that Cleveland's trading *S* to Miami for *OJ* is a potential Pareto improvement (A *Pareto improvement*—named for Vilfredo Pareto, Italian economist and sociologist—is a trade that makes at least one of the parties involved better off without making the other party worse off; it is a synonym for mutually beneficial trade.) An example of a possible set of mutually beneficial prices (1:2) is shown by the dotted lines in Figure 5.1. The potential consumption points for Cleveland (assuming it specializes in *S* and trades with Miami for *OJ*) are beyond the production possibility frontier (PPF—the amount a city can produce if it uses all resources efficiently given the available technology), indicating that Cleveland is no worse off as a result of specialization and trade. The same is true of Miami. In fact, if the two cities do trade at the given price, they are both better off. To see this concretely, suppose that Cleveland trades 50 *S* to Miami in return for 100 *OJ*. Now Cleveland consumes 50 *S* and 100 *OJ*, which is more than it could produce under autarky, while Miami consumes 50 *S* and 500 *OJ*, which is more than it could produce under autarky.

This potential improvement depends, though, upon the magnitude of the transport costs. If transport costs exceed the potential gains from trade, then the cities have no reason to engage in trade. Suppose, for example, that transportation costs take the form that a certain fraction of the good disappears en route to its destination. (This form of transportation costs is called "iceberg transportation costs"—some of the product melts along the way. You can think of this as payment to the person shipping the good.) If 50 percent of each product disappears en route, then Cleveland and Miami will no longer wish to trade. Return to our example. Now Cleveland consumes 50 *S* and 50 *OJ* (Miami exports 100 *OJ*, 50 percent arrives), which is no better than it could have done under autarky. Miami consumes 25 *S* and 500 *OJ*, which is actually worse than it could have done under autarky, since the PPF includes the point where Miami produces 500 *OJ* and 33.3 *S*.

FIGURE 5.1 Gains from Trade

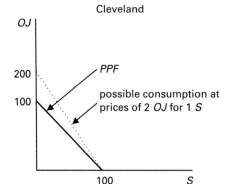

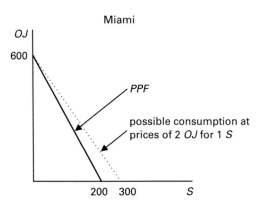

For much of history, high transport costs precluded much large-scale trade. The counterexample of trade between East Asia and Europe along the silk and spice routes proves this rule, as both silk and spice were extremely valuable relative to their weight.

The figure assumes that each city completely specializes in the good in which it has a comparative advantage. This clearly maximizes the available consumption for both cities, assuming that sufficient amounts of the good not produced locally can be obtained. In this simple example, where both cities have the same resources, such an assumption seems innocuous but may not hold, depending on the desired levels of consumption in the two cities. It is certainly not expected to hold universally under more realistic conditions of disparities among cities in resources and demand.

The potential gains from trade between Cleveland and Miami can be illustrated on one graph using a tool known as an *Edgeworth Box*, named for the English economist Francis Ysidro Edgeworth. An Edgeworth Box is shown as Figure 5.2 with an initial production of 100 tons of steel(S) in Cleveland and 600 (100 gallon) units of orange juice(OJ) in Miami. The width of the box is the total amount of S available, with Cleveland's allocation of S being read from left to right and Miami's from right to left. Because there are only two cities, any S that Cleveland doesn't consume is left for Miami and vice versa. The allocation of OJ between the two cities is read from the graph similarly. Every point in the box represents a feasible allocation of the current production among the two cities. The logic of the Edgeworth Box is that everything that Cleveland doesn't consume is left for Miami, and vice versa. Hence, you need only one point to illustrate the consumption of both cities. For example, if each city consumes only what it produces, then it is at the point labeled ①, with Cleveland consuming 100 S and 0 OJ and Miami consuming 600 OJ and 0 S.

If the cities wish to consume both goods, then they have a choice: produce both goods themselves or trade one good for the other. The dotted line in Figure 5.2 shows the PPF for Cleveland—in other words, the available consumption under autarky if Cleveland should decide to produce less S and more OJ. The dashed line shows part of the PPF for Miami. There are clearly allocations in the box that are not available to each city acting independently; these allocations are the area labeled "potential Pareto improvements." For example, it is possible for Cleveland to consume 150 OJ

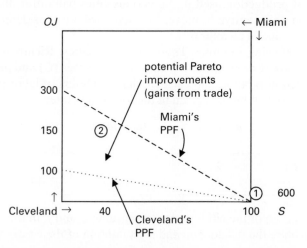

FIGURE 5.2 Edgeworth Box

and 40 S while Miami consumes 450 OJ and 60 S. This is the point labeled ②. Acting independently, neither city could consume that much.

The observant reader will note that I have again gotten a little ahead of the game by assuming that cities have formed. Therefore, comparative advantage alone is an insufficient justification for the formation of cities. Note, though, that scale economies in transportation and storage could lead to the formation of transport nodes in order to facilitate trade with other cities. Thus, trade can encourage the formation and development of cities.

Preferences, Relative Size, Transport Costs, and Trading Patterns

The discussion to this point has focused on the potential for Pareto improving trade between cities. The idea that comparative advantage can lead to gains from specialization and trade is important, but the extent to which trade actually occurs depends on several factors in addition to the existence of comparative advantage. These factors include the preferences for the products in the cities, the relative size of the cities' economies, and transport costs between the cities.

When cities decide to trade with each other, we can think of combining their PPFs to show the total production possibilities for the combined economies. The point chosen on this combined PPF will show both the pattern of production in the cities and the pattern of trade. But choosing a point at which to consume is a matter of preferences, so we need to say something about preferences in order to be definite about the outcome we observe.

The relative size of the economies is important because it affects the extent to which trade can be of benefit. If one city is much larger than another, it is unlikely that it will be able to import all its needs from the smaller city. The smaller city, on the other hand, will be able to completely specialize.

The role of transport costs is important for two reasons. First, as we have already seen, the addition of transport costs to a situation where a trade is Pareto improving can remove the trade from consideration. Second, the presence of transport costs implies that relative prices will differ in the cities. This in turn implies that the rewards to factors of production used in the various cities will differ, thus giving the factors of production an incentive to move. This issue will be considered at length in the rest of this chapter and in chapter 6.

Consider the following example. There are three cities: Richmond, Louisville, and Nashville. There are two commodities: consulting services (C) and paper (P). The only factor of production is labor, and each city has 200 hours of labor per day available. The output per hour of labor is given in the following table:

City → Good ↓	Richmond	Louisville	Nashville
Consulting Services (C)	2	6	4
Paper (P)	4	16	10

Suppose residents of each of the cities prefer to consume C and P in the ratio of 2 P to 1 C. Let us first calculate the production and consumption of the cities under autarky, then consider the effect of opening trade. Begin with Richmond. The PPF for Richmond can be written as $P = 800 - 2C$. The preferred consumption is $P = 2C$. If we substitute the preferred consumption into the PPF, we find that $2P = 800$, or $P = 400$. This in turn implies that $C = 200$. If you perform a similar exercise for Louisville and Nashville, you will find that Louisville produces and consumes 686 C and 1,372 P while Nashville produces and consumes 444 C and 889 P.

Now consider the effect of opening up trade among the three cities. Louisville has a comparative advantage in P over both Nashville and Richmond, while Richmond has a comparative advantage in C over both Nashville and Louisville. Nashville has a comparative advantage in C over Louisville and a comparative advantage in P over Richmond. If we combine the PPFs of the cities, we know that if we produce any P at all, then Louisville will be producing P. So the PPF starting from the C axis will have the slope of the opportunity cost in Louisville. This will continue until Louisville is completely specialized in P, at which point production of P will shift to Nashville. Richmond will start producing P only if Louisville and Nashville have completely specialized. The combined PPF is drawn below as Figure 5.3.

The preferred consumption for the combined economy is where the dashed line $P = 2C$ intersects the PPF. This is the point at which Nashville and Richmond are specialized in producing C while Louisville is producing both C and P. Total production equals 1,371 C and 2,743 P. Nashville produces 800 C, Richmond produces 400 C, and Louisville produces 2,743 P and 171 C. What is the consumption in the various cities? In order to determine that, we need to know what the relative price of P and C is.

Note that Louisville is both importing C and consuming the C it produces. This means that Louisville consumers make no distinction between imported C and locally produced C, so the relative price of C and P must be that in Louisville. In other words, each P can buy 0.375 C. In general, relative prices under trade will reflect the opportunity costs of cities that are not completely specialized, because of this need for indifference between local production and imports. With this relative price, both Nashville and Richmond gain from trade, while Louisville is indifferent. The pattern of production and consumption is summarized in Table 5.1. Because trade is simply the difference between local production and local consumption, the trade activities of the cities

FIGURE 5.3 Combined PPF

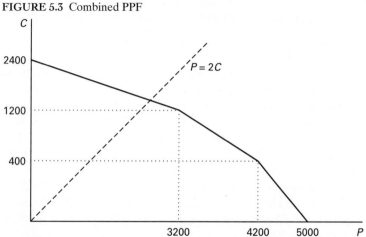

TABLE 5.1 Production and Consumption under Autarky and Free Trade

	Richmond		Louisville		Nashville	
Production						
Autarky	200 C	400 P	686 C	1,372 P	444 C	889 P
Free Trade	400 C	0 P	171 C	2,743 P	800 C	0 P
Consumption						
Autarky	200 C	400 P	686 C	1,372 P	444 C	889 P
Free Trade	226 C	464 P	686 C	1,372 P	459 C	907 P

are also illustrated on this table. (If local production exceeds local consumption, then the commodity is exported; if local consumption exceeds local production, then the commodity is imported.)

Transport costs would affect the pattern of trade by affecting the relative prices in the various cities. If the increase in the price of imports was sufficient, one or all of the cities could withdraw from trade. Note that Louisville and Richmond have the largest difference in their opportunity costs, and therefore the most to gain by trading with each other. If transportation costs gradually increased, Nashville would be the first to drop out and return to autarky.

We can change the example slightly to see the effect of differences in the relative sizes of the cities. Suppose Richmond has 700 hours of labor per day, while Nashville and Louisville continue to have only 200 hours available. What is the effect on the pattern of production and trade? Intuitively, we would expect that Louisville (and maybe Nashville) will now produce more P to trade for the additional C that the now larger Richmond can produce. If we go through the same steps as before, we find that total production is now 1,933 C and 3,867 P. This means that Louisville is now specialized in producing P, Richmond continues to specialize in C, and Nashville now produces both C and P. The relative price is now the opportunity cost in Nashville, rather than that in Louisville, so that P is relatively more expensive than it was before. This makes sense, because expanding Richmond means that the overall economy is now relatively better at producing C relative to P than it was before.

Trade and Wages

Let us now return to the example we developed earlier of trade between Cleveland and Miami in *OJ* and *S,* in order to analyze the effects of trade on the equilibrium price in the labor market. This is the simplest general equilibrium model possible, but it is worth developing in order to introduce this type of analysis. We will shortly be looking at models that include several factors of production and a nonlinear production possibility frontier, but the fundamental economic principles can be seen in a one-factor model with constant opportunity costs.

First, some notation. Let α_S, α_{OJ} be the labor requirements per unit of steel(S) and orange juice (OJ) in Cleveland; β_S, β_{OJ} be the labor requirements per unit of steel and orange juice in Miami; and L_S, L_{OJ} be the labor used for steel and orange juice production in Cleveland.

We can then write the equation for the production possibility frontier (PPF) in Cleveland using the following information: $L = L_S + L_{OJ}$; $L_S = \alpha_S S$; $L_{OJ} = \alpha_{OJ}$. Substituting for L_S and L_{OJ} and then solving for OJ, we find that $OJ = L/\alpha_{OJ} - (\alpha_S/\alpha_{OJ})S$, and the PPF is a straight line. The intercept, L/α_{OJ}, is the total amount of OJ that can be produced if Cleveland does nothing but produce OJ. If Cleveland produces steel, it reduces the amount of OJ by (α_S/α_{OJ}) for each unit of steel produced. Because α_S and α_{OJ} are constants, their ratio is constant, so there is a constant per-unit tradeoff—a straight line.

Since labor is the only factor of production, wages are the only cost. Price equals average cost in competitive equilibrium because there are no economic profits. Also, wages in the two sectors must be equal if labor is mobile between orange juice production and steel production. Therefore, $p_S = \alpha_S w$ and $p_{OJ} = \alpha_{OJ} w$, where w is the wage and p the price. So $p_S/p_{OJ} = \alpha_S/\alpha_{OJ}$; in other words, the relative prices equal the absolute value of the slope of the PPF. You can show that a similar situation prevails in Miami under autarky.

Suppose Miami specializes in OJ and Cleveland specializes in S. Then the price of S is the price in Cleveland ($\alpha_S w_{Cleveland}$) and the price of OJ is the price in Miami ($\beta_{OJ} w_{Miami}$). Since α_S and β_{OJ} are constants, if relative prices change (to equilibrate trade) then relative wages *must* change.

To further investigate the relation between product prices and factor prices, let us consider the "real wage," that is, the wage in terms of the amount of goods that it will buy. The real wage in Cleveland in terms of S is $w/p_S = 1/\alpha_S$. Real wages are inversely related to the amount of labor it takes to produce steel. This implies that a reduction of the necessary labor would increase the wage; in other words, wages reflect productivity. The real wage in terms of orange juice is $w/p_{OJ} = w/p_S (p_S/p_{OJ}) = 1/\alpha_S (p_S/p_{OJ})$. If the relative price of orange juice is lower under trade than under autarky, then real wages in terms of orange juice increase as a result of trade.

It is helpful in the midst of all of these algebraic manipulations to look at a numerical example. One possible situation is summarized in Table 5.2. The production parameters are the ones used earlier in the chapter to derive the PPF for the two cities, and the assumption that each city has a total of 100 units of labor is also maintained. The relative price of orange juice and steel after trade was arbitrarily selected, as were the consumption choices of the cities and the level of the wage rate (w) in Cleveland and Miami (although *not* the relative wage in the two cities). You can easily

TABLE 5.2 Trade and Wages: A Numerical Example

City	p_{OJ}	p_S	p_S/p_{OJ}	Production		Consumption	
				OJ	S	OJ	S
Cleveland ($\alpha_S = 1$, $\alpha_{OJ} = 1/100$)							
Autarky ($w_{Cleveland} = \$21$)	\$0.21	\$21.00	100	5,000	50	5,000	50
Trade ($w_{Cleveland} = \$7$)	\$0.035	\$7.00	200	0	100	9,000	55
Miami ($\beta_S = 1/2$, $\beta_{OJ} = 1/600$)							
Autarky ($w_{Miami} = \$21$)	\$0.035	\$10.50	300	30,000	100	30,000	100
Trade ($w_{Miami} = \$21$)	\$0.035	\$7.00	200	42,000	60	33,000	105

check that the real wage in terms of orange juice is higher in Cleveland as a result of trade and that the real wage in terms of steel is higher in Miami. A way of seeing this directly is that the total consumption of both steel and orange juice increases in both cities. Even though the level of the wage has fallen in Cleveland and remained constant in Miami, workers can afford to buy more, so the real wage has increased.

GAINS FROM TRADE—PARTIAL EQUILIBRIUM

Before turning to a general equilibrium model of the economy that includes more than one factor of production, I want to consider at some length the gains from trade in a single market. Since general equilibrium consists of equilibrium in many markets at once, it makes sense to look at one market in detail before tackling the general case.

Consider the case of Cleveland in the market for *OJ*. In Figure 5.4 the domestic supply and domestic demand curves are drawn and are assumed to have the familiar shape. However, the assumption that Cleveland is a small open economy leads to the existence of another supply curve, the "world" supply curve. This shows that Cleveland can import any quantity of *OJ* it wants at the existing world price, p_w.

The gains from trade are shown in the shaded area. These gains have two sources. The first is the "consumption effect," or the increase in consumer surplus because of the increased consumption of *OJ* relative to the autarky equilibrium. The second is the "production effect," or the increase in consumer surplus available because of the substitution of more efficient foreign sources of production for domestic production.

It is possible that this analysis understates the advantage obtained by trade. If *OJ* had been completely unavailable before trade was undertaken, then the entire consumer surplus would have to be included. This possibility is discussed at greater length later in this chapter, in the section entitled "Increasing Returns to Scale and Gains from Trade."

FIGURE 5.4 Gains from Trade

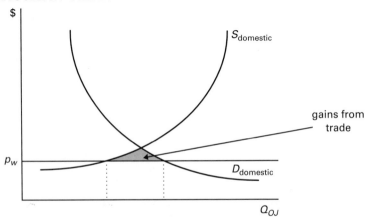

It is also possible to analyze the effects of transport costs using this diagram. Suppose a unit transport cost (τ) must be incurred to ship *OJ* from Miami to Cleveland. This causes the price of imported goods to increase to $p_w + \tau$, as shown in Figure 5.5. Then the quantity demanded falls from q_0 to q_2, the equilibrium price increases to $p_w + \tau$, the domestic (Cleveland) supply increases from q_1 to q_3, and imports fall from $(q_0 - q_1)$ to $(q_2 - q_3)$. This is a gain in revenues to Cleveland firms of the areas ① + ② + ③, as Cleveland production increases and the price of *OJ* increases. This is also a loss of consumer surplus to Cleveland consumers of areas ① + ② + ④ + ⑤ from two sources. The first source of loss is the reduction in consumption; the second source of loss is the higher price of *OJ*. Finally, the revenue of ④ to the providers of transportation services is equal to the amount of the unit transport costs multiplied by the quantity of imports.

The deadweight loss of ② + ⑤ is composed of two separate parts. First is the lost consumer surplus because of the increased price and reduced consumption, area ⑤. This is the standard loss from a monopolist's increase of price, with the monopolist in this case being the requirement to pay transport costs. Even if the market for transportation services is not a monopoly, this deadweight loss remains. The only way to reduce it is to improve the technology of transportation enough to lower unit costs.

Another loss is caused by the relative inefficiency of Cleveland production (higher marginal cost), area ②. The resources used to produce *OJ* in Cleveland have an opportunity cost that exceeds their value in *OJ* production in the absence of transportation costs. "Deadweight loss" is different from other losses. For example, the lost consumer surplus in area ④ is gained by the transport providers as revenue, so it is a transfer rather than a loss. However, the lost consumer surplus in area ⑤ does not represent a gain to anyone else; hence the term "deadweight" loss.

FIGURE 5.5 Effects of Transport Costs

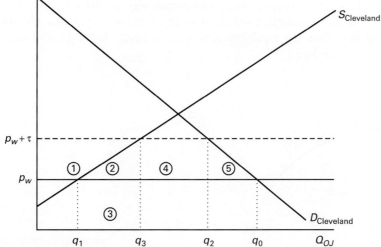

GAINS FROM TRADE—GENERAL EQUILIBRIUM

We are interested not only in the effect of trade on each individual market but on the overall economy. For example, the model in the previous section did not specify what happened to the factors of production in Cleveland that had previously been employed producing *OJ*. In this section we will show the effect of trade in the simplest possible general equilibrium model. The remainder of the chapter will turn to increasingly complicated models to more fully develop the relation between trade, product markets, and factor markets. All the models, though, illustrate the potential gains to all parties from a city that specializes in the production of the good in which it has a comparative advantage and that trades with other specialized cities.

The supply side of the model can be summarized through the use of the production possibility frontier. This assumes that all factors are fully employed, and this assumption is maintained throughout the chapter. If unemployment exists, then the economy is not on the production possibility frontier, so there may be potential Pareto improvements even in the absence of trade. Let us continue to assume that there are two goods, steel and orange juice. Then the PPF can be drawn as in Figure 5.6 below, assuming increasing opportunity cost. Unlike the linear PPF in which the opportunity cost is constant regardless of the level of production, the opportunity cost of producing each good increases as total production of the good increases. If the relative price of steel and orange juice is shown by the slope of the dashed line, then point *A* represents the maximum income that the city can achieve under autarky.

The demand side of the model will make an important simplifying assumption—that it is possible to aggregate the preferences of all the people in the city to form a "community indifference curve." This makes a strong assumption about people's preferences, but is a useful way of simplifying the exposition. This approach runs the risk of hiding important distributional issues (such as the case where gains in aggregate from some policy exceed losses in aggregate, but for some individuals the losses exceed the gains), but you will be reminded from time to time of their existence. For a criticism of the representative individual approach embodied in community indifference curves, see Kirman (1992). The community indifference curve is shown in Figure 5.7. If the available combinations (budget line) of *S* and *OJ* are given by the dashed line, then the equilibrium will be at point *A*, the highest indifference curve that can be reached.

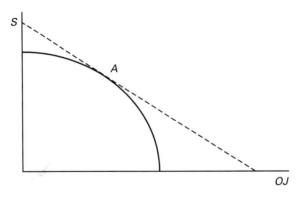

FIGURE 5.6 PPF with Increasing Opportunity Cost

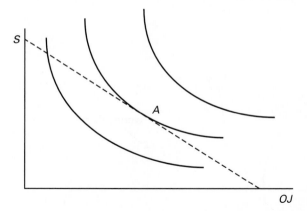

FIGURE 5.7 Community Indifference Curves

If people maximize utility at a set of relative prices, and if firms maximize profits at those same prices, then the quantities demanded will equal the quantities supplied for both *OJ* and *S*, as illustrated in Figure 5.8. The absolute value of the slope of the tangent line (the dashed line in Figure 5.8) equals the relative price of *S* and *OJ*. This is an important point that we will make much use of.

The slope of the dashed line represents the equilibrium prices under autarky, and point *A* shows the consumption and production of *S* and *OJ* under autarky.

If the economy is opened to world trade, then it is no longer restricted to its autarky prices. Suppose world prices are given by the dotted line in Figure 5.9. In this case, the income maximizing production point is point *P*, while the preferred consumption is point *C*.

The city has a comparative advantage in steel. Note that the autarky price of steel is lower than the world price, because the slope of the autarky tangent line is greater than the slope of the world price tangent line. (Recall that the absolute value of the slope of the tangent line gives the relative prices of *S* and *OJ*. If the absolute value of the slope is larger, then the relative price of *S* in terms of *OJ* is lower, because you can produce a greater amount of *S* for a given sacrifice of *OJ*.) This means that the opportunity cost of producing steel in Cleveland is lower than the opportunity cost in the rest of the world. Cleveland is producing more steel than it is consuming, so

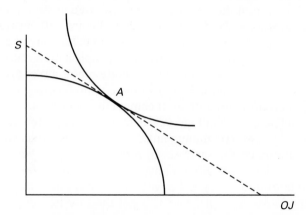

FIGURE 5.8 Production and Consumption under Autarky

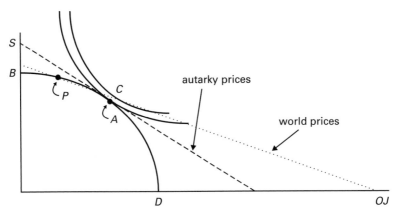

FIGURE 5.9 Production and Consumption under Free Trade

that it is exporting steel and importing orange juice. The gains from trade can be seen by the fact that the point C is on a higher indifference curve than point A. In other words, the representative person in Cleveland is happier under trade than under autarky. These gains from trade can be divided into two pieces. First, even if production remained at point A, the change in prices due to the availability of trade would lead to an improvement in utility. This increase is known as the "gains from exchange." The incremental benefit brought about by changing production to point P to exploit Cleveland's comparative advantage is known as the "gains from specialization."

It is important to emphasize that the only difference between the analysis in Figures 5.6 through 5.9 and the analysis presented at the beginning of the chapter is that the PPF is now allowed to be nonlinear. The concepts and general conclusions are identical to those developed earlier.

INCREASING RETURNS TO SCALE AND GAINS FROM TRADE

Paul Romer (1994) argues that the analysis of transportation costs above underestimates the potential losses from the absence of perfectly free mobility. Suppose there exists a good that requires some fixed costs to produce. Figure 5.10 illustrates this situation, where fixed costs equal to $x_1 - x_2$ must be incurred before any of good z can be produced. Depending on the level of fixed costs and people's preferences, it is possible that no z will be produced. If the community indifference curves are represented by the dashed line (---------) in Figure 5.10, then the city prefers to produce and consume x_1 rather than to produce any z at all. If community indifference curves are represented by the dotted line (·········) in Figure 5.10, then the city prefers to produce and consume both goods. (The two community indifference curves cross, which would be impossible if they represented the same set of preferences. However, each indifference curve represents a completely different hypothetical set of preferences.)

If the city is able to trade for good z with other cities, then the available consumption, given the relative price of z and x, is not the PPF but instead reflects the

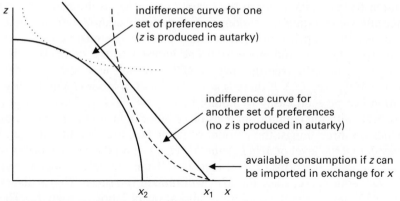

FIGURE 5.10 Fixed Costs in Production

terms of trade. One possible example is drawn in Figure 5.10. As you can see, even if the community indifference curves lead to production of no z, it is possible that the community will consume some z by trading x for it. All the consumer surplus associated with good z is a gain from trade, not only the small triangle illustrated in earlier diagrams (Figures 5.3 and 5.4). *The Economist* (16 July 1994) summarizes Romer's formal analysis. Note too, that the existence of fixed costs implies that if good z is produced, it will be produced in fairly large quantity. That is, the presence of fixed costs implies that a city will tend to specialize to an even greater extent than a simple comparison of opportunity costs (marginal costs) would suggest.

SPECIFIC FACTORS OF PRODUCTION

Suppose there are three factors of production: labor, which is used to produce both S and OJ; capital, which is used only to produce S; and land, which is used only to produce OJ. In this case, it is clear that a city will use all of its capital and land, so the important question becomes the allocation of labor between producing steel and producing orange juice. Capital and land in this model are referred to as *specific factors of production* because each is used only in the production of one type of product.

　　If the marginal product of labor decreases as more labor is devoted to producing steel (or orange juice), then the assumption of competitive factor markets (an exogenously given price of labor from the firm's point of view) lets us draw the *marginal revenue product* of labor in producing steel as a downward sloping curve. (The *marginal revenue product* is equal to marginal product multiplied by marginal revenue, a measure of the additional revenue generated by hiring an additional worker, and therefore the firm's demand for labor.) The quantity of labor used in steel is the quantity at which the wage (marginal cost of labor) equals the marginal revenue product (marginal benefit of labor). A similar analysis can be done of the demand for labor in orange juice production.

　　Define w as the money wage, w/p_S as the real wage (that is, the amount the money will buy) in terms of steel, MP as the marginal physical product (additional output from adding a unit of the factor), and *MRP* as the marginal revenue product. Because we maintain the assumption of perfectly competitive markets, marginal revenue is equal to price. In equilibrium, the real wage must be equal across industries; otherwise, labor would move from one industry to the other. Because $w = MRP_S = MP_S * p_S$, it must be true that $w/p_S = MP_S$. Further, $w = MRP_{OJ} = MP_{OJ} * p_{OJ}$; so that $w/p_S = MP_{OJ} * (p_{OJ}/p_S)$. If there is a fixed amount of labor (L) in the city, then the allocation can be seen easily by noting that $L_S = L - L_{OJ}$. This is diagrammed in Figure 5.11, with the equilibrium division of labor indicated as point L_0. Equilibrium depends on three things: the amount of labor (L), the quantity of fixed factors—since they define the level of $MP(L_S)$ and $MP(L_{OJ})$—and the relative prices of S and OJ.

Suppose the price of steel increases. Then the only change in the diagram is to the *OJ* labor curve, since the MP_S will remain the same. This is diagrammed in Figure 5.12, and the new equilibrium allocation of labor is point L_1. The real wage in terms of steel falls. The amount of labor hired to produce steel increases; therefore, the amount of steel produced increases. Similarly, the amount of labor hired to produce OJ falls, as does OJ production. The real wage in terms of OJ increases. This can be seen by the fact that a decrease in L_{OJ} implies an increase in MP_{OJ}. The return to capital (the specific factor in steel production) increases, while the return to land decreases. The effect of a change in p_S can be seen in the PPF diagram from before (Figure 5.9), and the increase in steel production and decrease in OJ production agree with the implied changes from the analysis of the labor market. This is not surprising (since it is general equilibrium, after all), but it is useful to emphasize, since in some cases it is easier to consider factor markets and in others product markets. Regardless of where you focus, you will get the same answer if you do the analysis correctly.

Now suppose the amount of capital increases. The effect of this change is shown in Figure 5.13. Because capital is used exclusively in the production of steel, the MP_S

FIGURE 5.11 Labor Market Equilibrium

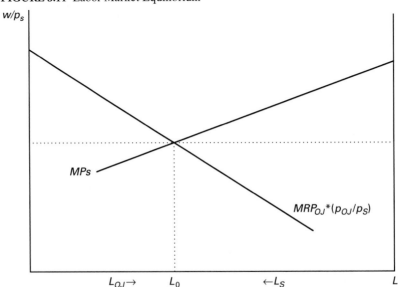

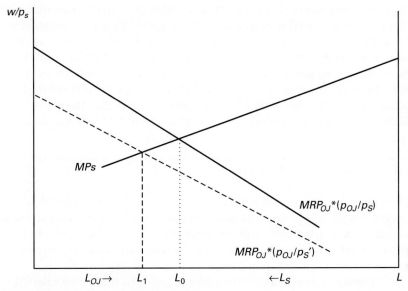

FIGURE 5.12 Increase in the Price of Steel

curve shifts up, although there is no change in the MP_{OJ} curve. The new allocation of labor is given by point L_1, and it is clear that the real wage in terms of steel increases. As with an increase in the price of steel, an increase in the amount of capital leads to an increase in steel production and a decrease in orange juice production.

The application of this framework to our ongoing example of Cleveland and Miami is straightforward. Suppose that Cleveland and Miami are initially identical but

FIGURE 5.13 Increase in Amount of Capital

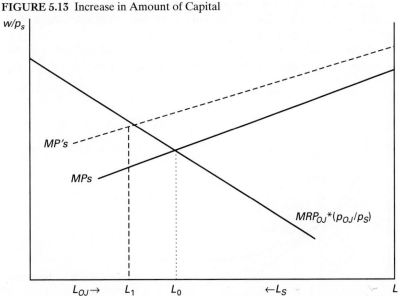

that Cleveland suddenly acquires some additional capital. This means that Cleveland is now relatively well endowed with the specific factor used for steel production, and Miami is relatively well endowed with the specific factor used for orange juice production. If p_s and p_{OJ} are equal in the two cities (as a result of free trade), then given identical amounts of labor, Cleveland will produce more S and Miami will produce more OJ. Recall the evidence on the specialization of cities presented in chapter 1. One explanation for the observed pattern of production is that the goods require a specific factor of production in which some cities are relatively well endowed.

FLEXIBLE FACTOR PROPORTIONS

Now consider the more general case in which various combinations of factors can be used to produce a given quantity of orange juice or steel. Simplifying for a moment, suppose there are two factors of production, capital (K) and labor (L), with factor prices r and w respectively. Then we can summarize the production function by the use of isoquants, as shown in Figure 5.14.

The cost-minimizing combination of factors is that point where the isocost line is tangent to the isoquant. At the relative factor prices (w/r) represented by the dotted isocost line, the production technique is relatively more capital intensive than the production technique chosen when factor prices are given by the solid isocost line. Define the capital-labor ratio, k, as the slope of a line from the origin to the tangency point. Note that k varies with relative factor prices w/r. As w/r increases, k increases. This is graphed in Figure 5.15.

Suppose steel production is more capital intensive than orange juice production. What does this mean? At any set of relative factor prices (w/r), the capital-labor ratio for steel (k_S) is greater than the capital-labor ratio for orange juice (k_{OJ}). This is illustrated in Figure 5.15. (It is possible that steel could be more capital-intensive than orange juice at some factor prices and less capital-intensive at other factor prices. This possibility, known as "factor intensity reversal," is interesting, but we shall omit it here for ease of exposition.)

Now consider the different allocation of capital and labor in the production of OJ and S. To simplify as before, we can use the fact that $L = L_{OJ} + L_S$ and $K = K_{OJ} +$

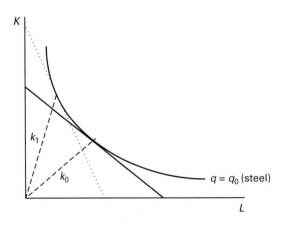

FIGURE 5.14 Isoquants and Isocost

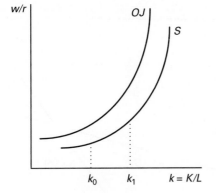

FIGURE 5.15 Factor Prices and Factor Intensities

K_S. At a given set of factor prices w/r, we know that k_{OJ} and k_S are the cost-minimizing techniques of production. This is drawn as Figure 5.16.

Suppose the total amount of labor available is L' and the total amount of capital available is K'. The capital-labor ratio for the economy as a whole is then K'/L', which is intermediate between k_S and k_{OJ}. Intuitively, then, production of S and OJ should be chosen so that the weighted average of the capital-labor ratios in the two goods equals the capital-labor ratio for the entire city. If we "slide" the k_S curve along the L axis, we can find an allocation of K and L between S and OJ such that all factors are fully employed.

Consider the following numerical example. Let $K' = 120$ and $L' = 60$. Suppose that the cost-minimizing capital-labor ratio at the given level of factor prices is $k_S = 4$ and $k_{OJ} = 1$. We can solve for the allocation of labor and capital that lead to full employment by substituting for K' and L' ($K_{OJ} + K_S = K'$, $L_{OJ} + L_S = L'$) and then using the capital-labor ratios to simplify. In the example, we find that $L_S = 20$, $L_{OJ} = 40$, $K_S = 80$, and $K_{OJ} = 40$.

FIGURE 5.16 Cost-Minimizing Factor Combinations

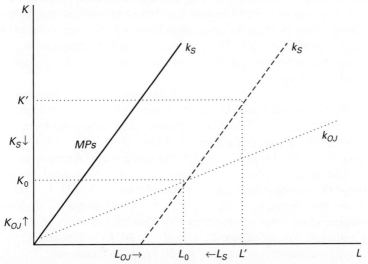

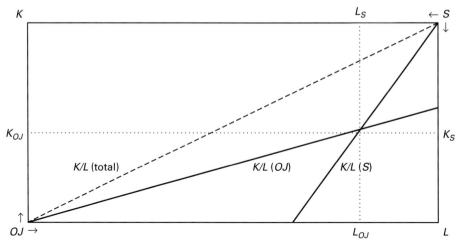

FIGURE 5.17 Edgeworth Box

This intuition can be further developed using an Edgeworth Box diagram. In the diagram in Figure 5.17, the horizontal axis shows the amount of labor, measured from the left for labor in *OJ* and from the right for labor in *S*. Similarly, the vertical axis shows the allocation of capital between *S* and *OJ*. Each point in the box is an allocation of capital and labor between *S* and *OJ* production. The capital-labor ratio for the entire economy is shown by the dashed line on the diagonal of the box. The capital-labor ratios for *OJ* and *S* for a given *w/r* are also shown. If all factors are to be employed, then the allocation of factors between *OJ* and *S* is given by the intersection of the two *K/L* lines.

The Edgeworth Box above has been derived assuming a given set of factor prices. Suppose the relative price of labor increases. From Figure 5.15 we know that the capital-labor ratio in both *OJ* and *S* will increase. The implication for the Edgeworth Box is shown in Figure 5.18. The amount of labor devoted to *OJ* production increases, as does the amount of capital devoted to *OJ* production, so the allocation of factors moves from point *A* to point *B* in Figure 5.18. Therefore, *OJ* production increases and *S* production falls. The complete set of full-employment points can be obtained by continuously varying *w/r*. Note that there are relative prices at which complete specialization occurs.

Suppose the amount of capital available in the economy increases. As is shown in Figure 5.19, this will have the effect of increasing steel production. This result is known as the *Rybczynski Theorem*, after the economist who formally developed it. An increase in the amount of a factor will lead, ceteris paribus, to an increase in the production of the good that uses that factor intensively. An increase in labor, for example, would increase production of the labor-intensive good, in this case orange juice. Recall the example from earlier in the chapter ($K' = 120$, $L' = 60$, $k_S = 4$, $k_{OJ} = 1$). Under those conditions, $L_S = 20$, $L_{OJ} = 40$, $K_{OJ} = 40$, and $K_S = 80$. Now suppose that the available capital stock increases to 150. You should verify that the new allocation of labor and capital is as follows: $L_S = 30$, $L_{OJ} = 30$, $K_S = 120$, and $K_{OJ} = 30$. This is exactly the type of change predicted by the Rybczynski Theorem.

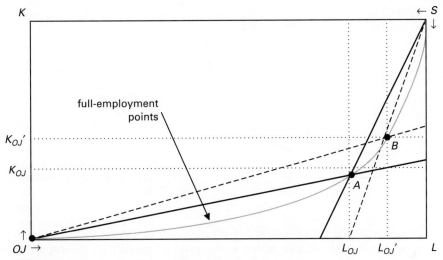

FIGURE 5.18 Full Employment at Varying Factor Prices

The allocation of factors in the Edgeworth Box can be related to the PPF. If $L_{OJ} = L'$, then you are producing no S and all OJ. This is point D on the PPF in Figure 5.9. Similarly, if $L_S = L'$, then you are at point B in Figure 5.9. Recall that equilibrium in product markets gives us a set of relative prices and a point on the PPF. This point can be linked through the Edgeworth Box diagram to equilibrium in factor markets. This relation between equilibrium prices is summarized in Figure 5.20.

We are now ready to simply characterize general equilibrium in terms of product market prices, factor market prices, and the capital-labor ratio for the various goods and the economy as a whole. The diagram in Figure 5.21 combines Figure 5.15 (showing the relation between factor prices and factor intensities) and Figure 5.20

FIGURE 5.19 The Rybczynski Theorem

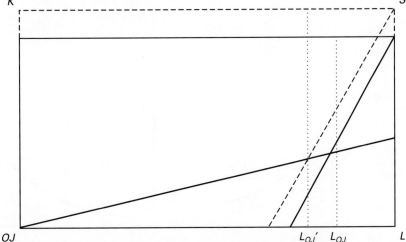

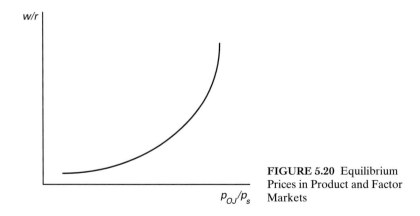

FIGURE 5.20 Equilibrium Prices in Product and Factor Markets

(showing the relation between product market prices and factor prices). Figure 5.21 shows that at relative prices in the product market p', the capital-labor ratio in OJ production is k_{OJ} and the capital-labor ratio in S production is k_S. The ratio of capital to labor for the entire economy is k'. Note that $k_S > k' > k_{OJ}$, as we saw above.

In the next chapter, we will use this model to analyze trade among cities. This model, in which trade is the result of differences in factor endowments among cities, is known as the *Hecksher-Ohlin* model of trade. Let me introduce at this point a bit of evidence on the applicability of this simple model at the level of the United States as a whole. Ziona Austrian and Susan Helper (1990) assert that the United States has long had a relative abundance of high technology and education. Hence, the Hecksher-Ohlin model would predict that the products exported from the United States would tend to be those made by educated workers using high technology, while imports would be made by less-educated workers. They used industry-level data from the U.S. Census Bureau to identify "export" and "import" industries and then examined the fraction of workers in each of the industries that had completed at least one year of

FIGURE 5.21 General Equilibrium

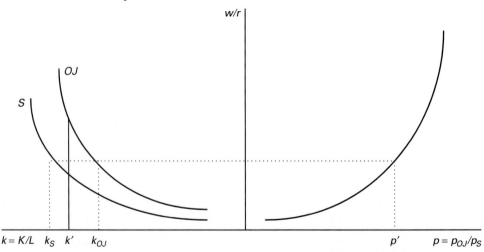

college. They found that the average for export industries was 41.3 percent of the workers with at least one year of college, compared with an average for import industries of 29.9 percent. The figures varied somewhat across region and industry but were consistent with the Hecksher-Ohlin model.

Moroney and Walker (1966) apply the Hecksher-Ohlin model to regional data from the United States. They relate capital-labor ratios to the levels of location quotients and to changes in location quotients. (A *location quotient* is the ratio of local production of a commodity to local consumption of that same commodity. If it is greater than 1, the good is an export; if it is less than 1, the good is an import. See chapter 8 for a further discussion.) Their statistical tests are inconclusive with respect to the Hecksher-Ohlin model, but they ascribe this to the importance of natural resources in determining comparative advantage. In the appendix to chapter 6, we will discuss how to extend the Hecksher-Ohlin model to include natural resources as well as capital and labor.

CHAPTER SUMMARY

- In this chapter we have developed the economic analysis of specialization and trade on the basis of comparative advantage. Comparative advantage exists when the opportunity cost of producing a product in one city is lower than it is in another city. Cities will export goods and services in which they have a comparative advantage in return for goods and services in which they do not have a comparative advantage. In the absence of transport costs and trade restrictions, the relative price of goods will be equal in all locations.

- The pattern of trade among cities reflects not only comparative advantage but also several other characteristics of the cities. Relatively small cities are able to specialize more completely than relatively large cities. The preferences of the population for various products determine the allocation of resources among various products. The existence of transport costs can reduce the volume of trade. Transport costs will also cause relative prices to differ across cities.

- Trade among cities affects not only product market prices but also factor market prices. If firms have a choice of production techniques, the changes in factor market prices will also lead to a change in the relative factor intensity of production. If a city is relatively well endowed with a factor of production used solely in producing one type of product, it will tend to export that product.

- If there are changes in the level of factors of production, then a city's production and trade will change. The Rybczynski Theorem states that an increase in one factor of production, ceteris paribus, will cause a city to increase its production of the goods whose production is relatively intensive in that factor.

EXCERPT: "PILGRIMAGE TO EARTH" (ROBERT SHECKLEY)

As technology has progressed, the set of goods and services that can be traded has multiplied. Sometimes this has happened because a reduction in transportation costs has made it profitable to exchange commodities that would have previously have been too expensive to ship. Sometimes it is because technological advance has made new products and services available that had been previously unavailable. The excerpt below from a short story by Robert Sheckley (1956) illustrates a little of both of these types of advances, where trade is between planets, and technological advances have made possible trade in previously inconceivable commodities.

Alfred Simon was born on Kazanga IV, a small agricultural planet near Arcturus, and there he drove a combine through the wheat fields, and in the long hushed evenings listened to the recorded love songs of Earth.

Life was pleasant enough on Kazanga, and the girls were buxom, jolly, frank, and acquiescent, good companions for a hike through the hills or a swim in the brook, staunch mates for life. But romantic—never! There was good fun to be had on Kazanga, in a cheerful open manner. But there was no more than fun.

Simon felt that something was missing in this bland existence. One day, he discovered what it was.

A vendor came to Kazanga in a battered spaceship loaded with books. He was gaunt, white-haired, and a little mad. A celebration was held for him, for novelty was appreciated on the outer worlds. And at last someone said "Tell us of Earth."

"Ah!" said the vendor, raising his eyebrows. "You want to hear of the mother planet? Well friends, there's no place like Earth, no place at all. On Earth, friends, everything is possible, and nothing is denied."

"Nothing?" Simon asked.

"They've got a law against denial," the vendor explained, grinning. "No one has ever been known to break it. Earth is *different,* friends. You folks specialize in farming? Well, Earth specializes in impracticalities such as madness, beauty, war, intoxication, purity, horror, and the like, and people come from light-years away to sample these wares."

"And love?" a woman asked.

"Earth is the only place in the galaxy that still has love. Earth specializes in the impractical, and makes it pay. Earth is old, her minerals are gone and her fields are barren. Her colonies are independent now, and filled with sober folk such as yourselves, who want value for their goods. So what else can old Earth deal in, except the nonessentials that make life worth living?"

The new worlds were austere, carefully planned, sterile in their perfection. Something had been lost in the dead reaches of space, and only Earth knew love.

Therefore, Simon worked and saved and dreamed. And in his twenty-ninth year he sold his farm and boarded the Kazanga-Metropole Flyer. At last he came to Earth, where dreams *must* come true, for there is a law against their failure. He passed quickly through Customs at Spaceport New York, and was shuttled underground to Times Square.

When he reached 44th Street he saw a tremendous neon sign flashing brightly. It said LOVE, INC. Simon frowned, for a terrible suspicion had just crossed his mind. Still, he climbed the stairs and entered a small, tastefully furnished reception room. From there he was sent down a long corridor to a numbered room.

Within the room was a handsome gray-haired man who rose from behind an impressive desk and shook his hand saying, "I'm Mr. Tate, and I'm here to help you to the best of my ability."

Simon said, "I don't want to be rude or anything, but . . . I think I'm in the wrong place. I mean, you can't really sell *love* can you? Not *love!*"

"But of course!" Mr. Tate said. "That's the whole point! *Love* is rare, *love* is special, *love* is found only on Earth! If we were selling simulated love, we'd label it as such. The advertising laws on Earth are strict, I can assure you."

"No sir, make no mistake. Our product is not a substitute. It is the exact self-same feeling that poets and writers have raved about for thousands of years. Through the wonders of modern science we can bring this feeling to you at your convenience, attractively packaged, completely disposable, and for a ridiculously low price."

"Unbiased scientific firms have made qualitative tests of it, in comparison with the natural thing. In every case, *our* love tested out to more depth, passion, fervor, and scope. We gave up natural selection years ago. It was too slow, and commercially unfeasible. Why bother with it, when we can produce any feeling at will by conditioning and proper stimulation of certain brain centers?"

Simon said, "I pictured something more—spontaneous."

"Spontaneity has its charm," Mr. Tate agreed. "Our research labs are working on it. Believe me, there's nothing science can't produce, as long as there's a market for it."

Source: "Pilgrimage to Earth" by Robert Sheckley. Copyright © 1956, 1979 by Robert Sheckley. Reprinted by permission of the author.

Questions for Review and Discussion

1. "Advances in transportation and communication make some goods and services tradable that were previously nontradable. Therefore, we expect cities in the United States to resemble each other more than they did in the past." Do you agree or disagree? Explain.

2. Suppose Cleveland can produce 2 tons of steel and 100 gallons of orange juice per hour and Miami can produce 1 ton of steel and 200 gallons of orange juice per hour. Each city has 100 hours of labor available.
   a. Draw the PPF for Cleveland. Draw the PPF for Miami.
   b. Suppose each city devotes 50 hours of labor to steel and 50 hours to orange juice. How much does each city produce? Draw an Edgeworth Box and illustrate whether there are gains from trade.
   c. Suppose there are "iceberg" transportation costs. How high would the transportation costs have to be to prevent trade from occurring between the two cities?

3. Suppose there are three cities: Richmond, Louisville, and Nashville. There are two commodities: consulting services (C) and paper (P). The only factor of production is labor, and each city has 200 hours of labor per day available. The output per hour of labor is given in the following table:

City → Good ↓	Richmond	Louisville	Nashville
Consulting Services (C)	2	6	4
Paper (P)	5	20	12

Suppose residents of each of the cities prefer to consume C and P in the ratio of 3 P to 1 C.
   a. Draw the PPF for each city and solve for the production and consumption of C and P under autarky.
   b. Draw the combined PPF and solve for the production and consumption of C and P in each city under free trade. Assume for the moment that there are zero transport costs.

c. Now suppose there are iceberg transportation costs. What is the effect on the equilibrium price and trading pattern?

d. Suppose now that Louisville has only 100 hours of labor available. Redo parts (a)–(c).

4. "An increase in labor productivity is like adding labor to the economy. The Rybczynski Theorem can therefore be used to infer that if labor is extremely productive, then the economy will produce a relatively large amount of labor-intensive products." Do you agree or disagree? Explain.

5. The model of trade developed in this chapter assumes that there is full employment of all factors of production. How would you incorporate unemployment in the analysis?

Appendix: Cost Minimization and Utility Maximization

The economic model of the world includes three main types of actors: households, firms, and governments. In this chapter, we saw how a formal model of household and firm decision making can be used to analyze the pattern of production and exchange among cities. This appendix reviews the elements of this formal model of household and firm decision making.

Cost Minimization by Firms

Firms are defined as the entities that transform resources into goods and services that they sell to other firms, households, and governments. Firms are assumed to be interested in maximizing profits, which are defined as equal to total revenues minus total costs. Firms must make four decisions: the quantity of goods and services to produce and sell, the price to charge, the quantity of inputs to demand, and the production technique to use. These decisions, of course, are linked. The amount that a firm can sell at a given price is constrained by demand, so the choice of quantity to supply and price are inseparable. Further, the amount produced and the inputs demanded are linked definitionally by the choice of production technique.

If many production techniques are available to produce a given amount of output, a firm will choose the one that requires the minimum total cost. After all, if a given amount is produced and sold, then the revenues are fixed, so that maximizing profits is simply a matter of minimizing costs. The cost-minimizing set of inputs depends on two things: the relative prices of the inputs and the technical ability to substitute one input for another. Graphical tools used to identify cost-minimizing input combinations are the isoquant, which illustrates the technical substitutability of inputs, and the isocost curve, which illustrates relative input prices.

The isoquant, as the name suggests, is the set of inputs that allows a given quantity of output to be produced. Suppose that 40 stories of office space is the output and that capital and land are the inputs. Different combinations of capital and land can result in the equivalent of 40 stories (where a story is a standardized number of square feet) of office space: for example, a 40-story building (say $50 million of capital on 3 acres of land), two 20-story buildings ($41 million of capital on 6 acres of land), and so on. If capital and land can be continuously substituted, one for the other, the result is a continuum of alternatives. This possibility is illustrated in Figure A-5.1, where 40 stories of office space can be produced in a variety of ways. If the desired output should change, then so would the isoquant. Figure A-5.1 also illustrates the capital and land combinations that can be used to produce 50 stories of office space.

Because the amount of output at each point on the isoquant is the same, it is straightforward to derive the slope. Let MP_L and MP_K represent the marginal product of land and capital respectively. Reducing the amount of capital by a small amount, ΔK, implies a reduction in output of $\Delta K \times MP_K$, while increasing the amount of land by a small amount implies an increase in output of $\Delta L \times MP_L$. Because along an isoquant the total output is constant, the decrease from the reduction in capital must be exactly offset by the increase from the increase in land. In other words $-\Delta K \times MP_K = \Delta L \times MP_L$. This can be rearranged to give the slope of the isoquant, $\Delta K/\Delta L = -MP_L/MP_K$. Because both MP_L and MP_K are greater than zero, the isoquant is downward sloping. Because there are diminishing returns to each factor in the short run, the isoquant curves outward from the origin. In other words, as the amount of land is reduced, the marginal cost of land increases in terms of the capital required to keep output constant.

Suppose the firm wants to produce 40 stories of office space. What combination of capital and land is the cost-minimizing one? To answer that question, we must consider the relative price of capital and land.

Suppose the firm takes the price of capital and the price of land as given. Then the total cost is just equal to the price of capital times the amount of capital plus the price of land times the amount of land. The set of points that have a given total cost form a straight line in capital-land space, as shown in Figure A-5.2. This line is defined as the "isocost curve." (If the cost per unit for the inputs is not constant, then the isocost may not be a straight line.) The slope of the isocost curve is the ratio of factor prices—that is, the opportunity cost of the inputs in the market. A shift in cost for a given set of factor prices leads to a parallel shift in the isocost curve; inward in the case of a reduction in cost, outward in the case of an increase in cost. An increase in cost relative to the solid line isocost is illustrated in Figure A-5.2 as a dashed line. If relative factor prices change, then the isocost curve will change its slope. A decrease in the price of land is shown as a dotted line in Figure A-5.2.

Now we are ready to put these two graphs together in order to identify the cost-minimizing combination of inputs. This is done in Figure A-5.3. The cost-minimizing combination will be the point of tangency between the isoquant and isocost curve. If

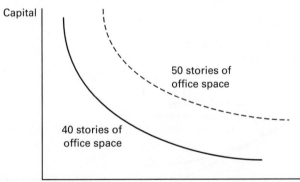

Land   **FIGURE A-5.1** Isoquant

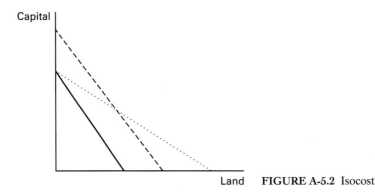

Land   **FIGURE A-5.2** Isocost

prices should change, then the tangency point will also change. This is shown in Figure A-5.3. The dotted line represents a set of factor prices in which land is relatively more expensive than capital, relative to the original situation. The firm, in this case, substitutes capital for land. This is known as the "factor substitution" effect.

Another possible effect, in addition to the factor substitution effect, of a factor price change is the so-called "output effect." Recall that a firm is interested not only in cost minimization but also in profit maximization. If input prices are lower, the firm's marginal cost is lower, suggesting that an increase in production is warranted. An increase in production means a move to a higher isoquant, as shown in Figure A-5.4. Even if the capital-land ratio is lower when the price of land falls, the total amount of capital demanded could remain the same.

Utility Maximization by Households

Households, like firms, use the resources at their disposal to advance their interests. Household preferences can be summarized by the use of indifference curves. These curves show combinations of goods and services that make the household equally happy. The idea is that the household can achieve the same level of happiness in a number of alternative ways. This idea is already familiar, as it is the same logic used to derive isoquants for firms. Like isoquants, indifference curves are downward sloping. The absolute value of the slope of the indifference curve, known as the marginal rate

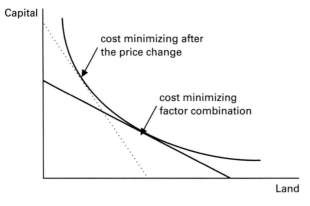

Land   **FIGURE A-5.3** Cost Minimization and Factor Substitution

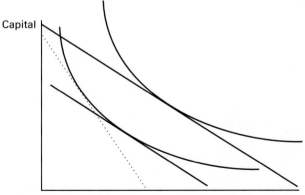

Capital

Land   **FIGURE A-5.4** Output Effect

of substitution, is the ratio of the marginal utilities of the goods being considered. An example is shown in Figure A-5.5.

Indifference curves representing higher levels of happiness are farther away from the origin. The goal of the household is to maximize utility—that is, to consume the goods that put it on the highest possible indifference curve, given its available resources. The available consumption possibilities are illustrated using a tool called the budget constraint. Consider a simple example. There are two goods, eclairs (E) and coffee (C). The household has a given amount of income, Y, to spend on the goods. Denote the price of eclairs and the price of coffee as p_E and p_C respectively. The household can afford any combination of E and C with a total cost less than or equal to Y. The budget constraint itself can be written as $p_C C + p_E E = Y$, which is a straight line. The absolute value of the slope of the budget constraint is the relative price of coffee and eclairs. The problem facing the household is illustrated in Figure A-5.5.

It is clear from Figure A-5.5 that the utility-maximizing consumption choice for the household is the point of tangency between the indifference curve and the budget constraint. This is the highest indifference curve that can be reached while not spending more money than the household has available.

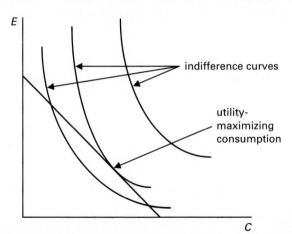

E

indifference curves

utility-
maximizing
consumption

C

FIGURE A-5.5 Household
Equilibrium

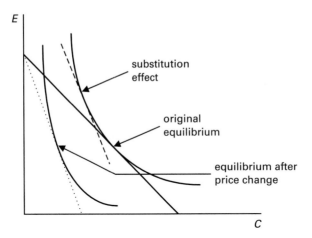

FIGURE A-5.6 Substitution and Income Effects of a Price Change

Suppose the price of coffee increases, all else being equal. In that case, the budget constraint pivots inward, as shown in Figure A-5.6. The new budget constraint is the dotted line with the same *E* intercept as the original budget constraint. The new equilibrium is also shown. As you would expect, the demand for coffee has decreased as a result of the increase in the price of coffee. This change in demand can be decomposed into two parts. The first part, the *substitution effect*, is the substitution of the now relatively less-expensive eclairs for the coffee. Suppose the household's income is increased so as to allow it to reach the same indifference curve it was on before the price increase. The result is shown by the dashed line in Figure A-5.6. The utility-maximizing point is the one labeled "substitution effect," with relatively more *E* and less *C* than previously. The second part, the *income effect*, is the change in consumption due to the effective reduction in income resulting from the price increase. If coffee is a normal good, this reduction in income will lead to a further reduction in consumption. If coffee is inferior, its consumption will increase as a result of a decrease in income. This change in demand is known as the "income effect" of a price change. In the diagram, it is the difference between coffee consumption at the "substitution effect" point and at the "equilibrium after price change" point. To check your understanding, you should verify that coffee is a normal good in this example.

CHAPTER

6

Factor Abundance and Specialization

In this chapter we continue to develop a general equilibrium model of a city's economy and show how cities will specialize and trade with each other based on relative factor abundance. This factor abundance theory (also known as the "Hecksher-Ohlin" model, after the two economists who first developed it) can be thought of as a complement to the central place theory discussed in chapters 3 and 4. Recall that central place theory was predicated on the location decisions of market-oriented firms; in other words, it was a world where inputs were cheap to transport relative to outputs. Hecksher-Ohlin theory, in contrast, models a world in which factors of production are expensive to transport relative to finished goods.

TRADE THEOREMS—HECKSHER-OHLIN AND FACTOR PRICE EQUALIZATION

The general equilibrium model of a city's economy developed at the end of chapter 5 can be used to analyze the effects of trade among cities. Consider the situation displayed in Figure 6.1. Cleveland has a higher capital-labor ratio than does Miami, and the autarky prices of goods and factors reflect this. For example, w/r is higher in Cleveland because labor is relatively scarce. Cleveland produces relatively more steel than Miami does.

Now consider the effect of opening up trade between the two cities. The price of orange juice relative to steel must be between the autarky prices in order for the cities to agree to trade. One possible set of prices is shown as point p in Figure 6.1. Trade affects prices, outputs, and factor usage. In Cleveland the price of orange juice and the price of labor fall, while the price of steel and the price of capital increase. In Miami the opposite occurs. Although both cities produced both products before the opening of trade, now Miami completely specializes in the production of orange juice.

The situation shown in Figure 6.1 illustrates the main idea of the economic analysis of trade. This analysis is summarized in the *Hecksher-Ohlin theorem*, which states that trade is based on differences in factor abundance among economies and

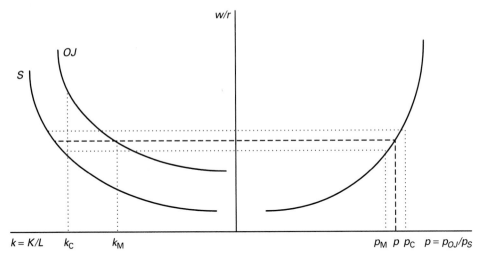

FIGURE 6.1 General Equilibrium with Trade

that trade serves to reduce the effect of those differences. In the example, Cleveland was relatively better endowed with capital, which gave it an advantage in steel but a disadvantage in orange juice. As a result of trade with Miami, which had the opposite factor endowment pattern, Cleveland lost its price advantage in steel but also lost its disadvantage in orange juice.

Factor Price Equalization

Return to the situation pictured in Figure 6.1. The diagram also illustrates the idea of *factor price equalization*, the idea that trade reduces differences among economies in relative factor prices as well as in relative product prices. The loci of capital-labor ratios for the two cities are identical, reflecting their common access to the same technology. Assuming that the trading partners have access to a common technology and that transport costs are zero, free trade results in identical factor returns so long as all cities produce all goods. This last condition is important, given our earlier focus on specialization as the source of gains from trade. If, for example, Miami completely specialized in *OJ* production, then the relative factor prices could be different in Miami and Cleveland even if there were completely free trade in *OJ* and *S*. The relative price of labor, shown as $(w/r)_C$ and $(w/r)_M$ for Cleveland and Miami respectively in Figure 6.2, is higher in Cleveland than in Miami, reflecting the continuing scarcity of labor relative to capital in Cleveland. This situation is illustrated in Figure 6.2, which shows that free trade has equalized product market prices but not factor prices.

The restriction that all cities produce all products is readily illustrated using the Edgeworth Box diagram introduced in the previous chapter. The solid lines in Figure 6.3 show the full employment capital-labor ratio in orange juice and steel production if all production was located in Cleveland, while the dashed lines show the same thing for Miami. This is called the "integrated equilibrium," because we can perform the thought experiment of starting with all the capital and labor in one city and then reallocating some to the other city while keeping total production the same. If capital

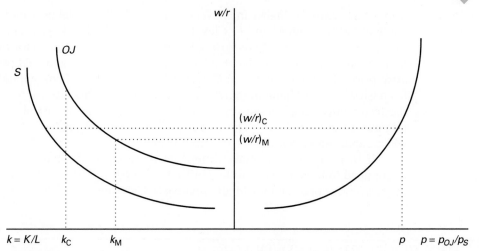

FIGURE 6.2 Complete Specialization and Factor Price Differences

and labor are allocated at any point in the "lozenge" formed by these lines, then both goods are produced in both cities, and the reallocation of factors is essentially offset by trade. Otherwise, one or both cities will specialize in either orange juice or steel production.

If both goods are produced in both cities, then the equilibrium price of the goods must be equal, implying in turn that factor prices are equal. Hence, the lozenge in Figure 6.3 is known as the *factor price equalization region* (Helpman and Krugman 1985). If the factors of production are distributed between the cities in a way that is outside the factor price equalization region, then at least one of the cities will specialize in producing one of the goods. In turn, this implies that factor prices can differ across cities. Consider a point such as α in Figure 6.3, where Cleveland has a lot of capital but little labor. In that case, Cleveland will produce only steel, and the relative

FIGURE 6.3 Factor Price Equalization in the Edgeworth Box

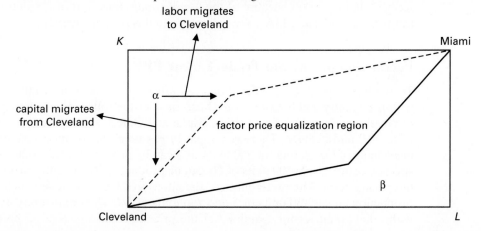

price of labor will be higher in Cleveland than in Miami. If labor is mobile, then people might move from Miami to Cleveland to get the higher wages. This mobility will cause the relative price of labor to fall as we move towards the factor price equalization region along the arrow labeled "labor migrates to Cleveland." At point α, the relative price of capital is lower in Cleveland than in Miami. Thus, capital might move from Cleveland to Miami in search of a higher return. This too will tend to lead us to the factor price equalization region, only this time along the arrow labeled "capital migrates from Cleveland." The actual path will depend on the relative speed with which capital and labor move from city to city.

If there are nonmonetary differences between Cleveland and Miami, people might need to be paid extra to live in Cleveland (or in Miami). At a point such as β, there is a wage premium for Miami relative to Cleveland.

LUMPY COUNTRIES AND TRADE

We have been focusing on cities as units of analysis to this point. Most trade theory, though, was developed using analysis at the national level. Even if one is unconvinced by my argument in chapter 1 that cities are economically equivalent to countries, there is an argument for focusing on cities rather than countries as the units of analysis. This argument was developed by Paul Courant and Alan Deardorff (1992, 1993), and is based on the idea of the integrated equilibrium introduced above. Courant and Deardorff show that an uneven allocation ("lumpiness") of factors of production within a country can cause the country to trade with other countries even if the rest of the characteristics of the country suggest that the country would not trade. Since a city is by definition an uneven allocation of factors of production, the existence of cities is a spur to and an explanation for international trade, in addition to the intranational trade we have been focusing on to this point. The interesting question also arises of the appropriate definition of a "country" for economic purposes. The definition I prefer is that a country's boundary is a discontinuity in transactions costs in factor or product markets. By this definition, a metropolitan area is a country if one considers land or labor markets (the definition of MSAs in the United States is one that describes a labor market because of the use of commuting patterns to identify the counties that belong to an MSA). We will return to this issue in chapter 7.

Factor Lumpiness and Trade: Linear PPF

To see how lumpy factor allocations can affect the pattern of production and trade within a country and between countries, consider the following example. The country of Greektome consists of two cities, Alpha and Omega. There are two goods, orange juice (*OJ*) and steel (*S*). There is a linear PPF, with an opportunity cost of 3 units of *S* per 5 units of *OJ*. A total of 300 units of *S* can be produced if the country completely specializes in *S*, while 500 units of *OJ* can be produced if the country produces nothing but orange juice. The preferences of the citizens of Greektome are such that current production equals 180 units of *S* and 200 units of *OJ*. The opportunity exists to trade with other countries for *S* and *OJ* at the price of 3 units of *S* per 5 units of *OJ*. At

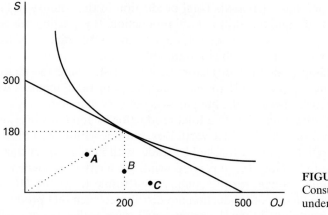

FIGURE 6.4 Production and Consumption in Greektome under Autarky

those prices, there is no advantage to trade, so that autarky is chosen. The situation as described is diagrammed in Figure 6.4.

To this point, nothing has been said about the allocation of production between the two cities of Alpha and Omega. Suppose that the capital-labor ratios are identical in the two cities but that Alpha is three times larger than Omega. In that case, Alpha will produce three-fourths of the total output of Greektome and Omega will produce one-fourth of the output. There is no reason for trade between the two cities, so there is autarky within the country as well as between the country and the rest of the world. The allocation of production between Alpha and Omega can be illustrated using an Edgeworth Box, as shown in Figure 6.5. Point A is the initial situation, with Alpha producing three-fourths of the output and Omega one-fourth. The dotted line shows combinations of production where there is no need for trade between the two cities, because the local production equals the desired consumption.

Now consider point *B* in Figure 6.5. To get to this point, we have shifted capital from Alpha to Omega, leading to an increase in *S* production by Omega. Omega has also reduced *OJ* production, while *OJ* production by Alpha has increased and *S* pro-

FIGURE 6.5 Allocation of Production between Alpha and Omega

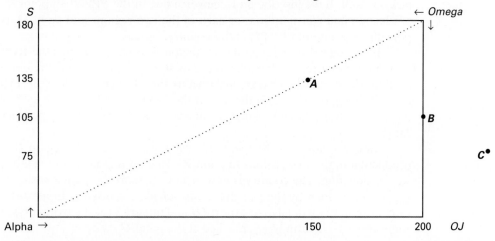

duction by Alpha has decreased. Total production in the country of Greektome has stayed the same despite this shift in local production. It is possible for consumption in each city to remain the same as well. If Alpha exports 50 units of *OJ* to Omega in return for 30 units of *S*, then both cities are able to consume at point *A* again. Point *B* represents a lumpier division of factors than point *A*, where the factors are equally distributed. The cities are able to undo the effects of the lumpiness without trading with other countries because the lumpiness is not very extreme.

Now consider point *C*, with a total production of 150 units of *S* and 250 units of *OJ*. This point is outside the Edgeworth Box, but it is within the PPF for the country. It seems that point *A* can be reached by trade, with Omega producing 105 units of *S* and −50 units of *OJ*. However, it is not possible for a city to produce negative units of *OJ*. It is possible, though, for the country as a whole to export *OJ* in return for *S*. Therefore, if the factors of production are distributed such that production in the two cities is given by point *C*, then the country will trade with other countries. This trade occurs despite the fact that there is no comparative advantage reason for trade—the opportunity cost of *OJ* and *S* are the same for local production and for international trade. The only reason for the trade to occur is the lumpy distribution of the factors among the cities within the country.

Factor Lumpiness and Trade: Nonlinear PPF

The analysis shown above used the simplifying assumption of a linear PPF in order to facilitate numerical calculations. There is nothing in the analysis, however, that relies on a linear PPF, so we will now take a more general approach to the same situation. The conclusions, of course, are the same, but the applicability is broader. Further, this analysis is an excellent exercise to be sure that you really understand the idea of trade among regions within a country as well as among countries.

Consider a country whose autarky prices equal world prices, so that there are no gains from international trade. The PPF for this country is shown as Figure 6.6. Suppose the country consists of two regions, *A* and *B*, whose factor endowments are equal and whose residents have identical utility functions. In that case, each region will produce and consume half of the country's output, and there will be regional autarky as well. If we inscribe an Edgeworth box in the PPF, then point Z_0 is the initial production and consumption for each of the two regions and point Q_0 is the production and consumption for the entire country.

If we begin moving capital from region *A* to region *B*, then the Rybczynski theorem implies that region *B* will increase its steel production while region *A* reduces its steel production. This change is shown as the "Rybczynski line" in Figure 6.6, with point Z_1 being one point on the line. If the two regions trade with each other, though, then they can still keep regional consumption at Z_0 and national production and consumption at Q_0.

Suppose, however, that so much capital has located in region *B* that it has led production in the two regions to point Z_2. Region *B* is now completely specialized in steel production. The country is now producing more *OJ* than it wishes to consume at Q_0, as can be seen by the fact that Z_2 is outside the original Edgeworth Box. Therefore, the country will have to export *OJ* and import *S* (at the world price ratio) to consume at the *S-OJ* ratio of Q_0, reached at the point C_2.

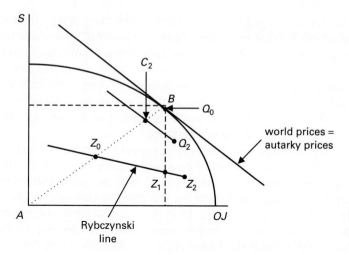

FIGURE 6.6 Uneven Factor Allocations and International Trade

The complete specialization of region B in the example above gives a hint to the general nature of the relation between regional factor allocation and international trade. Return to the Edgeworth Box showing the allocation of capital and labor among regions, shown as Figure 6.7. In the region of factor price equalization, there is no regional specialization, and the integrated (autarky) equilibrium can be maintained through trade among the regions. However, if factors are distributed outside the factor price equalization area, then the country will be a net exporter even though its autarky prices equal world prices. For example, the allocation of factors Z_0 corresponds to the identically labeled point on the production possibility frontier diagram in Figure 6.6. When capital is moved from region A to region B, eventually a point like Z_2 is reached where OJ is exported, as we saw above.

Courant and Deardorff examine at length whether any general conclusions can be reached about the pattern of trade resulting from uneven factor allocations. Their main finding is that countries will export the product that is intensive in the factor that is more unevenly distributed among the regions within the country. Consider point Z_2 in Figure 6.7. Capital is fairly evenly distributed between region A and region B, while

FIGURE 6.7 Lumpy Factor Allocations and Trade

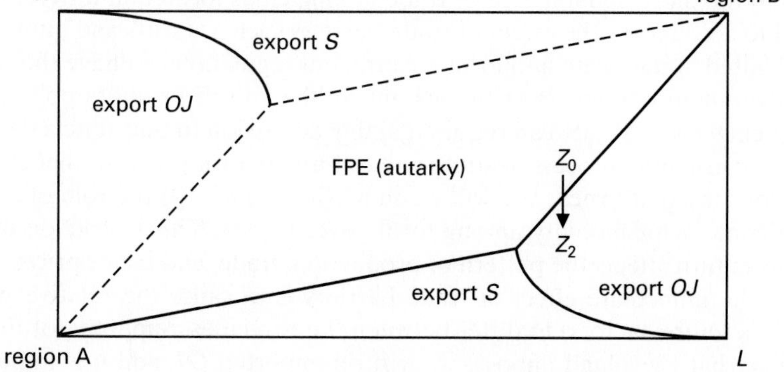

labor is concentrated in region *A*. Thus, labor is relatively lumpy, and Courant and Deardorff would predict that the country would export *OJ*, as we have found. A subtle point they emphasize is that even if the factors are evenly distributed among regions within a country, the country may be lumpy *relative* to other countries. (This is a point analogous to the idea of comparative advantage even in the case where a country has no absolute advantage.) Since the analysis was all done assuming there was no basis for trade other than lumpy factor allocations, it underestimates the degree to which we expect to see specialization and trade.

The final point to emphasize is that differences in amenities among regions within a country cause us to expect factors of production to be unevenly distributed. These amenities include those on the production side, such as agglomeration economies of scale and access to markets, and those on the consumption side, such as climate or quality of life. In the discussion of the factor price equalization region earlier in this chapter, we saw that differences in wages among regions could be expected to put the distribution of factors outside the factor price equalization region. The empirical evidence on systematic variation in wages presented in chapter 4 backs up this theoretical prediction, as does the evidence on city specialization presented in chapter 1. Neglecting the fact that countries are composed of collections of cities is a handicap in understanding their trade with other countries and thus is another reason for focusing on the cities themselves. As Courant and Deardorff conclude (p. 315), "countries are (except perhaps in the case of island nations) arbitrary aggregations of regions and cities, whose endowments of amenities and nontraded goods, both natural and produced, are the fundamental determinants of the location of production and the pattern of trade."

TRADE BARRIERS AND FACTOR MOBILITY

To this point, we have focused on the situation with free trade. Given our emphasis on intermetropolitan trade in the United States, this focus makes sense as a good approximation of the common market created in the United States by the interstate commerce clauses of the Constitution ("No State shall, without the Consent of the Congress, lay any Imposts or Duties on Imports or Exports. . . ." Article I, Section 10; "No Preference shall be given by Regulation of Commerce or Revenue to the Ports of one State over those of another: nor shall Vessels bound to, or from, one State, be obliged to enter, clear, or pay Duties in another." Article I, Section 9). However, when we turn to the more general case of trade among cities located in different countries, we need to account for the effect of trade barriers such as tariffs and quotas. Even within the United States, state and local government regulation can have the effect of reducing the mobility of goods or factors, much like a tariff or quota policy. For example, practicing law in a state can require gaining admission to that state's bar, which can be a time-consuming process, leading you to hire an attorney from that state rather than use your usual attorney. We will examine (in chapter 10) the role of zoning policy in restricting factor mobility among local governments. This restriction in factor movements in turn affects the pattern of production, trade, and factor prices.

The immediate effect of trade barriers is to cause the relative prices of goods (and therefore, factors) to differ between the two cities. Suppose, for the sake of illustration, that Cleveland imposes a tariff on imported *OJ*, and it is importing *OJ* from

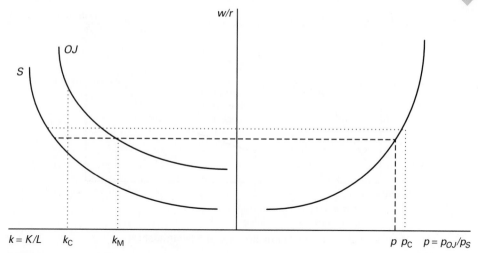

FIGURE 6.8 The Effect of Trade Barriers

Monterrey, a city outside the United States. The situation is diagrammed in Figure 6.8, with k_M representing the capital-labor ratio in Monterrey and k_C the capital-labor ratio in Cleveland. The relative price under free trade is p. The relative price of *OJ* will increase in Cleveland (to p_C) as a result of this tariff. Because Monterrey is already completely specialized in *OJ* production, given the relative prices prevailing under free trade, it will not produce any more *OJ* as a result; but Cleveland's *OJ* production will be higher than in the case of free trade. Also, as discussed above, the return to labor will be higher in Cleveland than in Monterrey, and it will be higher in Cleveland than it was under free trade. The return to capital, conversely, is higher in Monterrey.

Suppose, though, that people and capital can move freely between Monterrey and Cleveland. This does not strain credulity overmuch, although there may be restrictions on mobility depending on which country Monterrey is in. Since the return to capital is higher in Monterrey, we would expect to see capital leave Cleveland. Similarly, we would expect to see labor leaving Monterrey for Cleveland. Both of these changes will increase the capital-labor ratio in Monterrey and decrease it in Cleveland. In equilibrium, the factor prices will be equalized. Free factor mobility can be a substitute for free trade of goods. This, in turn, helps us to better understand the Hecksher-Ohlin theorem. A city, rather than importing the factors directly from another city, instead imports the services of those factors embodied in the goods they produce. However, should a city not allow this indirect trade in factors, the factors of production will move if they are free to do so.

NONTRADABLES

A "natural" trade barrier is the inability to trade some goods and services. Recall in chapter 4 that we identified several types of services that fell into this category. Nontradables enter the theory in a straightforward manner. Consider the Edgeworth Box

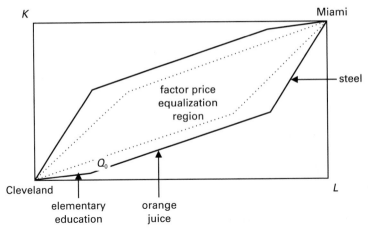

FIGURE 6.9 Factor Price Equalization with Nontradables

shown in Figure 6.9, which includes three commodities rather than simply two. As before, the commodities are ordered according to their relative factor intensity. The three commodities are elementary education, orange juice, and steel, in order of increasing capital intensity. Suppose that elementary education, the most labor-intensive good, is nontradable among cities. An endowment close to Q_0 in Figure 6.9 will not bring about factor price equalization, because all of Cleveland's labor will be allocated to producing the nontradable good, elementary education, leaving none to produce the tradable goods, orange juice and steel. However, a factor price equalization set can be constructed, even in the case of nontradables. This essentially involves finding allocations at which all three goods can feasibly be produced in both cities, as illustrated by the region within the dotted lines in Figure 6.9. This region is constructed by first removing from consideration the capital and labor required to produce elementary education in each city and then constructing a factor price equalization region for the other two goods. The important point is that the region is smaller than it would be if all goods were tradable.

As we have already seen in chapter 4, many goods and services are not tradable among cities. This means that even with free trade there may be factor price differences among cities. These differences are often called "compensating differentials," since the idea is that wages will be higher in cities that are less attractive to live in. The higher monetary wages, then, compensate for the lower levels of nontradable amenities.

Higher wages are both compensation for lower levels of amenities *and* a reward for higher levels of labor productivity. The importance of both positive and negative agglomeration economies of scale is thus seen again. When production clusters or capital intensity is high, then labor productivity is high, leading to higher wages. The clustering of production and capital also leads to negative externalities, such as congestion and pollution, necessitating the payment of higher wages to compensate mobile workers for the lower level of amenities available to them.

ECONOMIC DEVELOPMENT—CHANGES IN SPECIALIZATION AND TRADE

The discussion of factor mobility suggests that a city might change its pattern of production and trade over time. Factor mobility can alter the capital-labor ratio in a city, as was shown above. Further, factor mobility can remove the differences among cities that led to migration in the first place. The notion of compensating differentials in wages suggest an indifference curve between income and amenities for workers. The marginal worker will be just as indifferent to staying in one city as to migrating to another city. The adjustment to equilibrium could result from changes in wages. It could alternatively result from a reduction in amenities, such as an attractive vista having been spoiled by congestion and pollution.

Another reason that the pattern of production and trade might change is that technology could change either because of a general change affecting the entire economy or because the city acquires access to a technology that was previously unavailable. There is some evidence of persistence over time in a metropolitan area's specialization both because of fixed costs of entering an industry and dynamic externalities, such as a developed network of technological innovation and specific knowledge transfers. (Henderson et al. 1995) Some evidence suggests that the industrial adoption of university research findings, for example, is strongly linked to the proximity of the firm to the university. This link can operate in the following way. Companies adopt research findings from the local university. The companies then finance further research by the university, which they then adopt. (Does your university have a specialized research center? Is it in a field in which your city has an important economic stake?) Because the information being conveyed is often ambiguous, making trust important in such a relationship, we expect these relations to be strongest when the participants are in close spatial proximity. There is also the direct link: some innovations are used by their inventors to launch entrepreneurial ventures. If the entrepreneurs are researchers at a university, then they will be likely to start their ventures in the city where they live.

Patterns of Development—The Two-Factor Case

The model developed to this point has been one that includes only two factors of production, labor and capital. Economic development implies an increase in the productivity of labor, which means either a change in technology or an increase in the capital-labor ratio. Since we have maintained the assumption that all cities have access to the same technology, the only avenue for economic development is to increase the amount of capital available for each worker. If there are no factor intensity reversals, economic development entails increasing the capital-labor ratio, which in turn implies a change in the mix of production from more labor-intensive goods to more capital-intensive goods. Of course, if all cities follow this path, we would expect the equilibrium prices of goods to change over time, with labor-intensive goods (and services) becoming relatively more expensive and capital-intensive goods becoming less expensive.

William Baumol (1967) emphasizes the role of productivity change in explaining some of the problems facing city governments. Many government services are labor-intensive and have not seen much increase in productivity (think of a teacher in a classroom or a police officer walking a beat). Manufactured goods, however, have seen huge increases in productivity, with a concomitant increase in wages (simple competitive model: wage equals marginal revenue product). If labor is mobile between the manufactured goods sector and the service sector, then wages in the service sector must increase in order to attract and retain workers. But this means that the relative price of services in terms of manufactured products will continually increase.

Application: The Industrial Revolution

During the Industrial Revolution, the capital intensity of iron production in France increased. At the same time, the relative price of iron and wheat changed in exactly the way the Hecksher-Ohlin model predicts. (Strictly speaking, the model assumes a constant production technology at each point in time, so it is not rigorously applied here. The example is illuminating, nevertheless.) In 1790, the terms of trade were 1 kilogram of wheat for 0.6 kilograms of iron; in 1850 a kilogram of wheat bought 0.9 kilograms of iron; and in 1900 a kilogram of wheat bought 1.4 kilograms of iron. This change is illustrated by the points p_{1790}, p_{1850}, and p_{1900} in Figure 6.10. These changes in product market prices should, according to the model, be reflected in changes in factor market prices. Specifically, the wage relative to the cost of capital should increase. This in turn would be predicted to increase the capital-labor ratio in both wheat and iron production.

What does the evidence show? The capital intensity in iron production increased; and this fact, coupled with a decrease in transport costs, eliminated rural manufacturing as production concentrated in a few cities. Rural wages during this time increased as well. Finally, there was a reduction of small farm holdings and an increase in the capital intensity of agricultural production. The predictions of the model are borne out in this important example (data from Bairoch 1988, p. 337).

FIGURE 6.10 The Industrial Revolution in France

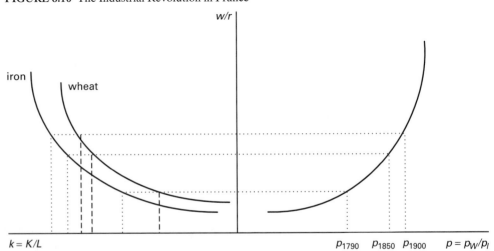

FURTHER ISSUES: TRANSPORT COSTS, IMPERFECT COMPETITION, AND PUBLIC GOODS

The theory developed in this chapter is a powerful tool for analyzing the economic development and interactions of metropolitan areas. There are (at least) three complicating factors that were introduced in chapters 3 and 4 that need to be integrated into the Hecksher-Ohlin model. These are (1) the role of transportation costs in determining trade and production location, (2) the implications of imperfect competition (especially monopolistic competition), and (3) the implications of economies of scale in public goods production for the predictions of the model.

Transport Costs and the Hecksher-Ohlin Model

The Hecksher-Ohlin model describes the role of trade in reducing the effects of differences among cities in their relative factor endowments. It assumes a zero transportation cost for produced goods and an infinite transportation cost for factors of production. In the terminology introduced in chapter 4, it is therefore a model that focuses on weight-losing (input-oriented) firms. The two models of urban growth seen to this point—central place theory and Hecksher-Ohlin—are therefore complementary. Which is the "right" model? The answer, as is so often the case in economics, is "it depends." In this case, it depends on the relative costs of transporting inputs and outputs. It also depends on the lumpiness of factors versus the lumpiness of markets. In the next chapter, we will explore this link, using the insight that markets for goods are large precisely where markets for labor are large because (by definition) a lot of people are located there.

There is another important implication of introducing positive (but not infinite) transactions costs for both goods and factors of production. The Hecksher-Ohlin model illustrates that trade in goods can substitute for factor mobility, and vice versa. If there are transport costs for goods, though, then trade in goods alone will not by itself equalize factor prices. Thus, we could see both goods and factor trade, depending on the relative transactions costs. Suppose product markets react to price differences faster than factor (labor) markets do. A difference in factor endowments could lead to trade in goods, as in the Hecksher-Ohlin model, but positive transport costs could prevent factor price equalization. This would then lead labor, eventually, to migrate to the place where it receives a higher reward. Then of course, this migration would reduce the need for trade in goods.

In some cases, transactions costs reflect not only transport costs but also legal constraints on the mobility of goods or factors. For example, there are restrictions on the ability of workers to get jobs in different jurisdictions, whether the jurisdictions be countries or states of the United States. Victor Norman and Anthony Venables (1995, p. 1502) suggest that "even a small reduction in the cost of [international] migration could induce immigration to a labour-scarce economy on a sufficiently large scale to turn the economy into an exporter of labour-intensive products. Conversely, liberalisation of goods trade . . . may be sufficient to remove the incentive for factor movements." We will return to this discussion in chapter 7 when we consider the likely impact of the North American Free Trade Agreement on product and factor markets in the United States.

Monopolistic Competition and the Hecksher-Ohlin Model

All the formal analysis in this chapter was done under the assumption that factor and product markets were perfectly competitive. This implies (among other things) that products are homogeneous, which is clearly an oversimplification. Further, we saw in chapter 3 that taking spatial location into account made monopolistic competition an appropriate model of market structure even for apparently homogeneous goods. We should therefore be concerned about whether the analysis in this chapter is robust enough for this more realistic level of analysis.

The good news is that the main conclusions from this chapter continue to obtain if we use a monopolistic competition model, but the bad news is that the level of analytical rigor required increases dramatically. Elhanan Helpman and Paul Krugman (1985) provide the most accessible introduction to this question, but their monograph is not easy to read (even for a Ph.D. in economics!). The main conclusions can be simply summarized, though.

First, some terminology. A *sector* of the economy is a set of firms with similar activities. Some of the sectors usually identified in analysis are manufacturing, services, retail trade, wholesale trade, agriculture, and mining. The idea is to group firms whose overall production methods—such as the capital-labor ratio—are likely to resemble each other. Thus, LTV Steel and Texaco both have high capital-labor ratios and produce manufactured goods, even though the type of goods (steel for LTV and petroleum products for Texaco) are quite different.

Differences in factor endowments among economies will serve as a good predictor of intersectoral trade because of the significant differences in relative factor proportions for the various sectors. For example, the agricultural and mining sectors are extremely natural-resource intensive, and thus it is unlikely that an economy without the appropriate natural resources will be a significant producer of those types of products. On the other hand, differences in factor endowments are not necessarily a good predictor of intrasectoral trade. Much intrasectoral trade involves trade in differentiated products. In the manufacturing sector, for example, the Cleveland metropolitan area exports steel that is used in the production of cars but imports petroleum products from other capital-intensive cities. In the service sector, the Cleveland metropolitan area exports medical services to patients from around the world who stay in its renowned hospitals, but it imports casino gambling from Atlantic City and Windsor, Ontario, neither of which is dramatically different from Cleveland except that they permit casinos to operate. The presence of economies of scale will cause autarky prices to be lower (in general) in larger markets, so that the pattern of trade is not necessarily predicted by the pattern of relative autarky prices. The combination of economies of scale and a desire for variety imply intrasectoral trade. This trade will likely be among "similar" cities because of the income needed to afford the goods and the likely similarity in factor endowments, given that both cities are specializing in the same type of product. On the other hand, intersectoral trade will be among "differing" cities, and the pattern of trade in this case will be that predicted by the Hecksher-Ohlin model—that is, it will offset the effects of differential factor endowments.

Public Goods and the Hecksher-Ohlin Model

Even if all private goods are produced under conditions of constant returns to scale, it is possible that public goods are produced under increasing returns to scale. For example, the average cost of providing public safety (police and fire) may be decreasing over some range of urban population. If people have different tastes for public goods and labor is mobile, then these differences provide another reason to expect specialization and trade among cities. This is perhaps most clear when we look at local governments within one metropolitan area, but it could also occur across city boundaries. Product trade, in this setting, occurs because some cities choose to produce greater amounts of nontradable public goods, which changes the marginal product of labor in the tradable goods. The most interesting result is that labor mobility and product trade are complements in this model rather than being necessarily substitutes for each other as in the basic Hecksher-Ohlin model. In the Hecksher-Ohlin model, product trade represents trade in embodied factors of production; it is not necessary for the factors themselves to move. With public goods providing a nontradable amenity, though, the mobility of the factors leads to a change in the local production conditions that provides an impetus for trade in goods (Wilson 1987). This analysis is clearly linked to the explanation of trade based on "lumpy" allocations of factors, in that the spatial variation in public goods provides an explanation for the lumpiness of the factors of production. Even if labor is evenly distributed throughout a metropolitan area, its marginal product (and the marginal product of capital) can vary because each of the constituent municipalities devotes a different amount of labor to producing its local public goods. This is an additional source of lumpiness beyond the mere uneven allocation of labor and other factors of production.

CHAPTER SUMMARY

- The *Hecksher-Ohlin theorem* states that trade exists due to differences in relative factor endowments and that trade offsets those differences. The *factor price equalization theorem* states that free trade (with no transport costs) will enable all factors of production to receive equal returns regardless of their location.

- Even if an economy does not have a comparative advantage in production of a product, uneven distribution of factors within the economy could lead to trade.

- If there are barriers to product market mobility, such as transport costs or trade restrictions, then factor prices will not be equalized as a result of product market trade. In that case, factor mobility might substitute for trade in products unless there are significant barriers to factor mobility. Changes in the extent of product market and factor market mobility will lead to changes in the pattern of production and trade as well as changes in relative prices.

- Economic development occurs as an economy changes both the available technology and the available factors of production. In a model of production incorporating capital and labor, economic development usually reflects an increase in the capital-labor ratio of the economy. Economic development will lead to a change in the pattern of production and trade. If all economies are developing, then relative prices of labor-intensive and capital-intensive products will change.

- The Hecksher-Ohlin model of trade can be extended to include several complications. In its simplest form, there is no factor mobility in the Hecksher-Ohlin model. However, allowing factor mobility in addition to trade in products does not alter the main conclusions of the model. The model can also be extended to the case of imperfect competition in the market for products. In that case, intrasectoral trade will occur among countries with similar factor endowments, and intersectoral trade will occur among countries with different factor endowments. Finally, the model can be extended to include local public goods as nontradable amenities. In that case, different preferences for public goods can lead to factor mobility as a complement to, rather than a substitute for, trade in products.

EXCERPT: EZEKIEL 27:3–24

The analysis in this chapter has taken the approach of examining an economy's factor endowments relative to other economies in order to predict the pattern of production and trade. This logic can be reversed, too. By examining the pattern of production and trade, inferences can be drawn about relative factor abundance in different places. It is also possible to make inferences about relative transportation and other transactions costs by considering the pattern of trade. The following passage from the Bible (King James Version), Ezekiel 27:3–24, describes the activities of Tyrus (modern Tyre, in Lebanon). Even if you are unfamiliar with the regions named, you should be able to make some well-informed inferences about the relative factor abundances in the regions and the ease of transport between them and Tyrus.

And say unto Tyrus, O thou are situated at the entry of the sea, which art a merchant of the people for many isles, Thus saith the Lord God; O Tyrus, thou hast said, I am of perfect beauty. Thy borders are in the midst of the seas, thy builders have perfected thy beauty. They have made all thy ship boards of fir trees of Senir: they have taken cedars of Lebanon to make masts for thee. Of the oaks of Bashan have they made thine oars; the company of the Ashurites have made thy benches of ivory, brought out of the isles of Chittim. Fine linen with broidered work from Egypt was that which thou spreadest forth to be thy sail; blue and purple from the isles of Elishah was that which covered thee. The inhabitants of Zidon and Arvad were thy mariners: thy wise men, O Tyrus, that were in thee, were thy pilots. The ancients of Gebal and the wise men thereof were in thee thy calkers: and all the ships of the sea with their mariners were in thee to occupy thy merchandise. They of Persia and of Lud and of Phut were in thine army, thy men of war: they hanged the shield and helmet in thee; they set forth thy comeliness. The men of Arvad with thine army were upon thy walls round about, and the Gammadims were in thy towers: they hanged their shields round about; they have made thy beauty perfect. Tarshish was thy merchant by reason of the multitude of all kind of riches; with silver, iron, tin, and lead, they traded in thy fairs. Javan, Tubal, and Meshech, they were thy merchants: they traded the persons of men and vessels of brass in thy market. They of the house of Tagarmah traded in thy fairs with horses and horsemen and mules. The men of Dedan were thy merchants; many isles were the merchandise of thine hand: they bought thee for a present horns of ivory and ebony. Syria was thy merchant by reason of the multitude of the wares of thy making: they occupied in thy fairs with emeralds, purple, and broidered work, and fine linen, and coral, and agate. Judah, and the land of Israel, they were thy merchants: they traded in thy market wheat of Minaith, and Pannag, and honey, and oil, and balm. Damascus was thy merchant in the multitude of the wares of thy making, for the multitude of all riches; in the wine of Helbon, and white wool. Dan also and Javan going to and fro occupied in thy fairs: bright iron, cassia, and calamus, were in thy market. Dedan was thy merchant in precious clothes for chariots. Arabia, and all the princes of Kedar, they occupied with thee in lambs, and rams, and goats: in these were they thy merchants. The merchants of Sheba and Raamah, they were thy merchants: they occupied in thy fairs with chief of all spices, and with all precious stones, and gold. Haran, and Canneh, and Eden, the merchants of Sheba, Asshur, and Chilmad, were thy merchants. These were thy merchants in all sorts of things, in blue clothes, and broidered work, and in chests of rich apparel, bound with cords, and made of cedar, among thy merchandise.

Questions for Review and Discussion

1. Examine the excerpt from Ezekiel that closes the chapter. Which regions that Tyrus trades with do you think are close to Tyrus? Which are far away? In which regions is labor relatively abundant? What is the comparative advantage of Tyrus?

2. "A subsidy to local production of goods has the same effect on a city's economy as an increase in the cost of transporting those goods from another city." Do you agree or disagree? Explain.

3. Are factors of production "lumpy" at the metropolitan area level? Give an example and discuss whether the pattern of trade within the metropolitan area and between the metropolitan area and other regions is affected as predicted by Courant and Deardorff.

4. "Differences in amenities among cities imply that it is impossible for factor price equalization to occur." Do you agree or disagree? Explain.

5. Although there are no tariffs permitted on products shipped within the United States, there are barriers to trade between the United States and other countries. What impact will these trade barriers have? Will it vary depending on which metropolitan area you consider?

6. Can you identify examples of cities that have developed over time and changed their specialization? Do all cities follow a similar pattern of development?

Appendix: Patterns of Development—The Three-Factor Case

The model of development sketched above is unsatisfying in that it implies that economic development can follow only one path. This clashes with even casual observation of production patterns of United States cities and, further, leaves little room for debate over policy. A richer set of possibilities appears when we extend the model to include a third factor of production in addition to labor and capital. We will call this third factor of production "land." This analysis follows that used by Leamer (1984, 1987), who used it to analyze trade among countries.

In order to look at different combinations of factor endowments, it is now necessary to use a three-dimensional diagram, as shown in Figure A-6.1. In the example, Cleveland has more labor and capital but less land than Miami. Table A-6.1 provides some information on actual factor endowments for cities in the United States. The

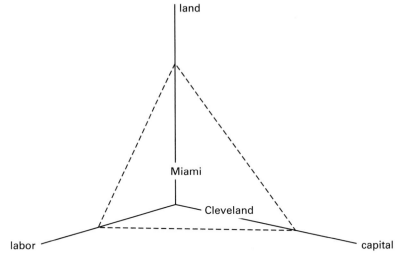

Note: Data for Figure A-6.1 taken from Table A-6.1. Miami has less capital and labor than Cleveland but more land than Cleveland.

FIGURE A-6.1 Factor Endowments

capital stock is in units of millions of dollars, the land area is in units of square miles, and the labor force is in units of thousands of people.

To make the diagram more useful, we will use the fact that all factor combinations on a straight line from the origin have the same factor ratios. Thus, we can intersect a plane with the positive orthant of Figure A-6.1 to look at the factor proportions of each city. The projection of the rays from the origin to the plane through the factor endowments of each city is shown as Figure A-6.2. Each point in the triangle represents a different combination of the three factors. A line from the land vertex connects points that have the same capital-labor ratio but different capital-land and

TABLE A-6.1 Factor Endowments for United States Metropolitan Areas, 1970

Metropolitan Area	Capital Stock (K)	Land Area (L)	Labor Force (N)	K/L	N/L	K/N
Atlanta	1,548	4,326	688.8	0.358	0.159	2.248
Baltimore	3,638	2,259	840.0	1.610	0.372	4.331
Buffalo	3,877	1,590	535.5	2.438	0.337	7.239
Chicago	15,249	3,719	2,954.2	4.100	0.794	5.162
Cleveland	5,285	1,519	858.8	3.480	0.565	6.155
Detroit	11,264	3,916	1,750.2	2.876	0.447	6.436
Houston	6,283	6,794	827.0	0.925	0.122	7.596
Miami	495	2,042	533.1	0.242	0.261	0.928
Pittsburgh	6,444	3,049	910.0	2.113	0.298	7.082
St. Louis	4,569	4,935	961.5	0.926	0.195	4.752

Source: L and N from U.S. Bureau of the Census; K from unpublished data provided by Gaspar Garofalo.

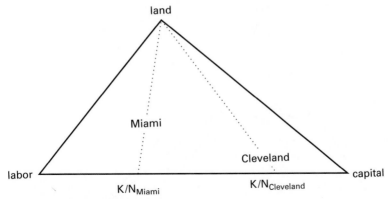

FIGURE A-6.2 The Endowment Triangle

labor-land ratios. The same applies to lines from the capital and labor vertices. The case of Cleveland and Miami is shown, and we see that Cleveland has a higher capital-labor ratio than Miami. (The data, again, are taken from Table A-6.1.) You should verify for yourself that the capital-land ratio and labor-land ratio are higher in Cleveland than in Miami.

The endowment triangle can be used to show different patterns of specialization and trade that depend on both relative factor abundance and relative prices. It is thus a three-dimensional analogue to the general equilibrium diagram we have already seen. In Figure 6.1, for example, as the relative prices of the goods changed, it would be possible for a city to specialize entirely in steel, entirely in orange juice, or in various combinations of the two goods. (Recall Figure 5.18 in chapter 5, showing all of the various combinations as a function of factor prices.) Suppose, for simplicity, that the city can engage in four different "activities," each of which corresponds to a different combination of factors. These activities are shown in Figure A-6.3 as *P*, *S*, *W*, and *OJ*. Two goods are manufactured: pharmaceuticals (*P*) and steel (*S*), which use labor and capital but not land as inputs. Two goods are agricultural: wheat (*W*), which uses labor and land but no capital, and orange juice (*OJ*), which uses land, labor, and capital. To check your understanding, verify (1) that the capital-labor ratio in *S* production exceeds the capital-labor ratio in *OJ* production and (2) that the land-labor ratio in *OJ* exceeds the land-labor ratio in *W*. The assumption that the factor proportions are fixed for each product is an important technical issue, but it does not alter the spirit of the analysis that we did in the two-factor Hecksher-Ohlin model.

A country's production pattern will depend upon its factor endowments and the relative prices of commodities and factors. One possible result is shown as Figure A-6.3. The endowment triangle is further subdivided into "triangles of diversification," in which one or more of the goods is produced. The areas are triangles (straight-line boundaries) because of the assumption that the factor proportions for each product were fixed. For example, in triangle 1, *W* and *OJ* are produced, while in triangle 2, *P*, *OJ*, and *S* are produced.

Just as in the earlier analysis, the price of a factor will depend on its relative scarcity. In Figure A-6.3, for example, capital will earn a higher return if the city's endowment is in region 1 than in region 2 because capital is relatively more abundant in

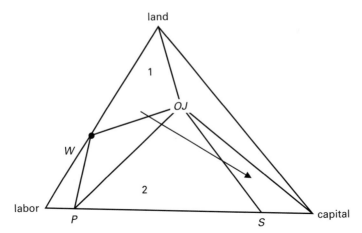

FIGURE A-6.3 Triangles of Diversification

region 2. The opposite is true for land. Of course, if factors are mobile, they will tend to move to the city where they receive the highest return (except in the case of land).

If the relative prices change, then the triangles will also change. For example, if pharmaceuticals become relatively more expensive, then more triangles including a greater fraction of potential endowments will include production of P as one of the activities engaged in. There are many different ways of dividing the endowment triangle into triangles of diversification, and in fact, there is a set of prices that supports any possible division. The important result is that an increase in the price of a product will increase the area of the endowment triangle in which it is produced. One alternative set of prices, with an increase in the price of S relative to Figure A-6.3, is shown as Figure A-6.4.

The richness of this setting, despite the restrictive assumption (constant factor proportions) on production technology, is immediately apparent. Consider a city whose initial endowment is in triangle 1, so that it produces W and OJ. If the city increases its capital, holding its land and labor constant, it will first (when it leaves triangle 1) begin producing P, then it will begin producing S and stop producing W, and

FIGURE A-6.4 Alternative Triangles of Diversification

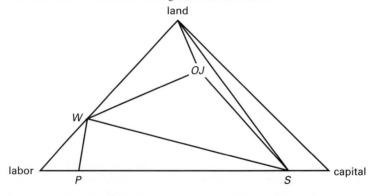

eventually it will be producing only *S*. This path is shown by the arrow in Figure A-6.3. A city that started in a different point in the endowment triangle might follow a slightly different path. Thus, there are different possible development patterns, and they depend not only on the capital-labor ratio for products but also on the land requirements and endowment of the city.

The approach above is very rich, but it is not the only way to model an economy's resources. For example, lumping all labor together masks the large skill differences among various components of the labor force and makes it impossible to address the implications of following a policy of worker education as opposed to capital attraction. Consider the following alternative. Let the three factors of production be land, professional labor, and non-professional labor and do the analysis on that basis. Leamer (1993) does this in order to find the differential effects of the North American Free Trade Agreement (NAFTA) on different types of workers in the United States. In order to do this analysis, Leamer focuses on long-run changes after production adjustments have taken place. Thus, his estimated effects are not instantaneous and should be interpreted as the predicted outcome of current trends in the absence of any change aside from NAFTA.

Leamer finds that the main cost of NAFTA in the United States will be an average $1,900 decrease in the wages of non-professional labor as production moves from the United States to more labor-intensive countries, including Mexico. The average wages of professional labor, however, are expected to increase by about $6,000 as a result of NAFTA. Finally, Leamer estimates that the return on $1,000 of capital will increase by $13. The advantage of this more disaggregated analysis is that it more clearly shows the differential impact of changes in production and trade on different types of workers. If we consider education to be a natural resource that can not only be renewed but expanded, then the analysis also suggests that rewards are available if more workers can be educated to a higher level than is currently the case.

CHAPTER

Agglomeration and Metropolitan Growth

W̶e have already introduced the idea of agglomeration economies of scale in previous chapters. In this chapter we consider formal models of both urbanization and localization economies of scale. Recall that *localization economies of scale* are economies of scale that result from being near related firms, while *urbanization economies of scale* are economies of scale that result from being located in a large city, regardless of the types of firms located there. The models presented in this chapter help to illuminate the manner in which agglomeration economies, introduced in chapter 1, operate. The models of specialized urban areas developed in chapters 5 and 6 were predicated on the existence of comparative advantage. This chapter "looks under the hood" to see where that comparative advantage comes from, and it adds agglomeration economies of scale to relative factor abundance as an explanation for the pattern of production and trade.

URBANIZATION ECONOMIES OF SCALE

The informal way of understanding urbanization economies of scale is "big is good." The intuition that city growth is based on urbanization economies of scale is well founded. Producers subject to economies of scale in production have an incentive to concentrate production in one (or a few) locations. To economize on transport costs, producers prefer to locate near large markets. (In addition to this transport cost advantage, large cities have the advantage of a wide variety of specialized services and amenities as well as the potential for cross-industry spillovers of knowledge and technology.) But markets are large precisely where other producers have located, so urban growth can be self-sustaining. This echoes both the principle of median location from chapter 4 and the discussion of market-oriented firms in chapters 3 and 4.

Chapter 4 introduced a model of urban growth that was based on transport cost minimization by a firm. That model did not include production costs explicitly, but we will now consider a simple extension that does so. This extension is known as the *core-*

periphery model because it features a concentration of economic activity in one place surrounded by a hinterland of less dense activity.

Suppose the possible locations for a city are along a unit line segment, and there are two types of production, agricultural and manufacturing. Further, suppose that a fraction α of the total population (divided equally between locations) is engaged in agricultural production, leaving $(1 - \alpha)$ to work in manufacturing. Let N represent the total population, x represent a given location, z represent the location of the city, and τ represent the unit transportation costs. Consumption of the manufactured good in each location is proportional to population in each location. The distribution costs to agricultural workers $t_A(x)$ and the distribution costs to manufacturing workers $t_M(x)$ are given by the following expressions, as in chapter 4.

$$t_A(x) = N\alpha\tau / 2 \, [x^2 + (1 - x)^2] \tag{1}$$
$$t_M(x) = N(1 - \alpha)\tau \, |x - z|$$

Now, though, we have to explicitly consider the production costs of the firm. Suppose they take the following simple form: fixed costs F to set up production at a location, with constant marginal production costs of c per unit of output. The firm has two problems: (1) whether to set up one plant or more than one plant (2) where to locate. If manufacturing firms cluster in equilibrium, then this model can explain urban growth.

Where will a firm locate? As in chapter 4, let us consider the case of a city that exists at point z and see whether a firm would wish to open a manufacturing plant in that city. Total production and transportation costs in the city are given by

$$TC(z) = F + Nc + N\alpha\tau / 2 \, [z^2 + (1-z)^2] \tag{2}$$

If the firm wishes to locate outside the city at some point x, its total costs are given by

$$TC(x) = F + Nc + N\alpha\tau / 2 \, [x^2 + (1 - x)^2] + N(1 - \alpha)\tau \, |x - z| \tag{3}$$

The firm's problem summarized in equations (2) and (3) is the problem of minimizing transportation costs already seen in chapter 4. Another possibility, however, is available to the firm. It could open two locations, one in the city and one somewhere else. Total distribution costs to the city would equal zero. The manufacturing firm would supply agricultural workers from the plant closest to them. Suppose that the second location x is to the right of z. In that case, all agricultural workers at a location less than $y = (x - z)/2$ would be supplied from the city z, and the remainder from the second plant x. Total costs would equal:

$$TC(\text{both locations}) = 2F + Nc + N\alpha\tau/2 \, [z^2 + (y - z)^2] + N\alpha\tau/2 \, [(x - y)^2 + (1 - x)^2] \tag{4}$$

A similar expression, of course, exists for x to the left of z.

Assume that if a firm only wants to open one plant, it will locate in the city. Under what circumstances would it wish to open more than one plant? The answer to that question is found by comparing equation (4) with equation (2). The condition is shown in equation (5) below.

$$F \leq N\alpha\tau/2 \, \{(1 - z)^2 - [(x - y)^2 + (1 - x)^2]\} \tag{5}$$

It is straightforward to show that the equation in brackets {} is always greater than zero. Whether or not a second location is optimal depends on three parameters. First, equation (5) will hold if the fixed costs of setting up a location, F, are small. This is trivially satisfied, for example, by setting $F = 0$, so that the firm will set up a separate plant at every location. Second, equation (5) will hold if there is a large fraction of the population in agriculture, α large. Third, equation (5) will hold if unit transport costs are high, τ large. Equation (5) also is consistent with a sudden increase in local production activity if any of the parameters should change. It is this possibility that we now turn to.

Krugman (1991a, ch. 1) uses this model to explain the emergence of a "manufacturing belt" in the United States in the 1800s. During that period, the economies of scale in production increased, the agricultural share of the labor force fell, and unit transport costs fell. These changes have already been discussed in chapter 2 as part of the Industrial Revolution. In the current context, it is sufficient to note that all these changes imply a greater concentration of production in the model. The model, though, does not explain why some city first comes into existence, since it is consistent with a range of locations z. Here we can use the analysis developed in chapters 5 and 6 to complete the story. Some locations have an initial advantage in production (in the model, lower F or lower c) due to the nonuniform distribution of factors of production. Cost-minimizing location decisions of firms faced with economies of scale in production make these early advantages sustainable and lead to the growth of cities. In other words, the "second nature" of urban development sustains and reinforces the "first nature" of locations.

One of the most important theoretical possibilities arising from this simple model is the idea that a small change in the parameters can lead to a large change in equilibrium location patterns. Return to the comparison in equation (5) and suppose that the right-hand side is $1 greater than the left-hand side. This implies that the only equilibrium location for the firm is in the city. A small decrease in the fixed costs of production can increase the range of optimal locations, leading to a sudden loss of concentration in the city and possibly even the development of a new city. This potential for sudden change is both disturbing and exciting. On the one hand, it implies that a city can never be secure in its relative status, regardless of its present success. On the other hand, it implies that a city that is close to success may need only a small change in its current conditions to reap a large reward. In chapter 8 we will return to the question of whether and how a city can alter its prospects.

Spurious Agglomeration and False Comparative Advantage

An old joke about economic analysis goes as follows: An economist and a friend are walking down the sidewalk when the friend spots a $20 bill on the ground. Excited, the friend tells the economist, who answers that there can be no $20 bill on the ground because if there was, someone would already have picked it up. This joke is relevant to the analysis of the location and specialization of cities, because an easy trap to fall into is the idea that all possible efficiencies have been taken advantage of. It is also easy to take the Panglossian approach that whatever is, is best.

In the context of cities, this type of analysis means that we assume that cities have formed in cost-minimizing locations and developed on the basis of agglomeration economies of scale. Gregory DeCoster and Will Strange (1993) present a cautionary counterexample. Suppose many firms must make location decisions based on their private information about the desirability of various sites. Some firms are better than others, but financial markets (banks) are unable to distinguish among them ex ante. Financial markets know, though, that good firms tend to think alike. Suppose one firm is the first to choose a location. The other firms have the choice of following that firm or moving to the locations that their own information suggests are best. If their private information agrees with the first firm's decision, there is no problem. If their private information disagrees, though, they must decide whether to risk going their own way. If they go their own way and fail, the banks will identify them as a bad firm and will stop providing financing. If they follow the first firm and fail, the banks won't know whether they failed because they were bad firms or because times were generally bad, and so the firm may continue to receive financing. DeCoster and Strange show that under these conditions it is possible for agglomeration to occur in the wrong places if firms cluster not for productivity advantages but in order to avoid being tagged as failures. Some desirable locations are thus left undeveloped, and some undesirable locations are overdeveloped. Clustering that results from informational reasons rather than in expectation of cost advantages is labeled *spurious agglomeration*. The model suggests, in effect, that some unclaimed $20 bills may well be lying about.

An example of the type of situation analyzed by DeCoster and Strange is suggested by Denis Brogan (in Handlin and Burchard, eds. 1963, p. 153). Brogan cites the location of Michelin—the famous tire company—in Clermont-Ferrand, France, "remote from ports, from coal, from river or canal transportation." The company located there because one of the founders married into a local family, and the area is now the center of the rubber industry in France. Brogan goes on to relate that when Dunlop, the British tire and rubber company, tried to break into the French market, it located nearby, although its location was similarly isolated from any natural advantage other than proximity to Michelin.

Another possible example of spurious agglomeration is found in major cities of developing countries. This is most likely to be true when the city is the capital of a highly centralized government that restricts trade with other countries, since strong forces push firms to locate there. These forces include a better-developed transport system, better education and other public services, and better access to powerful government officials (Henderson 1988, ch. 7; Krugman and Livas Elizondo 1996). This process, however, can proceed well past the point where agglomeration diseconomies of scale outweigh any agglomeration economies of scale. Cities such as Mexico City, Cairo, and Sao Paulo are natural urban centers, but the forces that created their current large size have mitigated against their reaching an efficient size.

This pattern of centralization that leads to abnormally large cities was noted by Mumford (1961, p. 362) as having occurred among the capital cities of baroque Europe. The development of the standing army as a tool of imperial policy also led to an increase in the attraction of the capital for market-oriented firms. As Mumford points out, "[a] standing army is a body of consumers making a mass demand." Thus, imperial policy led indirectly to phenomenal growth of capital cities relative to the other cities in Europe.

A less drastic but nevertheless important example of the care with which economic data should be interpreted is provided by Kelvin Lancaster (1980). Suppose we observe that the average costs of producing some product are lower in one metropolitan area than in another. A natural conclusion would be that the low-cost metropolitan area has a comparative advantage in the production of the good and that, if the two cities were to trade, the low-cost metropolitan area would export the good in question. In a constant-returns-to-scale world, this conclusion is reasonable; but in a world where some returns to scale (fixed costs) are increasing, this conclusion does not necessarily hold. The low-cost metropolitan area may be larger than the high-cost metropolitan area and, therefore, is able to take better advantage of economies of scale under autarky. If the two cities trade, though, then the high-cost metropolitan area before trade may in fact be the city with a comparative advantage in the production of the good since now it too can take advantage of economies of scale. Lancaster labels such a situation *false comparative advantage,* and it serves as a specific warning to economists of the difficulty in making predictions about the world on the basis of our simple models.

Increasing Returns to Scale and Trade: An Example

Although an abstract discussion of the possible implications of economies of scale is interesting, there is nothing better than a numerical example to illustrate what can happen. Suppose that there are two cities, Sodom and Gomorrah, and that there are two goods that can be produced, Recklessness and Abandon. Each good requires only one factor—labor—to produce, and each city has an identical production technology. The labor requirement per unit of Recklessness is $a_R = 1 + (4/R)$, where R is the amount of Recklessness produced. If L_R is the total amount of labor used to produce Recklessness, then we can write L_R as

$$L_R = a_R R = R + 4$$

Similarly, if the labor requirement per unit of Abandon is $a_A = 2 + (2/A)$, then the labor used to produce Abandon (L_A) equals

$$L_A = a_A A = 2A + 2$$

Suppose Sodom has 80 units of labor. In that case, we can find the production possibility frontier by substituting the expressions for L_A and L_R and noting that the total labor adds up to 80. If both R and A are greater than zero, we find that

$$L + 2A = 74; L > 0, R > 0.$$

If $R = 0$, though, $A = 39$. And if $A = 0$, then $R = 76$. The PPF for Sodom is sketched below in Figure 7.1. The "Xs" on the axes represent potential economies of scale.

What will the pattern of production and trade be? It depends on preferences, the relative size of Gomorrah, and transport costs. Begin with the simplest situation: Gomorrah also has 80 units of labor; preferences are such that each city devotes 40 units of labor to each commodity; and transport costs are zero. In that case, under autarky each city will produce and consume 36 R and 19 A. Total production and consumption in the two cities is thus 72 R and 38 A. However, if Sodom specializes in producing R and Gomorrah A (or vice versa), then 76 R and 39 A will be available, so that a Pareto-improving trade is possible. For example, Sodom could export 37 R to

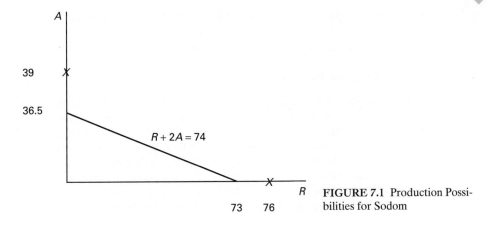

FIGURE 7.1 Production Possibilities for Sodom

Gomorrah in return for 19 A, leaving Sodom with 39 R and 19 A to consume. Gomorrah would have 37 R and 20 A to consume, so both cities are better off with the trade than under autarky. Economies of scale in production lead to a motivation for trade even in a case where cities have identical production technologies and factor endowments. This illustrates the importance of the assumption that there are no economies of scale for the Hecksher-Ohlin theory of trade developed in chapters 5 and 6.

Now consider the possibility of false comparative advantage. Suppose Gomorrah has 200 units of labor available while Sodom continues to have only 80. If each city devotes half of its labor to each commodity, then Sodom will have 36 R and 19 A while Gomorrah will have 96 R and 49 A. It might appear that Sodom has a comparative advantage in A—after all, 19/36 > 49/96, so if we "scaled up" Sodom's economy to be able to produce 96 R, it would produce over 50 A. (This is wrong, of course, but if you don't actually observe a production function, then how would you know?) Suppose Sodom decides to specialize in producing A, so that it produces 39 A that it is willing to trade at the rate of 37 R for 19 A, as above. Gomorrah can produce 30 A and 134 R, trading 37 R to Sodom in return for 19 A, and there is a Pareto improvement. Sodom has 37 R and 20 A, while in autarky it would consume only 36 R and 19 A. Gomorrah has 49 A and 97 R, while in autarky it would have only 49 A and 96 R. Note, though, that neither country truly has a comparative advantage. To see this, suppose Sodom had decided instead to specialize in producing R. Now Gomorrah can produce 58 R and 68 A, only this time trading at the rate of 39 R for 19 A. Again Sodom consumes 37 R and 20 A, while Gomorrah consumes 97 R and 49 A. As long as Sodom specializes, allowing it to take advantage of the economies of scale in production, the outcome is the same.

LOCALIZATION ECONOMIES OF SCALE

Alfred Marshall succinctly stated the reasons for localization economies of scale in his *Principles of Economics,* the first edition of which was published over 100 years ago. The three reasons can be simply described as: labor market pooling, variety and cost of intermediate inputs, and technological and information spillovers. The first two are (in principle) observable, while the last is inherently difficult to observe. We will consider each reason in turn, using Marshall's description as an introduction to each section.

Labor Market Pooling

> A localized industry gains a great advantage from the fact that it offers a constant market for skill. Employers are apt to resort to any place where they are likely to find a good choice of workers with the special skill which they require; while men seeking employment naturally go to places where there are many employers who need such skill as theirs and where therefore it is likely to find a good market. The owner of an isolated factory, even if he has access to a plentiful supply of general labour, is often put to great shifts for want of some special skilled labour; and a skilled workman, when thrown out of employment in it, has no easy refuge.
>
> ALFRED MARSHALL

Consider the following model. There are a fixed number of firms, a fixed number of identical workers, two locations, and two types of economic conditions ("good" or "bad"). There is some uncertainty as to whether a firm will face good or bad times in each period. Each firm desires more workers when times are good for the firm. It is possible that the fortunes of firms are positively or negatively correlated, but the model does not require any restriction on this matter. The more firms at a location, ceteris paribus, the greater the competition to retain workers, hence the higher the wage. The more workers at a location, ceteris paribus, the lower the wage. The question is: What is an equilibrium allocation of firms and workers across locations if mobility is unrestricted?

Figure 7.2 shows indifference curves for workers and isoprofit curves for firms. The figure should look familiar because it is just a variation on the Edgeworth Box diagram introduced in chapter 5. In this case, however, rather than showing various allocations of goods or factors between products, the diagram shows various distributions of firms and workers between two locations, labeled *E* and *W*, representing "east" and "west" respectively (and uninspiredly). The axes are labeled with the percentage of firms and workers at *E*; the percentage at *W* is simply 100 minus the percentage at *E*.

FIGURE 7.2 Location Decisions of Firms and Workers

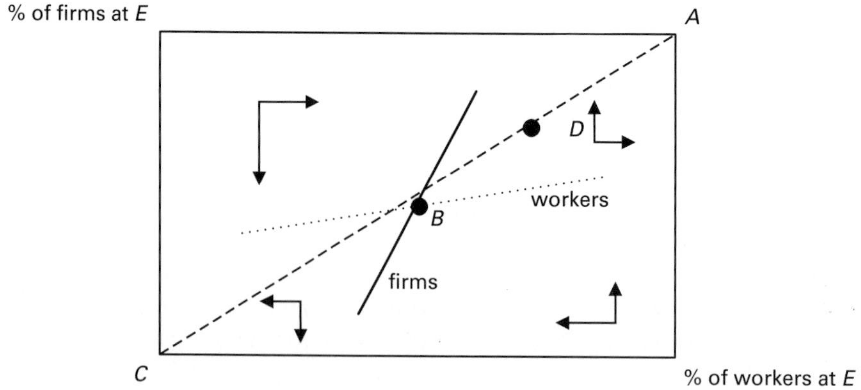

To see that the curves for firms and workers are as pictured in Figure 7.2, consider the following thought experiments. Begin at point *B*, where firms and workers are equally distributed between locations. Suppose the share of workers located at *E* increased from 50 percent to 55 percent while the share of firms stayed constant. The increase in workers represents a shift out in the labor supply curve at *E*, resulting in a lower equilibrium wage. Thus, workers at *E* are less happy with this situation than the situation at point *B*. What would it take for workers to be indifferent between *B* and the new point? Clearly, the share of firms in the east must increase beyond 50 percent, but how far? If the number of firms increases to 55 percent, then workers will actually be better off because a greater concentration of firms results in a more competitive labor market. Thus, in order to be indifferent, workers require an increase in the share of firms, but at a rate that is less than proportional to the increase in the share of workers.

The case of firms is a straightforward analogue to the case of workers. Starting from point *B*, an increase in the share of workers increases the profits of firms because of the firms' ability to pay a lower wage. Therefore, an increase in the share of workers in the east must be balanced by an increase in the share of firms in order for the firms to remain indifferent among locations—that is, for the profits to be the same in both places. The isoprofit curve of the firm must be steeper than the indifference curve of the workers. Consider point *D* in Figure 7.2. It has the same ratio of workers to firms as does point *B*, but it has the advantage of a larger pool of labor and firms than does point *B*. It is therefore preferred to point *B* by *both* workers and firms.

If the distribution of workers and firms is given by point *D*, then *E* is a preferable location, and both workers and firms will migrate there. This is reflected in the direction arrows in the upper right-hand part of Figure 7.2. If the distribution of workers and firms is at other points, it is possible to have workers migrating to or from *E*. Firms might also migrate. Each of these possibilities is shown using the arrows in Figure 7.2. An equilibrium is a point at which neither workers nor firms wish to change their location.

There are three equilibria: all employment located at *E* (point *A* in Figure 7.2), all employment located at *W* (point *C* in Figure 7.2), and employment equally divided (point *B*). The last equilibrium is unstable ("knife-edge"), while the other two are stable. To see the instability of an equal division, imagine that a large group of workers suddenly migrates east in a reverse "Horace Greeley effect." This would have the immediate result that firms in the east are better off than firms in the west, leading to migration of firms from west to east. This in turn would result in eastern workers being better off than their western counterparts, which would lead to further migration of workers; the ultimate effect would be that all the firms and workers would be in the east.

Keep two important points in mind about this result. First, pooling is not the same thing as "diversification," although diversification can add to the benefit of pooling. An advantage of having several firms whose performance is negatively correlated (diversified) located in one place can be that the firms don't experience downturns at the same time; thus the entire local economy may be more stable than the performance of each firm. This advantage has been known at least since Biblical times. For example, Ecclesiastes 4:9–10 (King James Version) says "Two are better than one; because they have good reward for their labor. For if they fall, the one will lift up his fellow: but woe to him that is alone when he falleth; for he hath not another to help him up." Nothing in the analysis presented above has relied upon the firms' experiencing good times and bad times at the same time or at different times. Even if the firms are identical, they have an incentive to locate together. Second, uncertainty alone is insufficient to justify labor market pooling. The existence of increasing returns to scale is crucial, since otherwise firms could reduce transportation costs by dividing in two and setting up plants in both locations.

The model above was informal in discussing the labor market. The same basic results can be readily obtained in the case where wages are determined in a standard model of the labor market, as will now be demonstrated. Figure 7.3 illustrates the demand for workers by a firm (equal to the marginal revenue product, MRP) in good times (MRP_G) and in bad times (MRP_B). If there are L workers in the town, and the firm is the only employer, then it will pay a total wage bill of $w_B L$ in bad times and a total wage bill of $w_G L$ in good times. If we assume that good times happen 50 percent of the time and bad times happen 50 percent of the time, then on average the firm will pay a total wage bill of $w'L$, where w' is the average of w_B and w_G. If the firm is not the only business in town, it must pay the prevailing wage, say w'. (To be indifferent across locations, risk-neutral workers need to get the same average wage in both situations.) Now, though, the firm is able to increase its employment in good times and reduce employment during bad times. If the firm hires L_B during bad times and L_G during good times, it pays on average $w'L$, where L is the average of L_B and L_G.

The average amount that the firm pays is identical regardless of location. Does this mean that the firm is indifferent between the two situations? No! Firms maximize profits, which are equal to revenues minus costs. Before deciding what the firm prefers, we have to look at the benefits of its being able to hire more workers in good times as compared to the loss from its hiring fewer workers in bad times.

Consider the following example: $w_B = 60$, $w_G = 80$, $w' = 70$, $L_B = 6$, $L_G = 8$, $L = 7$, $p_B = 300$, $p_G = 500$. Suppose the marginal product is decreasing with the level of employment, $MP = 0.32 - 0.02L$, and also suppose there is a 50-percent chance of good times or bad times. If the output is sold in a perfectly competitive market, then the marginal revenue product of labor is equal to the marginal product multiplied by the price. The marginal revenue product in good times exceeds the marginal revenue product in bad times because of the lower price in bad times, even though the physical

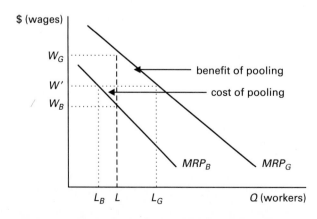

FIGURE 7.3 Labor Market Pooling

productivity of labor doesn't change. Assume that the labor market is perfectly competitive, so that the wage equals the marginal revenue product. If the firm is located by itself, it is able to hire seven workers at a wage that depends on the economic conditions: $60 in bad times and $80 in good times. On average, it will pay wages of $70. If the firm is located in a pooled labor market, it must pay the prevailing wage ($70) regardless of economic conditions, but it will be able to adjust its hiring. In the situation where the firm is by itself, it produces 1.75 units each period, earning revenues of $525 during bad times and $875 during good times. It pays labor costs of $420 during bad times and $560 during good times. Thus, its profits are $105 during bad times and $315 during good times, for an average of $210.

A firm in a pooled labor market produces 1.56 units of output during bad times and 1.92 units of output during good times. It earns revenues of $468 during bad times and $960 during good times. Its labor costs are $420 during bad times and $560 during good times. Thus, it makes a profit of $48 during bad times and $400 during good times, for an average of $224. Firms facing these conditions will prefer to cluster. The example above is summarized in Table 7.1.

What is the secret behind this result? The firm is, after all, hiring on average the same number of workers and paying the same wage regardless of location. The gain from being near other firms, though, is the possibility of increasing production when times are good and reducing production when times are bad. Further, the increase in production comes with no increase in production costs relative to being alone, while

TABLE 7.1 Labor Market Pooling: A Numerical Example*

	Alone	Pooled
Bad times	Labor = 7 Output = 1.75 Wage = $60 Labor Costs = $420 Revenue = $525 Profits = $105	Labor = 6 Output = 1.56 Wage = $70 Labor Costs = $420 Revenue = $468 Profits = $48
Good times	Labor = 7 Output = 1.75 Wage = $80 Labor Costs = $560 Revenue = $875 Profits = $315	Labor = 8 Output = 1.92 Wage = $70 Labor Costs = $560 Revenue = $960 Profits = $400
Average	Labor = 7 Output = 1.75 Wage = $70 Labor Costs = $490 Revenue = $700 Profits = $210	Labor = 7 Output = 1.74 Wage = $70 Labor Costs = $490 Revenue = $714 Profits = $224

*Assumptions are detailed in text.

the lower wage available when alone also does not reduce total production costs. Of course, the world doesn't always work out quite so neatly, but the basic principle remains.

The assumption that a firm will pay the marginal revenue product for labor even if it is the only firm in a city seems to ignore the possible effect of monopsony—in other words, being able to pay lower wages because the firm is the only buyer of labor services. This situation, known in popular culture as the *company town*, seems like a wonderful opportunity for the firm to increase profits by exploiting its monopsony power over the workers. *The Economist* (23 December 1995) looks in detail at the advantages and disadvantages of a company town in the past. The advantages included a paternalistic provision of social services in the days before the expansion of the welfare state. However, the disadvantages included a loss of individual autonomy and consumer sovereignty, since workers had no choice but to follow the directions of the company, including possibly shopping only at the company store. This notion of the exploitative town is familiar in popular culture, as seen in such sources as the song "Sixteen Tons," about an anonymous coal town, and the movie *Roger and Me,* about General Motors in Flint, Michigan. On a more personal note, Manassas, Virginia, where I grew up, had a large IBM facility that dominated employment in the town in the 1970s and 1980s. Cynics alleged that IBM stood for "I Be Manassas." (Full disclosure: I worked there for five summers.) One of the features of the IBM facility was a low-priced, high-quality cafeteria on site. This was good for employees looking for lunch, but it also had some built-in advantages for the company. If people eat their lunch on site, in company with their fellow workers, the length of the lunch hour is likely to be less than if they disperse, leave the building, and fend for themselves. Also, as a direct benefit for productivity, the cafeteria did not serve any alcoholic beverages.

The notion of profit maximization through worker exploitation is one with a lot of appeal. Economic theory, though, suggests a problem with such a scenario. In order to exploit workers, a company must attract them to a town and retain them there. In order to convince workers that they won't be exploited, it is useful to have enough competition to make this exploitation impossible. How, then, to explain company towns?

There are three possible explanations for company towns. First, the presence of unique natural resources explains the existence of mining towns and resorts. Unique resources can include "artificial natural resources," such as legalized gambling when other areas don't allow it, as was the case for many years in Las Vegas and Atlantic City. The second possibility is the existence of large economies of scale, where "large" means that one firm (or a few firms) can provide enough employment for an entire city. Possible examples include Kodak and Xerox in Rochester, Boeing in Seattle, and a whole host of university and state government towns. The third possible explanation is the existence of potential competition in the form of alternative company towns to which labor can relocate. Evidence for this last possibility is considered in the next paragraph.

William Boal (1995) examined coal mining towns in West Virginia between 1897 and 1932—the scene of "Sixteen Tons"—to see whether or not employers had been able to exploit their monopsony power. He finds little evidence in favor of such a hypothesis and, in fact, finds that the provision of company housing by coal-mining firms was associated with extremely high rates of labor turnover. Most of the turnover involved movement among employers as miners relocated along the rail lines in response to higher wages and other benefits offered by new employers. Company-provided housing reduced relocation costs because there was no need for a miner to search for a place to live. It also provided a dimension of competition apart from wages, further distinguishing employers from one another. Thus, even though an employer was a monopsonist in a given town, the competition provided by other employers in other towns put a limit on how much market power that employer could exert.

Intermediate Inputs

> The economic use of expensive machinery can sometimes be attained in a very high degree in a district in which there is a large aggregate production of the same kind, even though no individual capital employed in the trade be very large. For subsidiary industries devoting themselves each to one small branch of the process of production, and working it for a great many of their neighbours, are able to keep in constant use machinery of the most highly specialized character, and to make it pay its expenses, though its original cost may have been high, and its rate of depreciation very rapid.
>
> ALFRED MARSHALL

The second generic source of agglomeration economies is the access to specialized goods and services enjoyed by clustered industries. Like labor pooling, the intermediate inputs story requires increasing returns to scale in production, but this time in the production of the intermediate inputs. If there are not increasing returns to scale in production, then each region can duplicate the intermediate inputs at the same cost, so that there is no incentive to cluster production.

It is sometimes thought that the important characteristic of the intermediate inputs explanation is that the inputs themselves are nontradable. This is not true. If intermediate inputs are tradable, there is a "core-periphery" argument in the production of intermediate inputs that will lead their production to be spatially clustered, just as in the case of final consumer goods. Input-oriented firms will then locate near the core locations of intermediate input production, creating in turn a larger market for market-oriented firms. The possibility of clustering of intermediate goods production creates a "backward" linkage to final goods production that reinforces the "forward" linkage between goods production and the size of the market.

A homely example of spatial clustering can help make the point clear. My brother-in-law works in ceramics, using the so-called "raku" method of glazing. This involves firing the pottery and then covering it with sawdust. The ashes generated when the extremely hot pottery meets the sawdust cause the glaze to change color and develop patterns as the chemicals from the ashes react with the glaze to generate interesting effects. The school where he received his MFA, Rochester Institute of Technology, has a large woodworking operation in addition to its ceramics group. Woodworking, of course, generates large amounts of sawdust. Not only that, but it produces sawdust from many different types of wood. While the ceramicists presumably could import sawdust from elsewhere or even chop up trees themselves, having the kiln near the wood shop gives them real cost advantages as well as access to diversity.

One of the first systematic explorations of the idea of linkages among products is in a book by Helpman and Krugman (1985) in which they consider whether or not *industrial complexes* will form. They use the idea (introduced in chapter 5) of the integrated equilibrium to illustrate the importance of these linkages. If there are economies of scale in production, then the allocation of factors must be such that related industries are located in the same region or country. If related industries are not in the same region, then agglomeration economies of scale will be lost. This makes it impossible for trade alone to compensate for the uneven distribution of resources. This idea can be applied to creating a critical mass of production in any industry.

The observation that the core-periphery model also applies to the case of intermediate goods production has some immediate implications for likely changes over time. Suppose the unit costs of transport for intermediate inputs should fall. In that case, we would expect to see a greater clustering of production of intermediate inputs, with a concomitant increase in the specialization of locations as firms chose to be near their particular inputs. Thus, a decrease in transportation costs not only leads to an increase in the likelihood of a core-periphery pattern in general but also implies that each of the "cores" should be more specialized. This is exactly the pattern of development that we have observed in the United States over the last 150 years. For example, brewers relied on natural ice for cooling until the late 1870s. This input was both fairly ubiquitous (at least in the midwestern United States) and difficult to transport. When mechanical refrigeration was introduced along with the refrigerated rail-car, brewers could concentrate in large cities. There the brewers were able to take advantage of their proximity to coopers (barrel makers), bottlers, and other suppliers in order to expand even further. As a result of these changes, the number of brewers fell from 1,943 in 1880 to 640 by 1910 despite increases in total and per capita consumption (Pred 1966, pp. 65–68).

Technological Spillovers

> When an industry has thus chosen a locality for itself, it is likely to stay there long: so great are the advantages which people following the same trade get from near neighbourhood to one another. The mysteries of the trade become no mysteries; but are as it were in the air, and children learn many of them unconsciously. Good work is rightly appreciated, inventions and improvements in machinery, in processes and the general organization of the business have their merits promptly discussed: if one man starts a new idea, it is taken up by others and combined with suggestions of their own; and thus it becomes the source of further new ideas.
>
> ALFRED MARSHALL

The idea that there are special benefits in inventiveness from locating close together is a major part of the economic development mythology surrounding such well-known regions as Silicon Valley in California, the Route 128 area in Massachusetts, and the Research Triangle in North Carolina. It is alleged that high-technology firms are especially sensitive to the ease with which new technologies can be developed and adopted. This belief also colors the public-policy discussion of the value of academic research, with universities claiming an economic development role due to their promulgation of research findings. For example, Silicon Valley is near Stanford, Route 128 is near Harvard-MIT, and the Research Triangle gets its name from its central location among three universities with large research presences: Duke, North Carolina-Chapel Hill, and North Carolina State. Adam Jaffe (1986, 1989) has done the most to carefully identify the extent to which geographical clustering in specific fields leads to faster innovation or adoption of innovations. Using patents and patent citations, he finds some evidence that innovations tend to diffuse faster near their sources.

Richard Florida and Donald F. Smith, Jr. (1993) provide a financial explanation of the geographical concentration of technological diffusion. In order to produce and sell their products, firms require access to capital markets. Firms relying on new technologies are inherently risky, and specialized sources of venture capital have developed to supply them and reduce the problems of ambiguous information and uncertainty. Because the venture capital industry has spatially concentrated in a few areas, firms that would like access to venture capital have an incentive to concentrate near the sources of financing. They demonstrate that the venture capital market initially was concentrated in traditional finance centers such as New York and Chicago. Over time, the venture capital market migrated toward and concentrated in centers of innovation such as Silicon Valley in California and Boston. This change was the result of self-reinforcing cycles of innovation and successful commercial application.

The cycle of innovation and investment described above is not an invention of the late 1900s. It is also documented for U.S. cities during the post–Civil War period of the 1800s by Allan Pred (1966, p. 103), who found that "the cost-savings or profits resulting from one 'lumpy' innovation can provide the capital for another profit-enlarging 'lumpy' innovation at the same locus."

There are two reasons to be wary of the simple version of the technology-transfer theory, in which high-tech firms need to cluster together for reasons foreign to low-tech firms. The first reason is that localization is quite evident in low-tech sectors, not only in the high-technology sectors that are the focus of much public-policy discussion. The example of the garment district in Manhattan or the fashion industry in Milan shows that proximity can be an advantage even in the case of an industry whose main work is by hand. A common thread, so to speak, links the fashion industry and the computer software industry. This is the extent to which ambiguous information is transmitted among the people as well as the related issue of the extent to which coordination among the producers is desirable. Edwin Mills (in Mills and Mc-Donald, eds., 1992, p. 10) argues that geographical proximity is a virtue in any situation where the information to be transmitted is especially ambiguous. This is due to two factors. First, the extent of the ambiguity can be reduced by continuing interaction among the people transmitting it. Second, the information itself has the nature of a public good. In order to overcome the unwillingness of people to share information in that case, they must believe that they will get information (either in exchange or in the future) of sufficient value to make revealing their information worthwhile.

The second reason for skepticism is that the transmission of information, especially ambiguous information, is very difficult to measure. This is not only true in an absolute sense but also relative to the benefits of labor pooling or the benefits of proximity to specialized intermediate inputs. To the extent that economists rely on explanations that are empirically verifiable, the argument on the basis of technological spillovers remains at best weakly demonstrated. What effect will the communications revolution have on this source of localization economies? The short answer is that an improvement in the ability of people to communicate can be thought of as a decrease in the cost of trading information. This should lead to a greater concentration and specialization of information-generating activities. As with intermediate inputs, these changes could in turn be linked to greater regional specialization in production as well as a greater geographical diffusion of information.

The effect of technological change on urban growth presents another complication. Existing cities are, a fortiori, built on the basis of existing industries and existing technologies. Much of the cost advantage in information transmission in existing cities might be rendered obsolete by a technological change. This would imply that smaller cities would have an advantage in serving as hubs of growth of new technologies because their lower costs for factors are not offset by advantages due to existing informational networks in larger cities. This issue is theoretically developed in a paper by Elise Brezis and Paul Krugman (1993). One application of this idea that we have already seen is to the relative growth of small and large cities in England during the Industrial Revolution, which was discussed at length in chapter 2.

COUNTRIES AS COLLECTIONS OF CITIES

If external economies apply at the level of metropolitan areas, then how should one economically define a country? A strong candidate, introduced in chapter 6, is to define a country as a limitation on product and factor mobility (a discontinuity in transactions costs). How does this match with the idea that a country is a metropolitan area, or a collection of metropolitan areas? In fact, the two ideas are closely related, if not synonymous. Most obvious is the discontinuity in the land and labor market related to the idea that people live fairly close to where they work. If you change jobs within a metropolitan area, you might not need to change houses. If you move to a job in a different metropolitan area, you almost certainly need to change houses. On a larger geographical scale, in many ways it is easier to move from a job in Cleveland to a job in Atlanta than from a job in Cleveland to a job in Toronto, although Toronto is closer. The national boundary between the United States and Canada acts as a discontinuity in the factor market because of the necessity of obtaining special documents in order to work.

Recall that if factors of production are not too unevenly distributed, then regional and national boundaries can be ignored (offset) by trade. Moreover, trade in goods is a way of achieving localization economies even if factors are not completely mobile. While labor or capital (or especially land) might not move easily across national boundaries, the services of these factors can be embodied in products that can be more easily traded across national boundaries.

The discussion above suggests that national boundaries are an artificial construction with limited economic implications. Despite the basic theoretical accuracy of such an interpretation, there is evidence that national boundaries are still important, even in the case of neighboring countries with a long history of similar language and culture. John McCallum (1995) studied the trade flows within Canada and between Canada and the United States using provincial level data from Canada. Using a simple gravity model of trade within provinces, among provinces, and between provinces and states in the United States, (recall from chapter 3 that a gravity model predicts that trade will vary inversely with distance and proportionately with the size of the economy), he predicted that the largest province, Ontario, would ship 40 percent of its output to the United States. In fact, Ontario shipped only 19 percent of its output to the United States. For the entire country, he found an actual shipment percentage of 24 percent to the United States, significantly less than the 43 percent predicted by the gravity model. McCallum's data are for 1988, the year that the Canada–U.S. Free Trade Agreement was signed, so they do not reflect any increase in cross-border trade resulting from that treaty or from the succeeding North American Free Trade Agreement. Nevertheless, the results of this study illustrate the continuing importance of national boundaries.

This book begins by comparing metropolitan areas in the United States to countries in Europe. If we take that comparison to be valid, we would expect that the increasing economic integration in Europe would lead the economic relations among countries to resemble more closely the relations among metropolitan areas in the United States. Krugman (1991a, ch. 3) provides evidence that European countries are much less specialized than are comparable regions in the United States. Table 7.2 illustrates the case of the auto industry. We see that auto production in the United States, a region comparable to Europe in size, is far more specialized. The Midwest, where auto production in the United States is concentrated, produces almost two-thirds of the cars, while Germany, Europe's largest producer, produces less than two-fifths of Europe's cars. Over 90 percent of U.S. production is in just two regions, while less than 70 percent of Europe's production is in the two countries with the largest production.

Krugman's explanation for this difference between the continents is that, historically, tariff barriers between countries in Europe offset the decreases in transport costs and increases in efficient scale that led to the development of the U.S. manufacturing belt. As those tariff barriers are eliminated as a result of the European Union's economic integration policies, we should expect to see greater specialization of countries and increased trade among the countries.

More recent examples of clustering in Europe are provided in an article in *The Economist* (4 May 1996). In the case of textile manufacturing equipment, for example, the overall production patterns have remained roughly the same, but specialization has increased. "German firms have concentrated on making spinning and heavy duty machines. Italian firms have devoted themselves to fast machines and machinery for small firms. The Swiss make machines for weaving" (p. 63). In the case of services, animators are clustering in the Soho district of London, illustrating the way that people involved in transmitting ambiguous information gain from proximity. The concentration of mail-order retailing activity around Lille, France, is the result of access to excellent rail and road connections to French-speaking Europe. In addition to these

TABLE 7.2   Regional Distribution of Auto Production

U.S. Region	% of Production	European Country	% of Production
Midwest	66.3	Germany	38.5
South	25.4	France	31.1
West	5.1	Italy	17.6
Northeast	3.2	United Kingdom	12.9

Source: Krugman (1991), Table 3.3, p. 78.

anecdotes, there is also strong indirect evidence of greater specialization within Europe. Trade among countries within the European Union (EU) has been increasing faster than trade between the EU and the rest of the world. This suggests that countries have specialized and are now trading to obtain commodities they used to produce for themselves.

Political unification alone is not sufficient to cause a U.S.-style system of specialized cities to develop. Henderson (1988, ch. 11) provides evidence on the urban structure in the People's Republic of China in the 1980s, and finds that it is not analogous to that in the United States. Central planning, poor transportation, restricted labor mobility, and nonmarket prices reduce the opportunity for specialization in smaller cities and increase the relative importance of large cities.

Will Europe grow to resemble the United States? Maybe. First, recall that the core-periphery model allows for multiple equilibria, so the original pattern of production in Europe could persist. Second, there is evidence that manufacturing in the United States is becoming less localized than in the past, although services might be becoming more concentrated as a result of decreasing distribution costs. Third, there remains the question of how quickly such a transition would occur. The United States, after all, has been a common market for more than 200 years.

Sukkoo Kim (1995) examines "specialization" and "localization" of U.S. manufacturing between 1860 and 1987. Specialization is measured as the difference in the employment shares among regions, while localization is measured using an index constructed from the location quotient for various industries. The level of analysis is census regions, of which there are nine in the United States, each encompassing several states. Kim finds that specialization increased between 1860 and 1930 and has decreased since then. The trends in localization mirror the trends in specialization. Kim analyzes the data to see whether internal scale economies and resource intensity or external scale economies (including agglomeration) are a better explanation of the historical pattern of specialization and localization. He finds that the trends in regional specialization are consistent with internal scale economies and Hecksher-Ohlin explanations but inconsistent with an external scale economy explanation. In fact, he interprets his results as being most supportive of the basic Hecksher-Ohlin explanation of regional production and trade. Of course, all of this analysis is done using census regions as the basic geographical areas, though metropolitan areas are arguably more appropriate. Kim's results are cautionary, though, in reminding us not to be swayed by the elegance of the theory rather than the preponderance of the evidence.

"Giant Sucking Sounds" — The Effects of NAFTA

Maybe the most famous contribution of 1992 independent presidential candidate H. Ross Perot was the phrase that heads this section. He was referring to the flight of manufacturing firms from the United States to Mexico that he predicted would follow the passage of the North American Free Trade Agreement (NAFTA). We can use both the core-periphery model and the general equilibrium trade model to consider the likely effects of opening up trade between the United States and Mexico.

Consider a simple model in which there are six possible places, numbered 1 through 6, for manufacturing firms to locate. Suppose that regions 4 and 5 are in one country and regions 1, 2, 3, and 6 are in another country. Further, suppose that topography dictates that each place can only trade with two other places, as shown in Figure 7.4. Finally, suppose that no trade is allowed between countries and that manufacturing agglomerations develop in regions 1 and 4. What will be the effect of removing the barriers to trade among the countries?

After the removal of trade barriers, two results are possbile. First, region 4 will now develop to serve its "natural" hinterland region 3, reducing the size of the manufacturing agglomeration in region 1. Second, region 1 will benefit from its "head start" in development to attract manufacturing firms from region 4. Krugman and Hanson (1993) explore this question in regard to manufacturing location after NAFTA. They find that the benefit of free access to the U.S. market "turns Mexico inside out," from a country whose strong economic center is Mexico City to one whose economic center is the United States. Krugman and Hanson argue that NAFTA is likely to have greater impact on the internal location of production in Mexico than on the overall level and composition of trade. In particular, they expect to see the cities along the border with the U.S. grow faster than Mexico City. The recent economic dominance of Mexico City, they find, is due to the import-substitution policies followed by the Mexican government since the 1950s. The congestion and high cost associated with location in Mexico City have not been sufficient barriers to firm location in an economy where the bulk of the market was in Mexico City, but will be strong deterrents when the economic center of gravity shifts northward. The process of decentralization should continue as the core-periphery model predicts: As firms leave Mexico City for the border, the size of the market in Mexico City will fall and the size of the border markets will increase, leading other firms to relocate to the border.

We can also use the Hecksher-Ohlin model developed in chapter 6 to analyze the results of reducing trade barriers with Mexico. Consider the situation diagrammed in Figure 7.5. The United States has a higher capital-labor ratio than Mexico before NAFTA, and the relative prices of manufactured and agricultural goods differ due to protective tariffs, with the relative price of agricultural goods being lower in Mexico.

What are the effects of opening trade with Mexico? The relative price of agricultural products falls in the United States, as does the return to labor. Although the diagram is drawn at a high level of aggregation, we can also make some inferences about the implications of NAFTA for specific cities. Cities that specialize in the production of

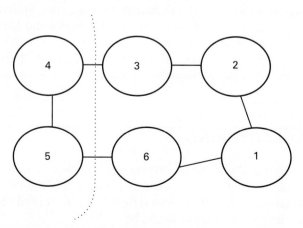

FIGURE 7.4 Core-Periphery
Model and Trade Barriers

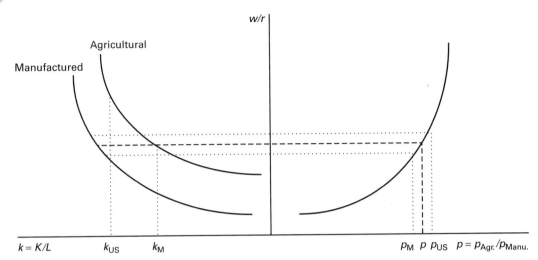

FIGURE 7.5 Effects of NAFTA

agricultural products will be harmed by NAFTA because of the increase in imports, while cities that specialize in the production of manufactured products will be helped by the increase in exports. The impact will be larger for cities close to Mexico because of transportation costs. The return to labor in the United States will fall, reducing the incentive for labor to migrate from Mexico. Vernon Henderson (1993) finds that the cities of Austin, Anaheim, Los Angeles, San Jose, Phoenix, and Dallas should see an increase in employment of more than 2,000 jobs due to expansion of industries there for the Mexican export market. His analysis also finds that cities specializing in products that can be produced more cheaply in Mexico, such as textiles or food processing, could lose employment as a result of NAFTA. Edward Leamer (1993) uses a three-factor (professional workers, nonprofessional workers, and capital) Hecksher-Ohlin model to analyze NAFTA. Leamer finds that the removal of tariff barriers will reduce earnings to low-skilled workers in the United States and could, in fact, have an adverse impact on the level of national income because of changes in the terms of trade. His policy prescription is to focus on developing the skills of workers in order to improve their ability to produce goods in which the United States has a comparative advantage.

The analysis applied to the integration of the United States and Mexico can also be applied to the recently possible economic integration between the countries of Central and Eastern Europe and the countries of Western Europe. It also can be applied to the relations between the Mediterranean European countries and the countries of the Maghreb.

SERVICES VERSUS MANUFACTURING

Most of the examples and analyses in this chapter have involved manufactured products. However, it is well known that services compose the bulk of the value of national income in modern societies. Hence, the reader is right to be concerned about what the effect of including services in our analysis would be.

The short answer is that there is nothing in the core-periphery model that relies on the commodity's being a manufactured good rather than a service. The entire model is thus applicable to analyzing the location decisions of service industries. The main difference is the transportation costs. For many services (a college class, for example), intermetropolitan trade is extremely expensive relative to production costs. However, the transportation costs for other services have been falling. For example, teleconferencing and fax machines now make it easier for a lawyer in Cleveland to help a firm in Switzerland close a deal in Brazil than ever before. This change in technology would lead in the model to an increase in concentration and specialization, and arguably that has been the case in services.

Because so many services are nontradable among metropolitan areas but tradable within a metropolitan area, we will return to this question again in chapter 9. The development of "edge cities" as a modern complement to industrial-era downtowns can be thought of as a result of the increasing transportability of services within and among metropolitan areas.

CHAPTER SUMMARY

- Firms prefer to locate near large markets, all else being equal. Markets are large where other firms have located, since the workers at the other firms live nearby. Thus, urban growth can be self-reinforcing. The core-periphery model provides a theoretical explanation of when we can expect such self-reinforcing growth to occur. Even a small divergence in initial conditions between two locations can be magnified greatly over time.

- Localization economies of scale arise from three sources. The first is the advantage of having a large number of workers and employment opportunities located in close proximity. The second is the advantage of having a broad range of intermediate inputs readily available. The third is the potential for the diffusion of technological advances among firms in the same industry.

- If trade barriers among regions are reduced, the new trade in products along with factor mobility can lead to the growth and decline of existing centers of activity. As trade becomes freer, we expect to find production concentrated in a few locations and exported elsewhere. One form of natural trade barrier that has been eroding over time is the nontradability of various types of services. Thus, we observe a number of service industries concentrating production relative to their earlier location pattern.

EXCERPT: "THE DEATH OF THE CITY" (KENNETH BOULDING)

The following excerpt from an essay by Kenneth Boulding (1963) is not so much a work of fiction as a work of speculation. Boulding, an economist, looked at the evolution of technology and predicted that what we now call cities would be replaced by something different. You may enjoy comparing our actual experience with the predictions he made over thirty years ago. The dynamic nature of cities as modeled in this chapter suggests that we should be unsurprised by changes, even revolutionary changes, in large and small aspects of urban life.

We are now passing through a period of transition in the state of man quite as large and as far reaching as the transition from precivilized to civilized society. I call this the transition from civilization to postcivilization. This is what we mean by the innocent term "economic development." There is something ironic in the reflection that just at the moment when civilization has, in effect, extended itself over the whole world and when precivilized societies exist only in rapidly declining pockets, postcivilization is stalking on the heels of civilization itself and is creating the same kind of disruption and disturbance in civilized societies that civilization produces on precivilized societies.

Just as civilization is a product of the food surplus which proceeds from agriculture, which represents a higher level of organization of food production than primitive hunting and food gathering, so postcivilization is a product of science, that is, of a higher level of organization of human knowledge and the organization of this knowledge into know-how. The result of this is an increase in the productivity of human labor, especially in the production of commodities, which is quantitatively so large as to create a qualitatively different kind of society. The food surplus upon which classical civilization rested was extremely meager. In the Roman Empire at its height, for instance, it is doubtful whether more than twenty or twenty-five percent of the total population were in nonfood-producing occupations.

In the United States at the moment, which is the part of the world furthest advanced toward postcivilization, we can now produce all our food requirements with about ten percent of the population and still have an embarrassing agricultural surplus. It is by no means impossible to suppose a world in which we can produce our whole food supply with one percent of the population, in which we can produce all basic commodities such as clothing, housing, and so on with perhaps ten percent, and in which, therefore, economic life revolves very largely around the organization of personal services.

Just as civilization almost always produces a disastrous impact upon the precivilized societies with which it comes into contact, it also seems all too probable that the impact of postcivilized on civilized societies will be equally disastrous. There are three major aspects of this breakdown of the institutions of civilization. The first is the breakdown of the system of national defense. The breakdown is partly the result of a diminution in the cost of transport of violence which, coupled with the increase in the range of the deadly missile, has rendered the cities of the world pitilessly vulnerable.

The second symptom of the disintegration of civilization is the population explosion in the civilized countries, and even in the incipient postcivilized countries. This puts a burden on developing societies in the current investment in human resources which may be more than they can bear. A poor, civilized society may prove to be incapable of devoting enough resources to education in the face of its enormous numbers of children. Under these circumstances, it can easily regress towards even lower levels of civilization.

The third aspect of the disintegration of civilization is the disintegration of what might be called the classical city. The classical city is a well-integrated social organization. It has clearly defined boundaries and limits and it earns its living by a judicious combination of politics, production, and trade. There is a sharp differentiation between the culture of the city and the country.

In postcivilization all the conditions which gave rise to the classical city have gone. The things which give rise to the need for concentrations all disappear. The city is now, for instance, utterly defenseless; it is a sitting duck for the H-bomb. The diminution in the cost of transport both of commodities and of communications has greatly diminished the value of concentrations of population for the purposes of trade and human intercourse. The classical city is based fundamentally on the necessity for face-to-face communication. For many purposes even today this necessity remains. The possibility of communication by means of modulated light beams, however, has opened up an enormous number of long-distance channels, and it may well be the case that in the not-too-distant future we shall each sit in our own studies and conduct long-distance televised conferences with people all over the world. We are very far from having exhausted the implications, both political and economic, of the communications revolution in which we are living. Stock markets and legislative assemblies, for instance, in a physical sense are civilized rather than postcivilized institutions, and one doubts whether they will survive another fifty or one hundred years with the present type of development.

Source: The Historian and the City, edited by Oscar Handlin and John Burchard. Copyright © 1963 by the Massachusetts Institute of Technology and the President and Fellows of Harvard University. Reprinted by permission of MIT Press.

Questions for Review and Discussion

1. Further improvements in transportation and communication have been made since Professor Boulding wrote the essay from which the excerpt above has been taken. Have we seen a decline in the role of cities as a result of these changes?

2. Could a prosperous city be the result of spurious agglomeration?

3. After more than forty years of economic separation, the countries of Central and Eastern Europe are becoming integrated with the countries of Western Europe. What implications does this have for cities in Europe? What implications does this have for trade between Europe and the rest of the world?

4. "The core-periphery model predicts that markets are large precisely where a lot of people are located. Therefore, China and India should be the core of the world's economy. They aren't, so the model is clearly flawed." Do you agree or disagree? Explain.

5. "Technological changes cause cities based on existing technologies to decline and cities that house the new technologies to prosper." Do you agree or disagree? Explain using an example.

6. Consider the following situation (analogous to that in Table 7.1): $w_B = 90$, $w_G = 120$, $w' = 82$, $L_B = 37$, $L_G = 37$, $L = 37$, $p_B = 300$, $p_G = 400$. Suppose that the marginal product is decreasing with the level of employment, $MP = 4 - 0.1L$, and also suppose that there is a 50 percent chance of good times or bad times.

   a. Calculate the firm's profits if it is in an isolated location.

   b. Calculate the firm's profits if it locates in proximity to many other firms.

   c. Under what circumstances would the firm prefer an isolated location?

7. "Improvements in communications technology that make it possible for people to attend classes in remote locations without leaving their homes or offices will lead to a significant consolidation in the market for college education. This reflects the pattern of consolidation observed in other industries as transportation costs fell relative to production costs." Do you agree or disagree? Explain.

CHAPTER 8

Government Policy and Metropolitan Growth

ocal governments throughout the United States are under great pressure to increase employment and investment in their areas. In this chapter we review the theory of business investment to see whether government policies exist that can affect business location decisions. We also briefly review the evidence on the effectiveness of government policy in this area and consider an approach to optimal design of policy. The theoretical construct of a city as a small open economy is revisited in order to investigate some constraints on the ability of governments to dictate policy. We conclude with an application of the analysis to a common situation in United States metropolitan areas—the construction or renovation of a stadium for professional sports teams.

BUSINESS INVESTMENT DECISIONS

The model of business investment we have used to this point has been extremely stylized. Economists have devoted a great deal of effort during the past decade to gaining a better understanding of the practical problems that face businesses when they make investment decisions. In particular, the role of ongoing uncertainty regarding the prospects for success and the choice of timing in making decisions has been emphasized.

Modern economic theory emphasizes three aspects of the investment decision. First, nearly all investment decisions involve some irreversible commitments of resources, or sunk costs. Second, there is ongoing uncertainty about conditions that may affect the profitability of the investment. Third, most investments include a decision about the timing of the investment; that is, a cmpany chooses both whether to invest and when to invest. (Avinash Dixit and Robert Pindyck, two of the major contributors to the academic literature in this area, summarize the modern theory of investment in their 1994 book.)

Begin with the simple idea of investment taught in any course in the principles of microeconomics. Consider a firm trying to decide whether to enter a market. If the price of the product exceeds the firm's average costs, then economic profits are to be made and the firm will enter. Similarly, if the price falls short of average cost for a firm currently in a market, it will exit. While this simple model does not preclude the possibility of sunk costs, it is clearly a static, complete information framework. Thus, it does not allow for the richness of the complete modern framework.

A slightly more sophisticated model of investment recognizes that costs and benefits of the investment extend into the future and that future costs and benefits are uncertain. The theory in this case is to calculate the expected (in a statistical sense) present discounted value of the costs and benefits and to invest if the benefits exceed the costs. This formulation recognizes uncertainty and irreversibility but does not explicitly account for the timing of the decision. To see how timing matters, consider the following simple example, adapted from Dixit and Pindyck (1994, chapter 2, p. 27). A company is considering opening a branch plant in a city. However, it is unsure whether the city's economy will do well ("boom") or do poorly ("bust"). If the city is a boom town, then the company will earn $300 per year forever; but if the city is a bust, the company will earn $100 per year forever. A sunk investment cost of $1,600 is necessary to open the branch plant; a 50-percent probability exists that the city will boom (and thus a 50-percent probability it will bust); and future flows of money are discounted at a rate of 10 percent. Finally, suppose the company would earn $200 this year if it opened the plant and that all uncertainty over the city's prospects will be resolved next year. What should the company do?

If we calculate the discounted present value of investing today, we find that the discounted present value of the costs clearly equals $1,600. The benefits are $200 today and have a 50-percent probability of being either $100 or $300 every year in the future. This represents an expected future return of $200 per year, and this expected return has a discounted present value of $2,000 at a 10-percent discount rate. The discounted present value of total expected benefits is $2,200. "Old-fashioned" investment theory would conclude that the firm should open the plant because the expected benefits exceed the costs by $600. Note, though, that if the firm waits a year, it will know for sure whether or not the city is booming. If the city is a bust, the firm won't invest. The discounted present value of the future benefits is only $1,000, which does not cover the costs of the investment. If the city booms, the firm invests because it gets benefits with a present discounted value of $3,000 in return for the investment of $1,454 ($1,600 next year has a present discounted value of $1,454 at a discount rate of 10 percent). However, there is a cost; the firm loses the $200 profits from investing today. Should the firm wait a year? Again calculating the discounted present value, we find that the firm earns expected profits of $773 by delaying the investment decision for a year. If the city booms (a 50-percent probability), then the firm earns $1,546 (calculated as $3,000 − $1,454). If the city busts, the firm does not invest and thus earns $0. The expected value is 50 percent times $1,546 plus 50 percent times $0, or $773. The benefits of avoiding a bust outweigh the lost profits from delay. In fact, the firm would be willing to pay up to $173 for the opportunity to maintain the flexibility of the investment decision. This example, although simple, captures the spirit of modern business investment theory.

There are two implications of the modern theory of investment. The first implication is that firms may rationally delay their entry and exit decisions relative to what a simple comparison of price and average cost would suggest. A move that entails large sunk costs requires either a high probability of success or the chance to earn extremely high profits. This in turn means that financial incentives offered by local governments are more likely to be successful if they can persuade firms that one of these two conditions will occur. The fact that local governments acting alone are unable either to guarantee success or to increase the rewards of success suggests that they will have a difficult time influencing firm location decisions. As we shall see later in the chapter, most studies do find that local government incentives have only a small effect on business location decisions.

The second implication is that if one firm's decision to invest provides information to another firm about the likely success of the investment, there can be "clumping" of investment. Suppose you are evaluating whether or not Kansas City is going to be a boom town in the future. Your information leaves you on the border between convinced and unconvinced. If you observe that other firms are moving to Kansas City, though, you can infer that their information convinced them that Kansas City has good prospects. This in turn might convince you and lead you to invest there. This can be a self-enforcing prophecy, of course. If enough firms move to Kansas City, it will certainly become a center for business activity.

The modern theory of investment reinforces the core-periphery model introduced in chapter 7 since it implies both that initial advantages can persist for a long time and that change, should it occur, could be sudden and drastic. We have already seen an example of this type of reasoning in chapter 7, when the signaling effect of one firm's investment led to the problem of "false agglomeration." These implications also reinforce the possibility that any given city will produce considerably less than the full spectrum of goods and services. Chapter 5 introduced this possibility to illustrate the idea that gains from trade could exceed differences in marginal costs among regions if large fixed costs discouraged the local production of some goods. The existence of sunk costs and uncertainty only increases the probability that a particular good will not be produced locally.

Industrial Parks and Firm Relocation

Rauch (1993a) analyzes the question of when a firm will leave a high-cost location in favor of a lower-cost location. The first firm to relocate has a disadvantage if there are agglomeration economies of scale, such as the demand externalities discussed in chapter 3. In the long run, a move to the new location could be to a firm's advantage, but the firm is uncertain about whether or not other firms will follow. Sunk costs are certainly associated with such a move, so that the conditions identified in our theoretical discussion above are met. A land developer can overcome the reluctance of firms to move first by using price discrimination—charging a lower cost to early tenants. Rauch presents evidence that this pattern of rents is found in private industrial parks. A city trying to achieve a "critical mass" of businesses can accomplish the same objective by providing tax abatement and other incentives to firms that locate in the city first. These incentives can offset the reluctance of firms to move into a place where the benefits of agglomeration economies will be realized only in the future, in the uncertain case that other firms follow their lead.

COSTS AND BENEFITS OF URBAN GROWTH

Before analyzing whether local government policy can affect business investment decisions, let us first review what effect a company's decision to locate in a city has on the city's economy. In what follows, we will focus on the decision of a company that exports goods or services to other cities.

An important concept in understanding local government decisions is the "multiplier," or the change in total local employment divided by a unit change in export employment. This is the total impact on the employment in a region caused by an initial investment of a firm (or an expansion by an existing firm) that exports goods or services. In the context of this analysis, it is important to define exports. A narrow definition of exports characterizes them as "commodities physically transported to purchasers outside the region" (Isserman 1980, p. 156). Even this narrow definition includes sales to purchasers within the same country, so long as they are not in the same region. A broader definition, and the one we will focus on, is that exports are "all goods and services produced for demand originating outside the region, including federal government expenditures, certain forms of transfer payments, and expenditures within the region by tourists and other nonresidents" (Isserman 1980, pp. 156–157). This broader definition of exports better accounts for the important role of services in the economy, noting that some services are exported to people physically located within the region. For example, a student from Djakarta, Indonesia, studying at the University of Minnesota represents purchases of services from Minneapolis-St. Paul and an influx of money into the region just as surely as the sale of Post-It® notes, manufactured by 3M in Minneapolis, to a company in Djakarta represents exports from the area.

The multiplier is really interesting only in an economy with some slack, which is not the type of economy our models have described to this point. The model of trade developed in chapters 5 and 6, for example, was predicated on the assumption that the economy was on the production possibility frontier. If there is unemployment, the economy can not be on the production possibility frontier. This implies that an opportunity exists for Pareto-improving government policy as previously unused resources are brought into production.

The multiplier may be estimated in three general ways (Isserman 1980). The first is so-called *export base* theory, in which industries are classified as either export or local. For example, a steel mill whose main customers are located in other metropolitan areas might lead steel manufacturing to be classified as an export industry, while the local government is likely to be classified as a local industry. The problem with this approach is that some local industries, such as restaurants, produce export goods, such as meals purchased by tourists. Similarly, the local government provides public safety services not only to residents but also to people just visiting the city. Conversely, some export industries produce local goods; perhaps the steel mill mentioned above also has a few local customers for its products. In the case of services, not only students from Djakarta attend the University of Minnesota but also students from Minneapolis. Even if the errors exactly offset for the region, the multiplier for any particular industry will not be correctly estimated. Suppose, for example, that the extent of exports is overstated by classifying all steel employment as export but understated by an equal amount by classifying all local government employment as local. Even if these errors cancel, so that total export employment in the region is correctly calculated, the multipliers for each industry will be wrong; as a result, policies designed to increase employment based on expanding export industries will not achieve their goal.

The second way to calculate the multiplier is through the use of *location quotients*. The idea here is to compare local production of a good with local consumption. If local production exceeds local consumption, then the good is defined as an export. The problem with this approach is that local consumption can't be observed in most cases. Thus, some assumptions must be made about consumption in order to implement this approach. The most common assumption is that consumption is proportional to employment. In that case, the metropolitan area's share of consumption is just equal to the fraction of national employment located in the metropolitan area. If the fraction of employment in a given industry in the region exceeds the fraction of employment in the industry for the entire country, then local production is assumed to exceed local consumption. This implicitly assumes that labor is equally productive in all regions in the country. Another assumption is that all local production goes first to satisfy local demand before being exported. If there is "cross-hauling" of goods and services—both imports and exports within the same industry—then the location quotient approach will underestimate the amount of exports. Return to the example of college students from outside the metropolitan area. If there is higher employment in colleges than the national average, then the location quotient approach will identify the production of higher education services as an export. However, the approach will only identify the *net* exports—the excess of exported services to imported services (local people attending college elsewhere)—not the total amount of exports.

The location quotient approach can be shown algebraically. Let E_{ir} be employment in industry i in region r, E_r be total employment in the region, and E_{in} and E_n be the industry and total employment for the nation, respectively. Then the location quotient (LQ) is defined as

$$LQ_{ir} = (E_{ir}/E_r) / (E_{in}/E_n) \tag{1}$$

Equation (1) can be rewritten to show the total amount of employment in an export industry. If $LQ_{ir} > 1$, then the amount of employment in the industry devoted to satisfying export demand is $X_{ir} = (1 - 1/LQ_{ir}) E_{ir}$, which can be written (substituting for LQ) as

$$X_{ir} = (E_{ir}/E_{in} - E_r/E_n) E_{in} \tag{2}$$

Equation (2) clearly highlights the assumptions of the location quotient approach. The first term (E_{ir}/E_{in}) is a proxy for local production because of the assumption that labor is equally productive everywhere. The second term (E_r/E_n) is a proxy for local consumption because consumption per worker is assumed to be equal everywhere. Another assumption is that the nation as a whole is not a net importer or exporter; otherwise, the consumption would have to be adjusted for that. A more general version of the location quotient that accounts for these possibilities is shown in equation (3) below, where v_i represents the relative productivity of the region, c_i represents the relative consumption, and e_i represents the net exports of the nation as a fraction of total production.

$$X_{ir} = (v_i E_{ir} / E_{in} - c_i (1-e_i) E_i / E_n) E_{in} / v_i \tag{3}$$

The other main empirical difficulty with calculating location quotients is that the level of aggregation of the data affect the results. This is intuitively clear when we think about the crosshauling problem identified earlier. The higher the level of aggregation, the more that crosshauling will be obscured by the aggregation process as imports and exports offset each other, leaving a smaller net import or export amount. This is illustrated in Table 8.1. Philadelphia is estimated to have exports of 5.8 percent of its economy when data are aggregated to the division level (manufacturing, services, wholesale trade, etc.) but exports of 19.3 percent—three times as large—when data are examined at the 4-digit SIC code level.

Table 8.2 gives two examples of calculating location quotients using data on employment in 1986. The total employment in a variety of sectors of the economy is given in the first section of the table. This allows you to calculate the percent of employment in each sector, which is shown in the second section of the table. The percent of employment in each sector for the entire country is also shown. The location quotient for a sector is then calculated as the ratio of the percent of employment in that sector in the metropolitan area to the percent of employment in the United States.

Spokane is identified as an exporter of retail services, distribution (wholesale activity), health, education, and social services, and "other." The latter employment category includes government employment. Spokane had a large military and civilian presence in 1986, with total Federal employment of 11,105.

The dominant presence of General Motors is clear in Flint's manufacturing location quotient of 196.1, although two other sectors are also identified as net exports. The heavy reliance on manufacturing can be both a benefit and a liability to a metropolitan area. The benefit, of course, is that specialization along with agglomeration economies of scale can lead to high productivity and, therefore, high wages for employees who live in the area. The liability is that the entire metropolitan area can suffer extreme economic hardship if there is a downturn in the business that it relies on

TABLE 8.1 Calculated Export Share at Different Levels of Aggregation*

Region	Division Data	2-Digit Data	3-Digit Data	4-Digit Data
Georgia	0.053	0.152	0.182	0.207
Kansas	0.097	0.154	0.209	0.233
West Virginia	0.120	0.239	0.287	0.318
Philadelphia	0.058	0.110	0.166	0.193

*Export share of economy is given in the table. Data are listed in order of increasing detail. Number of "digits" refers to the standard industrial classification (SIC) used to identify industries.

Source: Adapted from Isserman (1980, Table 1, p. 168)

TABLE 8.2 Calculating Location Quotients: An Example*

		Spokane, WA	Flint, MI
Total employment		144,312	193,723
Manufacturing		17,260	67,754
Retail		31,360	40,964
Financial and legal services		11,660	8,151
Business and professional services		5,808	8,508
Distribution		12,510	10,697
Health, education, social services		38,659	42,938
Other		27,055	14,711
Percentage of employment (% in entire U.S.)			
Manufacturing	(17.9)	12.0	35.0
Retail	(20.5)	21.7	21.1
Financial and legal services	(8.2)	8.1	4.2
Business and professional services	(6.7)	4.0	4.4
Distribution	(8.0)	8.7	5.5
Health, education, social services	(21.9)	26.8	22.2
Other	(16.8)	18.7	7.6
Location quotient			
Manufacturing		67.0	196.1
Retail		105.8	102.9
Financial and legal services		98.4	51.2
Business and professional services		60.5	66.0
Distribution		107.6	68.5
Health, education, social services		122.1	101.0
Other		111.9	45.3

*All data are for 1986. Location quotient equals 100 times the percentage of employment in the metropolitan area divided by the percentage of employment in the United States. For example, the location quotient for manufacturing in Spokane equals $100 \times 12.0\%/17.9\%$, or 67.0.

Source: Adapted from McDonald (1992, Tables 5.10 and 5.17).

so heavily. The documentary "Roger and Me," by Michael Moore, is an opinionated exploration of the effects of sustained problems at General Motors on the city and people of Flint.

Despite the problems identified with the location quotient approach, it is still a good way to learn something about a region's economy. For example, if an industry is identified as an exporter of a given sector's products despite the bias from cross-hauling, you can be confident of the result. This knowledge is useful in narrowing down further analysis to focus on the export industries in an area.

The third way of estimating a multiplier is through *input-output analysis.* This relates the amount of factors of production and intermediate goods needed to produce a given good. (Wassily Leontief won a Nobel Prize in economics for developing this type of analysis.) The basic idea is quite simple. All the analyst must do is trace the flows of inputs from their original sources to their ultimate destinations. The tables work by calculating a ratio of the required inputs for a given output, and then they can be used to show the ultimate impact on the economy of a change in the level of output. This approach has the advantage that it avoids some of the problems of aggregation that the other approaches are subject to. It does have two drawbacks, though.

First, it assumes constant coefficients production; that is, it allows no factor substitution. Second, it assumes constant factor prices, because the tables usually calculate the ratios in terms of dollar amounts of requirements rather than physical amounts.

All the measures above focus on export of goods and services as the source of urban growth. There is another source of urban growth—the local production of goods that were previously imported. This approach, or "import substitution," does not generally enjoy wide support by economists. The principal objection is that the product being imported may not be one in which a city enjoys a comparative advantage, and so it is inefficient to produce it relative to producing some other good. Also, a long-run consideration is that consumption patterns might shift by the time local production is in place. In fact, altering local production patterns can also alter local consumption patterns by affecting factor incomes. In defense of import substitution, consider the extreme example of the economy of the planet Earth. With the slight exception of some rockets being exported and moon rocks being imported, the economy is closed and therefore cannot grow on the basis of exports. How has the Earth's economy grown? Through technological progress, and through specialization and trade among the regions of Earth. Similarly, a metropolitan area can grow through increasing local productivity or intrametropolitan trade and by removing intrametropolitan trade barriers (zoning and growth controls being two prominent examples—see chapter 10), even if it does not increase intermetropolitan trade.

The most eloquent argument in favor of import substitution as a means of economic development is made by Jane Jacobs (1969). Her theory is that import substitution is a complement to export promotion in that the local production that replaces imports will also be a source of exports; after all, if the commodity is good enough to replace something already on the market, it is likely to be competitive in other locations as well. As the city gets larger, the locally produced set of goods expands as the local market gets large enough to support a variety of local activities. Although the volume of exports and imports may be larger as the city grows, its composition will vary as new industries are created to serve the local market. It should be emphasized that this argument for import substitution is not a justification for trade restrictions. It recognizes instead that cities may change the composition of their production over time as they grow and develop. (Recall from chapter 6 that changes in factor proportions over time as a city develops will lead to changes in production and trade by that city.)

A more general criticism of economic impact analysis is made by Bruce Seaman (1987). He points out that every business, by definition, has an economic impact. Further, it is often difficult to disentangle the separate impact of each business from those of the others. Note the absurdity of the extreme case—if we all have a multiplier of 2, why aren't we all twice as rich? This argument has a ring of truth to it, as Seaman illustrates by using economic impact studies from Atlanta. By combining the results of several studies, he finds that there was an estimated economic impact on Atlanta of $697 million in 1984 from three industries—professional sports, universities, and commercial music. Since the total personal income for Atlanta in 1984 was $32 billion, this means that there is room for no more than 138 ($32 billion/$232.3 million) separate industries that average the size of the three listed above—and the impact of Coca-Cola is likely to be bigger than average. The moral is not that economic impact is nonexistent but rather that we should be extremely careful in interpreting the figures that are reported for any specific firm or industry.

Who benefits from urban growth? Two obvious classes of beneficiaries are people who get jobs who were formerly unemployed and people who get jobs that pay more than the jobs they previously held. Tim Bartik (1991, chapter 4) uses a sample of cities to calculate that about 23 percent of the jobs created by reducing unemployment in a city would go to residents who were unemployed or out of the labor force, while the other 77 percent would go to new migrants to the city. This general finding depends on whether the city's residents are better qualified for the newly created jobs than potential migrants. If the welfare of the city's residents is the main concern of the local government, then job-creation policies should be closely coordinated with training policies for local residents.

An important empirical finding is that rapid urban growth is not the result of fewer jobs lost but rather the result of more jobs being created. Randall Eberts and Joe Stone (1992, Table 2.3) study job gains from openings of new businesses and expansions of existing businesses compared to job losses from closings and contractions in 34 metropolitan areas from 1984 to 1986. Their findings are shown in Table 8.3. Changes in net employment—gains minus losses—range from –8.19 percent of employment in Pittsburgh to 19.36 percent of employment in San Diego, with an average of 6.00 percent. All the metropolitan areas, though, had job losses from closings and contractions of at least 13.30 percent, with an average loss of 20.52 percent. Even San Diego, with the largest net employment increase, had a job loss from closings and contractions of 20.89 percent. The difference between the metropolitan areas that enjoyed employment gains and those that suffered employment losses was essentially in job creation.

Another study found a similar result by using detailed data for Dallas during the period 1986 to 1989. During this period, net employment changed very little, but 26.7 percent of the jobs existing in 1986 had disappeared by 1989. Most of these job losses were due to business closures; the rest were attributable to layoffs or business relocations. Only 1.6 percent of the lost jobs, however, was the result of companies moving to a new location. Of the jobs created, over 60 percent came as a result of new business formation, while only 3.3 percent were the result of companies moving into the area. The implication is that local government officials concerned with employment growth should concentrate on creating a hospitable environment for entrepreneurship rather than on attracting firms from other locations (*Fortune,* 26 July 1993).

What are the costs of urban growth? We hear, of course, the standard litany: crime, congestion, pollution. Note, though, that these are not caused by growth per se but by market failures that get worse as cities get bigger. If the market failures were corrected, in fact, we could expect cities to grow even larger than they are now. For example, a reduction in pollution, all else being equal, would increase the amenity value of the city. This would make it easier for firms to attract workers because they would not need to pay a wage that compensated workers for living amid pollution. This lower wage, in turn, would attract more firms, until profits and utility across the region were in equilibrium.

Paul Courant (1994) argues that the standard approach to measuring the benefits of the firm, which he characterizes as "counting jobs," is not a sound method of analysis. His argument is based on analysis that is captured in Figure 8.1. Suppose that a metropolitan area is attempting to attract firms by subsidizing capital. If capital is mobile and the metropolitan area is small relative to the world, then the supply of

TABLE 8.3 Percentage Employment Change from Various Causes, 1984–1986

Metropolitan Area	Net Change	Openings	Expansions	Closings	Contractions
Akron	0.46	16.20	6.43	−13.99	−8.18
Anaheim	6.88	19.44	11.42	−18.26	−5.72
Atlanta	15.58	22.18	12.61	−14.65	−4.55
Baltimore	8.93	19.00	10.82	−15.62	−5.27
Birmingham	8.73	21.12	10.25	−15.51	−7.13
Buffalo	2.57	15.36	7.26	−14.63	−5.42
Chicago	5.54	16.31	8.83	−13.67	−5.92
Cincinnati	3.16	13.27	8.25	−13.54	−4.82
Cleveland	0.64	13.31	8.48	−15.17	−5.98
Columbus	15.90	20.47	9.74	−9.56	−4.75
Dallas	5.68	20.03	10.44	−16.68	−8.10
Denver	6.16	20.18	8.87	−15.16	−7.72
Detroit	0.97	13.20	8.96	−15.40	−5.80
Greensboro	13.24	17.21	9.34	−8.73	−4.57
Houston	−5.41	16.75	7.54	−20.91	−8.80
Indianapolis	8.70	17.64	10.09	−11.05	−7.98
Kansas City	4.28	16.26	8.24	−14.76	−5.46
Los Angeles	3.95	16.78	9.78	−17.10	−5.52
Miami	2.18	15.48	8.72	−16.39	−5.63
Milwaukee	4.36	13.57	7.96	−11.71	−5.45
Minneapolis	15.29	19.42	11.22	−9.82	−5.53
New Orleans	0.86	15.41	6.03	−13.94	−6.65
New York	0.61	12.64	8.33	−15.38	−4.98
Newark	7.18	16.36	8.88	−12.61	−5.45
Philadelphia	−6.16	15.54	10.01	−13.87	−5.52
Pittsburgh	−8.19	11.46	5.82	−13.76	−11.71
Portland	5.43	20.12	8.14	−13.15	−9.68
Rochester	19.33	29.66	7.13	−12.12	−5.35
St. Louis	8.19	16.48	8.62	−11.72	−5.20
San Diego	19.36	27.32	12.93	−15.63	−5.26
San Francisco	2.26	13.48	8.81	−14.27	−5.76
San Jose	7.50	19.19	10.74	−16.21	−6.21
Seattle	11.08	21.58	10.02	−13.87	−6.65
Tampa	8.68	20.73	9.89	−17.25	−4.70
Average	6.00	17.74	9.14	−14.30	−6.22
Maximum	19.36	29.66	12.93	−20.91	−11.71
Minimum	−8.19	11.46	5.82	−8.73	−4.55

Source: Eberts and Stone (1992, Table 2.3).

capital to the metropolitan area is horizontal at the world price r_0. In the absence of a subsidy, the equilibrium level of capital (k_0 in Figure 8.1) is found at the intersection of the supply curve and the demand curve for capital, its marginal revenue product. Each unit of capital adds its marginal revenue product to the local economy, making the total contribution of the capital equal to the area under the marginal revenue product (*MRP*) of capital curve.

A subsidy to capital increases the supply of capital to the metropolitan area, as shown by the dashed line at the price r_1. The new level of capital is k_1, and the amount of the subsidy is $(r_0 - r_1) \times (k_1 - k_0)$. The total revenue in the metropolitan area increases by the area under the *MRP* curve between k_0 and k_1, which is less than the total amount of the subsidy. There is a deadweight loss illustrated in Figure 8.1, so the net effect of the subsidy is to reduce local well-being. The standard analysis, though, which measures only the change in local revenues, would suggest that the policy illustrated in Figure 8.1 was of benefit to the metropolitan area.

Courant argues that this type of result is quite general. In fact, he states a proposition showing the conditions under which subsidies to firm locations reduce local economic welfare.

PROPOSITION

If (1) the local economy exhibits diminishing returns—that is, diminishing marginal product for each factor of production; (2) the existing taxes on mobile factors of production are benefits taxes—that is, the taxes paid equal the benefits received from the local public services; (3) no nonfrictional unemployment exists; and (4) all subsidies are financed entirely by local taxes; then any subsidy to business location reduces economic welfare in the local economy.

Courant's proposition is crucial not only in its warning of the dangers of naively measuring the benefits of economic development policies but in the guidance it gives to finding policies that do benefit the local economy. For example, the proposition suggests that a policy that promotes the development of agglomeration economies of scale (so that the marginal product of some factor of production is increasing) can have a net positive effect on the region. Similarly, a policy that reduces nonfrictional unemployment can be of benefit, so that *sometimes* "counting jobs" is a reasonable

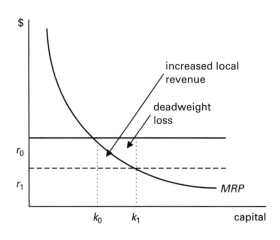

FIGURE 8.1 Effects of a Subsidy on Capital on a Local Economy

analytical approach. In general, Courant argues that the correct approach is to measure the economic well-being of individuals and groups in a region and to identify any changes in this well-being that result from a proposed policy. This is a much more difficult question than the usual question of the number of jobs created, but there is prima facie evidence that answering it correctly is important in determining the level of state and local government expenditures on subsidies designed to influence firm location decisions. Of course, if some people benefit from the policy and others do not, the local government must weigh the winners against the losers. If there is not a Pareto-improving policy, the actual policy followed by the government will depend on the relative political strength of various groups. (Even if a Pareto improvement is available, it may not be chosen if the dominant political group stands to gain more by adopting an alternative policy.)

DO TAXES AFFECT BUSINESS LOCATION?

Before answering the question that heads this section, let us first consider how taxes could matter to a firm. First, government services or the property tax could directly affect the cost of production. For example, good roads can reduce the cost of transporting intermediate inputs. The broad range of other public infrastructure can have a similar effect. Taxes on inventories add to the carrying cost of that form of capital. To the extent that publicly provided services are inadequate, firms must incur costs to supplement them. An example would be a lighted, fenced, and patrolled parking lot in a part of a city where police protection is perceived as insufficient.

Second, taxes can affect local demand for the goods and services a firm produces. This is perhaps most obvious in the case of the sales tax, which alters the relative price of taxed and untaxed goods. All taxes, though, have income effects, as do transfers of money from one household to another.

Third, taxes can affect factor costs. For example, income taxes can change the relative price of labor from place to place. A person earning a given salary in a state, such as Tennessee, that has no state income tax might require a higher salary to live in a state, such as Virginia, that has a state income tax. Taxes on capital, land, and natural resources that vary from place to place can also affect the prices those factors of production command.

Fourth, local government regulations that restrict a business can operate like a tax. For example, there is no analytic difference between forbidding an activity and levying a tax of 100 percent on the returns to the activity. Of course, by the same line of reasoning, regulations that reduce harmful externalities can be considered public services.

In order to infer the effect of taxes on firm location decisions, it is first necessary to estimate the economic incidence of local taxes. This is not a trivial task, especially when there are many firms and many small cities in which they can locate. David Bradford (1978) illustrates the difficulties that arise when taxes are introduced into a general equilibrium model of a small open economy. Consider the following model. There are many small communities, each of which produces an identical commodity by combining capital and land. Capital is mobile across communities, while land is not. Suppose one community imposes a tax on capital. If there are many communities, then the price of capital will remain roughly constant, implying that capitalists (owners of capital) in the taxing community require a pre-tax return higher than in other communities. If there are normally shaped isoquants, then there will be a substitution of land for the now more expensive capital in the taxing community, and some capital will exit the community. Bradford's contribution came in noting that this outflow of capital from one community is an inflow of capital to other communities, which should increase the relative price of land in those other towns, reducing the profits available to the capitalists. It is possible that the increase in land value in other towns resulting from this capital movement exceeds the reduction in land value in the taxing town. If the tax revenue is spent in a way that benefits landowners, then the only losers from the imposition of the tax may be owners of capital in the aggregate. This conclusion contradicts the standard partial equilibrium analysis that the supplier of the inelastic factor of production—land, in this case—bears the main burden of a tax.

We can use the general equilibrium model of trade developed in chapter 6 to analyze the effects of a tax (or subsidy) on capital. Suppose two commodities are being produced, health care (H) and ice cream (I). There are two factors of production, land (L) with price R, and capital (K) with price r. Health care is relatively capital intensive, and the situation before any incentives or taxes is depicted by the solid lines in Figure 8.2. All cities are assumed to be identical, and the equilibrium prices in product markets and factor markets are shown, as is the capital-land ratio in production.

A tax on capital imposed by one city will cause capital to go to other cities, all else being equal. This is illustrated by the dotted line in Figure 8.2, showing the capital-land ratio in the city imposing the tax after some of the capital leaves. The situation here is a bit more complicated than that described by Bradford, because now the city is able to shift the relative amount of goods it produces. In this case, it will produce more I and less H than before. If relative factor and product prices in the other cities do not change as a result of the capital flight, then it must be the case that production of H has increased in other cities to compensate for the reduction in the taxing city. The average capital-land ratio in the other cities has increased as illustrated by the dashed line in Figure 8.2. Bradford's point is that an increase in the capital-land ratio, holding the amount of land fixed, can be expected to increase the price of land

FIGURE 8.2 Effects of a Tax on Capital

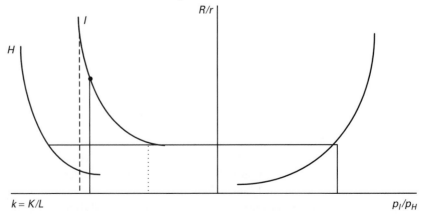

in the cities that did not tax land, even if the relative price of land and capital remains the same.

Economists have devoted countless time and effort to determining the effects of local government policy on business investment decisions. However, there is no completely convincing evidence on the subject. Bartik (1991), in the most thorough review of the literature, concludes that the elasticity of employment with respect to local taxes is approximately –0.3, so a 10-percent decrease in local taxes would be expected to increase local employment by 3 percent. This surely seems like a small amount compared to the amount and volume of political rhetoric over tax abatement, enterprise (and empowerment) zones, and other local government policies.

Why do most studies find little or no effect of local taxes or business investment decisions? There are four reasons. First, some taxes don't vary much across locations. Second, even if taxes vary, other factors (labor costs, transportation costs, and so on, as we saw in chapter 4) vary more. Third, taxes can be shifted from a firm to its consumers, so even a large difference in nominal tax rates does not reflect a difference in the actual tax burden borne by the firm. Fourth, higher taxes can be a reflection of higher-quality public services.

The four reasons above immediately suggest conditions in which taxes would be important for firm location decisions. First, taxes would be more important for intrametropolitan location decisions, in which the labor force is held constant and transportation costs are also roughly equal across locations. Second, taxes would be important in deciding among locations that have equivalent public services. Third, taxes would be more important to those firms that face an elastic demand for their product that prevents them from shifting the tax to their consumers. Table 8.4 illustrates the general range of findings in this area. Regardless of the design of the study, a majority of studies finds that business activity is negatively related to the level of taxation. The range of estimated relations is large, though, making it difficult to generalize from the experience of one city or region to another. The absolute value of the elasticity is

TABLE 8.4   Summary of Econometric Studies of Tax Effects on Business Location

Type of Study	Percentage of Studies With At Least One Statistically Significant Negative Tax Effect	Mean Elasticity of Business Activity With Respect to Taxes (Range)	Median Elasticity
Inter-area	70 percent (57 studies)	–0.25 (48 studies) [–1.40 to 0.76]	–0.15
Inter-area with controls for unobservable differences among areas	92 percent (12 studies)	–0.44 (11 studies) [–1.02 to 0.00]	–0.35
Inter-area with controls for public services	80 percent (30 studies)	–0.33 (25 studies)	–0.27
Intra-area	57 percent (14 studies)	–1.48 (9 studies) [–4.43 to 0.62]	–1.59
Intra-area using specific community data	70 percent (10 studies)	–1.91 (7 studies) [–4.43 to 0.62]	–1.95

Source: Adapted from Bartik (1991) Table 2.3, pp. 40–41.

larger for the intra-area studies as well as for the studies that have better controls for nontax differences among communities, providing some support to the theoretical arguments presented above.

Taxonomy of Economic Development Policy

A wide variety of approaches have been used by cities attempting to improve their economic conditions. One common way of grouping these policies is as so-called first-wave, second-wave, and third-wave policies. *First-wave policies* emphasize the attraction of new branch plants of large firms to an area, and include marketing programs, providing financial incentives to firms, and providing other incentives such as customized training or site-specific infrastructure. *Second-wave policies*, in contrast, emphasize the free provision of government services to small and medium-sized firms, including marketing assistance, technology transfer, capital market assistance (subsidized loans, for example), and workforce development. *Third-wave policies* emphasize the provision of services through private or quasi-private organizations (for example, user-fee-financed government agencies). The third wave is a reaction not only to the perceived failure of the other two approaches but also to a time of increased budgetary stringency at the local level.

An alternative typology is provided by Bartik (1994a, Table 1) and illustrated in Table 8.5. The distinction here is between policies that focus on attracting firms to an area and policies that focus on developing existing firms and creating a climate conducive to growth by local firms. The evidence presented earlier in this chapter suggests that the second type of policy is more likely to be successful in transforming the local economy because of the relatively small impact of firm relocation on the total level of output in most metropolitan areas.

TABLE 8.5   Economic Development Policies: Attraction versus Climate Improvement

Type of Policy	Examples
Attraction oriented	
Market area as branch plant location	Advertising area, marketing trips to corporate headquarters, provide information to prospects
Financial incentives	Industrial revenue bonds, property tax abatement, direct government loans, wage subsidies
Nonfinancial incentives	Customized training, site-specific infrastructure, regulatory help
Climate-improvement oriented	
Capital market	Government support for private loan programs
Small business information/Education	Small business information office, community college classes, small business development centers, small business incubators
Technology and research	Research-oriented industrial parks, applied research grants to business, technology transfer programs, university centers of business-related research
Export and marketing assistance	Trade missions, export financing, government procurement help, matching in-state suppliers with in-state businesses
Workforce development	Training grants, customized training programs, subsidies for on-the-job training

Source: Adapted from Bartik (1994a, Table 1).

Another prominent approach has been the development of *enterprise zones* or *empowerment zones*, used in at least 37 states and the District of Columbia. The idea here is to remove burdensome regulatory and tax burdens from businesses and also to provide subsidies for hiring people in economically distressed areas. Papke (1993) provides an overview of the programs, defining an enterprise zone program as a geographically targeted tax, expenditure, and regulatory inducement to firm location. If the enterprise zones are small relative to the metropolitan area where they are located, then simple partial equilibrium analysis predicts that the effect of the zone will depend on the relative elasticity of supply of factors of production to the zone.

Papke's analysis contains several immediate theoretical implications. First, a subsidy to capital could actually lead to a decrease in employment within the zone if firms substitute capital for labor or if capital-intensive firms choose to relocate to the zone. Second, if labor is inelastically supplied, the zone might increase wages without increasing total employment. Third, the benefits from the zones could be capitalized into property values in the area, benefiting landowners. This implies that the firm locating in the zone might not benefit from the subsidy at all, and it provides a rationale for local government policies of land acquisition and sale at below-market value. Fourth, some of the activity within the zone will involve a relocation of activity from elsewhere in the metropolitan area. Unless there are reasons for preferring firms to locate in one area or another, this is not a net benefit to the region.

Two main methodologies have been used to measure the effects of enterprise zones. The benefits are usually stated in terms of the number of jobs created, while the costs are the direct expenditures and indirect subsidies (reduced tax payments, etc.) that compose the policy. (Recall Courant's criticism of "counting jobs" as a way of measuring a policy's success.) The first method involves surveys or case studies of firms located within the zone. This technique has the advantage of providing information at the firm level, but it has several built-in biases. First, estimates of the jobs created specifically as a result of the zone are subjective, and they may be inflated by managers who perceive the survey as influencing future policy. Second, these surveys are unable to include firms that do not locate in the zone or do not stay in business until the survey date. The firms completing a survey are thus disproportionately successful and favorably disposed to the zone location, although they may not be representative of the firms in the economy as a whole. An example will illustrate the problems that can result. A survey of firms participating in New Jersey's enterprise zone program in 1988 yielded an estimate that 9,193 jobs were created between 1985 and 1988 as a result of the zones (Rubin 1990). However, data from the New Jersey Department of Labor indicated that the municipalities in which the zones were located had an increase of 4,305 jobs between 1985 and 1988. (Boarnet and Bogart 1996) The enterprise zones in New Jersey are smaller than the municipality, so the discrepancy may be the result of jobs shifting into the zones from elsewhere in the municipalities; but in any case, the result indicates the need for caution in interpreting survey evidence.

The second type of analysis is statistical (econometric) analysis of employment in enterprise zones. This type of approach typically includes a control group of areas that are similar to the enterprise zone areas but that do not have an enterprise zone. If zones were randomly assigned, then a simple comparison between places with and without zones would indicate the "treatment effect" of having a zone in place. Because zones are usually assigned on the basis of some policy goal, it is important to control for the differences among cities that may lead to one city receiving a zone while another does not. Some of these differences are unobservable, given the data available to the economist, so that fairly sophisticated statistical techniques must be used. The best statistical studies are Papke (1993, 1994) on enterprise zones in Indiana and Boarnet and Bogart (1996) on enterprise zones in New Jersey. Papke finds some evidence that enterprise zones have increased inventory investments and reduced unemployment in qualifying cities but that the economic well-being (estimated as income per capita) of enterprise zone residents does not seem to have improved. Boarnet and Bogart find no evidence that enterprise zones in New Jersey have increased employment in the municipalities where the zones are located.

Dowall (1996) combines statistical and survey data and finds little evidence that the enterprise zone program in California contributed to employment growth in the zones. He finds, using a survey of firms located in the zones, that 48 percent of the businesses did not even use the enterprise zone incentives. Only 23 percent of the firms reported that their location or expansion decisions were affected by the enterprise zones. Most troubling to advocates of enterprise zones, he found that employment growth was lower than predicted in 11 of the 13 zones.

Infrastructure and Economic Development

Governments use the tax revenue they collect to provide services. An alternative to tax abatement as a strategy to attract firms is to use the available revenue wisely. One way of using revenue is to construct and maintain the local infrastructure, including roads, bridges, sewers, and airports. Public sector capital is a large part of the nation's capital stock, representing about one-third of total capital in 1991 (Munnell 1992). This infrastructure affects private decisions in three ways. First, it provides consumption benefits to residents in the form of government services paid for with public capital. Second, expenditures on public works provide a short-run demand stimulus to the economy; of course, any government expenditure would have this effect. Third, public capital serves as an input into private production. It is this last aspect of infrastructure that has been the focus of research and the source of controversy in recent years. Dunphy (1993) provides a detailed look at the reaction of Houston to a perceived crisis in transportation, including increases in revenues for funding road construction and improvements in mass transit.

Some evidence, surveyed by Munnell (1992), indicates that investments in public infrastructure can increase private sector productivity by more than a comparable investment in private capital. These findings, however, suffer from some conceptual difficulties. The first difficulty is the possibility that higher levels of public capital are correlated with some unobservable difference among regions that is the true explanation of productivity differences. Holtz-Eakin (1993) summarizes this argument and the evidence in favor of it. When statistical techniques that account for this unobserved variation among regions are used, the estimated impact of public capital is reduced.

The second difficulty is that higher levels of public capital may be caused by higher levels of private productivity (analogous to an income effect in household demand) rather than causing them. Eberts and Fogarty (1987) examine this question and find some evidence in favor of both positions. In some cases, private productivity leads to higher public capital, while in other cases higher levels of public capital are found to lead to higher private sector productivity.

The third difficulty is that differences in the relative effectiveness of public capital among regions can be masked by aggregate analyses. In some regions, public capital may be a "better" investment than private capital, while in others the reverse may be true. Even if aggregate studies find a positive impact of public capital on local productivity, a policy maker in a particular region should be sure that public capital is the best available alternative. A related issue is the efficiency with which public capital is used. The largest form of public capital stock is highways, which are often congested. Boarnet (1995) presents evidence that reducing congestion on highways—for example, through the use of pricing policies—is likely to yield net benefits that are higher than those obtained by constructing new highways.

Most studies of infrastructure investment focus on the effect of the investment in the place where the investment is made. However, an investment in one place can affect other places. In particular, a capital improvement in one location could draw mobile factors of production from other locations, reducing production in those other locations. In that case, it is important to see whether or not the gains in the location of investment offset the losses in the other locations.

A model will illustrate the situation. Suppose that there are two cities, A and B, each producing an identical good that sells at a given price. Labor is freely mobile between the two cities, and location is the only difference between the cities; therefore, wages must be equal in the two cities. Highways are a free input into local production. (Highway construction can involve subsidy rates of up to 90 percent from the federal government, so this assumption is not as far-fetched as it seems.) Labor markets in A and B are competitive, so the wage equals the marginal revenue product (MRP). The situation is diagrammed in Figure 8.3.

Now suppose a highway is constructed in A. This will increase the marginal product of labor in A (this is similar to the specific factors model of trade we saw in chapter 5). Because the price of the good is taken as exogenous, the highway will increase the marginal revenue product (MRP) in A to MRP'. If the amount of labor in A remains L_A as in Figure 8.3, then the wage in A will increase to w_A as shown in

FIGURE 8.3 Labor Markets before Highway Construction

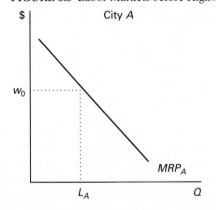
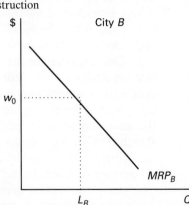

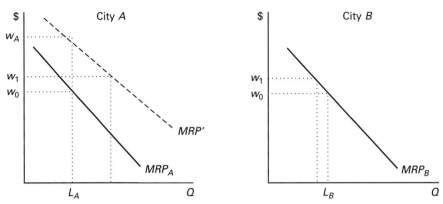

FIGURE 8.4 Effects of a Highway Investment on Labor Markets

Figure 8.4. However, this will induce migration from *B* to *A*, reducing the wage in *A* and increasing the wage in *B* until a new equilibrium is reached at w_1.

The highway investment at *A* increases wages at *A*, employment at *A*, and output at *A*. It reduces employment and output at *B*, so that estimates of the effect of the investment that examine only *A* will be biased toward finding an improvement. Wages increase in both cities. Because the price of the good stays the same and the *MRP* increases in both cities ($w_1 > w_0$ and $w = MRP$), the marginal product of labor increases in both cities. Because the marginal product is higher, total output in the two cities increases relative to what it was before the highway was constructed. As you can see, understanding the effects of highway construction even in a simplified framework does not imply a simple task of data analysis. Boarnet (1996) uses data at the county level in California to analyze the effects of highways in a model like the one described above. He finds that highways are an important determinant of the location of production, as we would expect from the model. He also points out that restrictions on factor mobility can make the outcome less favorable to those places that do not receive highway construction. In the model, workers in City *B* benefit from the highway constructed in City *A* because of the increase in wages. However, this improvement came about because of the implicit threat of the workers in City *B* to leave and go to City *A*. If they had been immobile, the outcome might have been different. Similarly, if agglomeration economies of scale are lost in City *B*, then the *MRP* might actually fall there, so that an initial investment in City *A* might spark a cycle of growth in *A* and a decline in *B*, as we saw in the core-periphery models of chapter 7.

One explanation for differences in productivity among metropolitan areas is that the education and skill levels of the workers vary. An intriguing possibility is that productivity advantages may be gained by clustering better-educated workers; in other words, the average level of education in a metropolitan area can be modeled in the same way as other public infrastructure. This assertion may seem surprising, but Rauch (1993b) used this idea to explore the likely effects on productivity of increasing the average educational level of the workers in a metropolitan area. He estimated that an increase of 1 year in the average amount of education would increase productivity (the amount of output generated by a given amount of inputs) by 2.8 percent. Why does average education matter? The defining characteristic of cities is the density of interactions among individuals. Thus, ideas can be created and diffused rapidly if people interact with other people of high ability. Increasing their average level of ability makes it likely that their interactions will be more productive.

Once we bring education into the picture, a local government is faced with an interesting set of decisions. The first decision is how much to spend on improving the infrastructure so as to encourage economic development. The second decision is how to allocate this spending between the physical infrastructure of highways and the intellectual infrastructure of education. Because the investments in education have a delayed payoff (you have to wait for the schoolchildren to grow up), a short-sighted government might overemphasize physical infrastructure with its short-term gains at the expense of education, even if education has a higher long-term payoff. The *Economist* (20 July 1996) argues that the city of Cleveland has followed precisely this path, building museums, offices, and stadiums while allowing the public schools to deteriorate.

Income Accounting and Constraints on Government Policy

An important constraint on the ability of a metropolitan area to operate an economic development policy is the basic accounting identity governing income in the metropolitan area. Income can be used for either consumption (C), savings (S), or taxes (T). Also, income derives from consumption (C), investment (I), government spending (G), and net exports ($X - M$). Algebraically,

$$Y = C + T + S = C + I + G + (X - M) \tag{1}$$

We can rearrange equation (1) to show the vital accounting identity that restricts all government policy.

$$X - M = (S - I) + (T - G) \tag{2}$$

Equation (2) says that net exports must equal the sum of the excess of savings over investment plus the government budget surplus. Suppose the government wants to use an export-promotion strategy of economic development. There are three (and only three) ways of increasing net exports. The first is to reduce imports. The second is to increase net savings either by reducing investment or by increasing savings. The third is to increase the budget surplus either by increasing taxes or by reducing government spending. Feldstein and Horioka (1980) find that savings and investment are correlated at the national level, leaving the government budget surplus or deficit as the only real policy variable. There is no such finding at the local level, but it is clearly a question worth investigating.

Strictly speaking, equation (2) holds only for each point in time, and doesn't account for the links between investment today and productivity increases tomorrow. Nevertheless, it is a useful "reality check" on the rhetoric surrounding local government economic development policy. For example, consider a policy designed to increase exports by abating taxes on export-oriented firms. If nothing else changes, then we can see immediately from equation (2) that this policy will lead in fact to a reduction in net exports as the government budget surplus decreases. Even if some export-oriented firms locate in the city, other sources of net exports will be displaced. Lawrence and Litan (1987) examine this question at the national level for the United States and find evidence that current account deficits are driven by government budget deficits. They find that subsidies and tariffs can affect the composition of trade but not the balance of trade. To my knowledge, a similar analysis has not been done at the metropolitan area level in the United States.

Short-Run and Long-Run Effects of Policy

In general, infusing money into an economy will lead to a short-term improvement in the measured performance of the economy. However, if there is a structural problem with the economy that is unaddressed, the economy will likely deteriorate again. An example would be a situation in which people have low incomes because they lack education and training that prepares them for high-paying employment. A one-time infusion of cash, while appreciated, does nothing by itself to alter the lack of education and training that are at the root of the low incomes. This distinction between short-run and long-run effects of policy have a strict analogy in the distinction between treating the symptoms of a disease and curing the disease. Oates, Howrey, and Baumol (1971) illustrate the problem using a simple model of deterioration.

Suppose that some measure of economic deterioration (D) is negatively related to the income of a city's residents (Y). For example, richer people are less likely to live in substandard housing. Further, suppose that the extent of deterioration in the present affects the income of the city's residents in the future. For example, if there is extensive substandard housing, then the richer people are likely to leave the city for more congenial areas. These two relations can be expressed as two linear equations:

$$Y_{t+1} = r - sD_t \quad s > 0 \tag{3}$$
$$D_t = u - vY_t \quad v > 0 \tag{4}$$

This system of equations can be solved for the long-run equilibrium level of income and deterioration in the city. Simply substitute equation (4) for D_t in equation (3), set $Y_t = Y_{t+1}$, and solve for Y_e, where Y_e is defined as the steady-state level of income. You will find that $Y_e = (r - su) / (1 - sv)$. It is also possible, given values for the parameters, to trace the dynamics of the system as it evolves from an initial value towards equilibrium.

The most important point about this model, though, is that a change in either D_t or Y_t has no long-run effect. If you reduce deterioration, say through a public works project, that will temporarily affect the incomes of the residents, but the process described by equations (3) and (4) will continue until the equilibrium is again reached. Similarly, a one-time change in the incomes of city residents will have only a temporary effect. If the city is deteriorating and we wish to reverse this deterioration, it is necessary to find some way of increasing Y_e, the steady-state income.

Oates et al. illustrate how government taxes and spending can be used in this type of model to change the equilibrium level of income. Suppose that the term u in equation (4) is linearly negatively related (higher spending means a lower level of deterioration) to city government spending E and that the coefficient on D in equation (3) is linearly positively related (higher taxes accelerate outmigration of rich people) to city government taxes T. In other words, we can write $u = a - bE$, where $b > 0$, and $s = f + gT$, where $g > 0$. Higher levels of government expenditure, E, will reduce the level of deterioration that occurs at any given level of resident incomes. However, higher taxes serve to accelerate the outmigration of higher income people from the city. Unlike policies that only affect income Y and deterioration D directly, local government spending and tax policy can affect the steady-state level of income because they affect the parameters u and s. Recall that the steady-state income, Y_e, is given by the equation $Y_e = (r - su) / (1 - sv)$. An increase in government expenditures will reduce the level of deterioration u, attracting more high income people back to the city, and increasing the steady-state income level. In fact, there is a familiar Keynesian multiplier of $1/(1 - sv)$ for the effects of government expenditures on the equilibrium level of deterioration, as you can find by substituting for u in the system of equations (3) and (4). We find the parameter s in the multiplier, so that local government taxes affect equilibrium by affecting the size of the multiplier. An increase in local taxes, all else equal, will increase the size of the multiplier as higher-income people become more quick to respond to any change in deterioration.

Oates et al. suggest that governments should consider the possibility of changing these structural variables (E and T) in order to improve the equilibrium outcome rather than opt for a policy that changes only the values of deterioration or income. Using data from 1960, they estimate that it would have required an increase in local government spending of $80 per capita to increase median income in the city by $1,000. The same increase in median income would have necessitated a $170 per person decrease in local taxes. This finding suggests that a balanced budget increase in local spending financed by local taxes within the range they consider would have increased the median income in the city because the spending increases would be valued more than the tax increases would be disliked. They also find that policies that directly affect the level of deterioration, such as constructing public housing, are inefficient relative to general tax cuts or spending increases. For example, the increase in median income achieved by one public housing program they consider could have been accomplished at only one-quarter of the cost if general tax cuts had been used instead. The general lesson is to examine not only the immediate impact of government policy but also the long-run effects as people adjust to changing conditions.

INTERNATIONAL TRADE POLICY AND METROPOLITAN GROWTH

Although we have been emphasizing the similarity between intermetropolitan trade and international trade, it is nevertheless important to recognize that international trade policy can have a separate effect on urban growth within an economy. In particular, tariffs on particular products increase the cost of importing those products, making it more likely that domestic cities will specialize in their production. For example, consider a tariff on a capital-intensive product. This will lead to an increase in domestic production of the product, which will (in the absence of factor mobility) increase the return to capital and decrease the return to labor. This has political implications in addition to the economic implications, in that owners of capital will favor trade restrictions and owners of labor will oppose trade restrictions. (Henderson 1988, ch. 7)

International trade, then, has implications for the pattern of domestic metropolitan specialization. This thought can be developed even further. Suppose that cities that specialize in the production of the capital-intensive good have a larger population than cities that specialize in the production of the labor-intensive good. Then a tariff on the capital-intensive good will lead to the formation of larger cities than would have formed in the case of free trade. While this result may seem innocuous, it could entail social costs from increases in administrative costs, uprooting of families, and the construction of infrastructure.

We saw in chapter 1 (Table 1.2) that many of the largest cities in the world are found in developing countries. Krugman and Livas Elizondo (1996) argue that many of the major cities in developing countries reached their large size due to import-substitution policies, including restrictive trade practices. The advantages of being located near the main city in a country are magnified if the country is the entire market but are diminished as the country becomes integrated with a regional or world market. They predict that giant Third World metropolitan areas will shrink in size as their economies become more open to international trade.

National Pollution Regulation and Local Business Activity

One of the unpleasant byproducts of dense economic activity is the pollution that accompanies the manufacture and consumption of modern industrial goods and services. This includes not only the dramatic but isolated examples of Three Mile Island and Love Canal but also the ubiquitous cumulative effect of automobile exhausts arising from the production and consumption of transportation services. In the United States, the primary approach to controlling pollution over the past 30 years has been the promulgation of standards by the national government. This approach has the advantage of creating a uniform system of rules throughout the country, but it has the disadvantage of inevitably imposing greater constraints on some regions than on others. Thus, like tariff policy, a uniform national rule can have the effect of favoring one or several metropolitan areas at the expense of others.

Why does a uniform set of rules cause disparate results? The reason is that some industries find it easier to comply with the rules, and so the cities that specialize in those industries are relatively advantaged. If a metropolitan area is a specialist in producing nuclear warheads, then rules about transporting plutonium will have a stronger impact than if the metropolitan area specializes in producing orange juice. (Although advances in the use of radiation as a bacteriological agent in food processing might soon change this situation.)

A recent example of the potential for disparate impact comes from the actions of the Environmental Protection Agency (EPA). In November 1996, the EPA announced stricter regulations on the level of particulate matter (soot) and on the chemicals that cause smog. Metropolitan areas in the northern part of the United States face colder winters than metropolitan areas in the southern states. As a result, many people in the North use fireplaces or wood stoves. These contribute substantially to particulate matter, making compliance more difficult for the metropolitan areas in the northern states even before industrial activity is taken into account. If the use of wood stoves for heating is discouraged as a result of the new regulation, the ironic outcome could be an increase in the use of fossil fuel and nuclear power in the name of environmental protection.

"MAJOR LEAGUE" ECONOMIC DEVELOPMENT POLICY

> If you are going to build a major sports stadium today, you start out by digging a hole. That is where you are going to put the stadium. And that is probably where the stadium is going to put you.*

One way that metropolitan areas attempt to distinguish themselves is on the basis of the professional sports teams that are located there. There is often rhetorical concern that the loss of a team to another city would mean the loss of "major league" status, resulting in an economic decline. Construction and renovation of stadiums for professional sports teams has long been a prominent and controversial feature of the economic development programs of many cities, as the above quote makes clear. A natural question to ask has been whether cities that have invested in stadiums to attract or retain teams have enjoyed greater economic success than cities that have not undertaken such a policy. Stadiums are an amenity, so theoretically they should help attract *only* amenity-oriented firms, and any study of their effects should focus on that area. The added complication is that they can be important in developing a "critical mass" of attractions in a city even if their presence alone is not responsible for a city's success. Hirzel (1993) illustrates this argument in the case of a new arena and baseball stadium in downtown Cleveland. Gottlieb (1994) surveys studies of the impact of amenities and concludes that the issue is most important at the level of the entire metropolitan area and that the most important amenities include the quality of schools, highways, the environment, and public safety. Of course, an economic development strategy that focuses on improving the quality of life for local residents has an obvious advantage—local residents presumably benefit even if there is no impact on the local economy.

A recent and thorough overview of stadium projects is a book by Baim (1994). He considers the direct costs and benefits of municipal stadium investments as well as some of the important indirect costs and benefits. The findings are summarized in Table 8.6. He finds that 12 of the 13 public stadiums that he studies require a subsidy; in other words, the costs outweigh the benefits. The per capita amount of the subsidy for the 12 unprofitable stadiums ranges from a high of $83 in New Orleans to a low of $0 in Minneapolis, with the only profitable stadium providing $4 per capita in Los Angeles. These costs do not include an estimate of the consumption benefits that city residents receive as a result of the prestige of being the home of a sports team. While these findings are not optimistic, cities continue to vie to attract professional teams. One other warning note: Baim finds that the median construction cost overrun in his sample is 26 percent, so that prospective stadium projects should be evaluated with this figure in mind.

A mutually beneficial trade can occur when a buyer is willing to pay at least as much as the seller is willing to accept. The interesting question, often, is whether the price that the buyer pays is less than the reservation price, the amount that the buyer

---

*From Charles Maher, "Major Sports Stadiums: They Keep Going Up," *Los Angeles Times*, 14 November 1971, quoted in Okner (1974).

TABLE 8.6 Present Value of Benefits and Costs of 13 Stadiums

City and Stadium	Years of Data	Present Value of Net Benefits	Per Capita Net Benefit
Anaheim			
Anaheim Stadium	25	−$4,268,715	−$30
Atlanta			
Fulton County Stadium	22	−$16,547,623	−$33
Baltimore			
Memorial Stadium	32	−$2,922,206	−$3
Buffalo			
War Memorial Stadium	20	−$836,021	−$1
Cincinnati			
Riverfront Stadium	20	−$4,846,388	−$11
Denver			
Mile High Stadium	22	−$2,010,631	−$5
Los Angeles			
Dodger Stadium	34	$7,992,568	$4
Minneapolis			
Metrodome	10	−$43,500	−$0
New Orleans			
Louisiana Superdome	16	−$47,729,356	−$83
Oakland			
Oakland–Alameda County Coliseum	25	−$10,534,636	−$30
Orchard Park, NY (Buffalo)			
Rich Stadium	10	−$16,454,233	−$17
San Diego			
Jack Murphy Stadium	23	−$9,000,723	−$13
Washington, DC			
RFK Stadium	25	−$10,780,339	−$15

Source: Baim (1994, Tables 17.2 and 17.4).

is willing to pay. If so, then we say that the buyer receives consumer surplus. Similarly, if the seller receives a price in excess of the minimum acceptable price, there is a profit on the sale. In a perfectly competitive market, the amount that the marginal buyer is willing to pay equals the price, which in turn equals the reservation price of the marginal seller, in turn equal to marginal cost. In imperfectly competitive markets, however, there will generally be a difference between willingness to pay and willingness to accept. The extent of market power is reflected in the ability of the seller to force the buyer to pay the full amount that the buyer is willing to pay—in other words, to transfer consumer surplus to profit.

The market structure for professional sports teams is not perfectly competitive. Entry barriers exist in the form of league rules on expansion, not to mention the simple expedient of the league's controlling the scheduling of games. Given that many cities are bidding for few teams, cities will be likely to pay their full reservation price rather than the team's reservation price. The financial loss estimated by Baim is one indicator of the nonfinancial benefits that cities believe they will receive as a result of gaining a professional sports team.

Why might the professional sports strategy make sense for a city? One reason is that a city choosing to specialize in the production of tourist services needs an added attraction for visitors as well as an advertising platform for their other tourist attractions. Perhaps the best example of this is the Anaheim Mighty Ducks of the National Hockey League. The team is owned by Disney, is named after a Disney movie, and is located in the same city as Disneyland. Even in less extreme situations, a sports team can contribute to the cultural life of a city in much the same way as can a ballet company, museum, theater, or entertainment district. In fact, a sports team can complement these other types of attractions. The development of Camden Yards in Baltimore near the Inner Harbor entertainment district and National Aquarium is an example. Another example is the so-called Gateway development in Cleveland, consisting of an arena that houses professional basketball and hockey and a stadium that houses the Cleveland Indians, all within walking distance of other major downtown entertainment areas. Hirzel (1993) cites several complementary downtown attractions, which are listed in Table 8.7. A very interesting example of this approach is Phoenix, Arizona, a city that grew without developing a "real" downtown. The city has spent almost $1 billion since 1991 on construction of cultural and sporting attractions in the downtown area. This has included attracting a new major league baseball team as well as a relocated National Hockey League franchise. These investments

TABLE 8.7   Downtown Attractions in Cleveland: Leveraging a Sports Complex

Type of Activity	Activity Center
Sports and entertainment	Gateway complex: 42,000-seat baseball stadium; 21,000-seat arena (basketball, hockey, concerts, other events)
Retail activity	Tower City: mixed-use retail and rail hub in the core of the city, connected to Gateway by a covered walkway
	Galleria: downtown shopping complex
Office activity	Existing and new high-rise office buildings
Theaters	Playhouse Square: four renovated theaters, originally constructed during the 1920s
Nightlife	The Flats: restored industrial area along the Cuyahoga River
	The Warehouse District: restored industrial area between downtown and the Flats
Residential	Warehouse District: conversion of buildings to apartments
	Hotels: tax abatement and other financing to encourage downtown pedestrian traffic from overnight visitors
Convention	Renovated convention center downtown
Public attractions	Rock and Roll Hall of Fame and Museum
	Great Lakes Museum of Science, Environment, and Technology
	Cleveland Aquarium (planned)

Source: Adapted from Hirzel (1993).

have been with the explicit goal of attracting and retaining residents and businesses (*New York Times*, 26 May 1996).

By providing business travelers and tourists with a reason to go to one city rather than another, a sports team can influence economic success. It seems clear, though, that a stadium by itself will not mean the difference between economic success and failure for a city, if for no other reason than the direct employment associated with professional sports is inherently limited by the number of games played. This is in contrast with employment in other industries, which do not have the same intrinsic limit.

Recall that in chapter 1 it was asserted and in chapter 7 modeled that a small change in a city's current situation could lead to a large change in the future. Stadium development can be viewed in that light as the last piece of the puzzle that creates a large change, even if the stadium alone does not yield tremendous benefits. The dynamic model of Oates, Howrey, and Baumol seen earlier in this chapter also illustrates how a stadium can affect the equilibrium by reducing the rate at which the city deteriorates as private businesses take advantage of the concentration of customers to earn profits for themselves.

Although much of the media attention is focused on major league teams, it is also possible to try to attract minor league professional teams for the same purposes. Arthur Johnson (1993, pp. 182–186) describes the experience of Harrisburg, Pennsylvania, which built a 4,300-seat stadium for its AA-level baseball team as the centerpiece of a recreational area on City Island. The city has used the success of the team in attracting people to City Island to make possible the construction of another sports field that is used for minor league football, community soccer, and concerts. A marina, a riverboat, and a food area have also developed on the island, thus making the baseball team only one of several attractions there. Harrisburg is far from the only city to use minor league baseball as a component of a downtown renewal project. The mayor of Toledo, Ohio, claims that building a new stadium for the Toledo Mud Hens "would be helpful for the mental psyche of the community" even if the actual dollar impact is small. (*Toledo Blade*, 24 November 1996) Norfolk, Virginia, opened a waterfront marketplace, a river walkway, a conference center, an opera house, and a maritime museum in addition to building a new riverfront stadium for their minor league baseball team.

Baim (1994, p. 219) warns that owners of professional sports teams who argue that they should receive public subsidies in return for the external benefits provided by their teams are setting themselves up for eminent domain if they should try to move their teams. In an interesting recent example, the city of Cleveland in the fall of 1995 asked for an injunction preventing a planned move of the Browns to Baltimore. Baltimore, which had lost its franchise in 1984 to Indianapolis, had offered to construct a new stadium for the Browns in addition to various other financial advantages. (Illustrating that this type of raiding is nothing new, consider that Glenn Martin moved his airplane firm—later to become Martin-Marietta and now Lockheed-Martin—from Cleveland to Baltimore in 1928 when Baltimore offered a free 50-acre site, as recounted in *Crain's Cleveland Business*, 4 December 1995.) The Browns wanted to leave for Baltimore after the 1995 season, although their lease at Cleveland's Municipal Stadium continued through the end of the 1998 season. Although the team offered to pay the costs of the lease in compensation, the city argued that the financial benefits from the presence of the team did not fully reflect the costs because the intangible benefits to having the team could not be compensated with monetary payments. On 24 November 1995, a judge in Cuyahoga County issued a preliminary injunction preventing the Browns from breaking the lease until after a trial. (Full disclosure: I was an expert witness for the city of Cleveland at the hearing, testifying on the economic impact of the Browns.) A trial was scheduled to begin on 12 February 1996, but the two sides reached a settlement that included approved of the Browns move white Cleveland retained the rights to the team name and colors. As of this writing, the former Browns play in Baltimore under the name of Ravens, the Ravens are treated as a brand-new team for purposes of NFL history, and an NFL team will be playing in a stadium to be constructed in Cleveland by 1999. This case, along with the recent moves of the Rams from Los Angeles to St. Louis and the Raiders from Los Angeles to Oakland (and the prospective move of the Houston Oilers to Nashville), has motivated widespread interest in the economic analysis of the costs and benefits of attracting professional sports teams.

CHAPTER SUMMARY

- Most investment decisions share three characteristics: sunk costs, uncertainty about future costs and benefits, and some flexibility in their timing. As a result, there is value to postponing decisions about whether or not to invest in order to learn more about conditions. Local governments and private developers have attempted to overcome the reluctance of firms to invest by providing various benefits, including tax abatement and rent reductions.

- The impact of new investment on the local economy can be estimated in several ways, including the use of export base theory, location quotients, and input-output analysis. Net employment changes result from four processes: hiring by local firms, contraction by local firms, relocation of firms from other areas, and relocation of location firms to other areas. Relocation of firms is not large relative to total employment, and the rate of contraction does not vary much among cities. The main source of variation in employment growth is the rate at which local firms create new jobs.

- One of the benefits of new investment is the expansion of employment opportunities for local residents. However, merely counting the number of jobs created in a city does not fully account for the true costs and benefits of a local development policy. If the policy takes the form of a subsidy to local firms, then a deadweight loss is possible as factors are allocated to uses valued below their optimum use.

- Local public capital can be modeled as a specific factor of production. While it can help one area to expand its infrastructure, much of its economic growth can come at the expense of other areas rather than representing a net increase to national product.

- Because investments are durable, firms and households are concerned with the long-run prospects for a city as well as the immediate situation. Not all government policies have the same ability to change the long-run situation for a city.

- Constructing stadiums for professional sports teams has been a widespread approach by cities to economic development. There is little evidence that the direct financial benefits from the stadium investments cover their costs to the cities. However, indirect benefits may make the investments worthwhile.

EXCERPT: *BABBITT* (SINCLAIR LEWIS)

This chapter has examined modern efforts to promote cities in hopes of attracting and retaining firms and boosting the local economy. Of course, civic boosterism is nothing new. George Babbit, the title character of the novel by Sinclair Lewis (1922), describes the glories of his hometown of Zenith in the following excerpt (pp. 151–154) and sets a high standard for all future civic boosters.

So! In my clumsy way I have tried to sketch the Real He-man, the fellow with Zip and Bang. And it's because Zenith has so large a proportion of such men that it's the most stable, the greatest of our cities. New York also has its thousands of Real Folks, but New York is cursed with unnumbered foreigners. So are Chicago and San Francisco. Oh, we have a golden roster of cities—Detroit and Cleveland with their renowned factories, Cincinnati with its great machine-tool and soap products. Pittsburg and Birmingham with their steel, Kansas City and Minneapolis and Omaha that open their bountiful gates on the bosom of the ocean-like wheatlands, and countless other magnificent sister-cities, for, by the last census, there were no less than sixty-eight glorious American burgs with a population of over one hundred thousand! And all these cities stand together for power and purity, and against foreign ideas and communism—Atlanta with Hartford, Rochester with Denver, Milwaukee with Indianapolis, Los Angeles with Scranton, Portland, Maine, with Portland, Oregon. A good live wire from Baltimore or Seattle or Duluth is the twin-brother of every like fellow booster from Buffalo or Akron, Fort Worth or Oskaloosa!

But it's here in Zenith, the home for manly men and womanly women and bright kids, that you find the largest proportion of these Regular Guys, and that's what sets it in a class by itself; that's why Zenith will be remembered in history as having set the pace for a civilization that shall endure when the old time-killing ways are gone forever and the day of earnest efficient endeavor shall have dawned all round the world!

I tell you, Zenith and her sister-cities are producing a new type of civilization. There are many resemblances between Zenith and these other burgs, and I'm darn glad of it! The extraordinary, growing, and sane standardization of stores, offices, streets, hotels, clothes, and newspapers throughout the United States shows how strong and enduring a type is ours.

Yes, sir, these other burgs are our true partners in the great game of vital living. But let's not have any mistake about this. I claim that Zenith is the best partner and the fastest-growing partner of the whole caboodle. Every intelligent person knows that Zenith manufactures more condensed milk and evaporated cream, more paper boxes, and more lighting-fixtures, than any other city in the United States, if not the world. But it is not so universally known that we stand second in the manufacture of package-butter, sixth in the giant realm of motors and automobiles, and somewhere about third in cheese, leather findings, tar roofing, breakfast food, and overalls!

Our greatness, however, lies not alone in punchful prosperity but equally in that public spirit, that forward-looking idealism and brotherhood, which has marked Zenith ever since its foundation by the Fathers. We have a right, indeed we have a duty toward our fair city, to announce broadcast the facts about our high schools, characterized by their complete plants and the finest school-ventilating systems in the country, bar none; our magnificent new hotels and banks and the paintings and carved marble in their lobbies; and the Second National Tower, the second highest business building in any inland city in the entire country. When I add that we have an unparalleled number of miles of paved streets, bathrooms, vacuum cleaners, and all the other signs of civilization; that our library and art museum are well supported and housed in convenient and roomy buildings; that our park-system is more than up to par, with its handsome driveways adorned with grass, shrubs, and statuary, then I give but a hint of the all-round unlimited greatness of Zenith!

Source: Excerpt from *Babbitt* by Sinclair Lewis. Copyright © 1922 by Harcourt Brace & Company and renewed 1950 by Sinclair Lewis. Reprinted by permission of Harcourt Brace & Company.

Questions for Review and Discussion

1. Specialization implies that every city should be relatively good at something. Sinclair Lewis describes the highlights of the fictional city of Zenith's economy. Can you identify the strengths of the city in which you live and relate them to the economic theory developed to this point?

2. "Because of the sunk costs of investment and uncertainty about the future, firms are wary of making investments in cities that have experienced difficult economic times. However, if a city offered very large incentives to the firms, then they would be willing to relocate." Do you agree or disagree? Explain.

3. Suppose a mayor told you, "I like my city's current size and industrial makeup. I'd like to keep things the way they are." If the mayor asked you for advice on how to maintain the status quo, what would you suggest?

4. "If I were the mayor, I'd make all professional sports teams pay their own way rather than caving in to their demands." Do you agree or disagree? Explain.

5. Suppose that you are the benevolent dictator of your metropolitan area. If you were given $100 million to spend on economic development, how would you allocate it?

6. In November 1996, the Environmental Protection Agency (EPA) announced that it would be imposing stricter air quality standards on particulate matter (soot) and chemicals that cause smog. The main impact of this change is expected to fall on cities in the northeastern and midwestern parts of the country. Why? How will business location decisions be affected? Should the EPA take this uneven geographical impact into account when it passes regulations? Should those areas that are affected be compensated?

PART

III

Intrametropolitan Analysis

CHAPTER

9

Clusters and Urban Form: Business Districts, Suburbs, and "Edge Cities"

I n the previous four chapters, we have considered an urban area as a monolithic economy and analyzed its interaction with other urban areas. In the following five chapters, we will turn to an analysis of the structure of a single urban area. In this chapter we will develop two theories of intrametropolitan location. The first is the "monocentric city model," a model that has enjoyed great prominence in urban economic analysis over the past thirty years. The second is a model of neighborhoods, business parks, and industrial clusters as small open economies that trade with each other. This second model, the same model we have been using to analyze intermetropolitan interactions, is now applied to intrametropolitan behavior. We will see that the monocentric city model is a special case of the small open economy model.

WHAT DO METROPOLITAN AREAS LOOK LIKE?

One of the best ways to begin the study of intrametropolitan location is by flying over a city. You can spot the downtown as a cluster of tall buildings, with lesser office buildings sloping away from it. Sometimes tall buildings cluster outside the historic downtown. Here is a suburb densely packed with townhouses and apartments; there, a shopping mall surrounded by cul-de-sac neighborhoods of large executive homes.

The urban form may be characterized in two basic ways. First is the *monocentric city*, in which there is a single center (the central business district, or CBD), around which the rest of the metropolitan area revolves. Second is the *polycentric city*, in which several centers interact with each other. These centers typically include the CBD as well as the "edge cities," or "suburban downtowns," documented by Garreau and others.

Recalling our picture of the city, we can summarize the monocentric city using a single graph, shown as Figure 9.1. The horizontal axis on the graph indicates distance from the CBD, while the vertical axis represents the height of buildings at various distances. As we will see when we develop the monocentric city model, the graph also

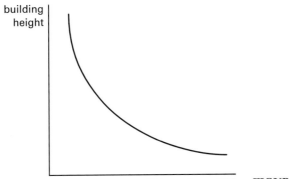

distance from *CBD*   **FIGURE 9.1** Monocentric City

shows the way that the capital-land ratio and the land rent vary with distance from the CBD. Figure 9.1 looks out along only one radius from the CBD, but this is acceptable if the city is symmetric in all directions. (Jackson [1979] illustrates how the actual rent gradient can be estimated in the presence of asymmetries such as topological irregularities or transportation routes.) The monocentric city model in its current form dates to the middle 1960s. Excellent primary sources are Alonso (1964), Mills (1967) and Muth (1969).

The basic idea of the monocentric city model is the tradeoff between accessibility and land cost. You can see this tradeoff yourself if you attend a sporting event or major concert at a city stadium. Parking at fairly remote locations is the least expensive, while as you get closer to the stadium, the parking rates increase. People are paying more because they do not have to walk as far to and from the stadium. In 1996, for example, you could observe parking fees ranging from $3 to $15 as you moved down Carnegie Avenue in Cleveland towards Jacobs Field, home of the Cleveland Indians. The $15 lot was immediately across the street from the stadium, while the $3 lot was about 15 blocks distant. Of course, on days when there are no baseball games, the accessibility to the stadium is worth much less, and the parking fees are reduced accordingly.

A slightly more complicated picture is needed for the polycentric city. The city is not symmetric, almost by definition. Thus, the analog to Figure 9.1 will vary depending on the radius considered. Figure 9.2 shows one perspective, looking out along a radius from the CBD toward a suburban center. The peak represents the suburban center, possibly located on a beltway or at the intersection of two major highways. Of course, as you move away from the suburban center, the picture looks much like it did in Figure 9.1. This makes it reasonable to explore the monocentric city in some detail, as the economic analysis of the area around each center in a polycentric city should be similar to that in a monocentric city.

Suburbanization: A Historical Perspective

> Our property seems to me the most beautiful in the world. It is so close to Babylon that we enjoy all the advantages of the city, and yet when we come home we are away from all the noise and dust.[*]

---
[*]From Letter to King of Persia, 539 B.C. (quoted in Jackson, 1985, p. 12).

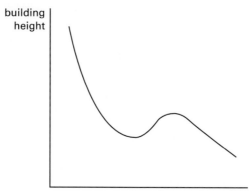

distance from *CBD*   **FIGURE 9.2** Polycentric City

It is by now a cliché that the central cities and central business districts play a declining role in United States metropolitan areas while suburbs play an increasing role. What is less well known is that this process is not a phenomenon of the recent past but has been occurring throughout the Industrial Revolution. Kenneth Jackson, in *Crabgrass Frontier: The Suburbanization of the United States* (1985, p. 20) calls the period from 1815 to 1875 "the most fundamental realignment of urban structure in the 4,500-year past of cities on this planet." He traces the ascendance of the suburb and the decline of the central city to the innovations in transportation of the time, including the steam ferry and various intra-urban wheeled transit vehicles (omnibus, horsecar, cable car, and elevated railroad).

The modern suburbanized U.S. metropolitan area is epitomized by Los Angeles, especially in its dependence on automobiles and freeways. Jackson (1985, p. 250) argues, though, that the general outline of the Los Angeles metropolitan area was determined well before the advent of the freeway. In the 1920s, the availability of cheap land promoted the construction of detached homes at a far greater rate than was common in other metropolitan areas at the time. The dispersed location of the oil fields and refineries in the Los Angeles area also promoted several isolated industrial centers, including Fullerton and Whittier. These dispersed centers, ironically, were provided a connection and given unity by the largest electric interurban railway in the world.

One difference between the earlier waves of suburbanization and the process seen since 1945 is that many cities are unable to annex their growing suburbs. New York, for example, added its early suburbs such as Brooklyn and Queens to its boundaries in the late 1800s, but suburbs in much of the rest of Long Island and up the Hudson River in Westchester County incorporated and preserved their independence. Like that of Los Angeles, the expansion of New York during the late 1800s and early 1900s was stimulated by the development of rapid transit, and the dispersed pattern of development led in turn to further transit construction. The population of Manhattan peaked in 1910 and then declined, while the total population of New York City continued to increase during the period between 1910 and 1940 (Hood 1993, pp. 179, 207).

Tables 9.1a and 9.1b show the population figures in the 1900s of two cities, Cleveland and Memphis, and the counties in which they are located. The dominant

TABLE 9.1a   Relative Population of Cleveland and Cuyahoga County

Year	Cuyahoga County Population	Cleveland Population	City Population/ County Population
1910	637,425	560,663	88.0%
1920	943,495	796,841	84.5%
1930	1,201,455	900,429	74.9%
1940	1,217,250	878,336	72.2%
1950	1,389,532	914,808	65.8%
1960	1,647,895	876,050	53.2%
1970	1,720,835	750,879	43.6%
1980	1,498,400	573,822	38.3%
1990	1,412,140	505,616	35.8%

Source: Census of Population and Housing.

status of Cleveland within its county has been eroding for a long time. In fact, Jackson (1985, p. 316) provides information that shows Cuyahoga County growing faster than the city of Cleveland as early as the 1840s. Memphis displays a contrast, since the city's population peaked in 1970, both in absolute terms and as a fraction of the county's; but it has fallen since that time. The situation in these cities is representative of the experience of most cities in the United States. For example, the population in the urban core of Philadelphia peaked during the 1820s (Jackson 1985, p. 308). The main difference between the post–WW II period and earlier periods was the dramatic size of the decentralization. Because of the increased extent of urbanization in the United States by the middle of the twentieth century, movements within metropolitan areas were that much more noticeable. Although Philadelphia had been decentralizing by some measures since the 1820s, Summers and Luce (1986, p. 136) provide data that show a large decrease in Philadelphia relative to its PMSA during the period from 1950 to 1980. During those 30 years, the city's share of PMSA population fell

TABLE 9.1b   Relative Population of Memphis and Shelby County

Year	Shelby County Population	Memphis Population	City Population/ County Population
1910	191,439	131,105	68.5%
1920	223,216	162,351	72.7%
1930	306,482	253,143	82.6%
1940	358,250	292,942	81.8%
1950	482,393	396,000	82.1%
1960	627,019	497,524	79.3%
1970	722,111	657,007	91.0%
1980	777,113	646,356	83.2%
1990	826,330	610,337	73.9%

Source: Census of Population and Housing.

from 56 percent to 36 percent, and its share of employment fell from 68 percent to 39 percent. Philadelphia was not alone in this change. Jackson (1985) shows that in 1980 14 of the 15 largest metropolitan areas in the United States had a majority of their populations in the suburbs. The one exception was Houston, a city that continued to engage in large-scale annexation of land even during the 1980s.

Mieszkowski and Mills (1993) present evidence that suburbanization has been a long-running development not only in the United States but also around the world. They suggest two broad classes of explanation for this phenomenon. The first, "natural evolution," emphasizes changes in transportation technology and the construction of new housing at the edges of urban areas. The second, "flight from blight," emphasizes the migration of high-income households to avoid the fiscal and social problems of central cities. The two theories have opposite implications for government policy, in that the first suggests a laissez-faire approach and the second a more interventionist strategy. Unfortunately, it is difficult to distinguish between them in practice. For example, both theories predict that richer people will move from the central city toward more remote suburbs.

Mills (1972) presents evidence consistent with the natural evolution theory. He finds that the density gradient for five U.S. cities became progressively flatter during the period from 1880 to 1940. Thus, suburbs have been gradually and consistently becoming more important. Further, he finds no evidence that the process speeded up after 1945, when central city problems got worse.

Adams et al. (1996) bring up the important point that there is intermetropolitan migration in addition to the intrametropolitan migration that both the flight from blight and natural evolution descriptions of suburbanization emphasize. They present evidence that much of the population increase in suburbs is the result of intermetropolitan migration rather than movement from the central city. They also find that higher levels of distress in the central city have been associated with higher levels of measured suburbanization. This last finding, though, suffers from the criticism that less-distressed central cities tend to be in the South and West, where central cities also have had the ability to annex much of the surrounding area, so that a large part of what in the Northeast and Midwest would be suburbs is contained within the central city.

Recall that the economic definition of a city hinges on density of development. Therefore, if the density of the city is declining, and the density of the suburb is increasing, at some point either the city ceases to be a city or the suburb becomes a city. It is this latter possibility that we now turn our attention to.

When Is a Suburb a "Center"?

The difference between the polycentric model and the monocentric model is relatively subtle. The basic question of identifying a center involves identifying concentrations of economic activity. But at what point is a concentration of economic activity large enough to merit a transition from one description of the city to another? The notion of suburban center has been broadly discussed for at least 15 years under a variety of names, including edge city, suburban downtown, and so on. Some of these subcenters have large concentrations of employment, in some cases exceeding those in the traditional CBD. Consider one measure of economic activity, the number of cars traveling past a point during the day. Table 9.2 illustrates the ten busiest intersections in Cleveland in 1995. (The locations of these intersections is shown in the map of Cuyahoga County in chapter 1.) Only one of these intersections is found in the historic central business district, and it is the third busiest in the county. Six of the top ten intersections are found in the Beachwood-Solon edge city to the east of Cleveland, including the busiest intersection in the county. Another one is in Mayfield Heights, near Beachwood. The other two of the top ten, including the second busiest, are found in the University Circle area of the city of Cleveland, about five miles east of downtown, home of (among other things) the Cleveland Clinic, University Hospitals, and Case Western Reserve University.

Genevieve Giuliano and Kenneth Small (1991) illustrate the size and density of employment in these subcenters relative to the CBD in Los Angeles. Their results are shown in Table 9.3. Before looking at the centers in detail, it is important to note that only about 1.5 million of a total regional employment of 4.7 million is identified as being within centers. These centers are peaks in employment density, not the only locuses of employment. The average density of employment outside the centers is 1.4 workers per acre, and the employment-population ratio is 0.32, so there is a distinct difference between most of the region and the centers.

Downtown Los Angeles has a total employment of 469,000, an employment density of 36.0 workers per acre, and 1.47 jobs per resident. Total employment in the subcenters is 922,000, almost double the employment in the Los Angeles CBD. Employment density in the subcenters averages 17.7 workers per acre, only half that in the CBD. However, the subcenters average 1.58 jobs per resident, a greater concentration of business relative to residential use than in the CBD. This last figure is especially high around the airports, but not only there, as the 4.97 jobs per resident figure in Fullerton indicates. It is important to emphasize the difference between economic boundaries and political boundaries—many of the centers identified in Los Angeles are within the city limits, but they are nevertheless identifiable as distinct economic units. The other main finding of Giuliano and Small is that the subcenters can be distinguished in terms of their economic specializations. They identify five types of cen-

TABLE 9.2 Most-Traveled Intersections in Cuyahoga County, Ohio: 1995

Intersection	24-hour Volume	Location
Chagrin Blvd. and Richmond Rd.	77,399	Beachwood
Carnegie Ave. and MLK Blvd.	73,360	University Circle
Carnegie Ave. and Ontario St.	68,466	Cleveland CBD
I-271 ramp west and Chagrin Blvd.	68,243	Beachwood
Euclid Ave. and MLK Blvd.	67,767	University Circle
Chagrin Blvd. and Warrensville Rd.	63,193	Beachwood
Solon Rd. and SOM Center Rd.	60,045	Solon
Mayfield Rd. and SOM Center Rd.	59,310	Mayfield Heights
Chagrin Blvd. and Park East	58,069	Beachwood
Chagrin Blvd. and I-271 ramp east	57,795	Beachwood

Source: Crain's Cleveland Business 3 July 1995.

TABLE 9.3 Employment Centers in the Los Angeles Area*

Rank	Center Name	Employment (thousands)	Employment Density (per acre)	Employment- Population Ratio	Distance from CBD (miles)
1	Los Angeles CBD	469.0	36.0	1.47	0.1
2	West Los Angeles	176.2	25.5	1.37	15.8
3	Santa Monica	65.1	16.9	1.11	16.7
4	Hollywood	64.2	21.4	0.73	7.3
5	LA Airport	59.1	16.7	4.32	18.8
6	Orange Cty Airport	47.7	16.1	1589.87	40.7
7	Glendale	43.0	15.5	1.07	12.3
8	Commerce	41.9	17.0	4.05	9.8
9	Vernon	39.2	33.2	2.42	4.9
10	San Pedro	37.6	15.7	2.74	23.3
11	Santa Ana	37.5	17.3	1.51	32.9
12	Inglewood	36.5	14.6	1.24	14.7
13	Pasadena	35.9	25.3	1.73	12.1
14	Long Beach Airport	33.2	15.5	3684.78	23.3
15	Marina Del Rey	31.7	11.4	1.28	14.0
16	Long Beach	29.7	18.0	0.84	25.3
17	Van Nuys Airport	27.8	12.6	2.04	22.1
18	Burbank Airport	26.2	28.4	10.86	16.5
19	Hawthorne	17.9	12.4	0.74	13.5
20	Canoga Park	17.2	11.2	1.21	27.4
21	Lawndale	16.9	17.1	1.36	20.5
22	East Los Angeles	16.3	37.3	2.30	6.8
23	Fullerton / Anaheim	16.1	11.4	4.97	27.3
24	Downey	14.6	17.3	2.38	14.8
25	Riverside	14.2	21.4	3.76	56.9
26	Santa Ana South	14.1	12.2	1.76	37.4
27	Sherman Oaks	13.3	11.9	1.04	18.6
28	Burbank SW	12.7	18.0	1.92	14.1
29	Orange / Gar. Grv.	10.5	11.3	1.06	30.2
30	Gar. Grv. / Stanton	10.1	12.9	5.60	26.6
31	Oxnard	8.3	10.3	0.98	63.0
32	San Bernardino	7.3	22.9	7.89	63.6
	Total	1,490.9	21.0	1.55	
	Total outside "core"	922.2	17.7	1.58	

*The "core" comprises the top four clusters. Data from Giuliano and Small (1991, Table 1, p. 168)

ter: specialized manufacturing (rank numbers 14, 18, 19, 21, 23, 24, 26), mixed industrial (5, 6, 8, 9, 10, 12, 15, 17, 30), mixed service (1, 3, 7, 11, 13, 16, 20, 25, 27, 31, 32), specialized entertainment (4, 28), and specialized service (2, 22, 29).

The chapter by Hartshorn and Muller in Mills and MacDonald (eds., 1991), defines a "suburban downtown" as an area containing a regional shopping center of at least 1 million square feet, at least three high-rise office buildings with a Fortune 100 regional or national headquarters, at least 5 million square feet of office space (as compared to 10.4 million in Miami's CBD, 11.6 million in San Diego's CBD, or 12.7 million in Baltimore's CBD), at least two major hotels with 400 rooms each, and at least 50,000 people employed in the area.

Joel Garreau's book *Edge City* (1991) defines an "edge city" as an area containing at least 5 million square feet of office space and at least 600,000 square feet of retail space, having a daytime employment greater than the resident population, having a perception as a destination for mixed use (a name), and having been overwhelmingly rural or residential 30 years ago.

Any definition of suburban downtown or edge city is arbitrary. In fact, recall from chapter 1 that even defining a city is rather arbitrary, given that the definition of a city is an area of relatively dense economic activity. The various definitions can provide guidance in identifying and analyzing similar phenomena, but it should always be kept in mind that they are chosen only for their usefulness.

The transition from residential suburb to edge city should happen with incredible speed rather than gradually. The key to understanding this transition is found in a set of "rules of thumb" for developers that Garreau chronicles in a chapter he calls "The Laws." One of the laws is the "one-story climb law," which states that the maximum number of flights of stairs that Americans will use is one. The sixth corollary to the one-story climb law states that residential structures must either be fewer than three stories (in order to build them without elevators) or high-rise. Because the fixed costs of accommodating an elevator are quite high, it does not make sense to build, say, a five-story residential site. In other words, when you pass a certain threshold, you need to build a lot bigger in order to be profitable. To put it in economic terms, there are economies of scale beyond a certain threshold of residential density. This suggests that there will be a discontinuity in the observed density of development; an area is likely to grow slowly until the "three-story" level is reached and then increase rapidly in density if zoning rules allow. Hence, the swift transition that Garreau records, in which farms become office buildings almost overnight, is to be expected given this structure of costs.

We have already seen an example of this type of transition in the section of chapter 5 on "Increasing Returns to Scale and Gains from Trade." Recall the situation in which there were fixed costs in producing a good. If a small change occurred in prices or preferences so that the good became worth producing, then its production began at a fairly high level. In other words, there was a rapid change in the use of resources, exactly as described above.

The discussion in chapter 8 of "Industrial Parks and Firm Relocation" should also be recalled at this point. There the idea that there was a "critical mass" at which a metropolitan area would become viable was introduced in the context of local government economic development policy. Here we see an intrametropolitan area application of that idea.

MONOCENTRIC CITY MODEL

The unifying intellectual concept for 30 years in urban economics has been the monocentric city model. The continuing decline of the CBD and the rise of the edge city have made this framework less appropriate to analyzing urban form than it once was. Nevertheless, there is much insight to be gained from it, and we will develop it here. The monocentric model is a special case of the polycentric model of small open economies that we will use for most of our analysis. In a monocentric city model, only the CBD specializes in business services, while all other areas specialize in residential services.

The monocentric city can be thought of as an artifact of a particular set of technologies. A streetcar that made rapid radial transit possible, combined with the elevator and steel frame construction that made high-rise building possible, together yield a great value to the place where all the radii meet. For an extreme example of the economic implications, consider that the one-half-square-mile Loop in downtown Chicago represented almost 40 percent of the assessed land value in the entire 211-square-mile city in 1910. (Jackson 1985, p. 114)

Classical Land Rent

The monocentric city model is a model of land use and land rent within a metropolitan area. It is useful, then, to begin with the simplest model of land rent. Interestingly, this theory, like the idea of comparative advantage and the model of trade based on specific factors of production, dates to David Ricardo. Ricardo can thus stake a real claim to being the true father of urban economics.

Consider the following simple model. Many identical price-taking firms are earning zero economic profits in equilibrium (perfect competition). Land is sold to the highest bidder. In order to sell its output, a firm must ship its product through a transport node located at the CBD. Aside from the transport node, all land is identical. A unit of output has a monetary weight of t, so that total transport costs equal tu, where u is the distance from the firm to the CBD. If we denote p as the output price, q as the amount of output, w as nonland costs per unit, $\Pi(u)$ as profit earned if the firm locates at a distance u from the CBD, and $R(u)$ as land rent at a distance u from the CBD, we can write the firm's problem as follows: maximize $\Pi(u)$ = revenue – costs = $pq - wq - R(u) - tqu$. Since profits equal zero, we can rewrite this condition as $R(u) = pq - wq - tqu$. Note that the first two components of the right-hand side do not depend on u. Combining them and denoting them as A, we obtain the *bid-rent curve* for a representative firm. This curve, as its name suggests, shows the amount of rent that a firm is willing to bid for a particular piece of land.

$$R(u) = A - tqu$$

The bid-rent curve for a typical firm is graphed in Figure 9.3.

This simple model produces two immediate results. First, land rent is higher at the CBD than at more remote locations. Second, the reason for this higher land rent is the savings in transport costs obtained by locating closer to the CBD.

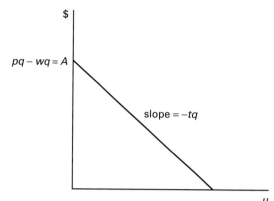

$pq - wq = A$

slope $= -tq$

u **FIGURE 9.3** Bid-Rent Curve

If all firms are identical, the actual land-rent curve will be identical to the bid-rent curve shown above. Suppose, though, there are several sectors (defined as a firm or set of firms with identical bid-rent curves). In this case, the land rent at any given distance will be the maximum (the "outer envelope") of the bid-rents of the various sectors.

For example, suppose that there are two sectors, offices and manufacturing, with bid-rent curves as shown in Figure 9.4. The bid-rent curve for offices is steeper than that for manufacturing, allowing office uses to outbid manufacturing uses at distances less than u_0, and manufacturing to outbid offices beyond u_0.

The pattern of land use implied by Figure 9.4 is one where zones of specialized activity lie at various distances from the CBD. If the city is symmetric, so that every radius looks just like Figure 9.4, the city will consist of concentric rings, each with a different activity. So, for example, there will be a ring of office buildings and, outside that, a ring of factories, followed by a ring of high-density housing and, last of all, a ring of low-density housing. This description of a city is precisely that of Manchester in Friedrich Engels's 1844 book, *The Condition of the Working Class in England.* Engels, coauthor four years later of *The Communist Manifesto*, describes the city (pp. 57–58) as follows:

FIGURE 9.4 Land-Rent Curve with Several Sectors

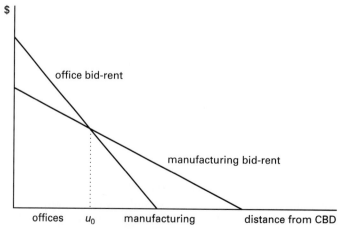

office bid-rent

manufacturing bid-rent

offices u_0 manufacturing   distance from CBD

Manchester contains, at its heart a rather extended commercial district, consisting almost wholly of offices and warehouses. With the exception of this commercial district, all Manchester proper is unmixed working-people's quarters, stretching like a girdle around the commercial district. Outside, beyond this girdle, lives the upper and middle bourgeoisie. And the finest part of the arrangement is this, that the members of this money aristocracy can take the shortest road through the middle of all the laboring districts to their places of business, without ever seeing that they are in the midst of the grimy misery that lurks to the right and the left.

—FRIEDRICH ENGELS

Fishman (1987, p. 75) quotes a visitor's guide to Manchester, published in 1857, that confirms—albeit with a positive tone rather than the negative tone adopted by Engels—this description.

Factor Substitution and the Rent Gradient

In the classical model of production, a producer has no opportunity to substitute one factor of production for another. The more expensive land closer to the CBD would provide an incentive for a producer locating closer to the CBD to substitute other inputs for land. We can use the isocost-isoquant diagram introduced earlier to consider the implications of factor substitution for bid-rent curves and therefore for the land-rent curve. The main difference is that the bid-rent curve for each sector will now be nonlinear rather than linear because of the ability to substitute capital for land.

Recall that factor market equilibrium is $MRP_{factor} = p_{factor}$. Since we now have to take transport cost into account, define $MR(u) = p - tu$ for each distance u. Then profit maximization implies that the MRP (marginal revenue multiplied by marginal product) at each distance is equal to the factor price. For example, $MRP_{land}(u) = MP_{land}(u)MR(u) = MP_{land}(u) \times (p - tu) = R(u)$. If $MP_{land}(u)$ is constant, then $R(u)$ is once again a straight line.

Why isn't $MP_{land}(u)$ constant? Factor substitution. Consider a firm that moves closer to the CBD. If we let r represent the cost of K, and C the total production cost, then the isocost in the original location can be written $C = rK + R(u)L$, with a slope of $-R(u)/r$. At the new location, the isocost is $C' = rK' + R'(u)L'$, where $R'(u) > R(u)$ due to the savings in transport costs. If the cost of capital is equal at all locations, then the slope of the isocost is steeper closer to the center of the city. Thus, the firm will choose to substitute capital for land at its new location, as shown below in Figure 9.5. It is straightforward to show that $MP_{land}(u)$ is higher at the new location. We know that $-R(u)/r = -MP_{land}/MP_K$, and since the slope is steeper closer to the CBD, either MP_{land} is higher or MP_K is lower. It must be the case, though, that MP_K is constant with respect to distance from the CBD, since r is constant.

At the location closer to the CBD, the firm chooses a more capital-intensive land use (a higher K/Land ratio). This is the second stylized fact that the model needed to explain. Further, a higher capital-to-land ratio represents a taller building, thus completing the model.

One observation that can be gleaned from Figure 9.5 might be troubling. The isocost line at the new location has a larger K intercept than the isocost line at the old location. But since the price of K stays fixed, this implies that total production costs at the new location are higher. Since output (hence revenue) is the same, this would

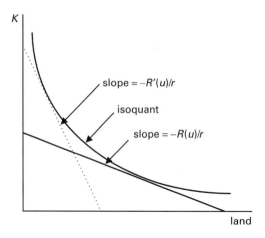

slope = −R′(u)/r

isoquant

slope = −R(u)/r

land

FIGURE 9.5 Factor Substitution

seem to contradict profit maximization. The puzzle is resolved by recalling that the closer location saves on transport costs. In fact, the difference between the two *K* intercepts is exactly the transport cost savings in equilibrium.

The analysis in Figure 9.5 can readily be translated into bid-rent terms. As a firm moves closer to the CBD, two factors change. First, transport costs fall, as they did before, increasing the amount the firm is willing to pay for land. Second, the firm substitutes capital for land, enabling it to produce the same output on less land, or in other words, more output per unit of land. The additional congestion caused by the increased density of activity can reduce profits or increase costs, but I have drawn the curve assuming that the productivity differences outweigh these negative agglomeration effects. If firms at each distance are to earn the same profits, then it must be the case that the firms must pay more for the land on which they are able to produce higher output. This second consideration implies that the land increases in value faster than the reduction in transportation costs. Because the change in transportation costs was linear, the change is now faster than linear and becomes nonlinear. The bid-rent curve for a single sector is shown in Figure 9.6. The diagram illustrates the two components of land rent—accessibility to the CBD and increased productivity. The

FIGURE 9.6 Bid-Rent Curve with Factor Substitution

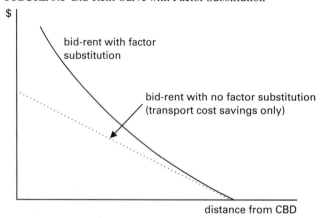

bid-rent with factor substitution

bid-rent with no factor substitution (transport cost savings only)

distance from CBD

difference between the bid-rent with no factor substitution and the bid-rent with factor substitution reflects the productivity advantage from more capital-intensive production. The land-rent curve for the city is found, as before, by allocating land to the highest bidder.

Complications: Building Height and Land Values at the Edge of the City

The basic monocentric city model introduced above has two predictions that are fairly easy to test. The first prediction is that building height should decline as we move away from the center. The second prediction is that land value at the edge of the urban area should equal that outside the urban area. If land outside the urban area is used for agriculture, then the land value at the edge of the urban area should be equal to (or slightly greater than) its value if it were to be used for agriculture. Unfortunately, both of these predictions are not very accurate. We often find relatively tall buildings away from the CBD. Even if we accept the possibility of edge cities, we can find tall buildings away from these centers of economic activity. As for the second prediction, there is usually a large difference between the value of land at the edge of the urban area and the agricultural value of the land. Even if we take into consideration the cost of preparing the land for urban use, the difference remains. We will now examine each of these issues in turn.

The basic monocentric city model, even if it acknowledges the existence of several sectors (manufacturing, office, etc.), retains the assumption that there is homogeneity in the production process used in each sector. In other words, all firms are assumed to be willing to trade off land rents and building height at the same rate. But some types of activity are more easily carried out than others in tall buildings. Consider a convention hotel, for example. It provides the services of rooms to its guests, but it also provides restaurants and meeting rooms. Is it easier to provide these services in a ten-story building or a two-story building? The answer will depend on the relative cost of vertical and horizontal transport. Vertical transport involves elevators. Horizontal transport involves either walking or vehicles. Driving from your hotel room to a meeting room is higher-cost transport than walking down the hall and riding the elevator. Thus, a hotel might reasonably build vertically even if land rents are relatively low. Hospitals and housing facilities for the elderly provide similar types of services. Arthur Sullivan (1991) provides evidence that intrabuilding transport costs can explain much of the otherwise anomalous presence of relatively tall buildings in relative isolation on relatively inexpensive land. For example, he finds that Sacramento, California, has 11 isolated tall buildings (at least six stories high and at least three times taller than surrounding buildings). Two of these buildings are hotels, three are hospitals, five are retirement homes, and one is a state government building. Many office buildings house a variety of firms, so intrabuilding transport costs are not particularly important. If a building is devoted to the activities of one firm (in this case the state government), then the ease with which people can move within the building can be important, just as it is for hotels.

Now consider the case of land values at the edge of the city. In the basic monocentric city model, land values have two components—opportunity cost in nonurban (agricultural) use and accessibility to the CBD. Dennis Capozza and Robert Helsley

(1989) show that finished lots (six per acre) at the edge of Vancouver sold in 1986 for about \$40,000 each and required about \$15,000 in servicing and conversion costs from agricultural use. This implies a land value of about \$150,000 per acre. Agricultural land value, though, was less than \$5,000 per acre. How to explain this gap? Their answer was to focus on the durability of capital combined with expected growth of the urban area. If the capital improvements to a piece of land are durable, then the value of the land reflects not only the current use but also the future uses. If the urban area is growing, the land will be more valuable in the future. Thus, the current value reflects the land market's judgment on the future prospects for the city as well as the current activities. Capozza and Helsley add the cost of converting land to urban use and the expected future growth in land rents to the agricultural land value and accessibility value in the basic monocentric city model. These considerations are especially important in explaining why cities of roughly equal current size have drastically different land values. Even more difficult to explain with the monocentric city model is why a smaller city could have higher land values than a larger city. The answer is that they are expected to grow at different rates.

The model of Capozza and Helsley can be viewed as a formalization of analysis that dates at least to the famous book by Henry George (1880), *Progress and Poverty*. Discussing land rents at the edge of a growing city, George (p. 257) presents a case very similar to that of Capozza and Helsley: "But when we reach the limits of the growing city—the actual margin of building, which corresponds to the margin of cultivation in agriculture—we shall not find the land purchasable at its value for agricultural purposes, as it would be were rent determined simply by present requirements; but we shall find that for a long distance beyond the city, land bears a speculative value, based upon the belief that it will be required in the future for urban purposes, and that to reach the point at which land can be purchased at a price not based upon urban rent, we must go very far beyond the actual margin of urban use."

Household Location

All the discussion to this point has focused on the location decisions of firms. However, households face a similar type of decision. Consider a household that has one worker who works in the CBD. The household must choose a distance from the CBD, u, to live; an amount of housing to consume, $h(u)$; and an amount of all other goods to consume, $x(u)$. The household earns a wage, w, and incurs commuting costs that vary linearly with the commuting distance, tu. The commuting costs include both the time and money cost of the commute. (We will investigate the commuting decision in detail in chapter 15.) The price of housing at a distance u is $p_h(u)$, and the price of all other goods is p_x. We will assume that the price of all other goods does not vary with location, so that we can write it as p_x, that is, it does not vary with distance to the CBD.

The household's budget constraint can be written as

$$p_x x(u) + p_h(u)h(u) = w - tu \qquad \textbf{(1)}$$

As the household moves further from the CBD, the commuting costs increase, which lowers the x intercept. If all households are identical, then in equilibrium they must achieve equal utility, so the price of housing must fall as we move away from the

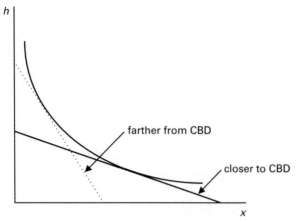

FIGURE 9.7 Household Location

CBD. This is graphed in Figure 9.7. When a household chooses a location, it chooses the position and slope of the budget constraint.

Recall that a price change has two effects on demand: the substitution effect and the income effect. The substitution effect involves movement along an indifference curve, as shown in Figure 9.7. The income effect involves movement from one indifference curve to the other. Where is the income effect? The answer is that the "extra income" gained from lower housing prices is used to pay the "extra commuting costs" associated with the more remote location. As we saw with the bid-rent function for firms, households too are trading off transportation costs and land prices.

Inspecting Figure 9.7, we see that the household closer to the CBD consumes less housing than the household farther from the CBD. This is an immediate result of the fact that change in demand is strictly a substitution effect.

Consider the following alternative way of deriving the land rent at a location. If a household is going to be indifferent about locating at varying distances from the CBD, then the sum of housing and commuting costs must be constant with respect to distance from the CBD. As the household moves away from the CBD, transportation costs increase, reducing the amount the household is willing to pay for the house. This is diagrammed below in Figure 9.8.

Now, suppose a profit-maximizing housing developer is considering what density of housing to construct. The choice of density is perhaps most clear in the case of

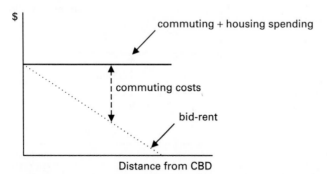

FIGURE 9.8 Bid-Rent Curve for Household

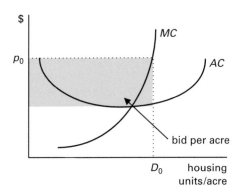

FIGURE 9.9 Bid-Rent for Housing Developer

choosing the number of units to build in an apartment building on a given size lot, but also applies to the case of detached housing. If the housing developer operates in a perfectly competitive market, then the profit-maximizing choice is to produce the density of housing at which the price equals marginal cost. Separate land rents from all other costs (including a normal rate of return). Then the profit calculated at the profit-maximizing density equals the amount the developer is willing to bid for land. This situation is illustrated in Figure 9.9. As the price of housing increases, the density of development increases, as does the amount the developer is willing to bid.

The developer's problem and the household's problem can be combined in one diagram through the simple expedient of "reversing" Figure 9.9. In Figure 9.10, we see the simple relationship predicted among proximity to the CBD, commuting costs, housing prices, site rents, and housing density. The tradeoff between commuting costs and housing costs that is the main feature of the monocentric city model is clearly illustrated in Figure 9.10.

The following numerical example will help clarify Figure 9.10 even further. Suppose the households are identical and are willing to pay $800 per month in combined commuting and housing spending. The round-trip cost per month of commuting is $40 per mile. Each household wants to consume 1100 ft^2 of housing. This housing can be produced at a marginal cost per unit (not including land) of $200 if the density is less than or equal to 4 units per acre, $300 if the density is greater than 4 but less than or equal to 10 units per acre, and $600 if the density is greater than 10 units per acre and

FIGURE 9.10 Housing Density and Land Rent in the Monocentric City Model

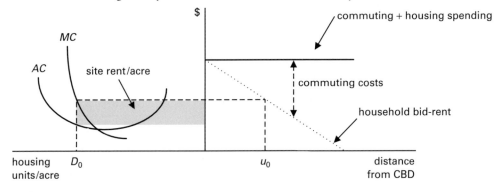

less than 30 units per acre (the maximum allowed by the city's zoning regulation). This marginal cost curve increases with density, as does that in Figure 9.10, but this one does so by steps rather than smoothly and continuously. We will assume that there are no fixed costs, so that average cost equals marginal cost. What will the equilibrium rent and density be as you move away from the CBD?

Begin with housing located just at the CBD. Commuting costs are zero, so households are willing to spend $800 per month on rent. The developer can build 4 units per acre at a marginal cost of $200 per unit. This would yield $600 ($800 – $200) per unit to pay for land, or a total of $2,400 per acre bid-rent. If the developer instead built at a density of 10 units per acre, the bid could be $5,000, since 10 units would generate $500 each after paying nonland costs. If the developer built at a density of 30 units per acre, then the bid would increase to $6,000 per acre. Clearly, the winning bid close to the CBD will be the one with the highest density of housing units.

Now consider a location 4 miles from the CBD. Households still pay a total of $800, but now $160 of that has to go for commuting costs, leaving only $640 for rent. At a density of 4 units per acre, a developer would be able to bid $1,760 (calculated as $4x (640 – 200)$); at a density of 10 units per acre, the bid would increase to $3,400; at a density of 30 units per acre, the bid is only $1,200. At a distance of 4 miles from the CBD, the housing density will be lower than at the CBD.

Finally, as you move even farther from the CBD, low-density housing is the dominant choice. For example, consider the situation 12 miles from the CBD, so that the rent paid by the household is $320 per month. At a density of 4 units per acre, the developer can bid $480 per acre. A density of 10 units per acre yields a bid of only $200 per acre, while someone developing at a density of 30 units per acre would actually have to be paid $8,400 per acre to proceed.

The above examples show the density chosen at just three locations. You can use bid-rent analysis to find the distances at which the density changes. Note that it was never optimal to build at a density other than 4, 10, or 30 units per acre, the upper bounds of the marginal cost ranges. If you graph density as a function of distance from the CBD, you will see it increase in large jumps. This result, although an artifact of the specific numbers used in the example, is suggestive of the way density can suddenly increase in response to a small change in economic conditions. We turn to formal analysis of changes using comparative statics in the next section.

Comparative Statics: Changing Commuting Costs, Changing Income

Before leaving the monocentric city model, it is interesting to use it to analyze the effects of changes in the economic environment. In particular, let us consider a change in the unit cost of commuting. After that, we will examine the predicted effects of an increase in household income.

A reduction in unit commuting costs is straightforward to analyze using Figure 9.10. The amount the household is willing to pay goes up at each distance from the CBD, leading to an increase in housing density and land rents at each point within the CBD. Note that the distance households are willing to commute increases (assuming positive land rents) in equilibrium, increasing the radius of the city. Of course, if the radius increases, the area available for settlement increases even faster (recall that the area of a circle is Πr^2). Thus, even a seemingly small change in the radius of a mono-centric city model can imply large changes in population and housing density in the city, along with large absolute increases in population. The most dramatic example of this increase is the revolutionary change chronicled by Warner (1962). He shows how concentrated residential development in Boston expanded from a two-mile radius before the coming of streetcars to a ten-mile radius after their introduction. This implies a roughly 25-fold increase in the area of the city (4Π square miles versus 100Π square miles, assuming that all the land is available for development).

An increase in household income is not as simple to analyze, but it is important for two reasons. First, the relative bid-rent curves at a point in time will determine whether the pattern of settlement in a monocentric city shows increasing or decreasing income with respect to distance from the CBD. Second, changing incomes over time could have implications for the relative centralization of households.

If income increases, two things happen. First, the unit costs of commuting increase. As we will see in detail in chapter 15, a large part of the costs of commuting are the time costs, which have been found to be valued at a fraction of a person's wage. Thus, higher-income people place a higher value on their time and so find a given commute more costly than do lower-income people. Second, the demand for housing increases, if housing is a normal good. We can analyze the effects of these changes using Figure 9.11. Suppose each household wishes to spend a total of 30 percent of its income on housing and commuting costs. Suppose further that unit housing costs differ by location, as shown, with housing being more expensive closer to the CBD. Finally, suppose each household wishes to purchase the highest-quality house it can afford. Under these assumptions, the choice of housing quality and the choice of location are synonymous, as shown. The intercept of the house-price curves plots the total commuting costs associated with the location. The higher commuting costs for the high-income household are reflected in the higher intercept outside the CBD. Both households have zero commuting costs at the CBD, so there is only one curve there. The higher-income household prefers the higher-quality house outside the CBD, while the lower-income household chooses to locate in the CBD.

Clearly, this result depends strongly on the relative slopes of the curves and on the difference in commuting costs between the two households. But as drawn, it allows two simple stories to be told. The first compares the location of high- and low-income households at a point in time. The analysis in Figure 9.11 suggests that high-income households will locate farther from the CBD than low-income households, a pattern commonly observed in the United States during the twentieth century. The second story is that rising income over time will cause households to choose more remote locations, even though housing price and transportation technology remain constant.

A formal way of stating the results described above is obtained by comparing the relative income elasticities of commuting costs and housing demand. If the income elasticity of commuting costs exceeds the income elasticity of housing, then the household moves closer to the CBD as a result of an increase in income. Conversely, if the elasticity of housing exceeds the elasticity of commuting costs, then the higher-income household will move farther away from the CBD. What is the empirical finding? It's inconclusive, with an estimated elasticity for commuting costs of between 0.3 and 1.2, while the estimated income elasticity for housing is about 0.7. Wheaton (1977) argues

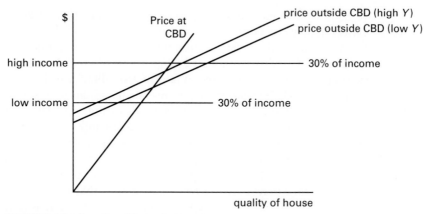

FIGURE 9.11 Location Choice by Income

that because the elasticities are approximately equal, then the pattern of income segregation cannot be explained by the tradeoff between land rent and accessibility.

In the United States, the typical pattern is for income to increase with distance to the CBD. However, this does not provide conclusive evidence for the relative elasticities, since there are other reasons for higher-income people to live farther away from the CBD. First, higher-income people occupy newer housing, which typically is farther from the CBD. Second, there has been a "flight to the suburbs" as higher-income households attempt to escape perceived central city problems. Third, strict zoning in the suburbs alleviates some externalities associated with housing, making the more remote locations more attractive.

INTRAMETROPOLITAN TRADE AND POLYCENTRIC MODELS

One of the important things to notice about urban areas is that people live, work, and shop in different areas. This specialization was already seen in its most basic form in the monocentric city model, since in that model every person works in the CBD but no one lives there. Further, different bid-rent curves for different types of firms implied that the metropolitan area would have "bands of specialization" where one type of firm would locate, as seen in Figure 9.4. The monocentric city model was predicated on the idea that the metropolitan area was a "featureless plain" with locations differentiated only on the basis of proximity to the CBD. We now extend the analysis to the more realistic case in which locations are differentiated in other dimensions as well. The result is a model of intrametropolitan specialization and trade that is conceptually identical to the model of intermetropolitan trade developed in chapters 5 through 7.

Tradables and Nontradables

Recall that about 60 percent of metropolitan employment is engaged in the production of goods and services that are not traded among metropolitan areas. Among the services that can be traded within a metropolitan area but not among metropolitan areas are haircuts and nice neighborhoods. At the metropolitan area level, though, some services that were nontradable now become tradable for our purposes. How does one trade a nice neighborhood for a busy office park? Simple—a person lives in one place and travels to the other. It is important, of course, for intrametropolitan transportation to be efficient relative to intermetropolitan transportation for there to be additional trade. The advent of the automobile made this mobility a fact for households; the truck reduced the cost of moving goods within a city so that manufacturing firms were not tied to a central transport node (Moses and Williamson 1967, p. 213).

The fact that a higher percentage of products are tradable at an intrametropolitan level than at an intermetropolitan level has some immediate implications for the pattern of production within a metropolitan area. In the basic core-periphery model of chapter 7, a higher percentage of tradables implies that firms are more footloose. Therefore, the model leads us to expect greater specialization within metropolitan areas than among metropolitan areas. Of course, if the metropolitan area is "lumpy" in its relative factor abundance, then the analysis of Courant and Deardorff introduced in chapter 6 implies that the intrametropolitan pattern of production and trade affects intermetropolitan trade.

Specialization and Trade among Suburbs

Consider the following simple model of a small open economy. This economy is a part of a metropolitan area, and for simplicity I will refer to it as a "suburb." However, the CBD is an example of what I mean by a suburb in this context. It has two factors of production, capital (K) and land (L), with the price of capital being denoted r and the price of land R. It produces two goods, offices (O) and houses (H). The general equilibrium for the suburb at product market prices p' and capital-land ratio k' is shown as Figure 9.12.

If this suburb is trading freely with other suburbs, there is again factor price equalization unless there is complete specialization. If a suburb, for example, completely specialized in housing, its relative land and capital prices could diverge from

FIGURE 9.12 General Equilibrium

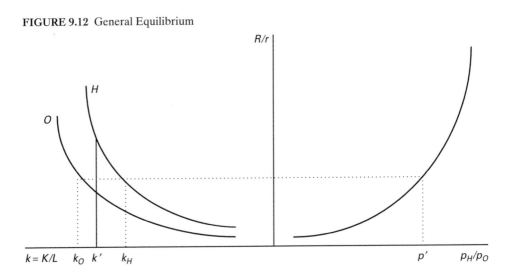

other suburbs, with land being relatively cheaper and capital relatively more expensive. Of course, this would provide an incentive for capital to flow into the suburb. The only way to prevent such a capital inflow is through a factor market restriction, such as zoning. In chapter 10 we will use this approach to analyze zoning.

An Example: Clustered Manufacturing in Cleveland

In order to see concretely the way in which suburbs specialize and trade with each other, consider the example of industrial employment in 1990 in the Cleveland CMSA. The Center for Regional Economic Issues at Case Western Reserve University used data from the Harris Industrial Directory to identify "clusters" of manufacturing firms within the CMSA, and further to refine these clusters into their areas of specialization as identified by the standard industrial classification (SIC) code of the firms within each cluster. The dominant manufacturing zone within the CMSA consists of Cleveland and the eastern parts of Cuyahoga County, and it accounted in 1990 for 38.9 percent of the total manufacturing employment in the CMSA. The center of each zone is illustrated in Figure 9.13. The "Flats" area of Cleveland, at the mouth of the Cuyahoga River, in turn accounted for 30.5 percent of employment within the largest zone, as shown in Figure 9.14. This area, the old industrial heart of Cleveland, thus accounted for about 12 percent of the manufacturing employment in the CMSA. Almost all the industries of Cleveland are located in the largest cluster, but the other clusters are more clearly specialized. For example, there is extensive automobile employment in only three (of ten) clusters within the zone. Another example of specialization is in the drug and medical instruments industry, where there is significant employment in only two clusters: the largest cluster and a second cluster containing two major research hospitals, the Cleveland Clinic and University Hospitals. Table 9.4 shows employment concentrations in some selected industries for this zone.

FIGURE 9.13 Top Six Manufacturing Zones, 1990
Note: County boundaries are shown with boldface outlines; lighter lines show interstate highways.

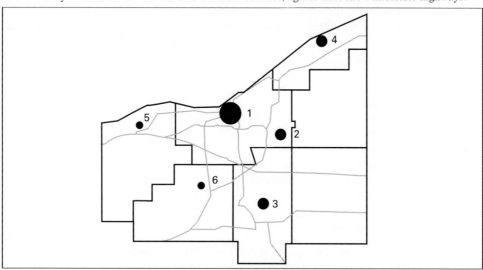

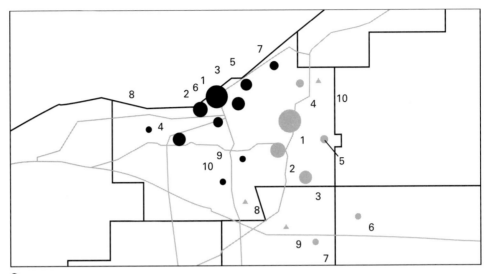

● ●: 10 largest manufacturing clusters in Zone 1
● ●: 10 largest manufacturing clusters in Zone 2

FIGURE 9.14 Manufacturing Clusters in Zones 1 and 2

The second largest manufacturing zone within the CMSA consists of the southeastern part of Cuyahoga County and the northern parts of Summit and Portage Counties; it is also illustrated in Figure 9.14. This zone contains 14.5 percent of the manufacturing employment in the CMSA. The largest cluster in the zone, an area around Solon (the intersection of I-271 and U.S. 422, just north of I-480), contains 36.6 percent of the employment in the zone. This cluster is just south of the edge city of Beachwood and illustrates that decentralization of employment is not strictly limited to services.

Because data were available for 1985 as well as for 1990, the relation of the growth of industry to the growth of clusters specializing in those industries could be seen. These results are reported in Table 9.5. The city with the fastest manufacturing growth during that period was Solon, home of Stouffer Foods. One of the fastest-growing industries during that period, unsurprisingly, produced preserved fruits and

TABLE 9.4 Establishments in Selected Industries by Cluster

Industry	Zone 1 Cluster						Zone 2 Cluster			
	1	*2*	*3*	*4*	*5*	*6*	*1*	*2*	*3*	*4*
Preserved fruits and vegetables	3		2		1		2	1	1	2
Commercial printing	109	34		15		22	28			
Medical instruments and supplies	5					6	8			5
Drug and medical instruments	6					7	10			6
Automobile	37	46			39			12	12	
Forging and stamping	20	21	12	17		8			4	
Metal services	46	19	22	6	11		11			

Source: Center for Regional Economic Issues, 1991, p. 12. Establishments are listed for those areas with greater than 5 percent of employment or establishments for that industry.

TABLE 9.5   Industries with Employment Changes of 1,000 or More: 1985–1990

Industry	1985 Employment	1990 Employment	Employment Change	Percentage Change
Miscellaneous plastic products	11,413	17,810	6,397	56.1
Preserved fruits and vegetables	385	2,980	2,595	674.0
Metal forgings and stampings	17,126	19,442	2,316	13.5
Miscellaneous paper products	3,623	5,627	2,004	55.3
Commercial printing	7,448	9,127	1,679	22.5
Electronic components	3,551	5,080	1,529	43.1
Plumbing and heating	3,503	5,002	1,499	42.8
Fabricated structural metals	10,081	11,500	1,419	14.1
Engines and turbines	3,833	5,135	1,302	34.0
Ordnance and accessories	1,514	2,542	1,028	67.9
Plastic materials and syntheses	2,025	3,035	1,010	49.9

Source: Center for Regional Economic Issues, 1991, p. 16

vegetables. The continuing decentralization of manufacturing employment was also demonstrated by the fact that nine of the ten cities with the largest employment growth were located outside the largest manufacturing zone.

Edge Cities and Services

Most of the discussion and formal modeling has focused on manufacturing industries. However, it is well known that the United States is overwhelmingly a service-based economy. What implications does this have for the pattern of urban growth?

Joel Garreau's book *Edge City* (1991) documents the changing urban form in the United States in the late twentieth century. The experiences he documents can be readily put into the general framework we have been considering if we change the focus of our analysis to services. Specifically, if there are changes in the way services are delivered within and among urban areas, then changes in urban form can result in turn.

Garreau's thesis in *Edge City* is that these "suburban downtowns" are exporters of services, including insurance, financial, architecture, shopping, university, medical, and office. The reason for the new concentration is that modern communication devices and decreases in intracity transportation costs combine to make services that were formerly nontradable, tradable. For example, the fax machine can be thought of as a matter transmitter, the teleconference as a teleporter, and computer numerically controlled tools (CNC) as a way of remote manufacturing. Garreau gives the example of a set of CNC instructions being shipped to a local producer instead of having a producer manufacture and ship a custom door. (Recall the effects of decreasing transport costs on specialization and concentration in the core-periphery model developed in chapter 7.) We therefore expect to see increasing concentration of services within metropolitan areas. This concentration can be thought of in turn as an increase in the "lumpiness" of metropolitan areas, with the result (recall the analysis in chapter 6) that we expect to see an increase in intermetropolitan trade of services as well. The

TABLE 9.6 Employment Patterns in Ohio Edge Cities, 1992

| Central City | Number of Edge Cities | Retail | Specialization | | | | |
			Social Service	Personal Service	Manufacture	Producer Service	Wholesale
Akron	1	0	0	1	0	0	0
Cincinnati	3	1	1	0	1	0	0
Cleveland	8	1	1	1	3	2	0
Columbus	6	0	3	0	1	1	1
Dayton	4	0	1	0	2	1	0
Toledo	4	1	1	1	0	0	1
Total	26	3	7	3	7	4	2

Source: Bingham and Kimble (1995, Table 5, p. 268).

findings of Giuliano and Small (1991) about specialization in goods and services of various centers in the Los Angeles area have been described earlier. Let us consider one other example, a recent study of edge cities in Ohio.

Richard Bingham and Deborah Kimble (1995) explore the range of specializations in Ohio's edge cities. Using Garreau's definition of edge cities, Bingham and Kimble identify 26 edge cities around six of Ohio's major cities. They then examine employment patterns to identify each edge city as specializing in one of several types of production: retail, social services, personal services, manufacturing, producer services, and wholesale. They demonstrate that edge cities are far from homogeneous, in that as a whole they specialize in a wide range of activities rather than only in producer services as a superficial reading of Garreau's thesis might suggest. They also find that the edge cities perform functions that are distinctly different from those of the central cities of the metropolitan area in which the edge cities are found. The pattern of specialization found among edge cities in Ohio by Bingham and Kimble is summarized in Table 9.6.

THE FUTURE OF URBAN STRUCTURE

Human society has been predominantly urban for less than two hundred years. The first century of the industrial era was a time of increasing density within the central city, while the second century has been marked by decreasing density within the central city despite the overall increase in the level of urbanization. Let us indulge in some speculation about what cities will look like in the future—not in a "Buck Rogers" sense, but in the sense of extrapolating on the basis of our analysis and current conditions.

Consider the following three hypotheses. The first hypothesis is that people like to live reasonably close to other people, where reasonably means at a density greater than rural areas but less than cities of the early 1900s. For the sake of argument, let us characterize a suburban density of two households per acre (roughly 8 people per acre, or 5,120 per square mile) as reasonable. This is roughly the population density in the cities in Orange County, California today (Downs 1994, p. 143). The second hypothesis is that people like to live reasonably close to their jobs, where reasonably close means that 75 percent of the people commute less than 40 minutes. This is comparable to current practice, as in both 1980 and 1990 about 70 percent of the population commuted less than 30 minutes to work (Downs 1994, p. 5). It is also consistent with historical data and may, in fact, constitute a basic "law" of human behavior, as it is observed repeatedly throughout history (Bairoch 1988) An interesting—and unsolved—question is the reason for this consistency. My students have suggested that one or two hours spent commuting plus eight hours of work is about the right amount of time away from home. But the eight-hour workday is a recent innovation, and the answer still doesn't explain what makes one amount of time more reasonable than another. The third hypothesis is that transportation costs for most goods and services will continue to decrease.

Combining these three hypotheses leads me to expect a future of "edge cities" within metropolitan areas as decreased transportation costs make agglomeration to exploit localization economies possible for a broader range of goods and services. The residential density suggested as reasonable is not that small relative to population densities in most cities, so that there is no pressing reason for a massive relocation of population relative to the massive relocation that has occurred over the two centuries since the Industrial Revolution. The idea that the population density in a metropolitan area could be about the same as it was in a monocentric city period, although more evenly distributed throughout the area, implies that people could find it easier to live at some distance from their jobs and still stay within the 40-minute commuting radius. Figure 9.15 illustrates how the construction of interstate highways extended the geographical range of a 30-minute commute to downtown Cleveland. Figure 9.16

FIGURE 9.15 How Edge Cities Expand the Metropolitan Area
Light shading shows the 30-minute commuting range from downtown Cleveland before freeways; darker shading shows how freeways expanded the commuting range.

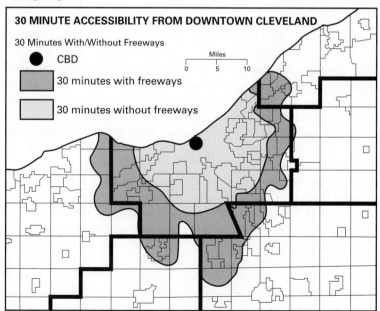

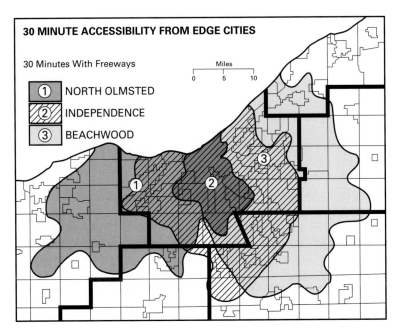

FIGURE 9.16 Greatly expanded commuting ranges from the area's three edge cities—North Olmsted, Independence, and Beachwood. Source: NOACA

illustrates how the area of settlement is extended even further by the development of edge cities. (Both figures were published in EcoCity Cleveland, 1996, p. 13. The original analysis was done by Howard Maier of NOACA.)

The Communications Revolution and Urban Structure

The lead editorial in *The Economist* on 30 September 1995 predicted that "within a decade or two, most ordinary telephone conversations will cost nothing extra, whatever their duration or distance. As a result, one of the most important limits imposed by geography on human activities will eventually vanish." The editorial goes on to predict that "cities, which have so dominated development for the past two centuries, will lose some of their clout." This editorial raises an interesting question for the student of urban economics—are you wasting your time? My answer, of course, is no. Cities will continue to play an important role even if communication costs continue their dramatic decrease.

We can use the models we've developed in this chapter (and in chapter 7) to predict the effect of a decrease in communications costs on location decisions by firms. Let us consider an extreme case, one in which communications have advanced to the point that people no longer have to travel to their workplace in order to work. In that case, there is no necessity for all the employees of a firm to live anywhere near the firm. Would cities exist in such a world? Yes, for two reasons. First, the decoupling from the physical location of their workforce makes the firms more footloose. As we saw earlier, if firms are more footloose, they are free to cluster together in order to take advantage of localization economies of scale. If there are still localization economies of scale for reasons other than labor pooling, there will be concentrations of economic activity. Second, there will continue to be agglomeration economies of scale in consumption even if there are not agglomeration economies of scale in production. People will still group together in order to consume products, assuming that face-to-face communication is not completely replaced by its digital counterpart. The presence of amenities that differ from place to place, such as climate, also makes it likely that these newly footloose workers will cluster together with others of similar consumption interests, forming neighborhoods that are much more specialized than today's can be. Of course, if people are located close together, then market-oriented firms will have an incentive to follow.

Suburb Today, Slum Tomorrow?

One interesting perspective on the familiar townhouse developments of modern edge cities is provided by Garreau (1991, p. 87), who likens them to tenements. "Tenements were tightly packed three- and four-story buildings in which each family occupied one floor. They were thrown up in a hurry . . . [and] were the cheapest and most efficient way of getting the highest number of people reasonably close to their jobs." Townhouses are also tightly packed, the only difference being that the families occupy a vertical rather than a horizontal space. They are constructed as a cheap and efficient way of providing housing that is accessible via freeway to the edge cities in which modern service workers spend their day. The problem implicit in this analogy is that today's shiny new suburban developments could be tomorrow's scenes of urban decay.

CHAPTER SUMMARY

- Two main types of city structure can be observed. The first is the monocentric city, in which there is one employment center (the central business district, or CBD), relative to which the rest of the city is defined. The second is the polycentric city, in which there are several employment centers. Cities in the United States are increasingly polycentric, although the historic CBD remains an important center.

- Land that is more accessible to desirable features has a higher value. Thus, we expect to see land rents decline as we move away from an employment or transport center. Higher land prices lead profit-maximizing firms to substitute other factors of production for land. Thus, taller buildings are built on higher-valued land.

- There has been a long-term trend towards decentralization in U.S. metropolitan areas. There are two main explanations of this trend. First, it represents a desire by people to escape perceived problems in the central city. Second, it represents a natural evolution in urban structure resulting from changes in employment patterns that in turn reflect changes in production and transportation technology.

- Regions within metropolitan areas specialize and trade with one another. The products traded within a metropolitan area include some products that are not traded among metropolitan areas.

- Urban structure is largely determined by production and transportation technologies. Thus, changes in these technologies could lead to changes in the typical metropolitan area. The revolution in communications has helped create the specialized business service areas known as "edge cities."

EXCERPT: *GLADIATOR-AT-LAW* (FREDERIK POHL AND C. M. KORNBLUTH)

A fictional version of the potential downward spiral of suburban housing developments appeared in a novel published in 1955, almost contemporaneous with the initial Levittown development on Long Island. The excerpt below shows how the authors see a bleak future for the Levittown-like subdivision Belle Reve, predicting its future transformation into the nightmarish world of Belly Rave (Frederik Pohl and C. M. Kornbluth 1955, pp. 27–31).

Reverse your telescope. Point the small end at a sign that is neither here nor now, a long way off in space and as many years past as it has been since the end of World War II.

The sign is in a dozen chromatic colors, a picture of a vine-covered cottage with a curl of smoke winding from a fieldstone chimney, and an impossibly long-legged girl waving from the door. The giant letters read:

BELLE REVE ESTATES
Gracious Living for America's Heroes
VETS! OWN YOUR OWN HOME!
$350 cash, $40.25 monthly pays all
F R E E !
3-speed washer, home freezer
Fifteen-Foot Picture Window

Before the paint on the sign was dry, three cars were parked in the muddy ruts in front of it and three couples were being guided through the model home by Belle Reve salesmen—estate managers, they preferred to be called.

A prospect got the dizzy impression that somehow he could move into the place tomorrow, furnished as it was, simply by signing his name and handing over the twenty-dollar binder. And a swimming pool would be on their lawn the day after to be shared with another nice couple like them, and the children could gambol on the grassy sward unmenaced by city traffic, and they would spit right in the eye of the city apartment-house janitor after telling him they were getting out of the crowded, evil-smelling, budget-devouring, paper-walled, sticky-windowed, airless, lightless, privacy-less hole in the wall forever. They were going Home to Belle Reve. They signed and paid.

Time passed.

The place isn't an expense, honey; it's an *asset*. Do you realize we have an equity of *eight thousand dollars* in this house we can recover at the drop of a hat if we can find somebody to buy the place and if there was some place else to go? It makes a man feel mighty good to know he has eight thousand dollars to his name. I know it runs a little higher than anybody figured, but things are up all over. Insurance, sewer assessment, road tax, fuel oil, interest, assessment in that stockholders' suit whatever it was about — it isn't more than a hundred twenty-five a month, if that. If I get the raise and swing that note on the car we can have the roof repaired before the November rains, and then get right to work on the oil heater — please don't cry, honey. Besides. There's. No. Place. Else. To. Go.

Time passed.

He owned the house outright, almost. In just a few years it would be his, as soon as he cleared up the sewer assessments outstanding. I'll sell, he schemed craftily, forgetting to cry. At the top of the market. Not right now; things were too dull. A few of the places on the street were empty, abandoned. A kind of funny element was moving in; not the kind of people you talked to much. Bad for the children. He was sure that passing the abandoned Samuels place he had smelled something like the raw reek of alcohol and glimpsed shiny copper pots and tubing through the ill-shuttered picture window. Sometimes police cars and copters descended on Belly Rave and left loaded—but that was just on the outskirts, the neighborhood would pick up, the old man told himself sternly. And then he'd sell at the top of the market.

Time passed....

More than a century.

There was no sizable city which did not have the equivalent of Belly Rave. The festering slums of Long Island were another New York problem; Boston had its Springfield; Chicago its Evanston; Los Angeles its Greenville. None was worse than Belle Reve Estates.

Source: Gladiator-At-Law by Frederik Pohl and C. M. Kornbluth. Copyright © 1955 by Frederik Pohl and C. M. Kornbluth. Reprinted by permission of Frederik Pohl.

Questions for Review and Discussion

1. "Fifty years from now, the new housing developments in edge cities will be sites of blight and decay. The fact that they are scattered throughout the region rather than concentrated in the central city will make it even more difficult to combat this problem." Do you agree or disagree? Explain.

2. "The reason 'edge cities' form is because it is extremely expensive to convert from one land use to another. If demolition and rezoning were free, the downtown would be readjusted to changing economic conditions, making edge cities unnecessary." Do you agree or disagree? Explain.

3. Ricardo developed his theory of land rent to describe agricultural land that had different productivity. This made sense because, using the same inputs, you could grow different quantities of crop on different parcels of land, depending on how productive it was. How is it possible to describe urban land as being "productive"? What is the marginal product of urban land, and why does it differ from place to place?

4. The monocentric city model analyzes the tradeoff between accessibility and land rents. What would be the effect on the rent gradient of:
   a. an increase in the number of households that had two workers
   b. an increase in the price of gasoline
   c. an increase in the percentage of trips by the household to destinations outside the CBD (shopping mall, etc.)

5. Are there restrictions on student housing in the area surrounding your college? Can you construct a rent gradient for students?

6. For what types of activities do you expect that it would be difficult to substitute capital for land? The monocentric city model would predict that these activities occur towards the edge of cities. Do you observe this?

7. "Downtown buildings are tall because downtown land is expensive. It is inefficient to have short buildings downtown." Do you agree or disagree? Explain. (Why do we observe both short and tall buildings downtown?)

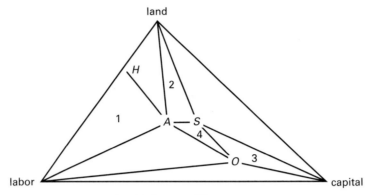

FIGURE A-9.1 Suburban Endowment Diagram

Appendix: Suburban Development in a Three-Factor Model

We can extend the basic model of suburban development in this chapter to include a third factor of production, labor. An endowment triangle (recall the appendix to chapter 6) is drawn as Figure A-9.1. Suppose there are four activities that suburbs can engage in: apartments (A), houses (H), offices (O), and shopping centers (S). Further, suppose that prices are such that the current triangles of diversification are as drawn in Figure A-9.1. In that case, we can consider a few representative suburbs. A suburb in area 1 produces houses and apartments, importing shopping centers and offices. This is the quintessential bedroom community. A suburb in area 2 also provides housing but in addition produces some shopping services. A suburb in area 3 produces only shopping and offices; an example would be the CBD. Finally, area 4, with apartments, shopping, and offices could be an "edge city." From the analysis in chapter 6, we know that land values will be higher in suburb 3, say, than in suburb 1 because of the differences in the relative scarcity of land.

A suburb could take a variety of paths over time, given a certain endowment of land. Although difficult to model formally, it is intuitively clear that there could be a "race to develop" as the development leads to changes in prices, which in turn causes the diversification triangles to change. Also, capital and labor mobility can change the position of the suburbs in the endowment triangle unless zoning prohibits suburban development. (This topic is returned to in chapter 10.) A suburb in area 1 that waited to add to its capital stock might find itself better off specializing even further in houses if extensive development of shopping centers and offices has occurred throughout the metropolitan area.

CHAPTER

10

Land-Use Controls

A lthough this book does not formally analyze the entire spectrum of local government policy, it would be a serious omission to neglect land-use controls. Especially in the suburbs, zoning and other controls on the use of land are an important and controversial matter for public policy. In this chapter, we first review the development of zoning in the United States in order to gain some historical perspective. We then use three different techniques to analyze the economic effects of zoning. First, we analyze zoning as a restriction on factor movements among local governments within a metropolitan area. Second, we analyze zoning as a way of alleviating the potentially harmful effects of externalities. Third, we analyze zoning as a community property right whose allocation is determined jointly through the political and judicial process.

LAND-USE CONTROLS: HISTORY
AND INSTITUTIONAL BACKGROUND

Before the advent of fast intraurban transportation, people lived within walking distance of their work. This implies that there was not a great deal of separation between residential and business areas, and it also implies that all income classes lived close to one another. (There is evidence that people were willing to walk several miles each way, so the possible extent of socioeconomic segregation shouldn't be minimized even in the absence of wheeled transport. See Harris 1996.) This spatial proximity should not be confused with social proximity. Mumford (1961, p. 47) argues that the reduction in spatial distance between people and classes associated with early urbanization was related to an increase in social distance among the classes. The development of wheeled transport only made such class differences larger—recall Engels's description of Manchester in chapter 9 or the behavior of the nobility in their carriages in Dickens's *Tale of Two Cities.*

The separation of residential from commercial/industrial land uses was a crucial innovation in the 1800s made possible by better transport; it encouraged the segregation of residences according to the socioeconomic status of each household. Levine

(1988, p. 207) argues that the process of residential segregation was part of a general fragmentation of society during the late 1800s. Thus, formal zoning, which legislated residential segregation by occupation and income class, was developed at the same time as many professional organizations that performed the same role in the workplace. This was also a time of extensive immigration, leading to increased heterogeneity in cities and possibly increasing the desire of people to segregate themselves. Warner (1962) provides a detailed look at the process of income and class segregation between 1870 and 1900 in three Boston neighborhoods that followed the introduction of the streetcar.

Fishman (1987, p. 135) argues that inaccessibility has been the key to suburban development. For a suburb to be attractive, it was not only important that the residents have easy access to their jobs, shopping, and other amenities, but it was crucial that the nonresidents not have easy access. The automobile, argues Fishman, destroyed the classical suburb by making it easy and affordable for anyone to get anywhere within the metropolitan area. The phenomenon of edge city, where residential and commercial land uses intermingle, is considered by Fishman to mark the end of a period in history that started with the early Industrial Revolution.

The first comprehensive zoning ordinance, passed in New York City in 1916, thus reflected an existing pattern of land use—de facto segregation of residential and business uses as well as segregation of types of residential uses—rather than introducing anything new. More recently, Siegan (1972) argued that land use in Houston, a city without zoning, is not substantially different from land use in cities with zoning. Anticipating an important policy issue, the question of whether zoning merely reflects market decisions or enforces nonmarket outcomes is one that is still argued about today. (Wallace 1988, is an example of this type of analysis.)

Before turning to a formal economic model of zoning, it is first necessary to define it and put it into context. *Zoning* is defined to be the division of a community into districts in which certain activities are prohibited and others are permitted. Zoning is done in two basic ways. The first type of zoning, *cumulative zoning*, sets forth a hierarchy of uses ranked from least restricted to most restricted, usually on the basis of perceived negative externalities arising from the land use. An example of this type of zoning is the 1923 zoning in the city of Chicago, outlined in Table 10.1. A parcel of property zoned R3 could be devoted to a park (an R3 use), a church (an R2 use), or even a single-family house (an R1 use), but it could not be used for an apartment building.

The second type of zoning, *prescriptive zoning*, prescribes the allowable use for each parcel of property. In this case, a special exception must be made if the property is to be used for anything other than its zoned use even if the desired use is ranked higher in the hierarchical sense. Return to the example of Chicago in Table 10.1. If the zoning was of a prescriptive form, a developer would not be allowed to build a single-family house on a parcel of property zoned R3 without special permission. Prescriptive zoning is the most common form of zoning used today in the United States.

The predominant land use in urban areas is housing. Charles Abrams (in Davis, ed., 1973, p. 228) found that over 32 percent of the land in each of seven large cities (Detroit, Pittsburgh, Philadelphia, Los Angeles, Cleveland, Chicago, New York) that he studied in 1960 was devoted to residential use, with 52.3 percent of Philadelphia being the largest. The next largest use of land was public rights-of-way, including

TABLE 10.1   Chicago Zoning Ordinance (1923)

Zone (ranked from least restrictive to most restrictive)	Representative Land Uses for the Zone
Residence districts	
R1	single-family dwellings
R2	golf courses, churches, schools
R3	public parks, public playgrounds
R4	farms, greenhouses
Apartment districts	
A1	apartment houses
A2	boarding houses, hotels
A3	public libraries, private clubs
Commercial districts	
C1	retail stores, restaurants, theaters
C2	small manufacturing establishments
C3	breweries, poultry killing, paint blending
Manufacturing districts	
M1	lumber yards, gravel storage, metal forging
M2	carpet cleaning, tallow rendering, paper mill
M3	asphalt or chlorine manufacturing, tanning
Special uses (can locate anywhere)	airport, hospital, police station

roads. By contrast, commercial and industrial uses accounted for at most 17 percent of the land used in these cities. The fraction of land used for housing is even higher in the suburbs. Hence, when we look at zoning, we will be mainly concerned about restrictions on residential use. The large externalities associated with commercial and industrial use imply that its location is also important, and so we will not neglect that question either.

We have already seen that the population of the United States is predominantly urban, regardless of which measure of "urban population" is used. A natural question is whether or not land use in the United States reflects this pattern. Table 10.2 summarizes land use in the 48 contiguous states. It is clear that urban land use is only a small fraction of the land use in the United States. Even if we include rural transportation, land devoted to "built up" purposes is only 3.2 percent of the total land in the country. Nevertheless, people are concerned that "urban sprawl" is encroaching on the last available land in the country. Is this an irrational fear? Not necessarily. Because so many people are living in urban areas, their daily experience is only with relatively dense urban land use. In other words, 100 percent of their experience is with 1.8 percent of the land. When a familiar local field or park is converted into an apartment building, this represents a relatively large loss of the land available to the urban resident.

The data in Table 10.2 are from the 1970s, and one might object that urban growth since then has changed the figures. It is true that the specific percentages of the land devoted to various uses changes over time, but the basic conclusion has not

TABLE 10.2   Land Use in the Contiguous United States

Land Use	Millions of Acres	Percentage of Area
Forests	598.5	31.5
Grassland pasture and range	595.2	31.4
Cropland	465.7	24.5
Wetlands, rock, desert, tundra	90.7	4.8
Rural parks and wildlife preserves	56.9	3.0
Urbanized areas and urban places	34.6	1.8
Rural roads, railroads, and airports	25.9	1.4
Military and nuclear installations	22.4	1.2
Farms and roads on farms	8.0	0.4

Source: Fischel 1985, Table 1.

changed. Table 10.3 presents evidence on land use in 1987. The categories are not identical to those in Table 10.2, but the overall conclusion is. Developed land is only 4.1 percent of the total land use in the United States, not including Alaska.

Taxonomy of Land-Use Controls

A variety of controls over land use are administered by all levels of government. At the local government level, those controls include zoning, subdivision regulations, building and housing codes, and provision of local public services. At the state government level, they include nuisance laws and provision of public services. Finally, the Federal government is involved, especially through the administration of environmental impact statements mandated by the National Environmental Protection Act. In addition to government involvement, private covenants (contracts) regulate land use.

Comprehensive zoning is a fairly recent phenomenon; the first city in the United States to adopt such a system was New York in 1916. The use of zoning spread quickly, and it was challenged by developers as a violation of the constitutional requirement that compensation be paid to people whose property was taken for public use. The U.S. Supreme Court affirmed the right of local governments to zone in the

TABLE 10.3   Land Use in the United States (excluding Alaska) in 1987

Land Use	Millions of Acres	Percentage of Area
Cropland	422.4	22.4
Federal land	404.1	21.4
Range land	401.7	21.3
Forest	393.9	20.9
Pasture	129.0	6.8
Developed land	77.3	4.1
Other rural uses	59.8	3.2

Source: Statistical Abstract of the United States 1991, Table 352, p. 204.

1926 decision *Euclid v. Ambler* (272 U.S. 365). The Ambler Realty Company had wanted to develop some property for industrial use, but the village of Euclid (a suburb of Cleveland) had zoned the property for residential use only. Despite the fact that this zoning reduced the value of the property, the Court upheld the authority of the village to zone without having to compensate the developer.

The U.S. Department of Commerce drew up a standard set of language that most states used in granting local governments zoning authority. This language, contained in the Standard Zoning Enabling Act of 1926, provided local governments the authority to zone "for the purpose of promoting health, safety, morals, or the general welfare of the community." Having given this broad authority to local governments, the Supreme Court did not make another major ruling on land use for 50 years. In the past 20 years, some court decisions have restricted the ability of local governments to use their zoning powers, but the presumption remains that local governments can zone as they wish.

Conflict Resolution

Zoning is a property right and/or a restriction on a property right. It is possible that people will disagree over who is entitled to the right. For example, a landowner may wish to allow a certain type of development that neighboring landowners object to. Disputes of this nature are generally resolved in two ways: political and judicial.

A political resolution occurs when the local government, either directly or through an elected or appointed zoning board, allocates the property right. One possible concern is whether the local government is a monopolist in the land market and therefore can "unfairly" exploit landowners. Fischel (1985, ch. 10) examines 25 metropolitan areas and finds little evidence that this is a widespread problem. Another factor influencing political outcomes is the size of the local government. If the town is large and diverse, it is more difficult to organize residents to exclude a particular land use.

Judicial resolution of zoning disputes can happen in place of or following a political resolution. The main U.S. Supreme Court case is the aforementioned *Euclid v. Ambler*. The Supreme Court has only recently revisited and begun to restrict the broad powers of the local government in allocating property rights. A 1992 decision by the U.S. Supreme Court on a case in South Carolina (*Lucas v. South Carolina Coastal Commission*) has made governments more wary, particularly with regard to land-use regulations that are motivated by a broad concern for the environment. This is especially important given the development during the past 25 years of a broad range of policies designed to give wide protection to endangered species and preferred land uses, especially wetlands. (*Business Week*, 13 July 1992)

Three constitutional issues are involved in land-use disputes. The first constitutional issue is due process (both procedural and substantive). The *due process* requirement is that there be a fair system for depriving someone of his or her rights. Substantive due process means that the zoning regulation reasonably advances some goal of the local government, and procedural due process means that the appropriate rules were followed in promulgating the regulation.

The second constitutional issue is *equal protection*. This has two parts: first, all landowners within a town must be treated equally; and second, people both inside and outside the town must be treated equally. One of the important questions in a legal proceeding is, Who has standing to bring a case? For example, if only residents of a town are allowed to bring a lawsuit, and if zoning prevents people from moving in, then the injured parties (the potential residents) do not have standing. The New Jersey Supreme Court found local practice to be a violation of equal protection on these grounds in the 1975 case *Southern Burlington County NAACP v. Mount Laurel* (336 A.2nd 713).

The third constitutional issue is the prohibition on *takings,* the requirement that governments pay for property taken for public use. This is obviously applicable in the case of land acquired to build roads but is more contentious when zoning regulations that are passed to promote a public purpose reduce the property values of a particular landowner. As we have already seen, the *Euclid* decision of the Supreme Court gave broad zoning powers to local governments without the requirement that landowners be compensated for a reduction in the value of their land. Even when the government indisputably has the right to take a parcel of land, the amount of compensation required can be a matter of controversy. If the owner of the land receives consumer surplus—values the land in excess of the market price—should the government be required to compensate the owner for the lost consumer surplus or for only the lost market value?

ZONING AS A TRADE RESTRICTION

We can easily adapt our model of suburbs as small open economies to include zoning. Consider a suburb that can produce one of two locally tradable products; housing (H) and offices (O). I refer to these products as locally tradable because although these products cannot be traded across metropolitan areas, they are tradable within a metropolitan area. The bedroom community that sends its residents downtown to work is importing offices and exporting housing, and vice versa for the central city.

Suppose that H and O are produced using two factors of production, capital (K) and land (L). Further, suppose that O is more capital intensive than H at any factor prices. Finally, suppose the metropolitan area contains many suburbs, so that we can approximate the markets for H, O, K, and L as perfectly competitive. Under these conditions, general equilibrium in product and factor markets can be summarized using the diagram in Figure 10.1, already familiar from chapter 9.

Suppose that the relative autarky price of H and O is p_1 in one suburb and p_2 in another. This would imply that relative factor prices differ between the two suburbs, as shown in Figure 10.1. If there is free trade between the two suburbs, then the equilibrium price will be intermediate between p_2 and p_1, and relative factor prices will be equalized. As we saw in chapter 6, factor mobility can lead to factor price equalization even in the absence of free trade in products. Land is clearly immobile (in the absence of annexation), but capital is mobile, so we would expect to see capital moving in order to equalize the relative return to land in all suburbs.

Zoning enters the model in a very simple way. Suppose that a suburb is free to set a maximum capital-land ratio. While a suburb could also conceivably set a minimum capital-land ratio, the immobility of land in the model makes that option unenforceable because capital is free to leave.

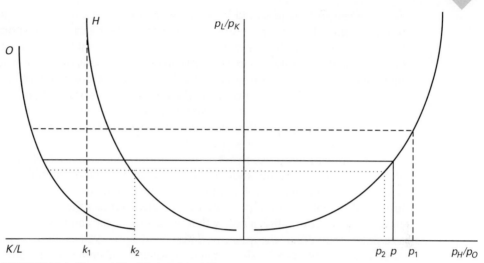

FIGURE 10.1 General Equilibrium Land Use

For example, suppose that suburb 2 in Figure 10.1 sets a maximum capital-land ratio of k_2. Suburb 2 remains completely specialized in producing housing and thus maintains its lower capital-land ratio, although the factor returns are equalized. (An interesting empirical question is the extent to which suburbs are specialized.) In the absence of any restriction, there would be an incentive for capital to flow into suburb 2 in order to earn the higher returns available there. The relative return to land (R/r) is lower in suburb 2 than in suburb 1, and the return to capital (r) is the same in both suburbs, so the price of land is lower in suburb 2. All else being equal, this means that production costs are lower in suburb 2, so that offices or more capital-intensive housing would like to locate there.

The return to land increases relative to autarky for suburb 2, but the restriction on capital inflows prevents the suburb from producing at the cost-minimizing capital-land ratio. This implies a deadweight loss from zoning. Why would a suburb willingly incur a loss of this sort? A plausible answer is that potential externalities from greater capital intensity exceed the deadweight loss of inefficient production (not using cost-minimizing factor proportions). Suburb 2 is free to import the services of offices from other suburbs and therefore gets the benefits of the services without having to bear the externalities. The residents of suburb 2 incur higher transportation costs because they must commute farther, but the net effect of the zoning should be to improve the welfare of the residents. Otherwise, they would presumably either move to a better suburb or vote out of office the people responsible for the zoning. The negative externalities from commuting, such as congestion and pollution (see chapter 15), could imply that the overall welfare of the metropolitan area falls due to the zoning restrictions, but residents of the suburb don't necessarily take those external costs into account.

Imposing a maximum capital-land ratio is equivalent in terms of the effect on suburb 2's output to putting a quota on offices, as can be immediately seen from Figure 10.1. Depending on the relative sizes of suburb 2 and suburb 1, it is possible that factor returns are not completely equalized by trade in housing and offices. In that case, the return to land would be lower in suburb 2 than in suburb 1, again implying that there must be some countervailing benefit to the restriction or suburb 2 would be foolish to approve it. Sivitanidou and Wheaton (1992) analyze zoning as a restriction on the capital-land ratio in order to investigate the effects on factor prices. They find that zoning that is too rigorous can actually destroy the possibility of employment in a suburb. They also find that increasing the restrictiveness of zoning tends to benefit the owners of commercial land at the expense of workers—an "artificial" scarcity of land has been created. Finally, they note the possible efficiency consequences of reducing agglomeration economies of scale.

A familiar theoretical result is that a quota policy can be replaced with an equivalent tariff policy. The intuition, of course, is that a market equilibrium consists of a related price and quantity. A quota policy controls the quantity and lets the price adjust. A tariff policy, in effect, controls the price and lets the quantity adjust. Thus, in controlling an externality, a policy that affects the price can lead to the same outcome as a policy that affects the quantity. This conclusion assumes, though, that the optimal price and quantity can be determined in advance of imposing the policy, so that the equilibrium outcome is optimal. Suppose there is uncertainty over the external benefits and/or costs. It is possible that price controls or quantity controls are unambiguously better in that case. We will consider this question now, following the analysis developed by Martin Weitzman (1974).

If costs are known with certainty but benefits are not, then the situation is as pictured in Figure 10.2. The expected value of the social marginal benefit is MB_{social}, but the actual marginal benefit will be somewhere between MB_H (the highest possible marginal benefit) and MB_L (the lowest possible marginal benefit). Suppose a quantity control of q^* is imposed. If the true marginal benefit is MB_L, then there is a social loss equal to area ②, where the marginal social cost exceeds the marginal social benefit. Moreover, if the true marginal benefit is MB_H, then there is a social cost in that the true optimal level of production is q_H, and the net benefits in area ① are lost. If a price control of p^* is imposed, then the equilibrium quantity is again q^*, and the potential losses are the same as under quantity controls. Thus, if the benefits (consumption externalities) are uncertain, it is still true that a control on prices is equivalent to a control on quantities.

Now consider the complementary case where benefits are known but costs are uncertain. This situation is illustrated in Figure 10.3 Consider first the effects of a

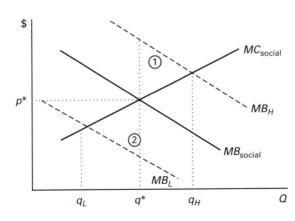

FIGURE 10.2 Known Costs, Uncertain Benefits

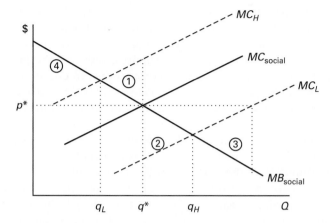

FIGURE 10.3 Uncertain Costs, Known Benefits

quantity control equal to q^*. If the true marginal costs are given by MC_H, then there is a loss equal to area ①. If the true marginal costs are MC_L, then there is a loss (lost opportunity for social benefit) equal to area ②. These are precisely the same types of social costs that we saw in the case of uncertain benefits.

Now consider the effect of a price control equal to p^*. If the true marginal cost is given by MC_L, then the equilibrium quantity will be where p^* and MC_L intersect. This represents a net social loss of area ③ because production exceeds the optimum amount due to the artificially high price. Similarly, if the true social marginal cost is given by MC_H, then there is a net social loss of area ④ due to the underproduction relative to the social optimum. As marginal costs become more and more uncertain (MC_H and MC_L get farther from MC_{social}), the expected social losses of using a price control get smaller and smaller. At the same time, the greater uncertainty in marginal costs, the larger the expected social loss from using a quantity control.

The conclusion is clear. If costs are known and benefits are uncertain, then price and quantity controls are theoretically indistinguishable. If costs are uncertain and benefits are certain, then price controls are superior to quantity controls, and this superiority is greater as costs are more uncertain. Therefore, there is no situation under which quantity controls are preferable to price controls.

Given the conclusion that price controls are better than quantity controls, why do communities impose a quantity control (zoning) rather than a price control, such as a maximum land price? There are three possible explanations. First, every community is being stupid. This is possible, but probably not a fruitful line for inquiry. Second, the main uncertainty about land use is the externalities in consumption (marginal social benefits) rather than the externalities in production (marginal social cost). If this were the case, communities could reasonably choose quantities over prices as the control variable, as their effects are theoretically equivalent. However, given that many of the items consumed locally are also produced locally (housing services and public school services are two important examples), this is also a weak reed to lean on. The third, and most likely, explanation is that quantity controls are legal and price controls are not. A local regulation imposing a maximum land value would almost certainly be viewed as a taking, while local zoning laws that effectively impose a maximum land value have been upheld as long as there is some general public justification for them.

If every suburb restricts capital inflows, the consequences can affect the entire metropolitan area. Intuitively, the metropolitan area might make it too expensive for offices to locate there and would suffer a concomitant loss of employment. This loss could reduce the demand for housing in the suburbs, reducing the price of housing and returns to land. This problem is just a variation of the "free-rider" problem familiar in public goods settings. Each suburb is trying to avoid the negative externalities of capital-intensive production while benefiting from being able to trade for the products with other suburbs.

Note that zoning in this model could actually decrease the returns to factors owned by residents rather than increase them, as is typically the case in trade restrictions. This is a consequence of the structure of the model, but it is not unrealistic. For example, minimum-lot-size restrictions can reduce the value per acre of land, and the political struggle over zoning is usually between the developer who wishes for less restrictive zoning and the current residents who want restrictive zoning. The situation in Avon, Ohio, a western suburb of Cleveland, is perhaps typical. Residents who moved there for its rural atmosphere wanted to change the zoning regulations to allow districts where homes must sit on lots of at least one acre, double the existing minimum. They were opposed by landowners, who argued that this would reduce the value of their land; the landowners included "a lot of old farmers" who planned to sell the land to finance their retirement (*Plain Dealer*, 5 March 1993). It is unrealistic to model local zoning officials as maximizing property values, except perhaps in the sense that they maximize (for political reasons) the property values of current residents for their property as currently used.

ZONING AS A RESPONSE TO EXTERNALITIES

A second way of looking at zoning is as a response to externalities. As was previously mentioned, nuisance laws are both a precursor of and a modern complement to zoning laws. The main effect of zoning is to separate land uses that generate externalities from other land uses, especially single-family residential, thereby reducing the total social cost of externality-generating production. The main problem with zoning is that it has no direct impact on the overall level of damage done and thus might only be "moving the problem around." Further, zoning could be superfluous if some direct way of mitigating the externality is available.

Table 10.4 summarizes the externalities associated with various land uses relative to middle-income single-family residences. The externalities associated with industrial, commercial, and high-density residential land uses are self-explanatory. Not all these uses generate equal amounts of negative externalities, as the hierarchy used by Chicago (shown in Table 10.1) clearly illustrates. An interesting study by Daniel McMillen and John McDonald (1993) examines whether the zoning regulations introduced in Chicago in 1923 could have had the effect of increasing land prices. If negative externalities had existed in the absence of the zoning that ended with the zoning (or if potential future externalities were averted), then land values should have increased. McMillen and McDonald estimate land values in 1921, two years before the zoning ordinance was adopted, and find no evidence that zoning increased property values above what they would have been in the absence of zoning.

TABLE 10.4 Externalities from Various Land Uses

Land Use	Externalities
Industrial	noise, odor, vibration, pollution
Commercial	noise, congestion, parking, obstruction of views
High-density residential	noise, congestion, parking, obstruction of views
Low-income residential	fiscal burden, deteriorating housing quality

Some land uses that were previously found innocuous have been facing increasing opposition as opinions change on what constitutes a negative externality. A common feature in towns across the United States is a McDonald's restaurant. The *Plain Dealer* (1 August 1994) reports on the increasing pressure placed on McDonald's by local governments to have the restaurants conform to ever stricter local architectural and building codes, even to the extent of forbidding the trademark golden arches in the building design. The story goes on to say that local officials often consider the opening of a McDonald's to represent a point of no return in local development, beyond which their community will become just one more homogeneous suburb.

The negative externalities associated with low-income housing need some comment. The first externality, *fiscal burden*, refers to the idea that low-income households pay less in local taxes than the value of the local public services they consume. This is an externality in that the housing decision by a low-income household requires higher-income households to pay local taxes that exceed the value of services that they themselves consume. The second externality, *housing quality*, refers to the idea that low-income households are likely to spend less on upkeep and external appearance of housing, since housing is a normal good. Because the value of a house depends in part on the appearance and quality of neighboring houses, lack of upkeep implies a potential negative externality from low-income housing.

All the externalities listed in Table 10.4 can be addressed using instruments other than zoning policy. For example, an apartment owner can be required to provide parking for the residents, thus reducing the negative externality of parking scarcity. Similarly, building codes can restrict the legal extent of quality deterioration in housing, thus reducing the negative impact of income-associated quality reductions. An interesting recent example was reported in the *Plain Dealer* (12 December 1995). The borough council of Indiana, Pennsylvania, agreed to write an ordinance preventing residents from using furniture outside that was not specifically designed for outdoor use. This ordinance was aimed at preventing people, especially college students, from putting old couches on front porches. Repeat offenders of the ordinance could face fines of up to $300. Another common type of local ordinance is a restriction on the number of unrelated individuals living in the same house. Originally targeted at controlling prostitution, it has more recently evolved into a way of preventing a group of college students from jointly renting a house in a residential area near a college. The original land-use restrictions, in fact, were building regulations aimed at reducing the negative externality of inadequate fire protection in medieval cities. Lübeck required fireproof roofing and walls as early as 1276, while London instituted special privileges for people building stone buildings after a great fire in 1189 (Mumford 1961, p. 283).

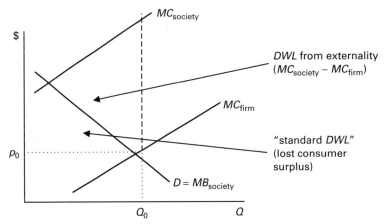

FIGURE 10.4 Production Restrictions and Externalities

As we saw in the previous section, zoning can be modeled as a restriction on local production of a good. If production is restricted in a world of autarky, the reduced consumption opportunities result in a deadweight loss for the population. However, if the external costs of production are large relative to the lost consumption opportunities, restricting production could still be a potential Pareto improvement. This situation is illustrated in Figure 10.4, where the production in the absence of a restriction is Q_0, but the production is assumed to be restricted to zero. As drawn, the external costs of production always exceed the foregone consumer surplus. If the good in question (say office services) can be obtained from other suburbs, then the deadweight loss will be lower than in the case of autarky. If the cost of obtaining these services is not very high, then the deadweight loss is correspondingly low, and it can make sense for any given suburb to restrict entry of capital-intensive production.

ZONING AS A COLLECTIVE PROPERTY RIGHT

The third way of analyzing zoning is to focus directly on its nature as a collective property right. This is complementary to the analysis of zoning as a control on externalities, since it is an application of the Coase theorem introduced in the appendix to chapter 1. It is worth treating this approach separately, though, since the analysis is extremely rich. (Fischel, 1985, presents the best comprehensive treatment of zoning from this perspective.) Much of the current research about zoning involves constructing and testing models of the endogenous determination of zoning as the outcome of a process involving utility-maximizing households and profit-maximizing developers. Pogodzinski and Sass (1990, 1991) critically survey the existing models and suggest productive avenues for future research.

Suppose that we can reduce zoning decisions to a single dimension called "restrictiveness." In the case of hierarchical zoning, this assumption is innocuous. In the case of prescriptive zoning, it is equivalent to saying that only one feature of land use is being restricted. For example, we could talk about the allowed density of development (housing units per acre) in residential areas as a one-dimensional zoning issue.

The nice thing about restricting zoning decisions to one dimension is that it makes it possible to clearly illustrate the tradeoff between the developer and the current residents that a zoning decision entails. Suppose that a parcel of property is to be zoned residential, the only question being the density of development allowed. For the reasons discussed in chapter 9, the greater the density of development allowed (up to some point), the higher the value of the land. As the zoning moves from less restrictive to more restrictive, the cost to the developer is equal to the reduced property value due to the lower density. This is illustrated in Figure 10.5 as the curve labeled $MC_{developer}$. An alternative way of viewing the curve is as a marginal benefit to the developer of relaxing the restrictiveness of zoning.

From the point of view of current residents, the costs associated with development include noise and congestion. The greater the density of development, the higher these costs will be. This is illustrated in Figure 10.5 (by the curve labeled $MB_{residents}$) as a marginal benefit to residents from increasing the restrictiveness of zoning. As drawn, the external costs of development decline as zoning becomes more restrictive, so the marginal benefit of additional restrictiveness declines with restrictiveness.

The point E in the diagram represents the point at which the marginal benefits and costs to the two sides are equal. This is the point that will be reached if property rights are clearly assigned and then trading allowed. Suppose, for example, that we start at point A. The developer is willing to pay $MC_{developer}$ for a reduction in the restrictiveness, which exceeds the marginal benefit to the residents of that degree of restrictiveness; so, starting from point A, the land use control will move in the direction of less restrictiveness. This process will continue until point E. In honor of Coase's contribution to developing this theory, point E is sometimes known as the *Coase point*. In the absence of transaction costs, any allocation of property rights will result in a zoning equilibrium of E.

Although the outcome in terms of the zoning rule is independent of the allocation of property rights, the outcome in terms of the net benefits to various parties depends strongly on the initial allocation. Suppose property rights are assigned so that developers are free to build residences at any density they want. In that case, residents would have to pay the developer to develop at the lower density E. On the other hand, if residents were able to arbitrarily restrict development, then the developer

FIGURE 10.5 Entitlements Diagram

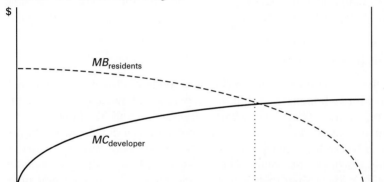

would be compensating residents in order to develop at the density *E*. Point *A* in Figure 10.5 represents a reasonable approximation of current practice, in which communities have great discretion to restrict land use. Recent court decisions (such as *Lucas v. South Carolina Coastal Commission*, referred to earlier in this chapter) have moved the endowment in the direction of less restrictiveness, but only marginally.

If the endowment is at point *A* in Figure 10.5, it is clear that the developer will be compensating the residents. The remaining question is the amount of compensation. There are two general possibilities. First, the developer may be forced to pay the marginal damage to current residents, that is, the area under the curve $MB_{residents}$. This is known as a *compensation rule*. In practice, this rule allows the developer to reduce restrictiveness of zoning at will but requires compensation from the developer. Second, the developer may be forced to pay whatever the residents are able to extract, which is the area under the curve $MC_{developer}$. This is known as a *property rule*, which requires residents' approval for any reduction in the restrictiveness of zoning. The second possibility clearly imposes higher costs on the developer. The standard imposed in *Euclid v. Ambler* is for all practical purposes a property rule because it gives broad powers to the local government to restrict the activities of developers.

The idea of property and compensation rules can be used to illuminate the question raised earlier in the chapter with regard to the amount the government must pay landowners in a takings case. If there is a compensation rule, the government is required to pay the fair market value of the property but does not have to pay a premium that reflects any consumer surplus the owner might receive from a private sale. If there is a property rule, the government must pay for the surplus in addition to the market value.

WHY IS SUBURBAN ZONING TOO RESTRICTIVE?

The typical suburban zoning conflict is between residents who prefer low-density uses and developers (or landowners who wish to sell to developers) who prefer high-density land uses. The title to this section presumes an answer to whether residents make it too difficult to develop land at high density—in other words, whether the outcome is to the right of point *E* in Figure 10.5. We can use the entitlements diagram to illustrate four reasons for expecting this outcome: transactions costs, wealth effect of endowments, illegitimate preferences, and monopoly control of development. This analysis closely follows that in chapter 7 of the book by Fischel (1985).

Transactions Costs

The first reason that suburban zoning is too restrictive is that there are limitations on the types of compensation that developers are allowed to pay residents. In particular, it is much more likely that a barter transaction will be allowed to occur than a cash compensation to current residents. For example, a developer might refurbish a public park in return for a change in the zoning restriction. Why does this lead to an inefficiently restrictive outcome? The answer is that the perceived benefit of an in-kind transfer is lower than that of a cash transfer of an equal amount of money. In other words, the cost per unit of reduced restrictiveness is higher if only in-kind transfers are allowed than they would be if cash transfers were allowed. This can be illustrated as a shift in the $MB_{residents}$ curve (to $MB'_{residents}$), as in Figure 10.6, because the marginal benefit of keeping the restriction in place is higher than previously.

There is a second type of transaction cost as well. The analysis to this point has assumed that the zoning discussion has been between one developer and one representative resident. In practice, the residents must come to some agreement among themselves about the extent of restrictiveness they wish to impose in any given circumstance. Achieving this agreement entails some costs, which again can be represented as a shift in the $MB_{residents}$ curve in Figure 10.6.

Wealth Effect of Endowment

The analysis in Figure 10.5 assumed that the marginal benefit and marginal cost curves were independent of the initial endowment of property rights. If the marginal benefit to residents of a certain level of restriction depends on the initial endowment, though, then the outcome is dependent on the initial endowment as well. Suppose that the $MB_{residents}$ is greater if the initial endowment is more restrictive. This is expected for two reasons. First, psychologists have found that people are less willing to part with something once they own it. Second, the endowment is an increment to individual wealth, and the marginal benefits from restrictiveness (such as the neighborhood ambiance) are expected to be wealth-elastic. The implication is illustrated in Figure 10.7, where $MB'_{residents}$ is the marginal benefits curve if the initial endowment was A'. The equilibrium amount of restrictiveness is lower if the initial endowment is A' than it is under the (current) endowment of A.

David Mills (1989) suggests that the wealth effect of the endowment combined with the restrictions on efficient trading of property rights make zoning a negative-sum game. In other words, the social costs of allowing zoning may exceed the social benefits, and there would be a net gain to society if broad trading of development rights were made easy.

Illegitimate Preferences

The analysis in Figure 10.5 assumed that all the reasons communities might use to justify zoning restrictions were legitimate in society's judgment. An example of an illegitimate preference would be a restriction justified by racial prejudice. Most states have

FIGURE 10.6 Transactions Costs and Zoning

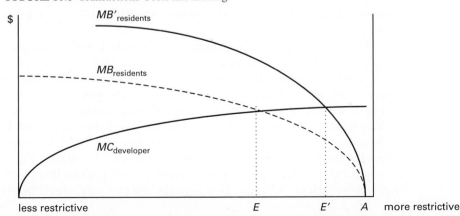

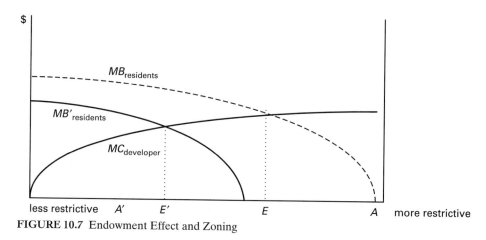

FIGURE 10.7 Endowment Effect and Zoning

not explicitly considered this question, but it is straightforward to analyze the implications of illegitimate preferences using Figure 10.7. This time, let $MB'_{residents}$ represent the legitimate preferences, and $MB_{residents}$ the preferences including illegitimate preferences. As with the wealth effect of initial endowments, illegitimate preferences for restriction will lead to an increase in restrictiveness through their impact on residents' willingness to permit development. This analysis has a clear policy implication. It suggests that suburbs should be endowed with few rights to restrict development but instead should have to acquire restrictions from landowners. Because the restrictions would have to be explicit, they could be more easily scrutinized to see whether or not they reflect preferences that society recognizes as legitimate.

Monopoly Control of Development

If the local government has some market power in the land market, it will have the ability to charge developers a higher price than it could charge in the absence of market power. This market power might arise because of some special characteristic of the community relative to other communities in the metropolitan area. More generally, all communities within a metropolitan area have some market power due to the comparative advantage of the metropolitan area relative to other metropolitan areas. This situation again can be illustrated using Figure 10.7. Now, the $MB_{residents}$ curve represents the situation with market power, while the $MB'_{residents}$ curve represents the situation without market power.

There are two theoretical objections to this result, both arising from the fact that land is durable. The first objection is that a community might restrict land use now but be less restrictive in the future because it will have more land left over in the future to dispose of. However, this objection founders on the grounds that even a postponement of development has costs to the developer; moreover, the town in the future will continue to withhold land for the same reasons it withholds land now. The second objection is that a developer might wait for land prices to fall in the future if it doesn't believe the local government will continue its restrictive policies. This objection fails on the grounds that local governments can undertake policies that commit them to restrictiveness, such as dedicating land to parks and thus removing it from the possibility of development. The objection also fails to take into account that expensive land developed today is occupied by voters, who will not want to undertake policies in the future that reduce land prices, because they had to pay the high prices to enter the town.

THE PROVISION OF LOCAL PUBLIC GOODS

Zoning is only one of the services that local governments provide. Its role in determining who is able to reside in a town, though, causes zoning to be inextricably linked to both the level of services provided and to the efficiency of these services. The main activities undertaken by local governments are the provision of primary and secondary education, public safety (police and fire), and infrastructure (roads, sewers, parks, etc.). All these services have at least some aspects of being "public goods." (See Fisher 1996, for a thorough introduction to the economic analysis of local governments.)

A *public good* is a good that is nonrival and nonexcludable in consumption. A good is *nonrival* if the marginal cost of adding a person to consume the good is zero. One example would be an uncrowded public park, where an additional jogger neither adds to the cost of park maintenance nor contributes to the costs of the park for others. (Why is it important that the park be uncrowded? Because if it is crowded, then there is the negative externality of congestion, so that the good is no longer completely nonrival. See chapter 15 for an analysis of traffic congestion in this light.) Another example would be a safe street. My taking a walk on the street doesn't reduce the amount of safety available for you to consume (in fact, it might even increase the amount of safety available for you). A good is *nonexcludable* if a person cannot be prevented from consuming it. Return to the example of a safe street. If it's safe because potential muggers know that the police will arrest them, then they will be deterred from mugging me even if I am not a resident of the town.

A public good is thus the opposite of a private good, which is both rival in consumption and excludable. Consider a Snickers bar, for example. If I eat it, there is no Snickers bar left for you, so it is a rival good. If I don't pay for the Snickers bar (assuming legal behavior) I will not have one to eat, making it an excludable good.

The problem that arises from the presence of public goods is the *free-rider problem*. Because people are able to consume the good even if they don't pay for it, it can be difficult to get people to pay for it. As a result, private markets will tend to provide too little of the public good, a result that is Pareto inefficient (Samuelson 1954). This is the usual argument for government intervention in the finance and provision of public goods, because the government by using the power to tax can force people to contribute to the financing of the public good. A natural response would be, Why not ask people how much they value the goods and then charge them accordingly? The problem is that people have an incentive to underreport their willingness to pay, again leading to underprovision.

Local Public Goods: The Tiebout Model

In one of the most influential papers in the economics literature, Charles Tiebout (1956) suggested that under some circumstances private markets could provide the efficient amount of public goods. In particular, he focused on the case of local public goods, that is, public goods that are nonrival and nonexcludable only over a limited geographical area. His essential insight was that if there were a wide enough variety of local governments and if each used local taxes to finance the production of slightly different levels and types of local public goods, then the decisions by households about where to locate would reveal their true willingness to pay. In effect, local public goods would be sold in a market, one in which households "voted with their feet" for their preferred combination of local public goods and taxes. If the market were perfectly competitive, if information were perfect, and if the local taxes were nondistortionary (did not cause the price to differ from marginal cost), then the equilibrium would be Pareto efficient even though public goods were present. The efficiency would come from two sources. First, people would be able to choose the level of public services that would best suit their needs. Second, the presence of competition for residents would force local governments to be efficient in their activities.

One of the predictions of the Tiebout model is that the population within a given suburb would be relatively homogeneous in its demand for local public goods. Note that this dimension of homogeneity does not necessarily correspond with homogeneity in socioeconomic dimensions such as income, education, or race. However, researchers investigating this prediction of Tiebout have often used these socioeconomic variables as proxies for demand and have found some evidence of relatively homogeneous communities. (Fischel 1985, ch. 14, surveys the evidence.)

The one glaring exception to this picture of homogeneous communities, of course, is the central city of the metropolitan area. Because the central city is a large and heterogeneous group of people, there is no efficiency gain from the provision of local public goods, because some people get more than they want and others less. Further, there is a concern that the residents of the central city are increasingly disconnected from the suburbs because of increasing income inequality, perhaps related to the quality of local public services (especially elementary and secondary education). An example of popular concern with city-suburban income inequality is the *USA Today* (23 September 1996) cover story.

Zoning, Property Taxes, and the Tiebout Model

The homogeneity in demand for local public goods predicted by the Tiebout model is reflected and enforced by the restrictions on land use prescribed by zoning. Bruce Hamilton (1975, 1976) first showed how a particular type of zoning could lead to an efficient outcome even in a world where the local government relied on an otherwise distortionary tax, the property tax. The property tax would be distortionary because there is a difference between the price paid by the purchaser of housing services and the price received by the provider of housing services. However, suppose all the households in a suburb desire $5,000 worth of local government spending. If the local government finances this spending by a 2.5% property tax *and* imposes a minimum house value of $200,000, then we expect all houses in the community to be worth $200,000. The tax, although collected as a property tax, is thus transformed into a user fee for the local government services.

The key assumption behind Hamilton's result is that the local government is able to impose a particularly strong type of zoning. It is illegal in the United States to pass a zoning regulation that specifies a minimum house value. Consider, though, a set of zoning regulations that require that the house be built of brick on a one-acre lot, include at least 2,000 square feet of living space and an attached garage, and have central air conditioning. The net effect of such regulations may well be to implicitly place a minimum value on the value of a house. An open question, despite a large volume of research, is the extent to which the zoning laws observed in practice are sufficiently strong to allow Hamilton's result to obtain. Mieszkowski and Zodrow (1989) argue that zoning is insufficient to prevent the property tax from being distortionary, while Fischel (1992) argues that zoning is sufficient. Much of the difficulty comes from the inability of researchers to know for sure the extent to which zoning actually restricts the decisions that households make, as opposed to the extent to which it reflects the decisions that households would make anyway.

The other key assumption behind Hamilton's analysis was that all local government spending was financed by the property tax on housing. Many suburbs, and all central cities, include nonresidential property that is also subject to the property tax. State and federal government grants to local governments provide another source of financing that can lead to distorted local decisions. Although a full analysis of these issues would take us beyond the scope of this book, the interested reader is referred to Fisher (1996) for further reference.

ZONING AND URBAN SPRAWL

> Instead of buildings set in a park, we now have buildings set in a parking lot.
> —LEWIS MUMFORD

We have already seen that urban land use is not particularly threatening to overwhelm the United States in an absolute sense. Nevertheless, the widespread concern about urban sprawl merits at least some consideration, especially an examination of the role of zoning in mitigating or exacerbating sprawl.

Irreversibility and Speculation

One criticism of land development patterns in the United States is the prevalence of so-called *leapfrog development*, in which high-density development and vacant land are interspersed as you move away from the CBD. The alleged problem with this pattern of development is that it is wasteful in the sense that people must commute farther (across the vacant area) to the CBD than they would if development occurred smoothly and continuously from the center of the city. Before considering the analytical problems with this attack, note that there is a fundamental empirical flaw: How can "sprawl" be distinguished from "green space," such as parks? In either case, there is undeveloped land in the midst of dense development. Arguably, the main difference is that one word is used to describe development patterns that a person likes and the other word is used to describe development patterns that someone doesn't like. Consider an extreme case. Commuting from the Bronx to downtown Manhattan could be much shorter if Central Park wasn't in the way. Does this make Central Park a contributor to "urban sprawl"?

There are two theoretical reasons to expect a leapfrog pattern of land development as an optimal outcome. The first theoretical reason is that the CBD is not the only center of activity in the metropolitan area. Edge cities, like any city, are distinguished by density of economic activity. The same cost-minimizing substitution of capital for land that occurs in the monocentric city will also occur in a modern polycentric city, so that development densities will decrease with distance from any of the centers. Of course, this may result in a measured decrease in density followed by an increase in density as we move from the CBD outward, but if the higher density is the result of cost-minimizing location choices made by people and firms, it may be optimal.

The second theoretical reason is that land development entails large sunk costs. The theory of investment developed in chapter 8 concluded that investments with uncertain benefits entailing large sunk costs should be undertaken only reluctantly, when it is clear that the expected benefits of the investment significantly exceed the costs. The option value of undeveloped land within a metropolitan area is high. Once the land is zoned and especially once there is construction on it, changing the land use is extremely costly. Hence, land speculators that withhold land from development can be doing the metropolitan area a favor by preserving the option of using the land in the future. Note that a profit-maximizing land speculator will withhold land from development only if the expected future benefits from developing it exceed the opportunity cost of developing the land now.

One minor empirical reason to expect the edge of a city to expand in irregular fashion, rather than smoothly along the border, is that much of the conversion from nonurban to urban land use occurs as a result of farmers selling their property. It is likely that this sale will accompany retirement, and so the exact transition time will depend, in part, on the relative ages of the owners of agricultural land.

Zoning can actually encourage urban sprawl. If negative externalities result from having high-density development in the town but positive externalities result from being close to high-density development in another town, each town may try to free-ride on the willingness of other towns to site dense development. However, if every town restricts the location and density of development, then the density of the metropolitan area is reduced, holding total metropolitan population and employment fixed. This is perhaps most easily seen by considering the analysis of zoning as a trade barrier. By reducing the capital-land ratio, zoning encourages sprawl. This can have macro effects as well. If agglomeration economies are reduced as a result of the reduction in density, then the equilibrium size of the metropolitan area might be smaller than in an uncontrolled setting, and equilibrium incomes could also be lower because of lower productivity.

Agricultural Land

A food surplus is the sine qua non of urban growth. At the extensive margin, cities grow by converting agricultural land. Does this reduce the land available for agriculture? There is an implicit belief that the conversion of agricultural land is a problem, as illustrated by the panoply of special treatment extended to farmland at the federal and state government levels. (This discussion follows Fischel 1985, ch. 13.) This includes property tax abatements and extremely generous zoning review. However, the problem does not stand up well to economic scrutiny, primarily because farmers can move. Suppose that there are two sites available and that one of them is better for farming than the other one. Suppose further that a housing development is built on the site that is better for farming. If the sites also differ in their relative attractiveness for housing, it is possible that the loss to the farmer (in the form of higher production costs or lower yields) is more than made up for by the gain to the housing developer.

Suppose that, rather than move, the farmer goes out of business. In this case, the price of food will increase. This can induce other farmers to increase production or people to convert their land to farmland. Even if that doesn't happen, there is a mitigating factor. The U.S. government provides subsidies to farmers based on agricultural prices. If prices increase, the amount of the subsidy falls. Thus, farmers receive the same revenue, consumers pay the same total amount (price plus tax-financed subsidy), and developers have lower costs.

Fischel (1985, p. 290) contends that the argument for preserving agricultural land is really a disguised exclusionary argument. While courts may frown on lot-size restrictions, they are likely to take a more benign view towards local policies claiming to advance farmland preservation. Also, some positive externalities are associated with agricultural use—driving home past an orchard or cow pasture—but those can be promoted in less extreme ways. In particular, the costs of providing these desired activities should be borne by the suburban residents who are able to enjoy them.

Jacobs (1969) is also sanguine about the impact of urban growth on agriculture, but for a different reason than Fischel. Her thesis is that agriculture really originated in and around cities and was later exported to rural areas. For example, the "medieval agricultural revolution" that saw the introduction of the three-field method of crop rotation (wheat/rye, oats/barley/peas/beans, fallow) first developed near cities and then diffused throughout Europe. Similarly, the modification of this system in the 1700s to use alfalfa/clover/sainfoin as ground cover during the fallow year was developed near cities. The modification had the dual advantage of fixing nitrogen in the soil and providing forage for cattle whose nitrogen-rich manure further enriched the soil. In fact, Jacobs argues that the origins of agriculture are to be found in prehistoric cities. The movement of what were once thought to be urban activities out of the city is thus a pattern that predates history. She argues that future generations will be amazed at the many services that were provided in cities, just as we are amazed that large-scale manufacturing and agricultural activities used to take place there.

Direct evidence on the relative efficiency of agricultural land conversion is provided by Brueckner and Fansler (1983). They show that higher agricultural land prices lead to smaller urban areas, all else being equal. In other words, the land market is taking into account the opportunity cost of land conversion from rural to urban uses.

PRIVATE ZONING

It is difficult to draw a man out of his own circle to interest him in the destiny of the state, because he does not clearly understand what influence the destiny of the state can have upon his own lot. But if it is proposed to make a road cross the end of his estate, he will see at a glance that there is a connection between this small public affair and his greatest private affairs.... Local freedom ... perpetually brings men together and forces them to help one another in spite of the propensities that sever them.

—ALEXIS DE TOCQUEVILLE

An important phenomenon is the growth of private covenants, often in the form of subdivision regulations or condominium/townhouse associations. Broadly speaking, these covenants replace local government services, taxes, and regulations with a set of private contractual arrangements. Because of their quasi-governmental status, private associations have faced strict scrutiny in their decisions. For example, many condominium associations do not use a "one person, one vote" system of government, instead assigning a vote or a fraction of a vote to each housing unit. In this, they are similar to private corporations who assign votes to shareholders based on the number of shares of stock they hold. Manson (1987) provides an overview of when such voting schemes are legal. Ellickson (1982) argues that homeowners' associations are able to do everything that city governments do, with the advantage that they are more homogeneous and composed solely of residents that subscribe to the association's management philosophy. This is a refinement of the Tiebout model developed above to include the possibility of private provision of local public goods. Cities (even relatively small suburbs) are more heterogeneous than are housing developments, and their diversity can lead to conflict and uncertainty over the provision of services and the assignment of payment responsibility. The advantages of private associations are their efficient decision making and the responsiveness of the "government" to local concerns. The legal and popular concern over private associations arises because of their exclusive nature and their "undemocratic" voting mechanisms.

An interesting theoretical question is under what conditions voting is an efficient way to make local decisions as opposed to the alternative of leaving things up to private contracts and the price mechanism. Barzel and Sass (1990) hypothesize that organizations will structure themselves in such a way as to minimize the expected costs of decision making. Further, they suggest that uncertainty about future wealth transfers—for example, low-income homeowners who vote to raise taxes on high-income homeowners—will be minimized. They examine condominium associations in New Mexico to see whether or not their hypotheses are verified by practical experience. They find that developers of condominiums frequently assign votes on the basis of either the market value of the condominium or the living area of the condominium. Because assessments (taxes) by the condominium association typically vary by value or area, these are different methods of allocating voting power on the basis of both relative payment and relative benefit. Barzel and Sass also observe that developers attempt to install any improvements that might cause controversy, such as the location of a swimming pool, in advance rather than leaving them to be decided by the association.

William Fischel (1994) considers an interesting hybrid of private and public zoning: the case of Foster City, California, a suburb of San Francisco (with a current population of about 30,000) whose land-use plan was laid out by a single developer in the 1950s and 1960s. The town incorporated in 1971, and the municipal government took over land-use control. The government has adhered to Foster's original scheme, so that we may properly speak of the zoning policy as a hybrid. Fischel finds that the ability of the developer to control land use throughout the suburb led to the absence of identifiable externalities in land use. Fischel goes on to argue that local government activities that restrict the ability of developers to engage in large-scale planning could actually lead to a less-efficient pattern of land use, even if the local government engages in zoning to compensate for the absence of large-scale private planning.

Garreau (1991, ch. 6) examines the growing use of "shadow governments" to provide local services in the United States. For example, he cites the case of Sun City, Arizona, near Phoenix. This is a development including 46,000 residents that is not incorporated into any municipality. It has a privately funded police force, the Sun City Posse, that has 183 members, more than any nearby government police force. It provides libraries, parks, and myriad other services, all financed by assessments (read "taxes") levied on the homeowners in the community. If the assessments are not paid, the association has the right to foreclose on the house and sell it at an auction. This is far from an anomaly. Garreau cites a figure of 150,000 such associations in the United States, and the number continues to grow. The importance of this type of collective organization is illustrated by comparing the number of shadow governments to the roughly 86,000 general- and special-purpose local governments in the United States.

A prominent recent example of this type of association is the town of Celebration, Florida. This town is being developed by the Walt Disney Company near Disney World, and it attempts to create small-town ambiance through the enforcement of a variety of controls. Among the rules are strict limits on renting and resale of houses, guidelines for the appearance of the gardens, and a prohibition against having broken-down cars outside the homes. The attraction of such a community can be seen by the fact that 4,550 entries were received for a lottery to be one of the town's first 350 homeowners (*The Economist*, 25 November 1995).

CHAPTER SUMMARY

- Comprehensive zoning in the United States dates only to 1916, when New York City introduced it. The United States Supreme Court legitimized the use of zoning in its 1926 decision, *Euclid v. Ambler*. Three constitutional restrictions govern zoning: the requirement for due process (both substantive and procedural), the requirement for equal protection, and the prohibition on takings.

- Only 4 percent of the land in the continental United States is used for urban purposes. The largest use of land in urban areas is for housing, while roads and parking also account for a large fraction of land use.

- Zoning can be analyzed as a trade restriction, specifically a quota on factor movements into a municipality. Most zoning can be summarized as either a restriction on the type of capital that enters a municipality or as a restriction on the capital-land ratio. Economic theory suggests that the use of tariffs (price restrictions) would be preferable to the use of quotas from an efficiency standpoint. However, the constitutional restrictions on imposing tariffs at the local level combined with the equal protection requirement make quotas (that is, zoning) the only feasible restriction available to local governments.

- Zoning can be analyzed as a way of preventing negative externalities in land use. There is little evidence that negative externalities are pervasive in practice. However, this could reflect zoning's effectiveness rather than the lack of a need for zoning.

- Zoning can be analyzed as a property right whose allocation is decided by local voters and landowners. We expect suburban zoning to be inefficiently restrictive for four reasons: the transactions costs involved in allocating the right, the wealth effect of endowments, illegitimate preferences, and monopoly control of development.

- Restrictive zoning can be argued to worsen the problem of urban sprawl by reducing settlement density in a metropolitan area. Analysis of urban sprawl is handicapped by the lack of a generally accepted definition. There is little evidence to support the hypothesis that problems in food availability are imminent because of the conversion of land from rural to urban uses.

- Private contracts (covenants) can serve as substitutes for government land-use controls. Covenants have proliferated in recent years. Covenants are viewed with suspicion because they are not subject to the same type of constitutional scrutiny that zoning decisions are; for example, there is generally no requirement that each person have one vote when determining a covenant.

EXCERPT: *UTOPIA* (THOMAS MORE)

In concluding our exploration of land-use controls, it is only fitting to turn from the Disney Corporation—creator of modern utopian societies like Disneyland—to the original Utopia authored by Thomas More (1515). This book examined every aspect of society, including the way to lay out a city in a perfect world. The excerpts below (pp. 73, 80–81) provide a look at housing and commercial activities respectively. The parallels between land use in More's world and in Disney's are perhaps instructive.

> The streets are well-designed, both for traffic and for protection against the wind. The buildings are far from unimpressive, for they take the form of terraces, facing one another and running the whole length of the street. The fronts of the houses are separated by a twenty-foot carriageway. Behind them is a large garden, also as long as the street itself, and completely enclosed by the backs of other streets. Each house has a front door leading into the street, and a back door into the garden. In both cases they're double swing-doors, which open at a touch, and close automatically behind you. So anyone can go in and out—for there's no such thing as private property. The houses themselves are allocated by lot, and changed round every ten years.
>
> They're extremely fond of these gardens, in which they grow fruit, including grapes, as well as grass and flowers. They keep them in wonderful condition—in fact, I've never seen anything to beat them for beauty or fertility. Certainly it would be hard to find any feature of the town more calculated to give pleasure and profit to the community—which makes me think that gardening must have been one of the founder's special interests.
>
> Every town is divided into four districts of equal size, each with its own shopping centre in the middle of it. There the products of every household are collected in warehouses, and then distributed according to type among various shops. When the head of a household needs anything for himself or his family, he just goes to one of these shops and asks for it. And whatever he asks for, he's allowed to take away without any sort of payment, either in money or in kind.
>
> These shopping centres include provision markets, to which they take meat and fish, as well as bread, fruit and vegetables. But there are special places outside the town where all blood and dirt are first washed off in running water. It's also forbidden

to bring anything dirty or unhygienic inside the town, for fear of polluting the atmosphere and so causing disease.

Every so often, as you walk down a street, you come to a large building, which has a special name of its own. That's where the Styward lives, and where his thirty households—fifteen from one direction and fifteen from the other—have their meals. The caterers for such dining-halls go off at a certain time each day to the provision market, where they report the number of people registered with them, and draw the appropriate rations.

There are four hospitals in the suburbs, just outside the walls. Each of them is about the size of a small town. The idea of this is to prevent overcrowding, and facilitate the isolation of infectious cases. These hospitals are so well run, and so well supplied with all types of medical equipment, the nurses are so sympathetic and conscientious, and there are so many experienced doctors constantly available, that, though nobody's forced to go there, practically everyone would rather be ill in hospitals than at home.

Source: Utopia by Thomas More, translated by Paul Turner (Penguin Classics, 1961). Copyright © 1961 by Paul Turner. Reproduced by permission of Penguin Books Ltd.

Questions for Review and Discussion

1. Compare land use in Celebration, Florida, and Utopia. The two towns are constructed under very different economic systems: one free enterprise, the other communist. Why is land use so similar?

2. How would you define "urban sprawl"? Is it a major problem where you live?

3. "Economic theory tells us that specialization promotes economic efficiency. Zoning promotes specialization within a community (and among communities) and therefore promotes efficiency." Do you agree or disagree? Explain.

4. How would you zone a city of 10 square miles that is being built from scratch close to a major city (in other words, within a metropolitan area)? Would you zone it at all?

5. Suppose a local government decided to use a tariff policy to control land use instead of using a quota policy (zoning). How would such a policy be implemented? What should be done with the revenue collected?

6. The Tiebout model predicts that a metropolitan area will consist of a large number of differentiated communities, each of which is relatively homogeneous. Is this an accurate description of the metropolitan area where you live?

CHAPTER

Intrametropolitan Competition and Economic Development Policy

We considered government policy that affected the economy of an entire metropolitan area in chapter 8. In this chapter, we analyze the relations among governments within a metropolitan area and the effect of their policies on firm location and economic development. As we saw in chapter 8, intrametropolitan location decisions of firms are strongly influenced by factors under the control of local governments. We especially focus on the case of tax abatement as a means of attracting firms.

An important set of policy issues revolves around the question of whether the relation between the central city and the suburbs is an equitable and efficient one. We briefly consider this question here, focusing especially on the possibility of an exploitative fiscal relation. Also, the role of zoning in helping the suburbs at the expense of the central city is examined.

HOW MUCH SHOULD A LOCAL GOVERNMENT PAY?

Recall from chapter 8 that economic development policies are more likely to affect a firm's location decision within a metropolitan area than a firm's decision among metropolitan areas. Also recall Courant's proposition, illustrating conditions under which subsidies to firm location can be a net benefit to the metropolitan area. The benefits include, for example, increased employment for city residents and increased tax revenue for the city, while the costs can include such items as increased local government service responsibilities, increased pollution, and increased congestion. In this section, we continue the analysis to examine how a local government within a metropolitan area can decide both the level of the subsidy and the targeting of the subsidy to a particular firm or type of firm.

Consider a metropolitan area composed of many small local governments. Suppose a local government is trying to decide how much to spend (directly or indirectly) to attract a firm. For simplicity, we will refer to generic policies of this type as *tax abatement,* although the policy might not explicitly involve reducing corporate tax lia-bility. Bartik (1994a) estimates that under a typical economic development policy, each job costs $6,000–$11,000 per year. The obvious approach would be to compare the benefits and costs of the tax abatement, where the costs include the opportunity cost of the subsidies as well as any possible deadweight loss from the taxes used to fi-nance the subsidies. A city might also want to take into account the effects of uncer-tainty and sunk costs on a firm's decision where to locate; every firm wants to be in a prosperous city, but the city can't be prosperous until the firms move there. We saw the same problem in the case of industrial parks in chapter 8, and it helps us under-stand local government investment incentives as price discrimination in favor of early firms. It also provides a quick test of whether or not a city has succeeded in improving its economic status—are firms willing to locate there without any additional incentive to do so?

The practice of towns competing for various activities is one with a colorful his-tory. Consider the following two examples from the Great Plains of the United States in the late 1800s. (I am grateful to Professor Andrew Morriss for bringing these to my attention.) In 1882, a group of influential people connected to the Northern Pacific Railroad decided to move the territorial capital from Yankton to Bismarck, where the Northern Pacific had an important station. To cloak this move in respectability, though, they created a commission that accepted bids from cities that desired to be the new capital. The following bids were made: Aberdeen, $100,000 and 160 acres of land; Pierre, $100,000 and 250 acres of land; Bismarck, $100,000 and 320 acres of land; Mitchell, $160,000 and 160 acres of land; Redfield, $100,000 and 240 acres of land; Ordway, $100,000 and 320 acres of land plus 160 acres of land for railroad; Canton, $100,000 and 160 acres of land; Frankfort, $100,000 and 160 acres of land; Huron, $100,000 and 160 acres of land; Odessa (Devil's Lake), $200,000 and 160 acres of land; and Steele, $100,000 and 160 acres of land. (See Kingsbury 1915, pp. 1301–1307 for more details.) The other cities did not know that the process was rigged, and it is in-teresting to see how important hosting the state capital was thought to be.

The second example, unsurprisingly for the period, also involves a railroad. The towns of Amarillo and Washburn, in the Texas Panhandle, were competing for a rail-road junction during the 1890s. The official history reports that the developer asked Washburn for $20,000 and Amarillo for $30,000—Washburn's railroad was more de-veloped than Amarillo's—so the developer required less inducement to build there. Washburn refused to pay, but Amarillo didn't; so Amarillo got the railroad and re-placed Washburn as the main city in the area. The willingness to advance money to at-tract business is familiar, but another version of the story makes clear the extent to which Amarillo was willing to go to win the competition. According to local legend, a railroad spur had already been built to Washburn, but an enterprising Amarillo booster tore up the track to prevent Washburn from successfully completing negotia-tions. (Both versions of the story are reported in Mojtabai [1986] pp. 27–28.) The last century has perhaps seen an increase in the subtlety of inducements; towns seldom ex-plicitly bid dollar amounts for businesses. The level of competition among cities, though, has certainly not decreased.

Comparing the benefits and costs of tax abatement is made more difficult by the inherent uncertainties involved. To be useful, the model has to account for the fact that a city does not necessarily know all of the relevant information about a firm.

Most important, the city does not know whether its incentives affected the firm's decision. Michael Wolkoff (1985) developed the following model of the city's decision.

Let p_α be the probability that a firm locates in the city if it is given a particular incentive (defined as a percentage reduction in local taxes) α between 0 and 1. Let D equal the incremental value (as a flow of benefits to the city) of the investment by the firm in a particular property, and let V equal the incremental value to the city of the next-best use of the property. Given these definitions, we can construct the expected value of a property at time t (Π_t) as

$$\Pi_t = p_\alpha (1 - \alpha) (D + V) + (1 - p_\alpha) V = p_\alpha (1 - \alpha) D - \alpha p_\alpha V + V \qquad (1)$$

Equation (1) is derived by combining two scenarios. The first scenario is that the firm moves to the property as a result of the tax abatement. This scenario occurs with probability p_α, and the value to the city in this case is $(1 - \alpha) (D + V)$. In other words, the expected return from the firm's locating in the city is the incremental value $(D + V)$ reduced by the fraction of this value that is returned to the firm as an abatement $(1 - \alpha)$ and weighted by the probability that the firm will move at all (p_α). The second scenario is that the firm does not move to the property. In that case, the value to the city is V. This scenario occurs with probability $(1 - p_\alpha)$. These two scenarios exhaust the possible outcomes, so the total expected value of the property to the city given an abatement level α is just the sum of the expected return from each scenario, which is the middle expression in equation (1). The expression farthest to the right simply rearranges terms to yield a version of the formula that is amenable to analysis.

The most important point to notice about the expression on the right-hand side of equation (1) is the second term, $\alpha p_\alpha V$, which explicitly accounts for the taxes that would have been collected by the city in the absence of the abatement. If the city's goal is to maximize its benefit from the property Π, then the optimal thing to do is choose a level of abatement α that maximizes the following expression for the present discounted value of the increase in property value resulting from the abatement, where β is the discount factor ($\beta = 1/1 + r$, where r is the discount rate) and T the planning horizon.

$$\text{Value} = \Sigma_{s=0, T} \beta^s [\Pi_s(\alpha) - \Pi_s(0)] = \Sigma_{s=0, T} \beta^s [p_\alpha(1 - \alpha)D - \alpha p_\alpha V] - \beta^s p_0 V \qquad (2)$$

Conceivably, a city could consider each firm, property, and value of α and use equation (2) to make an optimal offer. This sounds complicated, but the intuition is straightforward. Consider the following example. A city assesses the probability that a firm would locate there in the absence of abatement ($\alpha = 0$) at 20 percent ($p_0 = 0.2$). If a 50-percent tax abatement ($\alpha = 0.5$) were granted, then the probability increases to 80 percent ($p_{0.5} = 0.8$). The flow of benefits to the city in the absence of the firm (V) is $40,000 per year, while the firm would bring an extra benefit of $100,000 per year. If the planning horizon (T) is 10 years and the discount factor (β) equals 0.95, we can use equation (2) to calculate that the abatement brings the city a net benefit of $209,322. If the abatement were less effective, so that $p_{0.5}$ was only 0.4, then the benefit also falls, to $69,774. Using an approach like equation (2) lets a city government know how much it should be willing to "bid" for a firm; if the firm asks for an extra $100,000 worth of concessions in addition to the abatement, the city should acquiesce given the first set of parameters and refuse given the second set. Louisville, Kentucky, actually uses a more sophisticated model of this sort when deciding how much in the way of incentives to offer a firm.

Equation (2) can be simplified even further by assuming that $V = 0$, so that the property would yield no benefits in the absence of the firm's locating there (for example, an abandoned property). Then we obtain the following special cases. First, suppose that $p_0 = 0$, so that the firm would not locate in the city in the absence of an incentive. In this case, equation (2) is greater than or equal to zero for any $\alpha < 1$, and it is strictly positive as long as $p_\alpha > 0$. In other words, abatement is a good idea if it attracts firms that would not otherwise have come. Second, suppose that $p_\alpha = p_0$ for all α. In this case, equation (2) is always negative. In other words, abatement is not a good idea if you are just giving money to firms to do what they would have done anyway.

In addition to the theoretical work, Wolkoff reports some empirical findings, specifically in the case of Detroit's investments in the fabricated metals and electrical equipment industries. The cost of providing the services of capital has two components. The first is the amount the borrower must pay the lender to compensate the lender for the lost opportunity to invest in some other project. The second is the annual maintenance cost associated with the capital. One component of the maintenance cost is the property tax. In fact, a property tax of 1 percent is analytically similar to an increase in the interest rate of 1 percentage point (Bogart and Bradford 1990). Because taxes can be thought of as an increase in the carrying cost of capital, tax abatement is equivalent to a reduction in the user cost of capital, where the amount of the reduction depends on the amount of tax relative to the other costs of an investment. Wolkoff finds that the price elasticity of capital investment is about 0.5; in other words, a 10-percent reduction in the cost of capital leads to a 5-percent increase in investment. Local taxes represent about 4 percent of the cost of capital, so that even complete abatement would lead to an increase in investment of only 2 percent. Wolkoff goes on to show that these estimates imply that p_α is very close to p_0. In other words, the tax abatements offered by Detroit do not greatly increase the probability that a firm will locate there.

Five other issues should be considered. The first issue is that companies can lie about whether or not the abatement affects their location decision. This would certainly be a problem if you were attempting to estimate p_0 and p_α for each company, but might be less of a problem if you had a good estimate of the "average" p_α. A study of tax incentives using a survey of firms in Columbus, Ohio, by Morse and Farmer (1986) finds that as long as "enough" firms are affected, then abatement can be a good thing from a city's perspective. In their example, the additional taxes collected due to the increase in firm location exceeded the lost taxes due to abatement as long as at least 8.8 percent of the firms would not have located in the city in the absence of the abatement. Because their survey showed that 25 percent of the investments were influenced, the city's decision to grant abatements was rational.

The second issue is that there are often overlying or coterminous jurisdictions whose revenues are affected by the abatement but who do not have a direct input into the decision. To continue the example from Morse and Farmer, the tax being abated was property taxes, which are a source of revenue not only for the city but also for the local school district. The city benefited because it was able to collect payroll taxes from the firms it had granted property tax relief to, while the school district unambiguously lost. Morse and Farmer estimate that the benefits to both the city and school district exceed the costs only if at least 41.7 percent of the firms would not have located in the city without the abatement—and even in this case, there would be no requirement for the city to compensate the school district.

The third issue is the question of "targeting" firms or industries. If a city has limited resources with which to encourage business formation and relocation, how should it choose the firms and industries on which to focus? The arguments to this point suggest that a city should encourage the development of an area that specializes, but this does not necessarily identify the product in which the city or neighborhood should specialize. Even if a city correctly ascertains which firm or industry would be the best, there is no guarantee that changes in the economy might not make that firm obsolete.

The fourth issue is the "prisoner's dilemma" aspect of abatement policy, which we will examine in some detail in the next section. Imagine that all local governments offer the same incentive to a firm. In such a case, the firm will locate in the same place it would have in the absence of any incentives, only now it will pay lower taxes. This implies that local government officials have an incentive to cooperate in formulating economic development policy so as not to cause a destructive *race for ratables.*

The fifth issue is that incentives offered to individual firms can be considered as a substitute for a comprehensive reform of local taxes. If taxes need to be reduced in order to attract firms to the city, then maybe the government is better off restructuring the tax system rather than providing piecemeal inducements for individual firms. On the other hand, tailoring taxes for individual firms might allow a local government to collect higher total revenues. The idea is that the average cost of providing government services might exceed the marginal cost; by charging firms only marginal cost, the government might increase efficiency (Black and Hoyt 1989). There is no clear evidence that this approach works in practice, although it is a good theoretical argument. One policy that has received considerable academic attention is the idea of a "land value" tax to replace the property tax. The idea is that property values consist of two elements: the value of the site and the value of the improvements placed upon the site. If the elasticity of supply for sites is low (the quantity of land is fixed), then a smaller deadweight loss results from taxing land than from taxing the improvements. Improvements represent capital investments, and capital is assumed to be extremely mobile among locations. Oates and Schwab (1995) analyze the experience of Pittsburgh, Pennsylvania, which adopted a variation of land-value taxation in 1979. The tax rate on land value in Pittsburgh is more than five times the tax rate on improvements, so the system is intermediate between the standard property tax and a strict land-value tax. They find that the presence of the large land-value tax, by allowing other tax rates to remain fairly low, contributed to a significant increase in building activity in Pittsburgh during the 1980s relative to other cities in the same region.

Another alternative to tax abatement is suggested by Bogart and Bradford (1990). They point out that many of the incentive benefits of the land-value tax are also found in a system that permanently assigns a share of the local property tax to a property, which could be implemented by freezing assessed values in place. However, the transition to such a system would entail large redistributions as the change in future tax liabilities was capitalized into property values. This transition problem, by the way, also applies in the case of a shift to land-value taxation. Bogart and Bradford propose an alternative, which they call "separate treatment of new construction."

Under this scheme, any increase in property value due to improvements to the property is taxed at a fixed rate designed to capture the external costs to the community imposed by the development. This rate could be lower than the property tax rate in central cities, reflecting the social cost of idle infrastructure, or higher than the municipal property tax rate in areas where growth imposes large external costs. This approach was adopted as a recommendation by a state government tax study commission in New Jersey in 1988, but it has not yet been implemented anywhere.

COMPETITION AMONG LOCAL GOVERNMENTS AS A "PRISONER'S DILEMMA"

The model developed earlier considers the decision of a local government in isolation. In practice, a firm will generate offers from a variety of governments. Therefore, a city must consider not only its own action when formulating an offer, but must consider the actions of other cities as well. Because any given firm can entertain offers from a wide variety of cities, the greater bargaining power belongs to the firm. This power presents local governments with a dilemma. Suppose a firm is considering potential sites in three different cities, *A, B,* and *C,* in the same metropolitan area. In the absence of any tax incentive, the firm would locate in city *A* (recall the analysis of firm location in chapter 4). Now suppose each city, acting in isolation, offers the firm $3 million in incentives. Where will the firm locate? In *A,* only now it is $3 million richer.

The example above is not completely fanciful, and the lesson has not been lost on local government officials. So why don't all three cities agree not to offer the tax incentive to the firm? Suppose each city stands to reap $5 million in net benefits from the firm and that the firm's profits are $1 million higher if it locates in *A* than if it locates in *B* or *C*. If all three cities agree not to offer incentives, then cities *B* and *C* have a reason to renege on the agreement. If city *B* offers the firm $2 million, while cities *A* and *C* honor the agreement, then city *B* will gain $3 million while the firm will gain $1 million. Knowing this, city *A* will anticipate that cities *B* and *C* will make offers to the firm despite any agreement, and so *A* will prepare such an offer itself. This is an example of the general problem known as *the prisoner's dilemma.* The prisoner's dilemma—named after the situation where two prisoners are separated and each given a choice of confessing in return for a reduced sentence, but each prisoner keeps silent in the hope that the other one will also keep silent—is a well-known strategic situation resulting from the inability to make credible commitments. If city *A* really believed that cities *B* and *C* would not make offers to the firm, then city *A* would have no reason to preempt them. In turn, this knowledge could lead city *A* to work with cities *B* and *C* in order to promote the entire metropolitan area rather than to compete destructively with them. Rob Wassmer (1993) documents the proliferation of local government incentives in the Detroit metropolitan area in this analytical framework. Return to the example of the relocation of the territorial capital of Dakota from Yankton to Bismarck that I reported earlier in the chapter. It was widely accepted that the capital should move from Yankton (in the southeastern corner of the territory) to a more central location, but it was also widely accepted that any move should wait until the territory split (into the current states of North and South Dakota). If no other city had bid for the capital, thereby exposing the move by Bismarck for what it was, inertia might have kept the capital at Yankton for the few years before the split and promoted a fairer contest among the cities who wished to host the capital. In fact, the attempt to move the capital sparked editorial condemnation throughout the territory. However, the commission charged with choosing the new capital visited each of the cities, giving them all hope that they would be selected, and the condemnation turned instead to competition as the bids reported earlier were assembled.

Another practical example of a prisoner's dilemma for local governments is provided by Bartik (1991, pp. 28–30) who reports the findings of a case study of the location decision for the General Motors Saturn plant. These findings are summarized in Table 11.1. The cost-minimizing location in the absence of any government tax incentives was the Nashville, Tennessee area. This was also the location eventually chosen by Saturn, but only after the state of Tennessee had made tax concessions worth an estimated $34 per car. Note that had Tennessee refused to make concessions, Lexington, Kentucky, could have become the low-cost location by providing tax concessions of only $13 per car.

It is possible that even the "winner" of a bidding war for a firm might lose in the end. Garber (1990) argues that the residents of the town where Saturn located would have been better off had the plant not come at all, because all the residents got was an increasingly crowded infrastructure when most of the employees moved there from elsewhere. Other high-profile industrial location decisions (including BMW in South Carolina and Mercedes-Benz in Alabama) have involved hefty subsidies that would require incredible spillovers to justify, even if every employee in the plants had been an unemployed area resident.

One way that cities can credibly commit not to engage in destructive competition for firms is to have their ability to do so restricted by the state legislature. For example, the state of Michigan adopted a rule that essentially gave veto power over the use of tax abatement for intrastate moves to the city that the firm was leaving. A similar approach was taken by a bipartisan group around Cleveland known as the "Greater Cleveland Committee for Cooperative Economic Development." The group, co-chaired by the (Democratic) president of the Cleveland City Council and a

TABLE 11.1   Estimated Costs per Saturn Car

Location	Transport Cost to Market	Local Supplier's Labor Cost	State and Local Taxes	Total Costs
Nashville, TN	$426	$159	$118	$703
Lexington, KY	$423	$186	$106	$715
St. Louis, MO	$419	$172	$134	$725
Bloomington, IL	$417	$202	$162	$781
Kalamazoo, MI	$430	$244	$116	$790
Terre Haute, IN	$413	$209	$168	$790
Marysville, OH	$427	$219	$169	$815

Source: Bartik (1991), Table 2.2, p. 29.

Cuyahoga County Commissioner, included suburban Republican mayors as well. (Full disclosure: I participated in the deliberations.) It released a statement of principles in 1992 that began:

> (1) Cooperation among county and local governments to support regional economic development and job creation should be promoted. Economic development is a regional issue, not a local issue, and teamwork among governmental units will help ensure the economic viability of the region.
>
> (2) The use of tax abatement to support intra-state moves of businesses causes fierce competition among Ohio's local governments and is not consistent with the economic development goals of job creation and retention. Too often the motivation for this competition is to build the tax base of one community at the expense of another. Tax benefits that promote intra-state moves by firms should be discouraged because there is usually no obvious regional gain from these activities.

A second way of promoting cooperation is to directly link the fortunes of all the cities. Perhaps the most prominent example of this approach is the program for tax-base sharing in the Minneapolis–St. Paul area. Under this plan, in operation since 1974, 40 percent of the increase in the property tax base resulting from a business relocation or expansion enters a common pool. This lessens the incentive for destructive competition by reducing the private benefit to a city of attracting a firm. It also makes explicit the notion that the economy of the entire metropolitan area is closely linked, perhaps causing suburban residents to be more willing to support improvements to the central city. Over 30 percent of the total assessed value of commercial and industrial property is now in the common pool, and the pooling is estimated to reduce interjurisdictional fiscal disparities by over 20 percent (Macdonald-Taylor 1992; Reschovsky 1980).

Although the Minneapolis–St. Paul example is perhaps the best known, it is not the only one of its kind. For example, the Dayton, Ohio metropolitan area has operated, since 1991, a regional economic development program similar to that in Minneapolis. It includes in a pool for regional distribution not only tax-base sharing of commercial and industrial property values but also increases in residential assessments and local government income and property tax revenue. This sum of money is allocated partly as a set of monetary transfers among governments and partly to finance regional infrastructure investments.

The prisoner's dilemma, in its classical form, is a zero-sum game. In other words, the only way one prisoner can do better is for the other prisoner to do worse. Bartik (1991, ch. 8) asks, Are tax abatements a zero-sum game? If the only effect of tax abatement is to move businesses around, then Bartik's answer to this question is yes. However, social benefits can accrue from economic development policies of local governments. These benefits can come in two broad forms. First, if tax abatement results in the employment of previously unemployed people, and if this short-term employment has a permanent effect on these people, then it can be of benefit. Second, there may be productivity-enhancing competition among local governments trying to attract firms. As an exercise, you might want to show that these are specific instances of Courant's proposition about local government economic development policy.

CENTRAL CITY VERSUS SUBURBS

> Property is continually tending from our city to escape the oppressiveness of our taxation. . . . Thus, while every suburb of New York City is rapidly growing, . . . our City has no equivalent rapidity of growth, and unimproved property here is often unsalable at a nominal price."*

An ongoing debate in the United States focuses on the relation between the central city of a metropolitan area and its suburbs. The model we have developed in chapter 9 of a metropolitan area illustrates that some of this debate is misguided in the sense that it makes some incorrect assumptions about efficient urban economic structure. In particular, the increasing localization of services (and the associated rise of edge cities) is a natural development of the increased tradability of services and not necessarily the result of conspiracy or neglect.

The exodus of manufacturing from the traditional CBD to suburban or rural greenfield locations can be explained as resulting from a combination of changes in manufacturing techniques and revolutionary changes in federal liability for pollution. The possibility that exclusionary zoning policies by the suburbs create a pool of low-income households "trapped" in the city is not necessarily supported by the evidence. The notion that suburban residents "exploit" the central city through unjust fiscal relations is also not well documented. We consider each of these questions in turn.

Voith (1994) argues that central city and suburban growth can be complementary, and he provides statistical evidence to support his argument. The intuition behind the result is straightforward. Even if a suburb is prospering more than the central city, it might be doing relatively worse than it would if the central city were prospering. Therefore, suburbs have a self-interested motivation to promote central city development. These relative effects, however, are difficult to identify, and they are likely to be difficult to sell politically.

Pollution and Location: The Brownfields Problem

A longstanding phenomenon in the United States has been the decentralization of employment, especially in manufacturing (see chapter 9). Nevertheless, we have seen examples of government policies in many metropolitan areas aimed at stemming or reversing this "flight" of industry. One puzzle to economists has been the seeming ineffectiveness (or limited effectiveness, at best) of many policies that try to take advantage of existing infrastructure by concentrating fiscal incentives on the traditional industrial heart of the city. As we saw in chapter 8, statistical analysis of fiscal incentives by economists has found them to be of limited effectiveness in altering the location decisions of firms. In particular, enterprise zones—usually located in the industrial heart of cities—have not been successful at reversing the decline in employment.

One explanation of the limited effectiveness of these fiscal incentives is found in the change in liability promulgated by the Congress in the Comprehensive Environmental Response, Compensation, and Liability Act (CERCLA) in 1980, better known as "Superfund." This legislation mandated the use of an aggressive system that forces

---

*From the *New York Tribune,* 21 January 1847 (quoted in Jackson 1985, pp. 29–30)

a broad class of present, past, and future property owners to (potentially) pay for all cleanup costs. One way of thinking about the effect of CERCLA is as a local tax, in that the perceived potential liability on owners of property and their neighbors will vary depending on the extent of pollution in an area, which in turn depends on the history of land use in the area. The most important insight from economic analysis of the incidence of taxes is that the true burden of the tax is not necessarily borne by those assigned the incidence by statute. A standard incidence result is that the incidence of local taxes will be borne primarily by the owners of relatively immobile factors of production, such as land. A corporation, in this case, can reasonably decline even a generous financial incentive from a city to relocate if the relocation could potentially force them to become financially responsible for large cleanup costs and other environmental liabilities. Yount and Meyer (1994) argue that the characteristics of these *brownfield* sites makes potential investors likely to overestimate the risks associated with them, further reducing the chances that firms will choose to locate there. A study of industrial firm location decisions in Cuyahoga County, Ohio, by Bogart (1995) finds that the presence of a toxic waste site in a census tract reduces the level of industrial employment in the tract. He also finds that, controlling for the presence of toxic waste sites, designating the census tract as part of an enterprise zone leads to an increase in industrial employment.

These problems have led states and the federal EPA to try to make regulations and liability consistent with economic development policy. For example, several states have instituted policies in which firms that undertake remediation efforts receive from the state a *covenant not to sue*. This is a promise from the state government that the firm will not be responsible for lawsuits involving pollution that was not their responsibility and that the firm has cleaned up. Although the legal standing of such covenants remains in some doubt, they are credited with spurring redevelopment of brownfields in those states that have them.

Inclusionary Zoning

Low-income households and low-income housing are concentrated in central cities. This location pattern is not a problem per se, but some potential problems are associated with it. For example, if central city schools are worse than their suburban counterparts, children of low-income households could have worse prospects than otherwise comparable children of middle- and upper-income households. Also, low-income households might not have convenient access to jobs that are increasingly located in the suburbs. The pattern of income-based exclusion might also serve as a substitute for race-based exclusion as modern minimum lot-size restrictions replace the racial covenants of 50 years ago. (See chapter 14 for a detailed look at racial segregation in housing.)

The observed pattern of income segregation is alleged to result from exclusionary zoning practices by the suburbs. Theoretically, there are four explanations for excluding certain groups of people. First is "fiscal zoning," by which people are excluded who pay less in local government taxes than they receive in local government services. For example, if local government is financed by property taxes, zoning restrictions that effectively set a minimum house price can serve as a tool for fiscal zoning. Second is "public goods zoning," by which people are excluded because they increase the unit cost of producing public goods. For example, children of college-educated parents may be less expensive to educate than children of non-college-educated parents. Third is "consumption zoning," by which people who would impose negative consumption externalities in housing are excluded. For example, people who would let their house deteriorate and create a negative externality for their neighbors would be excluded on this basis. Fourth is "political economic zoning," by which people who might systematically vote against the status quo are excluded.

The implication of all of the theoretical explanations is that zoning will systematically exclude poor people. Fiscal zoning clearly works to exclude poor people. If poor people require greater public inputs to achieve the same level of service (the example of college-educated parents being particularly appropriate), then there is a public goods zoning explanation for excluding poor people. To the extent that poor people are willing to spend less on community norm decorations, there is a consumption reason to exclude poor people. Finally, if poor people systematically vote differently than middle-income and rich people, a political economic justification exists for their exclusion. Bogart (1993) uses a formal economic model to show that the different motivations cannot be distinguished solely on the basis of community economic composition, because their common prediction is that poor people will be excluded. This is troubling for policy makers attempting to alleviate undesirable motivations for exclusion while leaving in place the ability of communities to alleviate negative externalities in land use. Bogart likens this situation to that facing the Woodsman in Little Red Riding Hood, who must decide whether it's the Big Bad Wolf or Granny lying in bed. If it's the Wolf, then the Woodsman's ax yields a positive result for everyone (except the Wolf), but if it's Granny there, the outcome is less desirable. Rolleston (1987) presents the only empirical study to carefully distinguish among the various motivations. She examines zoning decisions in New Jersey and finds evidence that zoning decisions have been motivated for fiscal reasons. She also finds that some municipalities seem to be willing to zone an area for industrial use in order to prevent it from being used for low-income housing, which indicates that the perceived negative externalities from low-income housing could be substantial. Schwab and Oates (1991) show how equalizing intergovernmental grants—grants that vary inversely with some measure of local fiscal health—can offset the fiscal motivation for zoning. The intuition is straightforward: When poor people move into town, they pay less in local taxes than they receive in local spending, but they also bring an increase in intergovernmental grants to the town from the state.

There has been political and judicial pressure on suburban governments to remove the exclusionary zoning and adopt "inclusionary" policies instead. Usually the latter involve a combination of judicial review and legislative fiat in the form of a requirement that towns include a "fair share" of affordable housing. The most sweeping policy has been that adopted in New Jersey as a result of the Mount Laurel decisions discussed in chapter 10. Each municipality in the state is required to have a certain number of housing units that are affordable by low- and middle-income families as defined by the legislature. This requirement applies not only to municipalities with vacant land on which new affordable housing units can be built but even to suburbs whose land is completely occupied. Fanwood, a small New Jersey town 20 miles west of Manhattan, was ordered by the New Jersey Council on Affordable Housing to allow developers to go forward with plans to demolish existing single-family housing and replace it with apartment buildings, overruling the town's decision (*New York Times,* 19 October 1988). Municipalities that comply with the requirement without a legal struggle have sometimes tried to reduce any negative externalities by locating the affordable housing on the outskirts of town and/or by separating the affordable housing from the rest of town by a "moat" of commercial or vacant property. Lawrence Township (near Trenton), for example, built most of its units in a townhouse and apartment complex on the border with Hamilton Township and separated from the rest of town (including the prestigious Lawrenceville School) by a large shopping mall and U.S. Route 1. Princeton Township (home of Princeton University) located its affordable housing on the border with Montgomery Township in a new development.

The opening of a *market for exclusion* in New Jersey during the 1980s provides some direct evidence of the willingness of suburban residents to prevent the entry of low-income households, hence a measure of their perceived benefits from this action. This market was created by the New Jersey legislature in 1986, when it gave the ability to municipalities to satisfy part of their fair-share housing requirements by paying other municipalities to refurbish low-income housing. These payments were negotiated through a tool called a *regional contribution agreement* (RCA). The price per housing unit of an RCA has been found to vary from $20,000 to $27,500 in eight agreements reached before 1988 (Hughes and McGuire 1991). The mechanism creating the RCA allowed "donor" (rich) towns to negotiate with any potential "recipient" (poor) towns, thus eroding any ability of the recipient town to enforce favorable terms. This situation is analogous to the prisoner's dilemma identified earlier in the case of firm location. Hughes and McGuire argue that donor towns should be forced to negotiate with a particular recipient (for example, the closest neighbor that is a recipient) in order to increase the bargaining power of recipients. The problem facing recipient towns is strictly analogous to the problem facing cities in the earlier analysis (see chapter 8) of cities vying to attract professional sports teams. Hughes and McGuire do not have sufficient data to infer the amount that donor towns would be willing to pay, but it is reasonable to assume that it is greater than the amount that the recipient towns are willing to accept.

Suburban Exploitation of Central Cities

Another potential inequity in the relationship between central city and suburbs is the idea that suburban residents are exploiting the central city, where exploitation is interpreted as an "unjust relationship." This inequity can take several possible forms. One is that suburban residents use central city services but do not pay for them through taxes. Another is that homogeneous suburbs remove the potential for income redistribution. Still another is that if suburban residents are paying for central city services they are not paying a high enough price.

Measuring the extent of exploitation can be difficult even if we agree on the definition of an "unjust relationship." It is possible that people receive consumer surplus from a product or service. For example, suburbanites may value a visit to a city museum at $4 but have to pay only $2 in admission. It could be argued that the suburbanites are exploiting the city even if the costs of operating the museum are completely covered by admission fees. Measuring exploitation would require accurately assessing consumer surplus, which is not easy. And this example is actually simpler than many common situations, where the relationship is not as clear and direct between the amount paid and the city services received by the suburbanite.

There can be large efficiency gains from a fragmented metropolitan area. If there are many different types of local governments, each providing a distinctive set of services financed by local taxes, then people can "vote with their feet" by moving to the suburb that best suits their preferences. This provides an analog in local public services for a competitive market in private goods, with similar positive efficiency results. This analysis, originally due to Charles Tiebout (1956), has spawned 40 years of research into whether the positive effects of multiple jurisdictions outweigh their negative effects. (Recall the analysis in chapter 10.)

In a penetrating article, David Bradford and Wallace Oates (1974) carefully examined the theory in the case of a set of five central cities and 53 suburban municipalities in northeastern New Jersey. To do so, they compare the current fiscal relations with that of a counterfactual "unified system" in which all the suburbs and cities were combined into one single government.

The system defined by Bradford and Oates as the "Current System" is one with many small, independent local governments, each with its own taxing and spending authority. Each local government also has zoning authority, which effectively allows it to set a minimum price for housing in the local government. Under these conditions, a property tax proportional to the market value of the house amounts to a user fee for local public services. Given that the primary local tax for local governments is the property tax, this result is quite important. It says there is no deadweight loss from the local government tax system. The opportunity for mobility also implies that people live in the town whose level and composition of local government services best fits their demands. The combination of factors implies that suburbs are homogeneous in the demand for local services and in house value. In practice, these demands are correlated with the income of the household, implying income homogeneity among suburbs as well.

The one missing element in the model described above is a large, heterogeneous jurisdiction—the central city. The central city is too large to be inhabited by only one income group, and it also includes nonresidential land uses that impose costs on and demand services from the local government. The central city is the residual location for those unwilling or unable to live in any of the suburbs. There is no unanimity in the demand for central city services, so there is a deadweight loss from the property tax in the central city. Further, property tax rates in the central city typically exceed those in the suburbs. Because the deadweight loss of a tax increases proportional to the square of the tax rate, the deadweight loss in the city is especially high.

Even if we are not troubled by the existence of deadweight loss in the central city, there are nevertheless two reasons to be dissatisfied with the Current System. First, income segregation in the past could lead to income inequality in the future if the quality of local public schools is correlated with household income. This is not only inequitable but could be inefficient if talented young people are not getting the opportunity to fully develop their talents. Second, the centripetal effect of central city decline could lead to firms' leaving the city in favor of suburban sites, reducing the agglomeration economies that are the primary explanation for metropolitan area formation in the first place.

Bradford and Oates contrast the Current System with a hypothetical Unified System in which all of northeast New Jersey consists of one local government that is assumed to provide a level of services equal to the average of the current set of local governments. They discuss the effects of shifting to a Unified System as viewed from several perspectives. First, from the standpoint of vertical equity, the property tax rate would increase in the suburbs and fall in the central city, while expenditures would increase in the suburbs (because central cities provide a wider range of local services than do most suburbs). The overall impact on the income distribution from these changes is ambiguous. The relative population of the central city and the suburbs will determine whether the Unified System will undertake any explicitly redistributive policy. The ability to redistribute is limited, of course, by the extent to which high-income households are mobile between metropolitan areas and can escape any undesirable taxes. Further, redistribution is limited by the ability of high-income households to outbid low-income households for desirable locations (upwind of the landfill, for example), even if the per capita spending on the various local government services is equalized.

Second, they evaluate a Unified System from the standpoint of allocative efficiency. The shift implies that there is now a deadweight loss from the property tax in the suburbs, whereas before the tax had essentially been a user charge. This problem is ameliorated by the deductibility of property tax payments from the Federal income tax. It is also reduced to the extent that the tax rates in the central city fall. The *deadweight loss of taxation*—that is, the lost consumer surplus and producer surplus due to the presence of a tax—is proportional to the square of the tax rate. (A tax causes the price paid by the consumer to exceed the price received by the producer. This means that some Pareto-improving trades are not made. For example, if the consumer is willing to pay $60 for something that costs the producer $58, then there is an opportunity for a mutually beneficial trade with total benefits of $2 to divide between consumer and producer. If there is a tax of $3, though, the trade does not occur.) There is also a deadweight loss in consumption due to the loss of heterogeneity among governments in the level of public services. Bradford and Oates estimate a deadweight loss of $0.50 per $1.00 change in spending—in other words, lost consumer surplus of $1.50 for each $1.00 in tax revenue raised by the government. This finding suggests that the (presumed) increase in equity comes at a high efficiency cost. However, this efficiency cost is offset somewhat by the potential for income integration and agglomeration economies identified earlier as losses under the Current System.

Third, they consider problems arising during the transition from the Current System to the Unified System. The main issue is the windfall gains and losses that will accrue to landowners as a result of the changes in taxes and spending. Property values reflect the discounted present value of expected benefits less the costs of owning the property. (Any durable good can be valued in this way.) Shifting to a Unified System implies large changes in taxes and spending irregularly distributed throughout the metropolitan area. These transition costs could be "desirable" to some, especially to those who benefit, but the uncertainty associated with them only makes the political difficulties of moving to such a system greater.

Demolition Costs, Downtown, and Edge City

One explanation for edge cities is that they result from the difficulty in transforming central business districts to meet current needs. One of the important advantages of a greenfield location over a location downtown is that it is not difficult to change the

TABLE 11.2 Demolition Cost per Acre

Building height (stories)	2	3	4	5
Demolition cost per acre	$91,476	$137,214	$365,904	$457,380

previous land use in the greenfield location. If a building already occupies the land you wish to develop, it can be quite costly to remove. Table 11.2 summarizes information from Edwin Mills and Bruce Hamilton (1989, pp. 137–138) about the cost per acre of demolishing a building. Clearly, the existence of any such relics of prior use imposes a high cost on the prospective developer.

Suppose, though, that demolition was costless. Would this mitigate the creation of edge cities? Probably not. The theory developed in chapter 7 about localization economies implied that decreases in transportation costs should lead to greater spatial specialization. Edge cities are the products of the increased tradability of services. In fact, some of the more successful central business districts are precisely those that have specialized in providing services in which they have a comparative advantage.

MEASURING AND ALLEVIATING URBAN FISCAL DISTRESS

Although the notion of urban fiscal distress is a commonplace, it is important to distinguish among cities when designing policies. A thorough examination of both the extent of urban fiscal distress and policies with the potential to alleviate that distress is found in Ladd and Yinger (1989). The discussion in this section summarizes their findings.

The first empirical point they make is that the composition of employment varies substantially among the 86 cities that they study. They classify a city as belonging to a functional type on the basis of the broad nature of that city's specialization. Table 11.3 illustrates the variation among the averages in each functional type in the private-sector employment composition and in the public-sector employment as a fraction of total employment. This variation among cities implies that an urban strategy that focuses solely on one type of employment will not be uniformly effective.

In order to translate information about a city's economy into an indicator of the health of the local government, several assumptions must be made. The first set of assumptions deals with the set of taxes that can be imposed within the city and the size of tax rates imposed. Ladd and Yinger define the *revenue-raising capacity* of a city as the amount of money it could collect using a standard set of taxes and tax rates. The second set of assumptions deals with the level and composition of public services provided by the city government. The amount of spending needed to provide a standard set of services at a standard quality level is defined as the *standardized expenditure need* of a city. The first measure of fiscal health that Ladd and Yinger develop is the *standardized fiscal health* of a city, defined as the difference between the revenue-raising capacity of the city and its standardized expenditure need, expressed as a percentage of capacity. A standardized fiscal health that is less than zero indicates that

TABLE 11.3   Employment Mix in 1982 for 86 Cities

Functional Type	Number of Cities	Percentage of Private Employment in:			Public Employment as a Fraction of Total Employment
		Mfg.	Retail	Services	
Diversified centers					
National	6	20.8	15.8	30.3	16.0
Regional	23	21.5	17.6	28.5	14.3
Subregional	10	18.5	19.5	26.1	16.1
Functional and manufacturing	22	32.7	16.0	25.5	12.3
Government and education	6	17.4	20.5	38.1	27.7
Industrial, mining, and military	7	17.4	25.7	29.0	23.5
Residential, resort, and retirement	12	17.7	24.5	29.8	14.4

Source: Ladd and Yinger (1989), Table 2.4, p. 31.

the expenditure needs outweigh the ability of the city to pay for them using standard taxes and tax rates.

Ladd and Yinger calculated the standardized fiscal health for 71 cities in 1972 and 1982. They defined the index such that the average value of the index for 1972 was 0.0, so that the 1982 calculations illustrate how the overall fiscal health of cities had changed during the previous decade. They found that 35 cities had a standardized fiscal health greater than zero in 1972, while only 27 cities had a standardized fiscal health greater than zero in 1982. Further, the average value of the index in 1982 was −10.9, indicating that the overall fiscal health of the cities in their sample declined by almost 11 percent during the time period studied. There was large variation in the individual experiences of cities. In 1972, for example, the standardized fiscal health ranged from a high of 52.8 in Fort Lauderdale, Florida to a low of −81.5 in New York, New York. In 1982, the range was from 47.2 in Hollywood, Florida to a low of −109.7 in Newark, New Jersey.

The measure of standardized fiscal health does not account for variation among cities in the actual taxes that they are permitted to levy or for variation in the service responsibilities of different cities. In order to account for these variations, Ladd and Yinger developed a second measure of fiscal health that they call "actual fiscal health." They define the "restricted revenue-raising capacity" as the amount of revenue that can be raised by applying standard tax rates to the actual tax bases available to the city and adjusting for the level of intergovernmental grants available to the city. They also define "actual expenditure need," the level of spending needed to provide a standard level of quality for the public services that are actually the responsibility of the city government. The index of actual fiscal health is then calculated as the difference between the restricted revenue-raising capacity and the actual expenditure need of the city, expressed as a percentage of restricted revenue-raising capacity.

Again examining their sample of 71 cities, they found that 43 of them had an actual fiscal health greater than zero in 1972, with a range from 55.4 (Hollywood, Florida) to –71.1 (New York City). In 1982, the average for all cities had declined to –4.9 from an average of 0.0 in 1972. Only 32 cities had an actual fiscal health greater than zero, with the range from 56.4 (Hollywood, Florida) to –79.7 (Los Angeles, California).

Using both of their measures of fiscal health, Ladd and Yinger found that the worst problems were found in larger cities that had residents with relatively low incomes. What is perhaps most striking about their findings is the large variation in the measures across cities. The extent of urban fiscal distress varies substantially. They suggest that state and federal assistance should be targeted toward those cities that are most distressed rather than being spread across all cities regardless of fiscal health. They also suggest that indirect assistance in the form of extending the ability of local governments to tax or removing service provision responsibilities can be as helpful as direct assistance in the form of intergovernmental grants. In any event, policies that work to strengthen the economies of the cities and increase the incomes of city residents are an integral component of improving the fiscal health of the city governments.

A popular argument in the 1990s has been that central cities have been hamstrung by their inability to encapsulate the growth occurring in the suburbs and edge cities. The strongest statement of this hypothesis is by David Rusk (1995). He refers to "cities without suburbs" as being a laudable and achievable goal of public policy. By contrasting *elastic cities* (cities with the ability to expand through annexation) and *inelastic cities,* he argues that inelastic cities are doomed to decline. His methodology is suspect, though, because he uses economic criteria to compare politically determined boundaries. It is not clear, for example, that the low-income areas of his elastic cities are better off—or even a smaller part of the economy—than those in his inelastic cities. Adams et al. (1996) also argue for greater intervention on behalf of central cities because of their findings (discussed in chapter 9) that intermetropolitan migration is linked to the relative performance of the central city. Their argument, as does Rusk's, suffers from the criticism that the political boundaries of the central cities do not necessarily incorporate comparable economic entities. Rusk, as the former mayor of Albuquerque, can be forgiven for coming at questions from a political angle. However, this issue again illustrates the problem that since economic and political boundaries are not identical, analysis based on political boundaries (which is often the case, due to data limitations) can lead to inappropriate conclusions.

CENTRAL CITIES AS DEVELOPING COUNTRIES

A common criticism of cities in the United States is that they resemble—often unfavorably—developing countries. Given that the United States is predominantly an urban country and indisputably a wealthy nation, it can't be the case that all parts of all cities are comparable to developing countries. In fact, the principal concern that people have about U.S. cities is about the older, central cities rather than about the entire metropolitan area.

If we compare the central cities of U.S. metropolitan areas to other countries, we quickly see that a worthwhile analysis can really only be made vis à vis other wealthy industrialized countries. For example, consider infant mortality, a standard measure of basic health in a population. The infant mortality rate in the United States is 9.1 deaths per thousand, which is comparable to that for the European Union (8.3) and Australia (7.0), although much higher than that in Japan (4.6). This overall figure masks data from individual cities that can be much higher than average, such as Washington, D.C. (23.2) or Cleveland (17.0), or below average, such as San Francisco (8.4). The figure for Washington, while 150 percent above the national average, remains well below the average figure for Central America (38.8), South America (44.1), and the Middle East (57.9), and fails to compare with Africa (101.1) Central cities in the United States have worse infant mortality than do other parts of the United States, but they are not at levels found in developing countries.

An alternative basis for comparison is poverty, including housing conditions. Consider the case of a "traditional high poverty area" in Cleveland, the Hough neighborhood, site of a major riot in the 1960s. Data from the U.S. Census of Population and Housing indicate that all the people have access to safe water and almost all the houses have full kitchen facilities. The primary means of transportation to work in this area is private automobiles, although the use of public transportation exceeds average levels elsewhere in Cleveland. Poverty in the United States is unlike poverty elsewhere in the world.

Despite these rosy statistics showing that it's not so bad to be poor, the disparity between central city and suburb remains disturbing. For example, if the high-poverty neighborhoods are economically isolated from the remainder of the metropolitan area, opportunities for beneficial trade are being lost. Further, if this isolation leads to antisocial behavior (read crime), then deadweight losses are incurred in the form of protection of property and the costs of law enforcement. If the racial composition of high-poverty neighborhoods is systematically different from other parts of the metropolitan area, then economic isolation can be related to racial segregation with a concomitant increase in social tension.

A natural focus for government policy is the link between central cities and the remainder of the metropolitan area. Like developing countries, central cities have the option of following import substitution or export promotion strategies for economic development. An import substitution strategy would be to begin local production of a good or service currently being imported from other areas. An export promotion strategy would be to specialize in the area's competitive advantage and sell the resulting goods and services on the open market. If the area's competitive advantage is in a good currently being imported, then the two approaches have some similarities. Professor Michael Porter asserts that many government programs have amounted to import substitution, which only increases economic isolation for the inhabitants of the central city. He advocates instead that central city neighborhoods should seek greater connection with the metropolitan economy by following an export-based strategy. What is the comparative advantage of the central city? One of the main advantages is a central location, which can facilitate its use as a market. Another advantage is the large consumer base provided by high-density housing. Porter identifies several industries that are candidates for central city export, including food processing and storage, printing and publishing, commercial support services, storage and distribution facilities, and security services (Porter 1994).

An interesting and increasingly popular type of export industry is tourism. Although tourists come to your city, so they might seem like an import, the goods and services consumed by tourists are exports. Industrial areas in central cities, particularly those with a waterfront, have been revitalized in an attempt to draw visitors from elsewhere in the metropolitan area and even from other metropolitan areas. Examples abound, including Baltimore's Inner Harbor, Boston's Faneuil Hall, New York's Fulton Street Market, and Cleveland's Flats and North Coast Harbor. In the cases of Baltimore and Cleveland, shopping, museums, and sports stadiums have been combined to yield an attraction for a "critical mass" of people. By increasing the economic connection between the central city and the suburban areas, these types of developments can also remind suburban residents of the stake they have in a successful city. Also, the fact that central business districts are designed to handle rush-hour transportation and parking makes them the most capable part of the region to handle the large volume of traffic generated by, say, a professional sporting event. Because the peak hours for tourists and other visitors do not coincide with the normal business day, locating visitor attractions downtown is a way to make extra (efficient) use of the large downtown fixed investment in roads, public transportation, and parking.

CHAPTER SUMMARY

- When designing economic development programs, local governments need to balance the expected benefits against the expected costs. One reason that the benefits are uncertain is that it is difficult for local government officials to be certain that any particular incentive program actually led to a firm's decision to relocate or expand in their city.

- Local taxes and spending are more important for a firm considering sites within a metropolitan area than they are when it is considering sites in several metropolitan areas. If cities within the metropolitan area bid against one another, the firm will benefit relative to a situation where the cities do not bid. Cities are unable to credibly commit not to bid against one another in the absence of a regional or statewide program restricting their activities.

- Suburban zoning policy has contributed to the relative deterioration of the central city, but it is not the primary cause. Environmental problems due to industrial pollution have also contributed to the economic problems facing central cities. The change in environmental regulation begun in 1980 made firms unwilling to locate in areas that had been used for industrial purposes, and this change in regulation might even have offset the beneficial effects of various central city development policies.

- In order to determine the extent of distress a city is facing, it is necessary to calculate the needs and resources of the city. Every state has a different set of local taxes and responsibilities, so it is important to consider each city's individual circumstances. One way of alleviating fiscal distress is to reduce the responsibilities given to the city. A second way is to increase the resources available to the city. One way of increasing resources is to permit cities to annex surrounding territory.

EXCERPT: *THE ECONOMY OF CITIES* (JANE JACOBS)

In her book *The Economy of Cities*, published in 1969, Jane Jacobs argues that it is the continuous trial-and-error process of development, rather than the achievement of great productive efficiency, that is the secret to long-run urban growth and prosperity. In the following excerpt (pp. 86, 88, 92–93), she considers first the recent example of Manchester, England—one of the cradles of the Industrial Revolution—and then the ancient example of the Indus River Valley civilization centered on the cities of Mohenjo-daro and Harappa. As you read about these earlier cities, you may wish to consider whether the city in which you live is behaving like the examples discussed here.

Back in 1844, a character in one of Disraeli's novels said, "Certainly Manchester is the most wonderful city of modern times. It is the philosopher alone who can conceive the grandeur of Manchester and the immensity of its future."

What made Manchester seem the most advanced of all cities of the time was the stunning efficiency of its immense textile mills. The mills were Manchester. By the 1840s their work dominated the city completely. Here, it seemed, was the meaning of the industrial revolution, arrived at its logical conclusions. Here was the coming thing. Here was the kind of city that made all other cities old-fashioned—vestiges of an industrially undeveloped past.

Manchester's efficient specialization portended stagnation and a profoundly obsolescent city. For "the immensity of its future" proved to consist of immense losses of its markets as other people in other places learned how to spin and weave cotton efficiently too. Manchester developed nothing sufficient to compensate for these lost markets. Today it has become the very symbol of a city in long and unremitting decline.

Manchester's staggering productivity and efficiency were not so unprecedented as the observers of the 1840s thought. The machines were new, but history records a multitude of cities that poured their economic energy into repetitions of the same work with immense efficiency and which put no energy, or almost none, into development of new goods and services. Coventry had done this, also with textiles, in medieval times. Medieval Europe had an odd word, *dinanderie,* for brass vessels. Dinant, in the Lowlands, one of the most important and prosperous of medieval cities, had made such a success with its brass kettles and pots that, like Manchester, it had specialized merely in repeating its success. Dinant was extraordinarily productive—for a while.

At least as long ago as 2,500 B.C. there were cities of "terrible efficiency," according to the archeologist Stuart Piggott in *Prehistoric India.* He was referring to Mohenjo-daro and Harappa, the twin capital cities of an ancient empire of the Indus. Mohenjo-daro and Harappa were marvelously developed, to a point. But at some time before 2,500 B.C. development work had halted. They added no new goods and services from that time on, it seems, nor did they make any improvements in their old products. They simply repeated themselves. Their production must have been stupendous. The same standardized bricks were used in truly staggering quantities, not only in the cities themselves but throughout the scores of towns in the empire. The same wonderfully accurate stone weights, in multiples and fractions of sixteen, were turned out endlessly. And the voracious wood-fired kilns belonging to the two cities mass-produced so many identical pottery cups that Piggott speculates that it may have been the custom to drink from a cup and then break it. One suspects they had more cups than they knew what to do with.

But while other people were developing the spoked wheel and the light chariots made possible by spoked wheels, Harappa and Mohenjo-daro kept turning out only clumsy, solid wheels and cumbersome, heavy wagons. While other people were learning to strengthen bronze weapons and tools with a thickened central rib, and to make the heads of these with hollow hafts so handles could be fitted into them, Harappa and Mohenjo-daro kept turning out only one-piece, flat, easily broken implements. At length the Indus River at Mohenjo-daro became a lake of mud. The mud flows engulfed the city and undermined many buildings. The people seem to have been incapable of any response that involved changed ways of doing things, or new ideas. After every mud flood they rebuilt exactly as before, with their interminable bricks, and the quality of the work deteriorated steadily until it was no longer done at all. The mud floods cannot be described as the "cause" of Mohenjo-daro's decay because a similar decline was evident in the other city of Harappa and throughout the empire, alongside a similar, endless repetitiveness of old work. The response to the mud floods was merely one dramatic symptom of the all-pervading stagnation.

Source: The Economy of Cities by Jane Jacobs. Copyright © 1969 by Jane Jacobs. Reprinted by permission of Random House, Inc.

Questions for Review and Discussion

1. Jane Jacobs argues that specialization by a city leads to stagnation. Does this mean that analyses of urban economies based on comparative advantage are not useful? Explain.

2. Consider two almost identical metropolitan areas, Inelasticville and Annexia. Each metropolitan area has a total population of 2,400,000, per capita income of $24,000, and 372,000 people living in poverty. Each metropolitan area consists of three parts: the central city, the inner suburbs, and the outer suburbs. The central city has a population of 400,000, a per capita income of $15,000, and a poverty population of 160,000. The inner suburbs have a population of 800,000, a per capita income of $27,000, and a poverty population of 150,000. The outer suburbs have a population of 1,200,000, a per capita income of $25,000, and a poverty population of 62,000. The only difference between the two metropolitan areas is that the city of Inelasticville consists only of the central city, while the city of Annexia consists of the central city and the (annexed) inner suburbs.

   a. Calculate the city-suburban income differential (city per capita income as a fraction of suburban per capita income) for Inelasticville and for Annexia. Calculate the fraction of the respective metropolitan areas' population that lives in the city of Inelasticville and Annexia.

   b. Rusk (1995, Table 2.21, pp. 80–81) presents evidence that inelastic cities contain on average 31 percent of their metropolitan area's population and have a city-suburban income differential of 87 percent. Elastic cities contain on average 65 percent of their metropolitan area's population and have a city-suburban income differential of 106 percent. He argues that allowing annexation is imperative for improving the economic health of inelastic metropolitan areas. Comment on this argument given your findings from part (a).

3. "The amount of money a town is willing to pay (or the tax revenue it is willing to give up) to convince a firm to locate helps the firm to decide which location is best suited

for it. Prohibiting local tax incentives could thus reduce the efficiency of the economy because firms would be required to make location decisions with less information." Do you agree or disagree? Explain.

4. Why should middle-class suburban residents care about the conditions of poor city residents?

5. One of the debates in Cleveland (and other cities) has been the extent to which down-town development—with an emphasis on attracting and retaining firms—has come at the expense of the city's "neighborhoods." Should economic development policy focus more on firms or on households?

6. "Government subsidies to highway construction penalize central cities and inner-ring suburbs. The subsidies should either be stopped or matched by subsidies to the central cities." Do you agree or disagree? Explain.

C H A P T E R

Urban Labor Markets and Poverty

12

One way to think of a metropolitan area is as a set of interconnected markets for land, labor, and capital. The definition of metropolitan area used by the U.S. Census Bureau amounts to defining a labor market because of its emphasis on commuting flows among counties. The study of labor markets, of course, encompasses many topics that deserve more time than can be devoted to them in a text such as this. In this chapter we will explore a few topics that have either a spatial aspect or a policy link to cities. The former will include intrametropolitan wage differences and the "spatial mismatch" hypothesis, while the latter will include the issues of the underclass and homelessness that have received considerable attention from both researchers and politicians during the 1980s and 1990s.

INTRAMETROPOLITAN WAGE DIFFERENCES

In the simplest monocentric city model, all employment is located in the CBD and all workers are identical. In that case, there is no reason for workers in the same city to receive different wages. Wages might differ from city to city in order to compensate for varying amenities, as we saw in chapter 4, but each city would be uniform in its wages.

Once we relax the assumption that all employment is located in the CBD, though, the question of wage variability within a city arises. How should we expect wages to vary? Do we observe this in practice?

If we maintain (for simplicity) the assumption that all households are identical, then it must be the case that workers at all locations must receive equal utility in equilibrium. Thus, higher wages at a location must be compensation for higher costs to the worker or lower amenities arising from working at that location. Consider the workers in the CBD. They must purchase high-cost housing close to the CBD or face a long commute. Workers outside the CBD, though, can have a short commute and purchase less expensive housing. As a result, we would expect CBD workers to receive higher wages than suburban workers. As suburban employment centers (edge cities) grow, we would expect the wages in the center to increase relative to the wages in the CBD as land near the edge cities becomes more expensive.

Note that these wage differences have the same pattern as land-rent differences. Like land rent, wages are predicted to be high near the employment center(s) and decrease farther away. Two natural questions arise. First, why are firms willing to pay the higher wages? Second, is there greater variation among sites in wages or in land rents?

The reason firms are willing to pay higher wages in the CBD has an answer that is, by this point in the course, predictable. If there are agglomeration economies from locating in an employment center, then a firm is able to absorb some higher costs and still remain competitive. As we saw in the monocentric city model in chapter 9, a firm might also substitute capital for the more-expensive labor and land. The expansion of voice mail and computer networks has reduced the need for secretarial services at many companies, for example.

The question about the relative size of wage differences and rent differences is not so easily disposed of. Sivitanidou and Wheaton (1992) have carefully considered this question and found that in the absence of constraints on land use, wage differences exceed rent differences. This result is essentially due to the fact that people live on more space than they work in. Let me say that a bit less mysteriously. Recall that the wage differences within a city were needed in order to compensate workers for the commuting costs or housing costs they would incur to work at various locations. Of course, the housing costs and commuting costs are related, as we saw in chapter 9. The typical worker requires approximately 250 square feet of space. The typical household consumes much more than this, say 2,500 square feet. Unless there are agglomeration economies or other cost advantages on the order of ten times the variation in housing costs per square foot, then the wage differences can be expected to dominate rent differences. However, one complication is that the above discussion assumed that companies were free to substitute capital for labor and land. In practice, zoning restrictions constrain firms' choices, so that land can be scarce relative to what it would be in the absence of zoning. As a result, the price of land increases, and the restrictions may be severe enough to make the rent differences dominate the wage differences.

Some empirical evidence has been found of a wage gradient as predicted by the model. However, it has been difficult to completely study this question due to the large amount of data required. You need to know the wages paid to the workers, their characteristics, and the location of their residences. Most sources of data do not contain all three of these items. McMillen and Singell (1992) use detailed data from the Public Use Micro Sample (PUMS) of the 1980 Census of Population and Housing to analyze not only the change in wages over space but also whether residence and workplace location seem to be correlated. They find evidence that people choose their residence in part on the basis of proximity to work; they also find evidence that wages for identical workers decline with the distance of their job from the CBD. Their study is especially convincing for two reasons. First, it focuses only on cities that they argue to be monocentric in 1980: Cleveland, Columbus, Dayton, Detroit, Indianapolis, Philadelphia, and Pittsburgh. If a city is not monocentric, researchers may erroneously find that wages do not decrease much as firms move away from the CBD because the researchers have failed to account for the presence of other employment centers that also pay high wages. Second, the PUMS data contain detailed information on individuals, allowing McMillen and Singell to control directly for differences among workers that might lead to different wages. Previous studies have been forced to rely on aggregate or indirect measures, and so were not as convincing.

We have seen how constraints on land use by firms affect the analysis of intra-urban wage differences. Now consider another possibility, that households are constrained in their location choices. This is perhaps most clear in the case of racial discrimination, but recall that zoning can limit the housing options available for low-income households. If a firm is relying on a primarily low-income workforce, then we would expect higher wages to be paid by firms located farther from low-income housing. Ihlanfeldt and Young (1994) explore this possibility using data on employees at fast-food hamburger restaurants in Atlanta. Table 12.1 summarizes their findings. As one moves from the CBD to the north, there is an increase in the starting wage, average wage, and average commuting length for black workers, while the average commute for white workers remains roughly constant. On the other hand, as one moves from the CBD to the south, there is no evidence of any difference among locations. The average commute for blacks is longer than the average commute for whites in all but two cases, suggesting (though not proving) that location choices for black workers are constrained relative to location choices for whites. (We will return to this type of analysis when we consider the "spatial mismatch" hypothesis later in this chapter.) Knowing that the black population in Atlanta is historically concentrated to the south of the CBD completes the story. Ihlanfeldt and Young estimate that wages increase at roughly 1 percent per mile as you move north from the CBD.

Manufacturing versus Services

An intrametropolitan wage differential that has received a large amount of attention is that between employees in manufacturing and in the service sector. It is sometimes alleged that manufacturing jobs are "good jobs at good wages" while services amount to "burger flipping." As a service-sector employee—my firm, Case Western Reserve University provides teaching and research services—I of course take umbrage at this characterization. And the doctors, lawyers, and management consultants working in

TABLE 12.1 Constrained Location and Intrametropolitan Wage Differences

Miles from CBD	Starting Wage	Average Wage	Average Commute: Black Worker	Average Commute: White Worker
North				
0–5	$3.79	$4.16	2.58 miles	3.29 miles
5–10	$3.91	$4.20	3.32 miles	2.71 miles
10–15	$4.35	$4.79	4.27 miles	2.56 miles
15–20	$4.61	$5.05	4.77 miles	3.83 miles
South				
0–5	$3.82	$3.96	1.91 miles	——
5–10	$3.73	$4.03	2.51 miles	1.56 miles
10–15	$3.87	$4.19	2.13 miles	2.33 miles
15–20	$3.81	$4.20	2.48 miles	1.91 miles

Source: Adapted from Ihlanfeldt and Young (1994, Table 1, p. 429).

urban areas would be surprised to learn that they didn't earn good wages. Of course, not all service-sector employees are highly paid. The question of relative wages in manufacturing and services is important from an urban perspective because of the movement of manufacturing to the suburbs (and beyond) and the increase in the relative contribution of the service sector.

It is important to recall that the exit of manufacturing from the city is not a recent phenomenon (Frieden and Sagalyn 1989, p. 262). There were three main causes. The first was the advent of long, low buildings that replaced the multistory facilities in which manufacturing previously took place. Manufacturing became much more land-intensive, and the inexpensive and abundant land of the suburbs was attractive. The second was the advent of the intracity and intercity truck to carry freight, which made access to a port or rail terminal less important than access to highways. The interstate highway system, begun in the 1950s, solidified (through its pattern of bypassing central cities) the advantage of suburban manufacturing locations. The third was the advent of automobile commuting with the associated need for parking. The suburbs, with their abundant land, promised less-expensive parking lots than did downtown locations.

For the country as a whole, wage differences favor manufacturing, but the difference is not large, and it is not the case for all occupations. For example, in 1985 operatives, assemblers, and inspectors had median weekly earnings of $285, while administrative support and clerical workers had median weekly earnings of $286. The first set of occupations are the blue-collar bedrock of manufacturing, while the second set is the foundation for services. Office development can benefit a wide range of workers, not only the highly visible and highly paid professionals (Frieden and Sagalyn 1989, pp. 290–294). While it is true that highly paid, high-skilled professionals work in office buildings, it is also true that offices hire a wide range of employees. For this reason, most groups in the city stand to benefit from an expansion of the downtown office sector. In addition to the direct effect of office development on employment, it also has indirect effects. For example, if an increase in office employment leads to an increase in retail, hotel, and restaurant activity, it also creates additional entry-level positions in these areas.

Despite the potential benefits of the shift to a service economy, strong downtown economies might do little for city residents, for three reasons: (1) low-income people have inadequate access to information about job openings; (2) many city residents lack the education to function well in either a factory or an office; (3) many of the poor in the central cities are not in the job market at all. However, residents to whom these descriptions apply would be equally disadvantaged in a manufacturing economy, and so it is not clear that preserving manufacturing in the city will necessarily benefit low-income people.

Eberts (1995) surveys evidence on why some individuals are unable to qualify even for entry-level jobs. The main problem can be the fact that even "unskilled" jobs require a set of skills that most people take for granted. These skills include proper dress, arriving at work on time, coming to work every day, getting along with fellow employees, problem solving, and organization. The absence of these skills can create an "intellectual isolation" from the job market that can reinforce any physical isolation that residents of inner-city neighborhoods experience.

Legal and Illegal Activities

One source of intrametropolitan variation in observed wages is the differential ability of people to supplement their reported wages with earnings from illegal activities. Of course, it is difficult to obtain complete and accurate data on the extent of crime and its effect on the labor market, but the theoretical effects are straightforward. Crime can affect both labor supply (willingness of people to work at a given wage) and labor demand (willingness of employers to hire people at a given wage). Changes in the rewards of illegal activity affect the supply of labor by changing the relative price of illegal and legal labor. An increase in the expected cost of committing crimes, all else equal, would thus lead to a reduction in criminal activity and an increase in the supply of labor to legal jobs. Crime can also affect the demand for labor. The effect can be as simple as an employer's reluctance to hire a convicted felon or more subtle, as discrimination on the basis of statistics. *Statistical discrimination* occurs when a person is treated as though he or she has the average characteristics of their group. If young black males are on average more likely to commit crimes, then employers, not knowing whether the particular job applicant is likely to commit a crime, might be less likely to hire a young black male than an otherwise comparable white male. This penalizes those whose abilities are above average when the perceptions of employers are inaccurate. Of course, supply decisions and demand decisions are related over time. If the demand for black workers is low, for example, the supply of black workers may fall in the future as they become discouraged about their employment prospects (Holzer 1994, p. 711).

Richard Freeman (1992) analyzed the impact of crime on the urban labor market. He reached three main conclusions. First, the large majority of young black male high-school dropouts participate in illegal activities to earn income. Second, the pay-off to illegal activity relative to legal activity has increased over the past 10 years. Third, illegal activities, and especially incarceration, have severe long-term consequences on the employment prospects of an individual.

In general, ethnographic studies of the decision of people to engage in criminal activities support the simple labor supply decision described above. The reservation wage—the wage at which someone is willing to accept a job offer—has been shown to be related to the income that a person can earn in illegal activities. Thus, in designing policies to increase employment, it is important to find ways to make legal work more rewarding than crime. Otherwise, people will choose illegal activities.

An interesting application of the location theory developed earlier in the book is to the location of criminal activity. Recall that one of the reasons for close proximity of businesses is when ambiguous information must be transmitted. Close proximity builds trust and improves communication. Most illegal activities involve a great deal of ambiguity: What is the quality of the car or jewelry that was stolen or the drugs being offered for sale? We would expect the activities of buying and selling stolen property and drugs to cluster together.

We can actually say more about the likely location of these activities. Goods are stolen from people throughout the metropolitan area. In fact, nice neighborhoods scattered throughout a city and its suburbs are likely to be fertile ground for a thief. The ability to easily dispose of goods obtained throughout the metropolitan area dictates a relatively central location close to transportation (highways). Similarly, the consumers of illegal drugs come from throughout the metropolitan area. Economic theory suggests that illegal activities should cluster near major roads in the central city of a metropolitan area for the same reason that some high-level business service activities cluster—transmission of ambiguous information and access to the entire metropolitan area.

People develop their ideas about the relative benefits and costs of various types of activities based on the observations they make every day. If a person lives in an area with a high crime rate, and particularly if the criminals are seen to be relatively successful, then that person is more likely to engage in criminal activity. A number of studies have found these "contagion effects" among youth populations. It should be emphasized that not only negative outcomes are contagious—one study (Case and Katz 1991) found that church attendance among young people was strongly influenced by the behavior of neighbors. This finding should be kept in context—Case and Katz also found that drug use, unemployment, and gang membership was influenced by the behavior of neighbors—but suggests that people make decisions on the information available to them on the basis of daily observation.

RACE AND LABOR MARKETS: "SPATIAL MISMATCH" HYPOTHESIS

We have seen a theoretical argument and presented some evidence that residential location and workplace location are correlated. This finding can be interpreted in two ways. The first is that people prefer to live close to their job. The second is that people find jobs close to where they live. This second interpretation, when combined with a legacy of racial segregation in housing markets, leads to the so-called *spatial mismatch* hypothesis. This hypothesis simply states that blacks have less access to jobs than do whites because their housing options are more restricted. This implies that blacks do not learn of job openings and that they must commute farther to jobs they do find. In the case of entry-level positions, the extra commuting costs could even outweigh the benefits of employment, leading to higher unemployment among blacks. The decentralization of employment can exacerbate problems of spatial mismatch if blacks are prevented from moving to the suburbs and edge cities where so much employment growth now occurs.

To illustrate the potential for spatial mismatch, consider the results of a detailed case study of the move of a single employer (Fernandez 1994). This employer, a food-processor in Milwaukee, moved from the CBD to the suburbs in order to make a large upgrade in the plant. The location in the CBD was unsuited to the "long, low" type of building desired, and so the relocation was not a case of flight from blight or racial discrimination but was the type of industrial relocation that has become familiar over the past 50 years. Despite the nondiscriminatory cause of the move, Fernandez found that it had profoundly different impacts on workers of different races. He found that the least impact would be felt by white salaried workers, who were the highest paid. Among hourly employees, the least impact was felt by white males, while the largest impact was on Hispanic males. Black male employees were in the middle. This disparity was essentially the result of the grouping of neighborhoods in Milwaukee. Blacks are concentrated on the north side of the CBD, Hispanics on the south side, whites in the suburbs. The firm moved from the CBD to the northwestern suburbs, thus having the most impact on the commute for Hispanics. The questions that we will turn to now are the extent to which this finding is typical and, if it is, what can be done to resolve the problem.

Measuring Mismatch

The spatial mismatch hypothesis was introduced by John Kain in an influential paper published in 1968. This idea has been controversial, and repeated attempts have been made to carefully measure it. Holzer (1991) surveys much of this research. He identifies four approaches to measuring differential access to jobs by race. The first approach is to measure the extent of residential segregation. For example, Kain (1968) compared the fraction of jobs in an area held by blacks to the fraction of black residents in the area. He found that increasing housing integration would increase overall black employment. Other studies using a similar approach have found different results, so the evidence is inconclusive.

The second approach to measuring spatial mismatch is to examine residential suburbanization. Employment has been decentralizing, and blacks remain more concentrated near the central city than do whites, so measures of the extent of earnings differences between city and suburban residents provide evidence on spatial mismatch. The most influential study of this type, by Richard Price and Edwin Mills (1985), decomposed the difference in earnings between black workers and white workers into several components. On average, white workers earned wages that were 34.4 percent higher than black workers. However, Price and Mills found that 56 percent of the difference (a 19.2 percent difference in wages) was due to the fact that the whites in their sample had better qualifications, such as education and experience. This left a significant fraction (44 percent) of the difference attributed to discrimination. However, not all of that was the result of spatial mismatch, because some of the discrimination could have been employment discrimination rather than housing discrimination. Their best estimate was that a black moving from the central city to the suburbs would increase wages by about 6 percent. This finding is often cited as evidence that any spatial mismatch problems are small. However, Price and Mills focused only on people who had full-time jobs, so their results do not reflect any increase in unemployment or discouragement that might result from spatial mismatch.

The third approach is to focus on the suburbanization of employment, especially for service workers. A fairly consistent finding is that lower-educated people—both whites and blacks—have lower earnings in the central city than they do in the suburbs. However, this could be evidence of "crowding" (relatively high supply of low-skilled labor) in the central city, reflecting the prevalence of lower-cost housing near the central city, rather than evidence of spatial mismatch caused by racial discrimination.

The fourth approach is to measure the accessibility of jobs directly, for example by measuring average travel time among different areas in a metropolitan area. This approach has the advantage of focusing directly on the question at hand, but also has an important disadvantage. Recall from chapter 9 that the effect of increasing income on commuting times was theoretically ambiguous. In practice, commuting times increase as incomes increase. But high-income people—black or white—are the least constrained in their housing choices. Thus, simply looking at commuting times without further information on the individual workers is not completely convincing.

Choosing Mismatch

Before we consider ways of alleviating spatial mismatch, it is important to reflect briefly on whether the real problem of disparate labor market outcomes for blacks and whites results from spatial mismatch or some other cause. For example, if there is racial discrimination in the workplace, then improving access to jobs will not by itself improve the relative condition of black workers. Daniel McMillen (1993) returns to the first principles of location theory in order to investigate the potential benefits of relocation. Suppose there are two locations, the central city and the suburbs. All else being equal, people that work in the central city prefer to live in the central city because of the shorter commute. The same is true of suburban workers, who prefer to live close to their jobs.

Suppose that we observe that the average wage in the suburbs exceeds the average wage in the central city. Does this mean that workers who move from the central city to the suburbs will receive a wage increase? Not necessarily, and this is the key to McMillen's analysis. Not all workers are identical, and so not all workers will earn identical wages. If people choose to work in the central city, it might be the case that they are earning higher wages there than they would in the suburbs. McMillen finds evidence of racial discrimination, in that blacks with qualifications identical to those of whites receive lower wages. He also finds that blacks require a higher wage to work in the suburbs, which is indirect evidence of racial discrimination in housing markets.

The Housing Strategy, the Mobility Strategy, and the Jobs Strategy

If we believe there is a spatial mismatch, then three general approaches can be taken to alleviate the problem. The first is the *housing strategy,* which focuses on removing racial discrimination in housing markets and helping black households to move from the central city to the suburbs. The second is the *mobility strategy,* which focuses on improving the transportation between black central city residential areas and suburban job centers. The third is the *jobs strategy,* which focuses on reversing the decentralization of employment (Holzer 1994).

The housing strategy has the advantage of addressing social barriers to employment in addition to mobility barriers. If suburban employers have little knowledge of the residents of a city neighborhood, they might be reluctant to hire them even in the absence of racial discrimination. When residents of a city neighborhood become neighbors of the employers, they are more willing to hire them. Of course, this advantage is also the main disadvantage with the housing strategy. The resistance to income and racial integration in the housing market is, if anything, greater than that in the workplace. Recall from chapter 11 that most zoning policies have the effect, if not the intent, of keeping low-income people out. Overcoming the political support of such policies is expensive both in terms of money and time. However, in the long run this approach is vital, at least as far as promoting the flexibility in housing markets and labor markets that is necessary to adapt to changing economic conditions. The cities of today are not the cities of twenty years ago; why should we think the next twenty years will be any less tumultuous?

The mobility strategy has the advantage of being much less expensive in both monetary terms and in social adjustment required. However, this strategy's weakness is that it does nothing to improve the employability of people lacking education and job skills. An example of a policy in this vein is to ensure that bus routes run directly from central city neighborhoods to suburban job centers, especially to those that generate entry-level jobs in the service sector with some upward mobility. The philosophy is that once people find steady work in the suburbs they will find it easier both financially and socially to relocate to the suburbs. In other words, the long-run goal of this policy is similar to that of the housing strategy.

The jobs strategy is exemplified in the "enterprise zone" approach to urban development. This approach attempts to bring jobs back to the central city areas that they have left, improving access to employment for people still living in those neighborhoods. As we have already seen in chapter 11, this approach struggles to succeed because it runs counter to the economic forces generating employment decentralization. Thus, enterprise-zone programs do not do much to increase employment. They also implicitly accept racial discrimination, unlike the housing and mobility strategies.

If employers attempt to relocate away from perceived problems, spatial mismatch may actually represent flight from blight rather than discrimination per se. In that case, all the strategies outlined above have a chance of being successful. On the other hand, if employers racially discriminate, then all the strategies will fail.

CONCENTRATED POVERTY AND THE "UNDERCLASS"

Cities are defined as concentrations of population and economic activity. One of the major policy issues arising from cities during the past 15 years has been the question of whether spatial concentrations of poverty and deviance from social norms (not identical) have been becoming more widespread and more extreme. The popular and academic literature has focused on identifying and measuring the "underclass"—both the people and the places where they live. An important policy question is related to this issue of measurement—namely, whether poverty is synonymous with deviant behavior or not. If poverty is the result of bad luck rather than aberrant behavior, then social insurance policies should suffice in most cases to reduce the direct impact of poverty and assist people to restore their fortunes. However, if poverty is the result of behavior outside of normal society's expectations, then policies predicated on the assumption of normal behavior will be unsuccessful.

The extent to which poverty and deviance is concentrated is also a matter of concern because social norms are usually learned by observing and interacting with other people. Your idea of normal behavior is determined in part by the people you meet every day. If these people are not normal by society's standards, then you are likely to develop an out-of-the-ordinary view of normality. Hence, there is a concern about the extent to which people move in and out of underclass areas over time as well as a concern about the number of people living in underclass areas at any given time.

In the remainder of this section, I will first consider how to define the underclass and consider whether it has been growing over time. I will then examine some evidence on the extent to which people move into and out of poor neighborhoods.

Defining and Measuring the Underclass

The title of this section comes from a paper by Erol Ricketts and Isabel Sawhill (1988) that tries to identify the underclass population using data from the U.S. Census of Population and Housing. Because the term "underclass" carries so much political connotation, Ricketts and Sawhill are careful to define the word precisely. To them, the underclass population has two characteristics: (1) a large deviation from social norms and (2) spatial concentration. It is important to reiterate that "underclass" refers to more than poverty, or even extended poverty. For example, if people are poor but law-abiding, working, and married, then they are not members of the underclass. They might live in an area identified as an underclass area, though.

If underclass behavior is defined as departure from societal norms, then any measurement effort must begin by defining what the norms are. Ricketts and Sawhill propose the following four expectations of society, circa 1980. First, children will attend school and delay parenthood until at least the age of 18. Second, adult males under the age of 65 will work at a steady job. Third, adult females will either work or marry (or both). Fourth, everyone is law-abiding.

For measurement purposes, Ricketts and Sawhill define the norms as the national averages of each of four variables. First, the percentage of high school dropouts (16- to 19-year-olds who are not enrolled in school and are not high-school graduates) in the census tract. Second, the percentage of prime-age males not regularly attached to the labor force (males over the age of 16 who did not have a full-time or part-time job for 26 weeks) in the census tract. Third, the percentage of welfare recipients (households receiving public-assistance income). Fourth, the percentage of female-headed households with children. These measures do not perfectly correspond to the norms listed above, but are chosen to be related. For example, the measure of female-headed households is a proxy for early childbearing. An underclass area would be one with a high concentration of activities that deviate from the norms, and an underclass individual would be a person who lives in an underclass area and participates in underclass behavior.

The next step is to identify how deviant from the norms one has to be. After all, every area contains some unemployment, welfare, single mothers, and so on. Ricketts and Sawhill define deviance as an area whose measure in each of the four categories is at least one standard deviation above the national average.

The results of this definition are summarized in Table 12.2. The figures in Table 12.2 seem to indicate that high-poverty areas are also areas of concentrated deviance from social norms. Ricketts and Sawhill discuss the extent to which underclass and high-poverty areas overlap. They find that 39 percent of underclass areas are not high-poverty areas, while 72 percent of the high-poverty areas are not underclass by their definition. While there is a correlation between concentrated poverty and concentrated social problems, the two are not identical.

The estimates in Table 12.2 show about 1.3% of the U.S. population living in underclass areas in 1980. However, not all of the people living in underclass areas are members of the underclass. Ricketts and Sawhill go on to estimate that about 1.3 million people, or a little over half of the population in the underclass areas, are members of the underclass.

Needless to say, the Ricketts and Sawhill numbers are not accepted uncritically by everyone. Mark Hughes (1989) presents a criticism that focuses on both the mea-

TABLE 12.2 Underclass Areas and High Poverty Areas, 1980

	Underclass Areas	High Poverty Areas	United States
Total population (in thousands)	2,484	5,569	181,171
Female-headed households	60%	59%	19%
High school dropouts	36%	19%	13%
Welfare recipients	34%	33%	8%
Males not regularly employed	56%	57%	31%

Note: High poverty areas defined as census tracts with a poverty rate of at least 40%.

Source: Adapted from Ricketts and Sawhill (1988, Table 2, p. 322).

surement of norms and the measurement of deviance. It is important to emphasize, though, that he agrees with the basic definition of the underclass. The controversy, then, is in how to measure them. Hughes focuses not only on the level of underclass areas in 1980 but goes on to consider whether the underclass problem worsened between 1970 and 1980.

Hughes first says that the Ricketts and Sawhill approach of looking at deviance from national norms is misleading because it does not account for variation among metropolitan areas. He also argues that the "underclass hypothesis" really argues that certain areas of each metropolitan area have been becoming more deviant from the rest of the metropolitan area. Because norms will vary both by metropolitan area and by year—compare divorce in the 1940s and the 1980s—Hughes suggests using metropolitan area medians that are allowed to vary over time. Why the median rather than the mean? If some tracts have large departures from the rest of the metropolitan area ("outliers," in statistical jargon), then the mean will include these outliers and be large relative to the mass of tracts. The median, the point at which half of the tracts are higher and half lower, is less sensitive to the presence of outliers. Hence, using the median makes it easier to identify the outliers that truly exist.

The question of how to measure deviation from norms is a bit more subtle. All the variables being measured have variation around their mean. A possible example is shown as Figure 12.1. Point *A* is the median of the distribution, point *B* the mean. Point *C* is the mean plus one standard deviation, and point *D* is twice the median.

Hughes points out that every distribution will have some points that are at least one standard deviation above the mean because of the way that the standard deviation is calculated. However, not every distribution will have points that are at least twice as large as the median. He points out that Ricketts and Sawhill have essentially shown that the outliers from the various distributions are correlated with each other—an interesting finding but not convincing evidence of an emerging problem.

Hughes applies his definitions to five MSAs, and the results are shown in Table 12.3. He used three measures: one standard deviation above national means (the measure used by Ricketts and Sawhill), one standard deviation above metropolitan means, and two times the metropolitan median (his preferred measure). He finds that using his measure, New York and Los Angeles do not have nearly as large an underclass area as was found by Ricketts and Sawhill. However, Chicago, Philadelphia, and Detroit continue to show large numbers of underclass tracts. In fact, his measure of

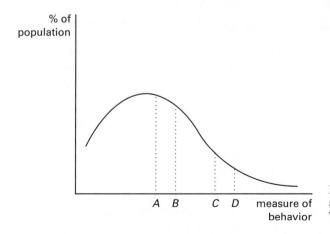

% of
population

A B   C D   measure of
                      behavior

FIGURE 12.1 Defining Deviance: Standard Deviation versus Twice the Median.

underclass tracts is higher than that of Ricketts and Sawhill for Philadelphia. The other main conclusion from Table 12.3 is that the change in the definition of deviance seems to matter the most. Using a metropolitan norm while continuing to measure deviance as the standard deviation does not appreciably change the results from those obtained using a national norm.

The other question that Hughes set out to address was the change in underclass areas over time. The results of this investigation are found in Table 12.4. Using a fixed norm leads to a measured explosion in the underclass areas. Using a variable norm and the standard deviation approach markedly reduces the measured change in the extent of underclass tracts, with only Detroit showing a major deterioration relative to national norms. The final measure shows a large increase in underclass area in Chicago, Philadelphia, and Detroit, a decrease in Los Angeles, and a small increase in New York. These figures suggest that a careful approach to measurement can distinguish among metropolitan areas, and it also suggests that changes during the 1970s were not uniform across cities.

As far as I know, the studies of the underclass have not been updated using 1990 census figures. This could make an excellent class project.

TABLE 12.3   Underclass Census Tracts in 1980: Alternative Measures

	One Standard Deviation above National Mean	*One Standard Deviation above Metropolitan Mean*	*Twice the Metropolitan Median*
New York	131 (5.2%)	84 (3.3%)	6 (0.2%)
Los Angeles	17 (1.0%)	13 (0.8%)	2 (0.1%)
Chicago	59 (3.9%)	29 (1.9%)	35 (2.3%)
Philadelphia	26 (2.2%)	46 (3.9%)	44 (3.7%)
Detroit	55 (5.3%)	50 (4.8%)	41 (3.9%)

Note: Percentage of metropolitan area tracts in parentheses.

Source: Hughes (1989, Table 1, p. 279).

TABLE 12.4 Change in Underclass Census Tracts between 1970 and 1980

	One Standard Deviation above National Mean, Fixed Norm		One Standard Deviation above National Mean, Variable Norm		Twice the Metropolitan Median, Variable Norm	
New York	105	(404%)	12	(10%)	1	(20%)
Los Angeles	4	(31%)	−8	(−32%)	−11	(−85%)
Chicago	42	(247%)	10	(20%)	20	(133%)
Philadelphia	14	(117%)	−8	(−24%)	36	(450%)
Detroit	50	(1000%)	24	(77%)	31	(310%)

Note: Percentage change in underclass tracts in parentheses. The measure using a fixed norm applies the 1980 standards in both 1970 and 1980, while the measures using a variable norm apply 1970 standards in 1970 and 1980 standards in 1980.

Source: Adapted from Hughes (1989, Table 2, p. 280).

Do People Move out of Poor Urban Areas?

Much of the discussion of poverty and the underclass has an underlying assumption that the population being discussed is fixed in number and location. However, it is possible that people move in and out of poverty—for example, if they lose or find a job. Similarly, it is possible that people move into and out of underclass and low-income census tracts. Distinguishing between people who are long-term residents in poor areas and those who are "just passing through" is important when designing policy. Again, if someone is poor temporarily, then the public policy likely to help that person is probably different from the public policy needed to help someone who has been poor for many years.

Gramlich, Laren, and Sealand (1992) used detailed data from the Panel Study of Income Dynamics (PSID), a survey administered by the University of Michigan, to investigate the mobility of households in low-income urban areas between 1979 and 1984. The PSID is a longitudinal survey; that is, it tracks families over time. Thus, it is an ideal instrument for investigating household mobility. Because it contains a great deal of detailed information about each household, it is preferred over the census, which often allows researchers to analyze aggregates only at the tract level (as you have seen in the discussion of the underclass above).

Gramlich et al. classified census tracts as low income, middle income, high income, and nonmetropolitan. They then investigated the degree to which poor people moved among the various types of tract. Table 12.5 presents the results of their estimation procedure, known as a "transition matrix." The numbers indicate the probability that a household living in one type of tract in the current year will move to the other type of tract in the following year. For example, a poor white household living in a middle-income census tract this year has an 87.4-percent chance of living in a middle-income census tract next year, a 3.0-percent chance of living in a low-income census tract next year, an 8.5-percent chance of living in a high-income census tract next year, and a 1.0-percent chance of living in a nonmetropolitan census tract next year.

The amount of mobility among areas is striking, but the patterns of mobility of white households and of black households differ considerably. For example, while

TABLE 12.5 Transition Matrix for Poor Families with Children, 1979–1984

Tract Type in Current Year	Tract Type Next Year			
	Low Income	**Middle Income**	**High Income**	**Nonmetro**
White household				
Low income	72.8%	19.8%	0.0%	7.3%
Middle income	3.0%	87.4%	8.5%	1.0%
High income	0.0%	14.0%	77.9%	8.1%
Nonmetropolitan	0.0%	0.6%	1.0%	98.4%
Black household				
Low income	90.4%	8.4%	1.0%	0.2%
Middle income	7.8%	88.0%	2.7%	1.5%
High income	5.6%	22.6%	71.6%	0.2%
Nonmetropolitan	2.6%	1.0%	0.5%	95.9%

Source: Adapted from Gramlich et al. (1992, Table 3, p. 280).

over 27 percent of poor white households moved out of low-income census tracts in a given year, less than 10 percent of poor black households did so. White households living in middle-income census tracts were more likely to move to a high-income tract (8.5 percent) than to a low-income tract (3.0 percent). The opposite pattern obtained for poor black households. These results imply that low-income census tracts are becoming increasingly black over time and that poor black households with children are becoming increasingly concentrated in low-income census tracts.

One of the prominent concerns about poverty is its effect on children. The results presented above are troubling in that they suggest a distinct racial difference in the residence patterns for children, since black children in poor families are becoming increasingly concentrated in low-income census tracts. If these areas have lower-quality public schools than do middle-income and high-income areas, then these poor children may find it difficult to escape poverty. Gramlich et al. also investigate the question of whether the people who move out of low-income areas leave permanently or return in a short time. They find that some of the apparent exit of black families with children is only temporary, which adds to the concern about the educational disparity between low-income areas and other areas.

HOMELESSNESS

> Home is the place where, when you have to go there,
> They have to take you in.
> —ROBERT FROST

The causes and prevalence of homelessness have loomed large in public debate throughout the 1980s and 1990s. Despite the amount of rhetoric on all sides of the issue, though, considerable uncertainty still exists about the definition of homelessness, the number of homeless people, the causes of homelessness, and the extent to which public policy has caused or alleviated homelessness.

Begin with the definition. Obviously someone who must sleep on the sidewalk is homeless, but what of someone who lives in a shelter? What about someone who is involuntarily sharing crowded conditions because of the inability to afford anything else? The very transience of the condition can also make it difficult to define. If someone is housed, on average, for five days a week and homeless for two days a week, is that person to be considered homeless?

The next problem is counting homeless people. Advocates for the homeless began circulating a figure of 2.5 million to 3 million homeless in the early 1980s. However, this estimate did not come from systematic analysis, but instead was essentially invented because reporters demanded a number. The department of Housing and Urban Development (HUD) estimated, using reasonable analytical techniques, that between 250,000 and 350,000 people were homeless in the United States in 1984. Most professionals estimate numbers closer to the HUD figures, but one can still find the 3 million figure quoted (Jencks 1994, ch. 1).

Finally, the question of the causes of homelessness have been fiercely debated. Is it the result of drug addiction and mental illness? The result of laziness? The result of a combination of a shift in labor markets and increasingly restrictive zoning policy? The result of cuts in public assistance to the needy? The result of the increase in homeless shelters? There are advocates for all of these positions, and we will consider briefly each of the arguments.

How Many Homeless?

Every ten years, the United States engages in a census designed to count every person living in the country. In practice, this is done by finding people at home either by mail or through the use of poll takers. How, then, to count someone who does not have a home? This problem was never really addressed before the 1990 census, and even then the coverage was spotty. Thus, researchers have had to resort to a variety of methods to estimate the number of homeless.

Rossi (1989) describes five alternative ways of estimating the number of homeless. First, there is the "key person survey." In this method, knowledgeable people (shelter directors, for example) are interviewed and their results combined. This approach is what HUD used in calculating its 1984 estimate of between 250,000 and 350,000 homeless. The problem with this approach, obviously, is that the interviewees may be biased or that they may be unfamiliar with some homeless people.

Second, there is the "partial count," which involves attempting to count only a portion of the homeless. For example, one could focus on the shelter population, rather than trying to estimate the number of people living on the street. This method is certain to undercount the total number of homeless, but it has the advantage of providing greater accuracy for the population actually studied.

Third, there is the "heroic extrapolation from a partial count." In this method, researchers make assumptions about the ratio of the uncounted homeless to the homeless tabulated using the partial-count method. For example, Freeman and Hall (1987) estimate a total of 279,000 homeless in 1983 by using a count of the homeless in shelters in New York and an estimate of the street-to-shelter ratio.

Fourth, there are "windshield street surveys and censuses." This method involves driving or walking through areas frequented by the homeless and counting the numbers. The strength of this method is that it provides direct evidence on the number of homeless not in shelters. The weaknesses are twofold. First is the fact that some homeless people will not be visible. Second is the problem that it is not always easy to identify a person as homeless just by his or her appearance. In interviews done with homeless people in Chicago, for example, Rossi (1989) found that 55 percent were described by the interviewers as "neat and clean."

The fifth method is an "adaptation of area probability designs." In other words, areas are designated by the probability of finding homeless people, and then a stratified random sample of these areas is carefully analyzed. This is the approach Rossi used in surveys of Chicago in 1985 and 1986. This method has the advantage of being a well-known design for sociological and ethnographic research, but it has the disadvantage that assigning the probabilities in advance is not a precise operation.

The good news, to one overwhelmed by the plethora of alternative counting methods, is that they all yield similar results. While the total number of homeless varies from study to study, the total for the United States is estimated at between 250,000 and 600,000 in the mid-1980s, with the modal figure being about 300,000 (Honig and Filer 1993, p. 249). The total shelter population increased fivefold between 1980 and 1990, suggesting that homelessness increased over this period. There is also a clear distinction between people that are homeless for a short time and those that remain homeless for a long time. One-half of the adults who become homeless are housed within a couple of months, while one-eighth remain homeless for over a year. Broadly speaking, women (especially women with children) are more likely to be homeless for a short time, while men are more likely to be homeless for a long time.

Rossi (1989, p. 8) argues that "homelessness is more properly viewed as the most aggravated state of a more prevalent problem, extreme poverty." He goes on to estimate that in addition to the roughly 300,000 homeless, between 4 and 7 million people are "extremely poor," defined as having an income that is less than two-thirds of the official poverty line. These people, according to Rossi, are at great risk for homelessness and should be considered when designing policy to alleviate homelessness.

The Causes of Homelessness

Every homeless person is different, but several broad generalities can be made about the homeless population. In this section I will discuss the various possible causes of homelessness, using evidence on the homeless population to illustrate these causes. (Jencks 1994 provides an excellent compilation of empirical analysis on the homeless, and I lean heavily on his work.) The key common pattern is one of alienation from society, although this alienation can come about for a variety of reasons. Jencks summarizes four characteristics of those who are most vulnerable to become homeless: too young for old-age assistance, no spouse, no steady job, and cash income less than $250 per month.

Five causes for the increase in homelessness among single adults are suggested by Jencks (1994, p. 103). The first cause was the drastic curtailment in involuntary commitment to mental hospitals. It is estimated that 142,000 people who would have been in mental hospitals in 1975 were elsewhere in 1990. While some of these people found homes with relatives, many others wound up on the street. The type of person who would cause a family to seek his or her involuntary commitment is not likely to be one they are comfortable having in their home.

The second cause of increased homelessness among single adults has been the eviction of patients from mental hospitals. Cuts in funding for mental hospitals were one reason for evictions. Another reason was a gradual change in philosophy among mental health professionals as to the relative benefits of hospitalization for their patients. Again, some of those evicted found other places to stay, but some wound up on the street. Despite these two causes, it is important to realize that a significant fraction, indeed probably a majority, of the homeless are not mentally ill.

The third cause was the advent of crack cocaine. Prior to crack, most street drugs were too expensive for a homeless person to afford. Alcohol was available, hence the stereotype of the wino. Although alcoholism rates among the homeless exceed those in the general population, a majority of the homeless are not addicts. The introduction of crack provided an alternative drug, increasing addiction rates among the homeless. And the fact that crack was inexpensive meant that addicts could continue their habit even as they became homeless.

The fourth cause was an increase in long-term joblessness, particularly among low-skilled workers. This cause was mainly a problem for men, because most public assistance programs are more generous to women, especially women with children. Skid Row, in most American cities, was a source of day labor for such businesses as railyards, construction, and general maintenance. After the 1940s, technological change in manufacturing reduced the reliance on unskilled day labor. The labor market in the United States continues to increasingly reward education, so that those who might have relied on day labor in the past for income are increasingly unable to find work. This change is related to the issue of mental illness as well. Day labor can be ideal for someone suffering from intermittent mental problems, allowing them to work on good days and not on bad days. If the only employment opportunity involves showing up for work every day, then this person is unlikely to find and keep a job.

The fifth cause is the political restriction on the creation of "flophouses," where a person can rent inexpensive housing for short terms. The classic version of this type of housing is the single room occupancy (SRO) hotel, once found in the Skid Row area of every major city. Many of these buildings were destroyed as a result of urban renewal programs in the 1940s, 1950s, and 1960s as the result of decreased demand for their services or just as the result of an expansion of downtown business activity. There is also an interesting political consensus that does not favor permitting construction of SRO-type housing. On the one hand, landlords who have some of the few remaining houses of this type are able to reap higher profits because of the restriction. On the other hand, "liberals" who advocate stringent building codes oppose the SROs as inadequate housing (a typical room was less than 6 feet by 10 feet, windowless, and had a shared bathroom). Urban renewal as slum destruction was not an invention of the post-World War II period in the United States. In the late 1800s, several cities converted tenement areas into public parks, including Grant Park in Chicago and Central Park in New York.

In addition to the spread of homelessness among single adults, homelessness among families also increased. Jencks identifies three causes: (1) an increase in single motherhood, which reduced the income available to the family; (2) the reduction in the purchasing power available to welfare recipients; and (3) the advent of crack.

Honig and Filer (1993) use statistical analysis to investigate the factors that are correlated with variations in homelessness among metropolitan areas. They find that higher rents for low-income apartments (possibly caused by a reduction in supply), changes in labor markets, changes in public policy towards the mentally ill, and reductions in public assistance to low-income people are the primary determinants of homelessness. Thus, their statistical analysis confirms the outline suggested by Jencks.

Notable by its absence in the causes of homelessness has been any change in government housing policy (with the possible exception of the treatment of SROs). This merely serves to reinforce Rossi's earlier statement that homelessness is a symptom of poverty rather than a problem in the housing market per se. For example, the vacancy rate in apartments renting for less than $250 per month was 7.7 percent in 1973, 7.4 percent in 1979, and 9.0 percent in 1989, surely not an indicator of excess demand in the whole country. The fact that landlords prefer to abandon some properties rather than rent them is further evidence that there is, if anything, an excess supply of low-income housing.

Reducing Homelessness: The Role of Shelters

The general answer to reducing homelessness is to remove its causes. Jencks, for example, suggests providing vouchers to low-income people so that they can choose services for themselves rather than relying on the government to decide whether their needs are being met (1994, p. 121). I want to focus, though, on the role of homeless shelters in alleviating, and perhaps exacerbating, the problem of homelessness.

By the late 1980s, shelters and soup kitchens served between 200,000 and 300,000 per day. Advocates for the homeless, though, argue that more shelters are needed. For example, studies find that the people who stay in shelters are more successful than those that do not. However, many homeless people do not make use of shelters, despite vacancy rates sometimes approaching 30 percent. If there is excess capacity in existing shelters, it is not clear that providing more shelters would lead to a large improvement.

Why do shelters have vacancies? There are two reasons, one related to demand and one related to supply. The demand-side reason is that many shelters are perceived as dangerous, leading some people to prefer to take their chances on the street. The supply-side reason has to do with the policies toward admission that shelters follow. In part due to concerns about the safety of their patrons, shelters tend to deny admission to those who seem most dangerous or disturbed.

The ideal candidate for admission to a shelter is someone who is sober, neat, and not obviously mentally ill (Rossi 1989, p. 99). If shelters do not turn away those who are drunk or disturbed, then the negative externalities from these people in the close quarters of the shelter can lead to the exit of less-disruptive people. A real conundrum faces the operator of a shelter. Either turn away people who might have no other alternative or face a deterioration in conditions that in the long run can leave the shelter attractive to none but the dangerously drunk and disturbed. It is not clear that constructing more shelters, in the absence of a solution to this conundrum, will markedly improve the condition of those currently being turned away.

There is also cause to believe that the expansion of shelters during the 1980s actually led to an increase in homelessness rather than the reverse. There are two reasons for this belief. The first reason is that some types of shelters, most notably shelters for battered women, are designed to help people escape intolerable conditions at home. If shelters for battered women are successful, then an increase in the number of homeless will result, but arguably society is better off as these women improve their lives. The second reason is that the availability of shelters reduces the cost of homelessness relative to uncomfortable or crowded living conditions. Economic theory suggests that if the price of a product falls, then people will choose to consume more of it. While homelessness is not the type of commodity that economists usually analyze, consider the specific ways that the substitution effect can be applied. For people who do not enjoy being forced to rely on friends or family, the fact that they can find shelter while remaining independent increases the probability that they will choose homelessness. For those who are hosting relatives or friends, the fact that shelters exist reduces the guilt incurred in evicting a guest who has stayed too long or who has overstepped the bounds of hospitality.

CHAPTER SUMMARY

- Wages vary among locations within a metropolitan area. Employment centers have higher wages, which are offset by productivity increases. Wages also differ among occupations. Service employment, which has been increasing as a proportion of the work force, does not always provide wages as high as manufacturing employment, although there is large variation among people. The extent to which people are willing to work at the going wage depends in part on the return they can expect to achieve by performing illegal activities.

- The spatial mismatch hypothesis states that black workers are less likely than white workers to find jobs, due to racial segregation in housing. There are three approaches to overcoming the problems of spatial mismatch. The first is to reduce racial segregation by encouraging black suburbanization. The second is to improve mobility from central city neighborhoods to suburban employment centers. The third is to attempt to reverse the decentralization of jobs by increasing employment in and near central city neighborhoods.

- One problem facing cities is concentrated deviance from accepted social norms. Some evidence suggests that this problem has gotten worse in some cities but not in others. There is also evidence that some people do succeed in moving out of low-income areas over time. However, the relative proportions of people in low-income areas who are black families with young children has been increasing over time.

- An extreme form of poverty is homelessness. About 300,000 people were homeless in the United States in the late 1980s. The number of homeless is believed to have increased since the 1970s for a variety of reasons, including changes in the labor market, changes in land use in central cities, and changes in the ease with which people can be involuntarily committed to mental hospitals. Little evidence suggests that the increase in homelessness is due to a shortage of housing.

EXCERPT: *THE CONDITION OF THE WORKING CLASS IN ENGLAND* (FRIEDRICH ENGELS)

The conditions of poverty in modern cities are difficult, even given the proliferation of public and private agencies to assist poor people both in daily life and in escaping poverty. These conditions were also observed in the early industrial cities of England.

Rather than use one of Dickens's familiar descriptions to describe life during those times, I instead present excerpts of a nonfictional account of neighborhoods in London by Friedrich Engels (1844, pp. 39–40, 43–45). What makes this description more astounding is the fact that it is meant not to apply only to the unemployed, but to describe the condition of a large segment of the population that was employed in creating both the height of the British Empire and the new urban society of the Industrial Revolution.

Every great city has one or more slums, where the working class is crowded together. True, poverty often dwells in hidden alleys close to the palaces of the rich; but, in general, a separate territory has been assigned to it, where, removed from the sight of the happier classes, it may struggle along as it can. These slums are pretty equally arranged in all the great towns of England, the worst houses in the worst quarters of the towns; usually one- or two-storeyed cottages in long rows, perhaps with cellars used as dwellings, almost always irregularly built. These houses of three or four rooms and a kitchen form, throughout England, some parts of London excepted, the general dwellings of the working class. The streets are generally unpaved, rough, dirty, filled with vegetable and animal refuse, without sewers or gutters, but supplied with foul, stagnant pools instead. Moreover, ventilation is impeded by the bad, confused method of building of the whole quarter, and since many human beings here live crowded into a small space, the atmosphere that prevails in these working-men's quarters may readily be imagined. Further, the streets serve as drying grounds in fine weather; lines are stretched across from house to house, and hung with wet clothing.

   Let us investigate some of the slums in their order. London comes first, and in London the famous rookery of St. Giles which is now, at last, about to be penetrated by a couple of broad streets. St. Giles is in the midst of a most populous part of the town, surrounded by broad, splendid avenues in which the gay world of London idles about, in the immediate neighbourhood of Oxford Street, Regent Street, of Trafalgar Square and the Strand. It is a disorderly collection of tall, three or four-storeyed houses, with narrow, crooked, filthy streets, in which there is quite as much life as in the great thoroughfares of the town, except that, here, people of the working class only are to be seen. A vegetable market is held in the street, baskets with vegetables and fruits, naturally all bad and hardly fit to use, obstruct the sidewalk still further, and from these, as well as from the fish-dealers' stalls, arises a horrible smell. The houses are occupied from cellar to garret, filthy within and without, and their appearance is such that no human being could possibly wish to live in them. But all this is nothing in comparison with the dwellings in the narrow courts and alleys between the streets entered by covered passages between the houses, in which the filth and tottering ruin surpass all description. Scarcely a whole window-pane can be found, the walls are crumbling, door-posts and window-frames loose and broken, doors of old boards nailed together, or altogether wanting in the thieves' quarter, where no doors are needed, there being nothing to steal. Heaps of garbage and ashes lie in all directions, and the foul liquids emptied before the doors gather in stinking pools. Nor is St. Giles the only London slum.

   I am far from asserting that *all* London working people live in such want. But I assert that thousands of industrious and worthy people—far worthier and more to be respected than all the rich of London—do find themselves in a condition unworthy of human beings; and that every proletarian, everyone, without exception, is exposed to a similar fate without any fault of his own and in spite of every possible effort.

   But in spite of all this, they who have some kind of a shelter are fortunate, fortunate in comparison with the utterly homeless. In London 50,000 human beings get up every morning, not knowing where they are to lay their heads at night. The luckiest of this multitude, those who succeed in keeping a penny or two until evening, enter a lodging house, such as abound in every great city, where they find a bed. But what a bed! These houses are filled with beds from cellar to garret, four, five, six beds in a room; as many as can be crowded in. Into every bed four, five, or six human beings are piled, as many as can be packed in, sick and well, young and old, drunk and sober, men and women, just as they come, indiscriminately. Then come strife, blows, wounds, or, if these bedfellows agree, so much the worse; thefts are arranged and things done which our language, grown more human than our deeds, refuses to record. And those who cannot pay for such a refuge? They sleep where they find a place, in passages, arcades, in corners where the police and the owners leave them undisturbed. A few individuals find their way to the refuges which are managed, here and there, by private charity, others sleep on the benches in the parks close under the windows of Queen Victoria.

I have referred to the refuges for the homeless. How greatly overcrowded these are, two examples may show. A newly erected Refuge for the Houseless in Upper Ogle Street, that can shelter 300 persons every night, has received, since its opening, 27 January to 17 March 1844, 2,740 persons for one or more nights, and a crowd of the homeless had to be sent away every night for want of room. In another refuge, the Central Asylum in Playhouse Yard, there were supplied on an average 460 beds nightly, during the first three months of the year 1844, 6,681 persons being sheltered, and 96,141 portions of bread were distributed.

Source: The Condition of the Working Class in England by Friedrich Engels. Oxford University Press edition 1993. Reprinted by permission of Oxford University Press.

Questions for Review and Discussion

1. Peter Rossi (1989) estimates that about 2,800 people were homeless in Chicago on any given night in 1985. Engels, in the excerpt above, estimates that there were 50,000 homeless in London on any given day in 1844. Why do you think the number has changed? Is this a sign that conditions have improved in low-income urban areas since 1844?

2. Engels reports that a homeless shelter that can house 300 people housed 2,740 people during a roughly three-month period. How is this possible? Would you expect a similar pattern for shelters in the United States in the 1990s?

3. "Black suburbanization has increased in the 1980s and 1990s. There is, therefore, no need to continue to worry about spatial mismatch." Do you agree or disagree? Explain.

4. "The return to drug dealing is high because it is illegal and therefore risky. Legalizing drugs would increase the labor supply in the legal sector and reduce the urban employment problem." Do you agree or disagree? Explain.

5. "Urban poverty is more of a threat to society than rural poverty because of the negative externalities resulting from spatial concentration of poverty." Do you agree or disagree? Explain.

6. "Shelters should not be allowed to turn people away if there are vacancies in the shelter." Do you agree or disagree? Explain.

CHAPTER

Housing Markets

13

ousing represents approximately 50 percent of the land use in urban areas. It is a unique commodity that looms large in the decisions of all households. Housing has also been an area of considerable policy intervention by both federal and local governments. In this chapter we consider several aspects of the housing market. We begin with a discussion of the characteristics of housing that make it unique. We then introduce a common tool of economic analysis known as "hedonic price analysis," which provides a basis for dividing the housing market into a set of submarkets that differ in important characteristics but are related through the cost of altering a house. The demand and supply for housing are then analyzed. The idea that the housing market is in fact composed of interrelated submarkets is further developed through the "filtering" model of housing.

HOUSING: A UNIQUE COMMODITY

As a good, housing is distinguished by five characteristics: heterogeneity, immobility, durability, large expense relative to income, and high adjustment costs. Many other goods and services share one or more of these characteristics, but none share all of them. Thus, housing is a unique commodity.

Housing is both a source of consumption and a means of investment. As a consumer, you enjoy housing services (including tax advantages), while as an investor, you accumulate equity in the house, which is an important investment vehicle for a homeowner. Housing contains both private and public good aspects. The private consumption aspects are clear, while the fact that living in a particular location brings with it a neighborhood (and a local government) implies that the housing decision also includes the choice of the level and composition of a variety of public goods. (The relation between housing choice and public goods was discussed in chapter 10.) This combination of attributes makes housing an especially difficult commodity to analyze. The effort to understand the housing market, though, promises great rewards; after all, if we can understand something so complicated, maybe other goods will be easier to analyze.

Heterogeneity

No two housing units are identical. This is trivially true in the sense that no two housing units can occupy the same space, but the matter is more profound than that. The heterogeneity of housing makes it difficult to characterize, for example, the amount that a household is consuming at any given time. If the amount of housing consumed is difficult to observe, then the price per unit clearly is difficult to observe; therefore, the whole notion of an equilibrium price in a market is empirically difficult. We will develop in the next section a way of measuring the quantity of housing consumed that alleviates (but does not completely eliminate) these difficulties.

Application: What Characteristics Are Important to People?

Because all housing units are different, and because it is not always possible for each person to live in a place that is ideal in every respect, it is interesting to examine what features are most important to people. The noted sociologist, Peter Rossi, used interview techniques on residents of Philadelphia neighborhoods to analyze this question in his classic book, *Why Families Move* (1955).

The preliminary question faced by many people is whether to purchase a house or rent housing. Table 13.1 illustrates Rossi's findings on this issue. Clearly, households have strong preferences for one or the other tenure status. Later in this chapter we will analyze in some detail the question of whether to rent or own.

Once the decision whether to own or rent has been made, a household still has to balance many competing characteristics. The people Rossi interviewed were asked about a set of characteristics in four groups: cost, space, location, and social composition of the neighborhood. People were first asked whether they preferred their current homes to the alternatives that they considered with respect to each group of characteristics. They were then asked which group of characteristics had been of primary importance in making their housing choice. The results of this survey are summarized in Table 13.2.

Table 13.2 shows that some characteristics seem to be more important to households than others. For example, 60 percent of the households rate their current unit better than alternatives on the basis of cost. Meanwhile, 42 percent of households identify cost as the most important factor in their decision, so that 70 percent of those preferring this characteristic actually made their decision on that basis. Rossi calls this measure the "index of effectiveness." We find that 50 percent of the people who prefer the amount of space in their current dwelling to alternatives made their decision

TABLE 13.1   Tenure Sought by Households Considering Moving

Tenure Sought	Current Renters	Current Homeowners
Purchase home only	——	75%
Rent only	89 %	——
Either own or rent	11%	25%

Source: Rossi (1955, Table 9.2, p. 156).

TABLE 13.2 Household Assessment of Housing Characteristics

Characteristic	Percentage Who Rate Their Current Unit Better Than Alternatives	Percentage Who Identify This Characteristic as Most Important	Index of Effectiveness (col. 3 / col. 2)
Cost	60	42	0.70
Space	36	18	0.50
Location	55	19	0.35
Neighborhood	31	6	0.19

Source: Adapted from Rossi (1955, Table 9.8, p. 167).

primarily on that basis, again indicating its importance. On the other hand, location (accessibility to work, friends, and family) and neighborhood composition are less crucial, with an index of effectiveness of 0.35 and 0.19 respectively.

The last question is whether it is possible for a household to have several of its desired characteristics at the same time, or whether it is only possible to have one at the expense of another. To examine that, Rossi calculated the extent to which different characteristics are correlated with each other and then constructed what he called an "index of incompatibility." This index is greater than 1 if the characteristics are incompatible and less than 1 if they are compatible. Table 13.3 illustrates the findings. The results in Table 13.3 should be read as follows. Each column indicates the most important characteristic for a household; for this analysis the characteristics include access to transportation, neighborhood composition, costs, appearance, and rooms. Reading down each column gives the compatibility of the remaining characteristics with that dominant characteristic. For example, if appearance is the most important factor to you, you will find that neighborhood (index = 0.55) and rooms (index = 0.76) are compatible, but transportation (index = 1.30) and cost (index = 1.29) are incompatible. So you can easily have a house with the desired appearance and the correct number of rooms, but you cannot also have easy access to transportation or pay a low cost for the house. It is probably not surprising to learn that the characteristic most incompatible with the others is cost—if you only have a limited amount of money to spend, you might have to compromise on your other desired characteristics.

TABLE 13.3 The Compatability of Different Characteristics: The Index of Incompatibility

	Transport	Neighborhood	Cost	Appearance	Rooms
Transport	—	1.27	1.09	1.30	0.73
Neighborhood	1.09	—	1.27	0.55	0.36
Cost	0.82	0.94	—	1.29	1.18
Appearance	1.18	0.68	1.46	—	0.64
Rooms	1.29	0.82	1.18	0.76	—

Note: Each row indicates the compatibility of other characteristics with the characteristic heading the column. A value less than one indicates compatibility, while a value greater than one indicates incompatibility.

Source: Rossi (1955, Table 9.10, p. 171).

Immobility

Once a housing unit is constructed, it is almost impossible to move (trailers and mobile homes being the exceptions that prove the rule). Further, it is expensive to extensively renovate housing, and it is expensive to demolish it and replace it with some other house or business. There is a large element of irreversibility in the construction of housing, and this will affect the supply decisions of firms as well as the consumption decisions of households.

Recall the discussion in chapter 8 about the effect of sunk costs and uncertainty on investment. There we saw that investment might be delayed past the short-term break-even point because the investor wants to be more certain about recouping sunk costs. In the case of housing, this implies that we expect to see the construction of new housing that will sell quickly and for a fairly high price. In other words, newly constructed housing can be expected to be relatively expensive.

Durability

Housing lasts a long time. A well-constructed house can last hundreds of years, and even the least-expensive new construction is expected to last at least 30 years. Therefore, expectations about market conditions that will obtain in the future will have a strong influence on the supply of housing. Further, a person buying a house will also take into account its value in the future, since the lifetime of housing units can reasonably be expected to include several different occupants.

Durability also makes the question of the future quality of the neighborhood more salient. Yes, there is a lovely field across the street now, but will it still be there in five years? If the land across the street is zoned for commercial development, today's view might become tomorrow's traffic jam. We have already seen in chapter 10 the importance of zoning for a city's economy. The long-term nature of the housing investment leads homeowners and developers to work intensely on zoning. I have to take into account the expected quality of the neighborhood 20 years from now, whether or not I'll still be living in this house, because the future neighborhood will affect how much I can sell my house for. Thus, the current value of my house—my largest investment, if I'm a typical American homeowner—depends on zoning. It's no wonder people get very involved in local land-use decisions.

High Expense Relative to Income

This is self-explanatory. Housing expenditures represented over 30 percent of average household expenditures in 1988 in the United States. The equity in a house is also the largest asset in the net worth of families in the United States, representing 32.2 percent of assets in 1989. This large expense means that the typical person can live in only one place and thus will face tradeoffs in the location decision among the various dimensions of the housing service.

Large Adjustment Costs

It is expensive, both financially and psychologically, to move. Moving, then, can be thought of as a large sunk cost to the household of making an investment in a particular location. Therefore, like firms that must make investment decisions in an environment of uncertainty and irreversibility, households will adjust their housing only if there is a large advantage to doing so. The fact that costs are involved in obtaining information about alternative housing makes it even more unlikely that households will want to move unless the difference between their current situation and desired situation is large. At any given time, many (maybe most) households are not in their "ideal" housing situation but rather are close enough to it that the costs of adjusting make adjustment undesirable.

Application: Adjustment Costs and the Rent Gradient

In chapter 9 we developed a model of housing rents based on the idea that households trade off accessibility against housing costs. The formal statement of this idea was couched in the monocentric city model, in which all employment is located in the CBD and there were no issues of accessibility except for the commute. If we broaden the analysis, though, the tradeoff is not so clear cut. Suppose, for instance, that there are two employment centers within a metropolitan area and that a person thinks there is a chance of working at each center at different times. If moving would entail large adjustment costs, then changing the job location will not necessarily lead to changing the house location. After all, if you change jobs once, you might change again, and you don't want to keep incurring adjustment costs. When purchasing (or renting) housing, the household will want to take into account not only the commuting distance to the current place of work but also the accessibility to other potential employment sites. This makes the benefit of being located near to the CBD less than it was in the simple monocentric city analysis (closer to CBD is not necessarily closer to other workplaces). There are several immediate implications. First, the rent gradient will be less steeply sloped than it is in the monocentric city model because land close to the CBD commands a smaller accessibility premium. Second, households will commute farther on average than they do in the monocentric city model. Because the job location might change, households will choose their location on the basis of their expected commute over a period of time rather than minimize their commute given their present job. Third, an increase in job stability will lead to a shorter commute and a steeper rent gradient, since people no longer have to take the chance of future moves into account (Crane 1996).

Even if employment is concentrated in the CBD, the idea that households value accessibility to different places more at different times makes sense. Consider a young, newly wed couple. They might value access to their jobs very highly now but not really care about how close they are to day-care services and schools. However, they might take those factors into account when buying a house so that they won't have to move when they have children.

HEDONIC PRICE ANALYSIS

How much housing are you consuming? One dorm room, you might answer. Fine. How many dorm rooms would be equivalent to one apartment? to one house? Is my house equivalent to 0.82 of my neighbor's? Answering these difficult questions is important if we want to systematically analyze housing markets. Recall that our basic supply-and-demand diagrams illustrate a relation between quantity and price—if we do not know what the quantity is, we cannot diagram supply and demand. (To illustrate the difficulty, compare the questions about housing quantity to the following question: "How many Snickers® bars are you consuming?")

The approach that economists use to compare housing units is known as *hedonic price analysis.* The idea is as follows: A housing unit is completely described by number of characteristics; for example, it has a certain number of rooms, a certain number of square feet, a certain style of roof, and so on. Each of these characteristics has an implicit price—$400 per room, say—and the total price of the house is just the sum of the implicit prices. If the price per room is $400, and the house has eight rooms, then that represents $3,200, and so on. If the characteristics of your house have implicit prices that add up to $80,000 and the characteristics of my house have implicit prices that add up to $120,000, then I am judged to be consuming 50 percent more housing than you. Alternatively, suppose we define a $100,000 house as 1 unit of housing. In that case, you are consuming 0.8 units of housing and I am consuming 1.2 units of housing.

Housing Price Indices

People care about the price of the typical house and how much this price changes from year to year. These figures provide information about the rate of return on investments in residential capital relative to other forms of investment. The National Association of Realtors (NAR) publishes such an index regularly, comparing the median sales price of houses sold in one year to the median sales price of houses sold the previous year. For example, if the median sales price this year is $82,000 and the median sales price last year was $80,000, then the NAR index would show that housing prices increased by 2.5 percent. However, there is a problem in comparing the sales prices of houses that sold in 1996 to those that sold in 1995. The houses that sold in 1996 might have a different set of characteristics than the houses that sold in 1995. If the typical 1996 house has a more attractive set of characteristics than the typical 1995 house, then part of the price increase reflects this more attractive set of characteristics rather than an increase in the implicit prices of characteristics. This difference is important to the homeowner because (in the absence of remodeling) it is only a change in implicit prices that will lead the price of an existing house to change.

Correcting for this problem of comparing houses across years is done in two principal ways. The first is to calculate a *repeat sales price index.* This index compares the sale prices of houses that sold this year with the prices of the houses when they sold in earlier years. If the characteristics of the houses have not been changed, then this approach will yield a better estimate of the changes in implicit prices than the approach of comparing the median sales price of all houses. The repeat sales price index does suffer from two problems, though. First, the houses that sell repeatedly are not necessarily representative of the total housing stock. If they are included in the total, the repeat sales price index can be an inaccurate estimate of the change in price for most houses. Second, the characteristics of houses can change over time, as can the relative value of those characteristics. Some studies attempt to address this problem by measuring the extent to which the houses are remodeled between sales. This approach does not solve the problem that the implicit prices themselves might have changed.

The second principal way of correcting the problem with the NAR price index is to calculate a *hedonic price index.* This approach involves calculating the implicit prices of characteristics each year. Then the price of a house consisting of a given set of characteristics can be calculated each year. This approach has the advantage of directly estimating the change in value of existing houses that have not been remodeled. It has the disadvantage of requiring more detailed information over a reasonably long period of time. However, as property transactions and tax assessment records increasingly are stored on computerized databases, the data needed for calculating hedonic price indices are more widely available than before.

How much of a problem is caused by ignoring changes in characteristics when calculating changes in house prices? Edwin Mills and Ronald Simenauer (1996) used data obtained from the NAR to compare the median sales price index with a hedonic price index. Their results are summarized in Table 13.4. The table compares the hedonic price index for the period 1986 to 1992 to the change in median sales price over the same period for each of four regions. In all four regions, the hedonic price index was lower over the period, illustrating the upward bias on house prices inherent in the median sales price technique.

An alternative question is which method of estimating housing-price changes provides the best forecast of future changes in house prices. After all, the durability of housing implies that people care not only about current prices but also about future prices when making decisions. Crone and Voith (1992) compared the median sales price index, the repeat sales price index, and the hedonic price index on the basis of the accuracy of their predictions. They found that the median sales price index is the least accurate forecaster of price appreciation. They conclude that either the repeat sales price index or the hedonic price index is a reliable approach. Under some prediction criteria, repeat sales was more accurate, while under other criteria the hedonic price was more accurate. Regardless, the importance of taking into account changes in house characteristics is unquestionable.

Calculating Hedonic Prices

In order to estimate the implicit prices used to calculate hedonic prices, economists use statistical analysis. Consider Figure 13.1, which shows a scatter plot of sales prices of houses against the living area of the house, using data from Schworm (1995).

Undertaking this type of analysis presents several technical difficulties. One of particular interest is the "specification" of the hedonic price equation—in other

TABLE 13.4 Hedonic Price Index versus NAR Median Sales Price Index, 1986–1992

Region	Percentage Change in House Price: Hedonic Price Index	Percentage Change in House Price: NAR Median Sales Price Index
East	4.96	32.42
Midwest	16.65	25.76
South	13.03	16.60
West	10.25	37.46

Source: Adapted from Mills and Simenauer (1996, Table 2, p. 214).

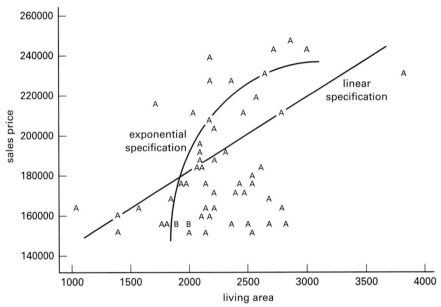

Legend: A = 1 obs, B = 2 obs, etc.

FIGURE 13.1 Plot of Sales Price against Living Area

words, the assumed functional relation between the price of a house and its characteristics. One possibility is a linear specification; that is,

$$\text{Price} = \beta_0 + \beta_1 * \text{Age} + \beta_2 * \text{Rooms} + \beta_3 * \text{Living Area} + \ldots + \varepsilon \qquad (1)$$

The βs are chosen to minimize the unexplained portion of the variation in price. In Figure 13.1, the relation between Sales Price and Living Area, using a linear specification, is shown. The ε represents an error term; not all the variation in prices will be explainable by the observed characteristics. Another possibility is an exponential specification; that is,

$$\text{Price} = \alpha_0 \text{Age}^{\alpha_1} \text{Rooms}^{\alpha_2} \text{LivingArea}^{\alpha_3} \ldots \eta \qquad (2)$$

Equivalently, equation (2) can be written as $\ln(\text{Price}) = \alpha_0 + \alpha_1 \ln(\text{Age})$ and so forth. The curve in Figure 13.1 labeled "exponential specification" shows the estimated relation between Sales Price and Living Area that best explains the observed data. This time, the η represents the error term. The main difference between specifications (1) and (2) is the marginal benefit of adding more of a characteristic. In specification (1), each additional unit has an identical value. In specification (2), it is possible to have diminishing marginal returns to a characteristic.

Any characteristic or set of characteristics can (in theory) be altered. The only question is the cost of the alteration. Thus, any particular house or even neighborhood can be changed in large or small ways to accommodate changing market conditions. This is an important source of housing. Note that although we speak of a "housing market," it probably makes more sense to think of a variety of submarkets. The very heterogeneity of housing makes it difficult to compare some houses to others.

The retired couple is likely to be looking for a different set of characteristics than the young professional couple. These submarkets are linked, though, through the cost of converting one type of housing to another. Rothenberg et al. (1991) provide a detailed analysis of the housing market using the approach of linked submarkets.

Application: House Prices in Brecksville and Broadview Heights, Ohio

Consider the following example of a hedonic price study. Lisa Schworm (1995) gathered data on recently purchased homes in two neighboring suburbs of Cleveland, Brecksville and Broadview Heights. Her data included the style of the house (ranch, split-level, bungalow, colonial, contemporary, or condominium), the construction materials (frame, brick, or vinyl siding), the type of garage (attached or detached), the number of parking spaces in the garage, the area of the garage, whether the basement was finished or unfinished, the size of the basement, the area of the lot, the living area of the house, the number of bedrooms, the number of bathrooms, the total number of rooms, the year the house was built, the type of heat (forced air or heat pump), and whether or not the house had central air conditioning. The mean values for all of these variables are shown in Table 13.5. The standard deviation, a measure of the extent of variation in the variables, is also shown in Table 13.5. Schworm's study focused on the question of whether houses in Brecksville were worth more than houses in Broadview Heights, all else being equal. In order to hold all else equal, she estimated the following hedonic price equation:

ln(SalesPrice) = −2.14 + 0.12 * Brecksville + 0.12 * ln(Living Area)
    + 0.006 * YearBuilt + 0.05 * Rooms − 0.32*Condominium + 0.11 * Colonial
    + 0.17 * AttachedGarage − 0.07 * AirConditioning + 0.06 * ForcedAirHeat
    + 0.08 * Bedrooms + 0.05 * Bathrooms − 0.02 * Brick + 0.16 * Frame
Number of observations = 199   Adjusted R^2 = 0.77

Interpreting these results, a house in Brecksville is worth 12 percent more than an identical house in Broadview Heights. She went on to investigate reasons for this difference, and you will be unsurprised to learn that differences in zoning policy between the two towns turned out to be important. Brecksville had concentrated its nonresidential activity into a single town center, thereby reducing the negative externalities of traffic from most of the residential areas. Broadview Heights, on the other hand, had commercial areas scattered throughout the suburb, which was less desirable to potential residents, as illustrated in the difference in house prices.

The effect of changing other variables can also be investigated by using the data from Table 13.5. For example, if the living area of the house increases by 10 percent, then the value of the house will increase by 1.2 percent. The mean living area is 2,044 square feet and the mean house price is $137,443. All else being equal, a 2,200-square-foot house (about 10 percent larger than the average house) would sell for about $139,000 (about 1.2 percent higher than the average price). You can evaluate the impact of changing other attributes in the same way. The adjusted R^2 is a statistical measure of how good a job the equation does explaining the variation in house prices. An adjusted R^2 of 0.77 means that over three-fourths (77 percent) of the variation in house prices is explained by the equation.

TABLE 13.5 Variables Used in Hedonic Price Analysis: Descriptive Statistics

Variable	Mean	Standard Deviation
SalesPrice	137,443.5	72,922.98
ln(SalesPrice)	11.722	0.460
Brecksville (0–1 variable)	0.460	0.500
Living Area	2,044.28	4,150.07
ln(LivingArea)	7.419	0.449
YearBuilt	1967.5	17.216
Rooms	6.23	1.513
Condominium (0–1 variable)	0.345	0.477
Colonial (0–1 variable)	0.180	0.385
AttachedGarage (0–1 variable)	0.680	0.468
AirConditioning (0–1 variable)	0.620	0.487
ForcedAirHeat (0–1 variable)	0.885	0.320
Bedrooms	2.92	0.810
Bathrooms	1.855	0.609
Brick (0–1 variable)	0.20	0.401
Frame (0–1 variable)	0.24	0.428

Source: Schworm (1995).

Although the statistical techniques may seem formidable (and the technical issues are considerable), the basic idea of hedonic pricing is to compare houses similar in every dimension but one in order to identify the effect of changing that one dimension. Schworm (1995) illustrates such an experiment, comparing the sales prices of houses in Brecksville and Broadview Heights that met a variety of selection criteria. She considered the prices of houses that shared the following characteristics: They were built between 1980 and 1990, had a lot size between 20,000 and 30,000 square feet, had a living area between 2,000 and 3,000 square feet, a finished basement, an attached garage, a fireplace, forced air heating, and three or four bedrooms. The four houses in Brecksville that met these criteria had an average sales price of $208,875 in 1994. The three houses in Broadview Heights that met these criteria had an average sales price of $185,250. The houses in Brecksville are thus estimated to be worth 11.3 percent more than the comparable houses in Broadview Heights, very similar to the result obtained using regression techniques.

DEMAND AND SUPPLY IN THE HOUSING MARKET

> I do not mean to insist here on the disadvantage of hiring compared to owning, but it is evident that the savage owns his shelter because it costs so little, while the civilized man hires his commonly because he cannot afford to own it; nor can he, in the long run, any better afford to hire.
>
> —HENRY DAVID THOREAU

The analysis of demand and supply in the housing market is complicated not only because of the difficulty in determining the quantity of housing consumed or produced but because of two other important issues. First, there is the question of whether a household chooses to own its house or rent from someone else. Second is the complication that the price that determines demand is not the same as the price that determines supply, although there is a straightforward relation between the two prices.

Renting versus Owning

Why would a household choose to rent rather than own (or vice versa)? Clearly, the answer is that a higher level of utility can be achieved from one or the other tenure status. Putting to one side such intangible benefits as pride of ownership, let us consider the financial aspects of the choice between renting and owning.

Two preliminary issues will help us in this analysis. First, note that homeowners, in effect, rent from themselves. Thus, the question of renting versus owning can be rephrased as renting from someone else versus renting from oneself. Second, in a perfectly competitive or monopolistically competitive housing market, a landlord will make zero economic profit. In other words, rent will equal average cost. Thus, we can look at the rental determination problem from the landlord's (cost) perspective. As we will see in chapter 14 when we discuss rent control, the exact nature of the market structure in the market for rental housing is a matter of some contention. To anticipate, the controversy will be over the question of whether monopolistic competition is a better description than perfect competition. Without prejudging what the answer to that question will be, note that both market structures have a long-run equilibrium in which firms (in this case landlords) earn zero profits because of the lack of entry barriers. Thus, the equilibrium price of rental housing will equal the average cost, the only question being whether or not the price is equal to or greater than marginal cost.

We wish to compare, then, the average cost of renting a housing unit from someone else with the average cost of renting a housing unit from oneself. A landlord has several costs that must be covered.

The first cost is the *maintenance* of the housing unit, which we will denote M. This cost includes the purchase of labor and materials to clean and operate the house, the purchase of utilities, and the time of the owner spent in maintaining the housing unit. Maintenance costs also include repairing and preventing the physical deterioration of the house.

The second cost is the *property tax liability* of the house, PT. The property tax liability is determined by the local government and is usually calculated as a tax rate applied to an assessed value that reflects the market value of the property. Property tax payments are deductible from federal income taxes, so this deduction must be accounted for in calculating the user cost of housing.

The third cost is the *interest payment on the mortgage* used to finance the house, MI. Few people are able to pay cash for a house and so must borrow money to do so. The interest rate they pay will reflect both the opportunity cost of the money ("real interest rate") and expected inflation. Mortgage interest payments, like property tax payments, are deductible from federal income taxes.

The fourth cost is the *capital gain* created by an increase in the value of the house, CG. Capital gains on housing are taxable, but three important provisions of the federal income tax code reduce the tax implications of this form of capital gain. The first provision is the fact that capital gains are taxed only upon their realization, in this case when the house is sold. As the value of the house increases from year to year, no capital gains tax liability is generated in the absence of a sale. The second provision is the ability to "roll over" capital gains from the sale of a house if a house of at least the same value is purchased within two years. This provision allows a homeowner to postpone capital gains taxes for as long as they are "trading up" in housing, and it also gives people an incentive to buy increasingly expensive houses over the course of their lifetime. The third provision is the ability to completely exclude from taxation some capital gains arising from the sale of housing. This provision is limited (currently to $125,000) and can only be used once (currently only after the person reaches the age of 55). The combination of these three provisions implies that capital gains on housing are taxed, if at all, at a very low effective rate. For the sake of simplicity, we will set this tax rate equal to zero, which is not inaccurate for many people.

The cost of housing can therefore be written as $C = M + PT + MI + CG$. The next step is to compare the costs to a person who rents housing to others (rental housing) with the costs to a person who rents housing to himself or herself (owner-occupied housing). For ease of comparison, suppose that maintenance, property taxes, mortgage interest, and capital gains are all a given fraction of the value of the house, V. These fractions are denoted m, t^P, i, and g respectively, where i is the real rate of interest. For simplicity, we will assume that the actual interest rate is the real rate plus the rate of inflation (Fisher's law). We allow for the possibility that the maintenance costs and interest rate vary systematically between owning and renting, using the subscripts O and R to denote owner-occupied and rental housing respectively. Then we can write the cost of owning C_O and the cost of renting C_R as follows, letting Π equal inflation, and t^F the federal marginal income tax rate.

$$C_O = \{m_O + t^P (1 - t^F) + (i_O + \Pi)(1 - t^F) - g\} V \tag{3}$$

$$C_R = \{m_R (1 - t^F) + t^P (1 - t^F) + (i_R + \Pi)(1 - t^F) - g\} V \tag{4}$$

There are four reasons that the cost of renting from someone else could be expected to be higher than the cost of renting from yourself. First, the externality of renting could imply that maintenance costs are higher. The absence of clear property rights to common areas along with the more transitive nature of rental occupiers could further depreciate the property. Second, rental property is riskier than owner-occupied property, making the carrying cost of the mortgage higher for rental housing because the real interest rate paid by homeowners is lower. Third, the fact that some people enjoy maintaining the house and property means that maintenance costs can be lower in the case of homeowners than in the case of renters. Fourth, owner-occupied housing enjoys a tax advantage in that the rent implicitly paid by homeowners to themselves as landlords is excluded from the income tax base.

Consider the following example of the relative costs of renting and owning, using reasonable parameters to fill in equations (3) and (4). Let $m_O = 0.02$, $m_R = 0.03$, $i_O = 0.05$, $i_R = 0.06$, $t^P = 0.02$, $t^F = 0.28$, $\Pi = 0.03$, and $g = 0.04$. These numbers reflect both the renter externality and the greater risk of rental property by having $m_R > m_O$ and $i_R > i_O$. From equation (3) we calculate that $C_O = 0.052V$, while from equation (4) we calculate that $C_R = 0.0608V$. In other words, renting is almost 20 percent more expensive than owning, all else being equal. This is a significant difference, especially when we recall that housing expenditures are a relatively high percentage of most people's income.

One item that may surprise you by its absence in this list of cost advantages for homeownership is the tax deductibility of mortgage interest. This is often cited as a major incentive to own rather than rent. However, the differential between owners and renters is reduced by the fact that landlords can deduct mortgage interest. If the rental market is perfectly competitive, this cost reduction is passed along to renters. If the rental market is not perfectly competitive, some of the advantage may be retained by the landlord. In equilibrium, though, the marginal landlord will continue to make zero profits. The value of any tax deduction depends upon the marginal tax rate of the person claiming the deduction. A graduated set of income tax rates implies that the value of the tax deduction is greater for high-income than for low-income people, so we might expect to see high-income landlords renting to low-income renters to take advantage of this "extra" tax benefit. A situation where a financial advantage is available on the basis of the tax code is known as *tax arbitrage.*

Rental property has another advantage over owner-occupied property. Landlords can deduct maintenance expenditures from their federal income tax liability. The ability to claim *accelerated depreciation* has greatly enhanced this advantage. Under U.S. law, owners of an asset used in a business are allowed to claim a deduction on the basis of the depreciation over time of that asset. Note the asymmetric treatment of capital gains in this respect. Accrued capital gains are not taxed by the federal government, while depreciation (accrued capital losses) is deductible from federal taxes. A rental housing unit might have a useful life of 40, 50, or even 100 years. However, for tax purposes, it is possible to claim that it depreciated over a much shorter time period. Once the property is completely depreciated for tax purposes, there is an incentive to sell it to a new owner who can then start the process over again. However, the Tax Reform Act of 1986 lengthened the period of time over which owners of rental property were allowed to depreciate it, thus reducing this incentive for property turnover (Pellechio 1988).

Who rents? Low-income people rent because of down-payment constraints and because of tax arbitrage given the progressive income tax structure in the United States. Table 13.6 illustrates the different income distributions of owners and renters in the U.S. The median income of renters in 1990 was $20,772, while the median income of homeowners was $36,298. High-mobility people rent because of the high

TABLE 13.6   Owners versus Renters

1990 Income (thousand $)	Owners	Renters
0–5	2.7%	9.4%
5–9.9	6.5%	15.4%
10–14.9	7.7%	12.5%
15–24.9	15.5%	21.7%
25–34.9	15.5%	16.3%
35–49.9	19.6%	14.0%
50–74.9	19.0%	7.7%
>75	13.5%	3.1%

Source: Statistical Abstract of the United States, 1992, table 697, p. 446.

transactions costs of purchasing and selling a house relative to moving from one rental unit to another. College students, with their combination of (relatively) low income and high mobility, are almost uniformly renters.

An intermediate case between single-family, owner-occupied housing and rental apartments is the condominium or cooperative apartment building. In this type of institution, people own their own housing units as well as share joint ownership of common areas. Condominiums and cooperative apartments have become increasingly common since 1960. Henry Hansmann (1991) points out that owning rather than renting a unit in multiunit housing suffers from several disadvantages, including illiquidity, high transactions costs of changing residences, poor diversification of risk, and collective choice problems (such as management of common areas) that require costly decision making. He concludes that the ability to avoid local rent-control ordinances is the main reason for the proliferation of this type of occupancy. This might not seem like an advantage for the renters. Recall, though, that an owner is someone who is both a renter and a landlord. If there is enough benefit from being able to collect sufficient rents to maintain a high-quality housing unit, then the additional rent paid will be worthwhile.

Deterioration and Maintenance

A properly maintained housing unit can last for over 100 years. How much will a landlord spend on maintenance? The profit-maximizing amount, by assumption. This answer, while theoretically unquestionable, is in itself unenlightening. To see in more detail how the profit-maximizing amount can be determined, consider the following diagram. The quality of the housing unit can be increased at some cost; in other words, there is a production function for housing quality. There are some fixed costs of the housing unit, even if the quality is allowed to equal zero. It is also assumed that the marginal cost of increasing house quality is rising. The cost function is curve TC in Figure 13.2. For simplicity, suppose the demand is such that there is a constant amount that people are willing to pay per unit of housing quality. This is shown by the total revenue curve TR in Figure 13.2. The profit-maximizing level of maintenance is found by maximizing the difference between TR and TC, and in this case it is shown by q^*.

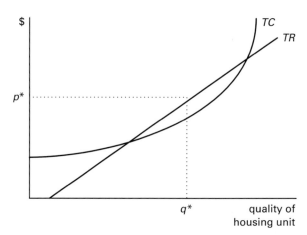

FIGURE 13.2 Optimal Maintenance

The optimum level of maintenance can change over time. For example, as the housing unit ages, the variable costs could go up, in turn shifting up the *TC* curve. All else being equal, this implies that the landlord should reduce maintenance and that the number of housing units (the quality of housing) provided by the dwelling should decrease. Theoretically, the optimum level of maintenance could be zero, so that the landlord incurs only the fixed costs of owning the unit (including property taxes). Alternatively, the *TR* curve could shift, possibly as a result of a change in demand. If demand increases, there are three supply responses. First, build new housing (see below). Second, reduce deterioration of some units, as shown here. Third, remodel some units to move them from one submarket to another.

There is an externality with maintenance, so that private market outcomes might not be Pareto efficient. This issue has arisen earlier, in the discussion of zoning in chapter 10. In this context, it should be noted that this externality is important not only in the current maintenance decisions of landlords but on the market value of the house and hence the future decisions of landlords. A neighborhood where there is deteriorating and abandoned property is not one that a risk-averse investor uncertain of the future will wish to enter. The issue of neighborhood deterioration is one of ongoing policy interest; especially salient is the question of whether a government policy should attempt to halt or reverse neighborhood decline. Stegman and Rasmussen (1980) define a stable neighborhood as one in which normal profits can be earned; in other words, one in which an investor in housing is compensated for the opportunity cost and risk of the investment. They suggest that reversing the process of decline through normal market adjustments is not possible in some neighborhoods. The analysis of urban decline due to Oates, Howrey, and Baumol (1971) introduced in chapter 8 illustrates that changing the long-run equilibrium conditions is essential if a policy is not to have only a short-run positive impact.

The most extreme form of reducing maintenance is to abandon the property altogether. Many of the factors that contribute to abandonment, such as the physical characteristics of the building or the characteristics of the people living in the neighborhood, are not under the control of the local government. White (1986) analyzes the effect of property taxes, which are under the control of local governments, on the decision by landlords to abandon property. She finds that property tax rates are a significant determinant of abandonment rates. City governments can reduce the rate of abandonment by initiating foreclosure immediately on a property that goes into arrears on tax payments rather than allowing a grace period. They can also slow down the rate of abandonment by lowering tax assessments in blighted areas. This is a possible counterexample to the analysis seen in chapters 8 and 11, which suggested that tax policy is not an important determinant of economic activity.

The problem of poor maintenance and deterioration of housing as they affect public policy is not of recent origin. Engels (1844, pp. 70–71) describes the poor construction and lack of maintenance of working-class housing in Manchester, England. He ascribes the lack of care to the fact that the contractors building and maintaining the housing do not own the property but lease it for terms of from 20 to 99 years, at the end of which time it reverts to the owner, who pays nothing for any improvements upon the property. Of course, this gives little incentive to the builder to construct a dwelling that is worth anything at the end of the lease as well as little incentive to maintain the dwelling through the term of the lease. The result, according to Engels

(p. 71), is that "the niggardliness of the original expenditure, the neglect of all repairs, the frequent periods of emptiness, the constant change of inhabitants, and the destruction carried on by the dwellers, accomplishes the complete ruin of the cottages by the end of forty years."

Demand for Housing

The discussion of the relative costs of owning and renting makes it clear that the price that matters for the demand for housing at any given point in time is the *rental price,* that is, the annual cost of renting the house (whether from someone else or from yourself). The most important question about demand curves in practice is the elasticity of demand with respect to price and with respect to income. The estimated price elasticity of housing demand is about 1, so that housing is neither particularly inelastic nor particularly elastic. The income elasticity is about 0.75, so that housing is a normal good. Note that the relevant income for housing demand is *permanent* income, rather than the income in any given year. Given the large costs of moving and the large capital commitment and transactions costs when purchasing a house, it is unlikely that a household would wish to adjust their housing consumption as often as their annual income changes. Because permanent income must be inferred rather than observed, estimating the income elasticity of demand for housing is a difficult process.

It is worth emphasizing again the other main difficulty in estimating the demand for housing. A demand curve shows the relation between quantity demanded and price, ceteris paribus. In the case of housing, the quantity demanded is not directly observable due to the multidimensional nature of the product. Thus, any estimation of the demand curve for housing requires first quantifying the amount of housing that each household is consuming—for example, by using the hedonic analysis introduced earlier in the chapter.

Supply of Housing

In the short run, the supply of housing is essentially the standing stock. New construction accounts for about 3 percent of the existing stock, and about 1 percent of the stock is retired (abandoned or demolished), for a net change each year of about 2 percent. Using this figure, it is readily observable that about 80 percent of the housing stock is over 10 years old.

A firm (or household) that considers constructing a house must take into account not only the current rental price that the house could generate but also the expected future stream of rentals. In fact, the *market value* of a house (like that of any durable asset) is just the present discounted value of the future stream of net benefits. The formula for calculating discounted present value is shown in equation (5) below, where β is a discount factor (assumed constant over time for simplicity).

$$\text{Value} = \Sigma_s \, \beta^s \, (\text{Benefits}_s - \text{Costs}_s) \tag{5}$$

In equations (3) and (4) earlier, we saw in detail a single year's flow of benefits and costs associated with a house. Those equations can be written simply as $C = \eta V,$ where η is the term in brackets {} and V is the value of the house. If the house is infinitely-lived and the benefits and costs are constant every year, then the discounted present value of a house is $V = C/\eta$. In the more realistic case where a house does not last forever and the benefits and costs vary over time, the formula is more complicated, but it keeps the same basic pattern. We will make use of this relation between rent and value when analyzing housing market equilibrium.

A firm will construct a house if its value will exceed the construction costs. In general, there may be many different houses for which this is true, and given limited resources, a firm will actually construct those for which the difference between value and construction cost will be greatest.

An important source of variation in the nature and quantity of housing available is the remodeling and renovation of existing housing. Another source is the conversion of nonhousing property, such as a school or warehouse, into housing. Baer (1986) calls these activities "the shadow market for housing" and provides evidence of their importance. In 1980, for example, developers spent \$47 billion on new construction. In the same year, owners of existing property spent \$46 billion on maintenance, alterations, and additions. Baer argues that governments should encourage these activities, since they are particularly important sources of affordable housing for low- and middle-income households.

The idea that maintenance and alterations are a source of revitalization to neighborhoods is examined in great detail in a book by Barbara Kelly (1993) describing the evolution of the original Levittown development on Long Island. You might recall that the fictional excerpt at the end of chapter 9 suggested a dismal future for this type of development, and many analysts at the time had similar views. Kelly does not find the dire predictions of Levittown's critics to have played out, though. "Contrary to the expectations of its critics, Levittown did not become a slum. Rather, the houses evolved into a solidly middle-class suburban development of homes complete with country kitchens, center halls, second and even third baths, dining rooms, vestibules, family rooms, computer rooms, and dens" (p. 147). She goes on to argue in favor of government subsidies for construction of new housing for low- and middle-income families, because once it is built, people will improve and customize it. In the next chapter, we will return to the question of the best way to provide housing for low- and middle-income families.

Housing Market Equilibrium

Equilibrium in the housing market, as in any market, consists of a price such that the quantity demanded equals the quantity supplied. Awkwardly, though, we have two different prices in the housing market, one for demand and one for supply. The key to determining equilibrium is to use our earlier observation that the two prices are simply linked through the cost of capital. This lets us convert demand, which is a function of rent, to a function of the value, if we are given a cost of capital η. Similarly, we can convert supply from a function of value to a function of rent. In equilibrium, the rent R_0 equals the cost of capital multiplied by the value V_0. Figure 13.3 illustrates equilibrium in terms of both the rental price and the value price.

The market equilibrium illustrated in Figure 13.3 was derived assuming a given cost of capital η. Suppose the cost of capital decreases, for example, as a result of a decrease in mortgage interest rates. What is the effect on equilibrium? Looking first at the market in terms of the rental price, we see that there is no effect on demand. Demand is a function of the rental price, regardless of the cost of capital. Supply, though,

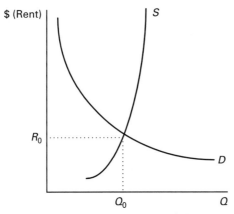
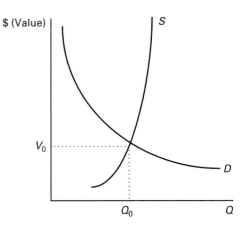

FIGURE 13.3 Housing Market Equilibrium

shifts, because a change in the cost of capital implies that a given rental price is now associated with a different value. If the cost of capital decreases, then a given rent is associated with a higher value, so the supply curve as a function of rent shifts out. This is graphed in Figure 13.4. The shift in supply implies an increase in the equilibrium quantity to Q_1 and a decrease in the equilibrium rent to R_1.

The effect on the equilibrium value of housing can be similarly calculated. The supply curve remains constant, while demand shifts out because any given value is associated with a lower rent. Thus, the equilibrium quantity increases to Q_1, and the equilibrium value increases to V_1, as shown in Figure 13.4.

Return to the numerical example of η that we used earlier. Recall that the cost of capital for owner-occupiers was calculated to equal 0.052 (5.2%) for the parameters that we used. If V_0 equals $120,000 (for example), then R_0 must equal $6,240. Now suppose that mortgage interest rates fall by 1 percentage point, so that i_O in our earlier example goes from 0.05 to 0.04. The cost of capital also falls, by 0.72 percentage points, from 0.052 to 0.0448. The rental price for a house with a market value of $120,000 is now $5,376, lower than it was earlier. This means that demand for houses

FIGURE 13.4 Decrease in the Cost of Capital

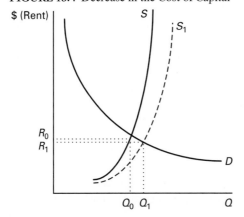
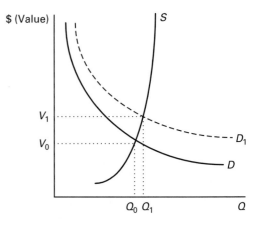

with a market value of \$120,000 will increase. The market value for a house with a rental price of \$6,240 is now \$139,286, so that supply of houses with a rental price of \$6,240 will increase. In equilibrium, we expect that the new rental price will be less than or equal to R_0 and the new market value will be greater than or equal to V_0.

REAL ESTATE AGENTS

One of the interesting features of the housing market is the large role played by intermediaries known as real estate agents. Housing is not the only commodity where intermediaries play a large role; other examples include insurance markets and executive labor markets. The relationships among the intermediary, the buyer, and the seller can be expected to play an important role in determining the outcome of the market.

Why are real estate agents needed? There are two answers. The first reason is that they provide information. An agent is someone who specializes in real estate. We have already seen how difficult it is to judge housing without going into voluminous detail. Most people do not have the time or desire to learn as much about the market as their real estate agent does, so that you are hiring knowledge and expertise when you hire an agent. The agent also has access to a wide range of buyers (if you are a seller) or sellers (if you are a buyer); therefore, hiring an agent to identify a set of houses for you to consider is less costly than undertaking the search on your own. The second reason is that an agent will assist in completing the many legal documents that are part of the transaction.

Traditionally, real estate agents have legally been agents of the seller. As such, they are legally required to represent the best interests of the seller, even if it is the buyer who approaches the agent. More recently, there has been a proliferation of buyers' agency agreements. Buyers' agents represent the interests of the buyer, and they claim to be able to identify and negotiate better prices. For example, buyers' agents are legally able to keep confidential any information the buyer gives them, which sellers' agents are not legally able to do. When negotiating, the more information you have about the other side, the better you will be able to set your terms. The change in information represented by a shift to buyers' agents can make it tougher for sellers to call the bluff of buyers, which can help buyers get a lower price. Curran and Schrag (1996) find that buyers' agents in Georgia have led to a reduction in house prices of usually about 5 percent, with an extreme estimate in one county of 15 percent. Their findings are consistent with the advertising claims of buyers' agents, who claim to be able to reduce the price by 4 to 7 percent.

In order for buyers' agents to operate, state legislatures must pass a law making it legal to do so. One would expect that sellers' agents would prefer a system under which buyers' agents do not exist and in which their responsibilities are poorly understood by buyers. After all, the higher the sales price, the higher the commission the agent earns (a typical commission is 7 percent of the sales price). In Georgia, though, the sellers' agents actually lobbied for the law legalizing buyers' agents. Why? They feared large lawsuits by homebuyers who believed that their interests had not been well served or who had been misled about the role of agents. This fear was grounded in fact, since one case involving a Minnesota firm had led the National Association of

Realtors to ask (in 1993) for every state legislature to clarify the responsibilities of agents. In effect, sellers' agents buy insurance for themselves when they lobby for the creation of buyers' agents. The premium for the insurance is the lower commission that they receive; the payoff is the freedom from the possibility of a catastrophic loss from a lawsuit.

FILTERING

Because housing is durable, a single housing unit will probably be occupied by several different households during its lifetime. A general framework for analyzing this process is known as the *filtering model* of housing. As the name suggests, the filtering model is one in which housing is constructed for high-income households and over its lifetime is passed on to ever-lower-income households. Table 13.7 illustrates this idea by comparing the median sales price for existing single-family houses with that for newly constructed single-family houses.

If incomes are increasing over time, then the existing stock of housing will not exactly meet the demand of the existing homeowners. There will be a shortage of housing for high-income households, in particular. The highest value opportunity for home builders is likely to be in new construction for high-income households. Because new construction is such a small fraction of the housing supply, this implies that the average new house will not be constructed for the average homeowner. Rather, the new houses will be constructed for higher-income households, who in turn will sell their homes to middle-income households, who in turn sell to low-income households.

The filtering model has some important public policy implications. First, it illustrates why constructing new housing for poor people can be inefficient. To be affordable, the new housing can't cost so much that poor people can't buy it. There is again the question, Why restrict assistance to housing rather than simply increase the ability of poor people to purchase housing *and* all other goods by increasing their income? Further, the characteristics of housing that are demanded can vary systematically by income. Finally, if costs are reduced by reducing the durability of housing, then society loses because the resources devoted to constructing this housing are wasted relative to their use to construct more durable housing. To whom will new construction for low-income households filter?

TABLE 13.7 Sales Prices for Existing Houses and for Newly Constructed Houses

Year	Median Sales Price, Existing Homes	Median Sales Price, New Construction	Difference
1973	$28,900	$32,500	12.5%
1978	$48,700	$55,700	14.4%
1983	$70,300	$75,300	7.1%
1988	$93,100	$112,500	20.8%
1993	$106,800	$126,500	18.4%

Source: Statistical Abstract of the United States, 1994, Tables 1206 and 1208, p. 732.

Second, the model can be used to argue that subsidies to new construction of housing for "rich" people can benefit many others. (This is "trickle-down economics" with a vengeance!) There are three important caveats to this argument, though. First, there are transaction costs in converting housing from one market to another, not to mention externalities as neighborhoods change their composition over time. Second, the benefits to lower-income households depend on a fairly rapid turnover of housing; if the filtering process operates only with a substantial lag, then current low-income households may not receive much benefit from current subsidies to housing construction. Third, the existing housing for, say, middle-income people may be poorly located from the perspective of the lower-income people to whom it is supposed to be filtering.

The negative side of filtering, in that some neighborhoods slip in status, is illustrated by the fictional piece at the end of chapter 9. However, the process does not have to be only one of decline. If the neighborhood has some advantages, at some point it may be economically worthwhile for a developer to take it over and renovate it. Jackson (1985, p. 286) argues that neighborhoods have life cycles just as people do, with the exception that neighborhoods can be reborn. He illustrates this idea with examples from the United States and England in the nineteenth and twentieth centuries. The popular idea of *gentrification* is an illustration of the potential for renaissance in deteriorated areas that have locational advantages. The typical gentrified area is one close to the CBD, implying a short commute for workers who live in that area. This convenience makes the area desirable for young professionals, such as lawyers, who work in the CBD. The postponement of marriage and childbearing also makes gentrification more likely, since people are able to make their housing decision without regard for the necessity to be in a particular school district or near play areas for children. Looking briefly at the suburban future, the prospects of gentrification for the future slums of edge city seem bleaker than they do for the central city. Prefabricated construction techniques imply that the new housing being built is less durable than tenements of brick and plaster. Today's beautiful new townhouses are likely to be the urban blight of fifty years from now, without much prospect for renovation short of demolition and reconstruction.

CHAPTER SUMMARY

- Housing is a unique commodity. It provides both public and private good consumption as well as being an investment. Housing is heterogeneous, durable, immobile, and expensive, requiring large adjustment costs to alter its consumption.

- Determining the quantity of housing consumption is difficult because housing is heterogeneous. Hedonic price analysis is a way of comparing houses with different characteristics. Hedonic price analysis involves placing a price on each characteristic and adding up the various prices. The housing market is composed of a variety of submarkets, each linked by the cost of converting a housing unit from one submarket to another.

- People choose to own or rent based on their individual characteristics. A person who owns a house can be thought of as someone that is both landlord and renter. A renter tends to have a lower income, be less inclined to perform home maintenance, and be more mobile than a homeowner.

- The demand for housing depends on the rental price of housing, that is, the price for housing during a given time period. The supply of housing depends on the market value of housing, that is, the discounted present value of the net benefits provided by a housing unit over its entire life. The market value and the rental price are linked by the cost of capital, which includes not only the mortgage interest rate but also the future tax consequences and the other costs and benefits of owning a housing unit.

- Because housing is heterogeneous, people must search for the unit that best suits them. Real estate agents can help in this process by matching buyers with sellers. Recent years have seen an increase in the use of agents who represent the buyer's interest rather than only the seller's.

- Most new housing construction is for higher-income individuals. Because housing is durable, when these people move into their new homes they must sell their existing homes to others. This leads to the filtering of housing from high- to low-income households. The filtering process implies that the typical new house is not built for the typical homeowner.

EXCERPT: *THE SOCIAL CONTRACT* (ROBERT ARDREY)

Although economists recognize the importance of neighborhood in determining people's housing decisions, they perhaps underestimate the strain placed on human interactions as a result of that *recent* invention, the city. Recall that cities have existed only as long as agriculture—a long time by historical standards, but a very short time ecologically. In the following excerpt from *The Social Contract*, Robert Ardrey (1970, pp. 227–228, 236–238, 245–246) explores the idea of neighborhood from an anthropological standpoint.

Any consideration of the problems of human space must begin and end nowhere if we deny the territorial propensities of man. If man is infinitely malleable, then urban concentration should offer no dismay. We can adapt to anything, even to the crawling masses of insect life. It is a proposition that few would accept. The territorial principle has been evolution's most effective implement in the distribution of animal space. And if man is a being biologically equipped with territorial patterns, then at least we have a premise to work from. Urbanization is deterritorialization in the classic sense of denial of land. But perhaps there may be conceptual substitutes or symbolic channels that will preserve our biological sanity. We may be sure, however, that we must somehow preserve NO TRESPASSING signs.

Xenophobia has been little written about. What we consider here is the proposition that xenophobia keeps socially integrated groups separated. Whether that separation is accomplished through active territorial defense, through sophisticated acceptance of territorial rights, through active group antagonisms wherever space may lie, or as in a herd through indifference, group identity is effected and social space affirmed. It is an animal rule, and it has reasons. We may find it a human rule as well.

One would think that with all the studies that have been made of densely packed slums, little could be left for discovery. Yet Edward Hall of Northwestern University's anthropology department has in the past few years found and traced invisible territorial boundaries. What in Chicago would seem to any eye the endless, amorphous, indivisible geometry of the South and West sides becomes through close inspection a mosaic of territories. And they contribute to social order.

Hall's most recent field of study has been the black neighborhoods. Since he is white and our times are incendiary, most direct observation has been done by his Negro graduate students at Northwestern. And what they found were territories each normally including two adjacent blocks. Boundaries fell at the middle of the surrounding streets. You might have a friend around the corner in your territory, but not across the street. Fellow inhabitants knew each other, whether personally or through gossip. Any nearest adult had the right to punish a misbehaving child, whatever family he might come from. Anyone regarded as undesirable attempting to move into the territory was subtly discouraged; if he succeeded, then perhaps with less subtlety he would be convinced that he should leave. A definite although unofficial structure of authority invested the group. One or several individuals respected by all mediated quarrels, made final decisions regarding social attitudes. The rotting, packed Negro ghetto was in truth a series of independent villages.

It was a time when the city of Chicago, with belated conscience and all civic urgency, was replacing the infested slums with hygienic, high-rise apartments. And Hall's group found that the apartments, destroying the old territorial social structure, were in truth factories of disorder. No longer could adults on their broken stoops bring neighbors' children to heel. Now the young vanished downstairs into space to form their gangs beyond parental reach. The perceptions, the quick communication of gossiping neighbors, the reaches of unofficial authority were lost in the mathematical anonymity and isolation of tall concrete honeycombs.

As gradually deterritorialized man loses the exclusive space that once protected him, so gradually he proceeds through continuum's tunnel into the urban battlefield. We lose space as an ally. We enter the arena where man faces man and alliances are temporal.

Few strains on the social contract can today compare with the urban challenge. Space has been devoured and can be recaptured only with the romanticism which regards the summer cottage, occupied four weeks a year, as territorial reincarnation. The urban environment demands that we compose our bodies, our movements, our fecal matter, our gaseous extrusions, our aggressions, our drunken excursions, our noisy adventures, our quarrels man and wife, parents and children, our sexual dalliances, our ambitions, our frustrations, our personal loves, our personal hatreds, our political affinities or political aversions into an urban whole which approximates social order. If I am correct in describing the biological social contract as a balance between necessary order and necessary disorder, then the urban challenge must be described, with most delicate understatement, as a large order.

Source: The Social Contract by Robert Ardrey. Copyright © 1970 by Robert Ardrey. Reprinted by permission of Daniel Ardrey.

Questions for Review and Discussion

1. Ardrey argues in the excerpt at the end of this chapter that people naturally align themselves into territories. Can you identify the neighborhood that you live in? Do most of your friends live there? Are you nervous about venturing out of it?

2. What characteristics of a house are most important to you? If your tastes differ from the general population, how is that likely to affect how happy you are with your house?

3. "The filtering model of housing suggests that the poor benefit from construction of housing for the rich. Therefore, we should subsidize the construction of housing for the rich." Do you agree or disagree? Explain.

4. "Because only a small part of the housing stock is built each year, new construction is unimportant in the housing market." Do you agree or disagree? Explain.

5. Use advertised prices and characteristics of housing from the real estate pages of your local newspaper to construct a hedonic price index for a neighborhood or suburb.

6. Does your landlord do a good job maintaining your building? Why or why not? Can you think of ways to encourage your landlord to do a better job? (Recall that if you own your own house, then you are your own landlord.)

7. "High local tax rates encourage abandonment of housing, but they are not an important determinant of location decisions by manufacturing firms." Do you agree or disagree? Explain.

CHAPTER

Housing Problems and Policies

14

Housing markets are important and complicated, as we saw in the previous chapter. Their importance has led to government intervention in several areas, two of which were discussed in earlier chapters—local zoning in chapter 10 and the problem of homelessness in chapter 12. In this chapter, I consider three additional areas of the housing market in which both governments and nonprofit organizations have intervened. I begin by describing the intervention of the federal government in the housing market, including activities that affect demand, supply, and financing of houses. Next is a look at rent control, a local government intervention that has until recently been almost universally condemned by economists but has now become the subject of some revisionist thinking. The chapter concludes with an extended look at the problems of racial prejudice, discrimination, and segregation.

FEDERAL HOUSING POLICY

The government of the United States has intervened both directly and indirectly in housing markets for many years. In 1992, $20.5 billion was spent on direct payments to individuals with limited income to assist them in renting or buying housing. This figure was dwarfed, though, by the implicit subsidy given to owners of housing (including both owner-occupiers and landlords) via special tax treatment. In 1993, the tax deductibility of mortgage interest decreased revenue to the Federal government by an estimated $48.7 billion; property tax deductibility decreased revenue to the federal government by another $13.1 billion; and accelerated depreciation of rental housing cost $1.2 billion in foregone revenue. In other words, over three times as much money is devoted by the federal government to tax relief for owners of homes than to direct subsidization of housing for low-income households.

Federal housing policy has had two broad goals over the past 60 years: to encourage home ownership and to upgrade the quality of housing for poor people. The first goal has been largely achieved, with home ownership rates in the United States increasing to 64.2 percent in 1991 from a level of 47.8 percent in 1930. Table 14.1

TABLE 14.1   United States Homeownership Rates over Time

Year	All Races	White	Black and Other
1920	45.6%	48.2%	23.9%
1930	47.8%	50.2%	25.2%
1940	43.6%	45.7%	23.6%
1950	55.0%	57.0%	34.9%
1960	61.9%	64.4%	38.4%
1970	62.9%	65.4%	42.1%
1980	64.4%	67.8%	44.2%
1991	64.2%	67.9%	43.2%

Source: Statistical Abstract of the United States, 1994, Table 1215, p. 735.

shows home ownership in the United States for the period 1920 to 1991 and also reports the figures for whites and other races separately. The percentage of the population who are homeowners increased rapidly between 1940 and 1960 but has remained just over 60 percent since 1960. You can see clear divergence between the tenure status of white households and that of all other households. Despite increases over time, the home-ownership rate for nonwhite households in 1991 (43.2%) is less than the home-ownership rate for whites in 1920 (48.2%).

The second goal has been achieved in some ways, has fallen short in some ways, and is impossible to achieve in some ways. The quality of housing overall has increased in the sense that the physical characteristics of low-income housing today are better than they were in previous years. For example, 55 percent of the housing stock lacked complete plumbing in 1940, while only 1.1 percent of the housing stock lacked complete plumbing in 1990. However, the quality of housing for poor people relative to that for wealthy people has not improved so dramatically. (A good survey of federal government housing policy that focuses on the political reasons for the adoption of various policies is Hays 1995).

Home Ownership and the Mortgage Market

The federal government has been indirectly involved in housing markets since 1913, when the income tax was first imposed. Property tax payments and mortgage interest have been exempt from the income tax from the start, reducing the carrying costs of housing relative to other assets. However, the first large-scale direct intervention by the federal government did not take place until the 1930s.

In 1933, with the banking system in turmoil in part because of massive defaults by homeowners, the Home Owners Loan Corporation (HOLC) was created to provide emergency loans to homeowners facing foreclosure. This agency was designed to assist not only home buyers but also the people employed in the banking industry and construction trades who were negatively affected by the high rates of eviction and foreclosure during the Depression. In 1934, the HOLC was superseded by the Federal Housing Administration (FHA), created by the National Housing Act of 1934. The FHA introduced a system of mortgage regulation and insurance that continues to operate to the present time.

The main innovation provided by the FHA was the long-term, self-amortizing, level-payment, low down-payment mortgage. It is by now commonplace that loans for the purchase of homes are for terms of 15, 20, or, most often, 30 years. Further, it is generally understood that the mortgage will be repaid with constant monthly payments that include both interest and principal repayment. Most mortgages require a low down payment; 20 percent of the purchase price is the standard, but it is not infrequent to see houses purchased with as little as 3 or 5 percent of the purchase price up front. Prior to 1934, though, the standard loan contract for purchasing a home was a short-term (less than 10 years) mortgage with a high down payment (typically 50 percent) and a balloon payment of the balance of the price due at the end of the loan. In other words, during the term of the loan only interest was paid, and the entire principal was due at the end of the loan. These conditions clearly made it much more difficult for people to be able to afford houses, since they had to save longer to accumulate the down payment and to ensure that they could meet the balloon payment in just a few years.

The FHA also provided mortgage insurance for banks and other lending institutions. This not only helped prevent a chain reaction of financial problems but also made mortgages less risky, so that banks could charge a lower interest rate. Of course, this made home ownership that much more attainable for a broad spectrum of people.

Another New Deal innovation was the creation of a secondary market for mortgages through the institution of the Federal National Mortgage Association ("Fannie Mae"). The FNMA helped financial institutions by letting them diversify their portfolio of holdings. A mortgage has a particular set of risk characteristics: for example, the probability of default by the home buyer and the chance that the home buyer might pay off the mortgage early and deprive the bank of some interest. In the absence of a market where a bank can sell mortgages and buy other securities, a bank is forced either to take on more mortgage-type risk than it prefers or to restrict the amount of mortgage lending it does. The existence of a secondary market means that the bank originating the mortgage can exchange the risk with some other institution that doesn't have as much mortgage-type risk as it is able to assume. This helps home buyers in two ways. First, their local bank—which has the best information on the local market and is thus most likely to make loans—is not restricted by risk considerations in underwriting home ownership. Second, the ability to diversify the risk makes it possible for banks to charge lower interest rates than they could in the absence of a secondary market.

Supply-Side Housing Policy: Public Housing

In addition to intervention in financial markets, the federal government has also been in the business of building and renting housing to people. One justification for this policy is that even the innovations in home mortgages do not make private home ownership affordable to poor people. The first public housing was funded in 1937, although for political reasons (opposition in Congress followed by World War II) large-scale construction did not begin until the late 1940s. By 1970, there were 1,155,000 low-income public housing units available and another 126,800 under construction. This figure, although impressive, implied that public housing was about 2 percent of the total housing stock of about 63 million units in 1970. The total number of public housing units in 1992 was about 1.3 million, about the same as in 1980. Because the total housing stock continued to grow (to 80 million in 1980 and 93 million in 1991), the fraction of the housing stock provided by public housing shrank during this time. The demolition in 1972 of the Pruitt-Igoe project in St. Louis, only 15 years after its construction, has been taken as symbolic of the failure of government-supplied housing. As the figures above indicate, new construction of public housing essentially ceased after the 1970s. Public housing has not received much favorable review during the past decades, but that does not mean the approach could not be successful. Let us consider the problems that have arisen in designing and operating public housing.

The first question when planning to build a housing project is where to place it. Recall the filtering model of the housing market described in chapter 13. This model suggests that plenty of housing is available for lower-income households as higher-income households move to newly constructed dwellings. However, these houses might not be in the "right" location. For example, they may lack access to public transportation, a serious problem for low-income people who do not own cars. This seems to dictate that public housing should be built in areas where poor people live. However, this approach has its own drawbacks. The first problem is the disruption caused by demolition and construction. The second, and perhaps more important problem, is the social stigma that can be attached to living in a "slum," "ghetto," or other pejoratively termed low-income neighborhood. This stigma might prevent people who could use the benefit from taking advantage of it. Since the people who would want to avoid the stigma of living in a low-income neighborhood (and can afford to stay out) are likely to be upwardly mobile relative to other poor people, the housing project becomes a home for only the people with no place else to go.

When public housing projects became completely filled with people who had no other option and no promising future, the problem was exacerbated by the income limitations that were placed on the residents. The rent charged in public housing is typically a fraction (say 20 percent) of the renter's income, up to a certain maximum rent (that is, the maximum income was five times the maximum rent, if the fraction for rent was 20 percent). Before 1959, the maximum rent was set so low that the housing was available only to the very poor. Even after 1959, when the regulations were altered, the fact that the housing projects had a high proportion of very poor made them less attractive to other poor (but not quite as poor) people.

Another problem with public housing as administered was that only the construction costs were funded by the federal government; operating costs and maintenance were expected to come from local residents and rents. When the housing was first built, maintenance costs were low. However, as the housing aged, maintenance costs increased without, however, a commensurate increase in the ability of the residents to finance repairs or perform repairs themselves.

Arguably, the real problem with public housing is that it does not address the true problem facing poor people living in substandard housing. The true problem is that they can't afford better housing, so that the best policy is one that addresses incomes rather than only housing. When we turn to demand-side policies, the same issue arises, as most of the programs require any income supplement to be spent on housing rather than leaving the decision to the household. Why, then, do people advocate policies that focus on housing rather than increasing incomes? There are several answers. First, positive externalities may result from consuming better housing. Second, the construction industry may lobby for building that benefits its members, using the assistance of poor people as its argument but not really its goal. (A similar statement can be made about farmers who lobby for food stamps.) Third, there may be paternalism on the part of the government and the public—"if they're poor, then they'll just squander money"—that leads to severe restrictions on what people are allowed to do with public subsidies.

Demand-Side Housing Policies: Subsidies and Housing Allowances

The year 1974 marks a dividing line in the approach taken by the federal government to housing assistance for low-income people. Before that year, the programs were designed to benefit the poor indirectly, usually by making it less expensive for developers to construct and rent housing to poor households. Since that year, the focus has been on making direct payments to supplement the rent paid by poor households.

An early demand-side policy was the Section 221(d)(3) program, introduced in 1961. This program subsidized mortgages taken out by low-income homebuyers. A related program, Section 235, was introduced in 1965 to supplement rents paid by low-income renters. The major criticism, as you might expect, was that the beneficiaries were not particularly poor. Although the participants in this program had incomes that were low relative to most home buyers, the fact that they could afford to buy a house rather than rent one implied that they were not without financial resources. Another objection to subsidizing low-income housing for people who were not destitute was the stigma attached to public housing that now transferred to *any* government program. Moderate-income neighborhoods were concerned that recipients of government aid would move in, and they lobbied to restrict the extent of the policy. In practice, the rent supplements were paid only to those who qualified for public housing (that is to say, households with quite low incomes).

The reason that these programs are all named "Section xxx" is that each program is authorized by an act of Congress, and the part of the act that contains the particular program is used to identify the program. It might be less confusing to call them by some other name, but I prefer to follow the standard convention. Now, when you read the newspaper, you'll know what is meant when Congress debates increasing Section 8 authorization.

Section 236 was created in 1968. This program was designed to benefit low-income renters. It operated by reducing the interest rate paid by developers who constructed or renovated housing for low-income renters. Note that it required the assumption of a fairly competitive rental market, since developers were expected to pass the interest rate subsidy through to renters. A number of problems with Section 236 were identified. The first problem was site selection; the housing tended to be concentrated in already poor areas, as was public housing. The second problem was its method of motivating investors. Most of the returns to investing in Section 236 housing were in the form of tax reductions rather than in rental income. This gave little incentive for investors to provide a competitive product—in fact, the more money they lost, the greater the tax benefit, in some cases. These considerations also led to overbuilding. Finally, some developers artificially inflated costs or rents. Section 236 also raised the same general question that had been asked about public housing: Why subsidize new construction for low-income people when most new construction is for high-income people?

Before moving to the post-1974 era of direct subsidies to renters, consider the following postscript to the story of Section 221(d)(3) and 236. In the 1980s, developers began to pay off their obligations to the government in order to convert the housing built in the 1960s and 1970s to condominiums or market-rate (unsubsidized) apartments. Congress passed legislation in 1987 to restrict this activity, but it illustrates the fundamental difficulty with these indirect approaches. If the housing is good enough to be a viable business at market rates, developers have an incentive to use it in that manner, which does not help poor people. However, if the housing is not good enough to be viable, then it is not likely to be attractive to poor people either.

The problems with the indirect approaches led to the Housing Act of 1974, which created the Section 8 program of housing allowances. A *housing allowance* is, in its pure form, a cash grant to a household to use for any type of housing and not any other purpose. In practice, there are restrictions on how housing allowances can be used. They include not only a requirement that the money be spent on housing but also restrictions on the type of housing, such as a requirement that it meet certain safety standards.

The Section 8 program consisted of four related parts: subsidies for renting in newly constructed housing, substantially rehabilitated housing, moderately rehabilitated housing (added in 1978), and existing housing. The program is very close to a pure housing voucher. The grant is calculated as the difference between the "fair market rent" for a unit—determined by using what amounts to hedonic price analysis—and a household contribution of 25 percent of the household's income. For example, if you rent an apartment with a fair market rent of $400 per month, and your income is $750 per month, then your contribution is $187.50. The Section 8 grant will then amount to $212.50 ($400 – $187.50).

Unlike other federal government programs, such as Medicaid, Section 8 is not an entitlement. (The welfare reform proposals being considered as of this writing in 1996 could remove some of the current entitlements.) In other words, there is no requirement that everyone who qualifies for it receives payment. The basic qualification is an income less than 80 percent of the median income in the region. In practice, most of the housing assistance under this program goes to people with incomes of less than 50 percent of the median income. Allocating Section 8 allowances is thus a classic economic question: how to distribute a scarce resource among competing uses. Khaddurri and Nelson (1992) describe the targeting system that, although legislated by Congress in 1979 and 1983, did not take effect until 1988. This system targets families that are paying over 50 percent of their income in rent, are living in substandard housing, or have been involuntarily displaced, putting those families at the top of the waiting list for Section 8 allowances. They find it to be quite effective at focusing the resources on the most critical cases, although more recent legislation would reduce targeting.

The Department of Housing and Urban Development (HUD) administers Section 8. In the 1980s, senior HUD officials from the Reagan administration were involved in a major scandal. The scandal involved the moderate rehabilitation part of the Section 8 program. The funds for this part of the program were relatively small and so were not allocated by formula but rather at the discretion of HUD. Developers would pay large "consulting fees" to influential people in order to get their projects funded. A number of officials were convicted of influence peddling in these cases. This example again illustrates how difficult it is to administer a program properly even if it is well-intentioned.

The most recent legislation regarding housing is the Cranston-Gonzalez National Affordable Housing Act of 1990. This legislation continues the housing allowance focus of the Housing Act of 1974 but includes a few modifications. The first, arising at least in part from the 1980s HUD scandal, is an emphasis on local control of housing production. The second is a renewed emphasis on home ownership for households regardless of their income level. The third, and potentially the most important, is an attempt to integrate the delivery of other social services with housing. If people are in substandard housing because they do not have the skills required to get better-paying jobs or because they lack day care for their children, then improving the housing alone will not solve the true problems. The new legislation attempts to bring together all of the various government programs that attempt to improve the well-being of low-income people.

RENT CONTROL

One local government intervention in housing markets that has received persistent attention from economists is the practice of imposing a price ceiling on the rental price of housing. The attention from economists has primarily been negative, in that the objectives typically sought by rent control—income redistribution and a sufficient supply of "affordable" housing—are only poorly served by it. If rent control is to have any effect, the price ceiling imposed must be less than the equilibrium price of housing. This is illustrated in Figure 14.1, which shows the demand and supply for rental housing in a suburb. The equilibrium price is p_e, while the price ceiling is p_c. If the price is prevented from increasing to clear the market, there is an excess demand for housing, by definition. In Figure 14.1, this is illustrated by the fact that the quantity supplied at a price of p_c, denoted as q_S, is less than the quantity demanded (q_D) at that price. Of course, people must find some way to allocate a scarce product if the price is not allowed to adjust. This can involve a black market, queuing, or moving to consume a substitute that does not have the same restriction. People who are already renters when rent control is introduced may gain from it, since they are already in a housing unit that they now pay less for. However, they may also face increased costs if landlords reduce maintenance to make up for their inability to charge market rents. Landlords may also attempt to convert housing from the price-controlled sector to an uncontrolled sector. One way of doing this is by changing the building to

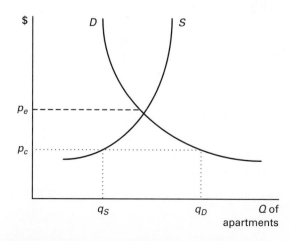

FIGURE 14.1 The Effects of Rent Control: Competitive Market for Rental Housing

owner-occupied housing ("going condo"). Another way is by converting it to commercial use or abandoning it altogether. None of these actions particularly benefits low-income tenants. Moreover, the longer wait for apartments implied by the excess demand resulting from the price ceiling can also be bad for tenants.

A recent article by Richard Arnott (1995) presents a revisionist view of rent control. The analysis hinges on the question of the market structure of the rental housing market, which we earlier saw to be an important issue. Arnott argues that housing is heterogeneous, so that monopolistic competition is the appropriate analytical construct. In monopolistic competition, profit-maximizing landlords charge a price such that marginal revenue equals marginal cost. Because marginal revenue is less than price, this implies an equilibrium price greater than marginal cost, which is inefficient in a Pareto sense. Rent control can be imposed so that price is equal to marginal cost, improving efficiency, and also so that price is equal to average cost, in which case landlords earn normal profits but no economic profits. Arnott presents some evidence that rent controls set in this fashion do not harm efficiency, but there is no evidence that the outcome under rent controls is a Pareto improvement over the market outcome. And the question remains: If the concern is for increasing the income of poor people, why not do so directly with an income transfer program instead of indirectly through rent controls? (*The Economist*, 8 April 1995)

Hubert (1993) studies the substitution of housing not covered by rent control for rent-controlled housing. It would seem that rent control would lead to an increase in the price of housing in the "uncontrolled" sector, as the demand shifted out. However, it may be the case that some "high demanders" are consuming rent-controlled housing, so that the demand curve for uncontrolled housing may be lower than it would be in the absence of rent control. Hubert shows that the effect of rent control on prices in the uncontrolled sector depends on the rationing mechanism in the rent-controlled sector and also on whether the people in rent-controlled housing are consuming more or less housing than they would in the absence of the price controls. The key issue is that there is an indivisibility—people live only in one place—that makes the analysis difficult, because people consuming rent-controlled housing are "irrelevant" to the market for uncontrolled housing.

RACE AND HOUSING MARKETS

Driving down the concrete artery,
Away from the smoky heart,
Through the darkening, blighted body,
Pausing at varicose veins,
The white man pressed the locks
*   on all the sedan's doors,*
Sped toward the white corpuscles
*   in the white arms*
*   hugging the black city.**
                                    —JAMES KILGORE

*Source: "The White Man Pressed the Locks" by James Kilgore. Copyright © 1970 by James Kilgore. Reprinted by permission of Ashland Poetry Press.

The United States is not a homogeneous society. It comprises many ethnic and racial groups. A long-lasting tension has been that between racial groups, although there have also been difficulties among ethnic groups (the Irish immigrants and earlier arrivals in Boston, for example). In this section we will introduce the economic analysis of race in housing markets and apply the analysis to the case of segregation and integration in Cleveland neighborhoods.

Prejudice, Discrimination, and Segregation

Economists are precise about the meanings of the three words that head this section. Prejudice is defined to be an *attitude* held about members of an identifiable group solely on the basis of their belonging to that group. For example, I am prejudiced in favor of otherwise indistinguishable individuals wearing the uniform of the Dallas Cowboys, and I am prejudiced against people wearing the uniform of the Washington Redskins. Discrimination is defined to be differential *behavior* toward members of an identifiable group. Continuing with my football example, I might ask a Dallas Cowboy player for an autograph but not a Washington Redskin player. Segregation is defined to be an *outcome* in which members of identifiable groups are separated. On the football field, we see the Cowboys and Redskins occupying benches on opposite sides of the field. (These definitions and much of the following general discussion are based on Yinger 1979.)

All the discussion above is predicated on the idea that we can separate people into groups on the basis of some observable characteristic. What is the appropriate characteristic to analyze in the case of housing markets? A number of candidates are immediately apparent, including race, socioeconomic status, age, and religion. While all of these are legitimate areas for analysis, none has stirred more controversy than prejudice, discrimination, and segregation on the basis of race.

Racial Segregation in Housing Markets

Cities in the United States are highly segregated by race. This statement probably doesn't surprise you, but underlying it are two important theoretical questions. First, how do we measure the extent to which a city's population is racially integrated? For example, should we consider the city as a whole? census tracts within the city? neighborhood blocks? or some other geographical area? Further, which races should be distinguished when measuring the extent of segregation? Most studies of U.S. cities distinguish "white" and "black," but in some cities "Latino" and "Asian" people represent significant population groups. Second, how integrated does an area have to be? If integration represents a 50-percent share for both groups, then vanishingly few places will be integrated. If integration represents anything other than 100 percent for one group and 0 percent for the other group, almost every place is integrated.

The usual measure of the extent of racial segregation is the so-called dissimilarity index, which we will denote as D. The index, which takes on values from 0 to 100, measures the extent to which the racial composition of each neighborhood reflects the aggregate racial composition of a city, county, or metropolitan area. If we let B_i and W_i represent the black and white populations respectively in a neighborhood and let B and W represents the black and white population in the entire city, then the formula for the index is

$$D = 100 \ (1/2) \ \Sigma_i \ | \ (B_i / B) - (W_i / W) \ | \tag{1}$$

The dissimilarity index for the city of Cleveland and several of its suburbs is presented in Table 14.2. The dissimilarity index can be interpreted as the percentage of the black population that would have to be moved in order for each neighborhood to reflect the racial composition of the city (or county). Cleveland is known as an extremely segregated city, and this is backed up by its index of 87, second only to that of Garfield Heights. Garfield Heights is almost perfectly polarized racially, with one part of the city almost entirely white and the other entirely black. While its index of 92 is high, this actually reflects a decrease from the level in 1980, when it was 96. The change was caused by an increase in the percentage of blacks in the city from about 5 percent to about 15 percent.

The dissimilarity index is straightforward to calculate, but it suffers from the drawback that it cannot distinguish between a pattern of integration and a pattern of segregation where there is an equal amount of above-average integration and below-average integration. An alternative measure of segregation that does not suffer from this drawback is the "exposure index," which calculates the average proportion of the other group in each subarea. This index must be calculated separately for each racial group, because it is nonlinear in the racial composition of each neighborhood. To calculate it, we need one more bit of notation. Let b_i represent the fraction of the population in neighborhood i that is black. Then the exposure index for E is

$$E = 100 \ \{1 - \Sigma_i \ B_i \ (1 - b_i) \ / \ [B \ (1 - b)]\} \tag{2}$$

The exposure index for the city of Cleveland and suburbs is also shown in Table 14.2.

In addition to the other conceptual difficulties in measuring the extent of segregation, there is the problem that the measures vary depending on how *neighborhood* is defined. For example, the data in Table 14.2 focused on the census tract as the definition of a neighborhood. An alternative definition would be the census block. The census block is smaller than the census tract, so that segregation measured using the census block would be higher. For example, the dissimilarity index for Shaker Heights

TABLE 14.2   Segregation Indices for Cleveland and Suburbs, 1990

City	Population	Percent Black	Dissimilarity Index	Exposure Index
Cleveland	505,616	46.5	87.0	80.2
Cleveland Heights	54,052	37.3	45.7	25.1
East Cleveland	33,096	94.0	49.1	9.7
Euclid	54,875	16.2	60.2	38.1
Garfield Heights	31,739	14.6	91.9	82.5
Shaker Heights	30,831	38.8	55.3	43.2
South Euclid	23,866	8.8	45.3	10.6
University Heights	14,790	16.0	47.8	17.7
Cuyahoga County	1,412,140	24.8	77.8	77.2

Source: Author's calculations based on data from the U.S. Bureau of the Census.

using census blocks to define neighborhoods is 57.9, which is 25 percent higher than it was using census tracts. This disparity implies that these measures are subject to manipulation: If you want the data to make the neighborhood look segregated, make the neighborhood as small as possible, and vice versa. This example illustrates the difficulty in making definitive statements about the degree of racial segregation.

Why does segregation matter? One reason is that segregated housing may reduce the access of blacks to jobs (according to the "spatial mismatch hypothesis" discussed in chapter 12), although there is some evidence that the place of residence does not affect earnings once other characteristics of an individual—such as education—are taken into account (Price and Mills 1985). Another is that segregation may perpetuate ignorance and fear among racial groups, thus weakening the cohesion of American society. A final reason is that the segregation may be the result of illegal activities (such as discrimination) prohibited by the Constitution and by law.

An important question for public policy is whether the segregation that occurs is the result of prejudice or of discrimination. If it is discrimination, there is a clear case for government intervention. If the outcome reflects prejudice, though, government intervention might not be warranted. A 1992 decision by the United States Supreme Court (quoted in Keating 1994, p. 11) made this point explicit: "Where resegregation is a product not of state action but of private choices, it does not have constitutional implications. It is beyond the authority and beyond the practical ability of the federal courts to try to counteract these kinds of continuous and massive demographic shifts."

Racial Discrimination in Housing Markets: "Redlining"

Race and ethnicity have long been factors in the housing market. One method that has been used to enforce racial segregation is the discrimination in mortgage lending known as "redlining." This term dates to the 1930s, when the Home Owners Loan Corporation (HOLC) was created by President Roosevelt to insure mortgages issued by banks and savings and loans to homeowners. (The discussion of the HOLC and FHA is based mainly on Jackson 1985, p. 197 ff.) Like any insurance agency, the HOLC was concerned with assessing the riskiness of activities, in this case the question of whether a home buyer would or would not default on a mortgage. One factor in the default calculation is the general character of the neighborhood; a good neighborhood is defined to be one where the probability of default is lower. The HOLC created a rating system for neighborhoods that classified them using a letter and associated color as A (green), B (blue), C (yellow), and D (red). The top classification of A went to new neighborhoods with a homogeneous population of "American [white Protestant] business and professional men." The red D neighborhoods were older and more heterogeneous, both economically and ethnically. Neighborhoods inhabited by blacks were zoned as red regardless of their other characteristics, hence the term "redlining" to mean racial discrimination in lending.

The HOLC ratings had a large influence on the decisions of loan officers about mortgage applications. A survey of loan officers in Newark, New Jersey, in the late 1930s found a clear preference for lending in A and B neighborhoods and a clear pattern of automatically refusing to lend in D (redlined) neighborhoods. The guidelines of the HOLC were adopted and continued by its successor, the Federal Housing Administration (FHA). The FHA continued the practice of redlining into the 1960s. Because redlining is a self-fulfilling prophecy of neighborhood decline—areas where people are unable to get loans to purchase or renovate houses are likely to deteriorate and not see any new construction—the FHA contributed to the racial segregation of the United States. Redlining also contributed to a disparate amount of decline in black neighborhoods relative to white neighborhoods.

More recently, there has been a renewed concern about mortgage-lending practices that discriminate on the basis of race. In 1989, the Home Mortgage Disclosure Act (HMDA) was amended to require the release of detailed information about loan applications, acceptances, and defaults at each financial institution. The Federal Reserve Bank of Boston started a huge controversy by releasing a study in 1992 (a revised version of the study was published as Munnell et al. 1996) that found evidence that banks systematically rejected a higher percentage of black applicants than comparable white applicants. The findings were controversial because of the extreme difficulty in identifying whether or not the banks' decisions were based solely on race or were justified for other reasons. Consider the following recent example from Cleveland. National City Bank was accused of racial discrimination because it was 3.8 times as likely to reject a black mortgage applicant as a white mortgage applicant in 1994, up from a ratio of 2.1 in 1992. The bank countered that the rejections were the result of increased applications due to the bank's increased activity in primarily black neighborhoods, and it pointed out that 157 blacks had received mortgages in 1994, up from 31 in 1992. Further, 21 percent of all the bank's loans were to blacks in 1994, up slightly from 20 percent in 1992. Is the bank racially discriminating? (*Plain Dealer,* 21 December 1995)

Carr and Megbolugbe (1993) put the Boston study into a broader perspective. They describe five stages of the lending process, each of which is subject to racial discrimination. The first stage is the definition of the "lending territory" of the bank. This territory is the area where the bank is presumed to be interested in making loans, and is thus the geographical area of interest in a study of racial discrimination. The second stage of the loan process is the advertising and marketing done by the bank to encourage loan applications. The third stage is the prescreening of applicants, in which applicants are informally told of their prospects for loan approval. The fourth stage is application processing, in which the application is formally reviewed and approved or rejected. The fifth stage is product steering, in which the successful loan applicant is led to choose among mortgages of various lengths and interest rates.

Carr and Megbolugbe identify a hierarchy of three types of discrimination: blatant discrimination, disparate treatment, and adverse impact. Blatant discrimination involves making a loan approval decision based on the race of the applicant. Disparate treatment involves treating applicants of different races differently—for example, giving different prescreening advice to otherwise comparable individuals depending on their race. Adverse impact occurs when "reasonable" lending practices have a differential impact on applicants of different races. For example, if blacks have, on average, lower income than whites, and the bank is more likely to approve the mortgage for a higher-income applicant, then blacks will be rejected more often than whites. Table 14.3 illustrates how each type of discrimination can occur at each stage of the process. The Munnell et al. study examined disparate treatment at the application-processing stage.

TABLE 14.3   Racial Discrimination in the Mortgage-Lending Process

	Blatant Discrimination	*Disparate Treatment*	*Adverse Impact*
Lending-territory selection	Excluding minority areas	Implicit policy of excluding minority areas	Selecting territory on the basis of a criterion that disproportionately excludes minorities
Advertising and marketing	Discouraging minority loan applications	Using media targeted to whites	Targeting advertising on the basis of a criterion that disproportionately reaches whites
Prescreening	Explicit policy of offering whites better information or discouraging minority applicants	Implicit policy of offering whites better information	Applying prescreening criteria that result in giving different advice to white and minority applicants
Application processing	Explicit policy of favoring white applicants	Implicit policy of favoring white applicants, such as using different approval criteria	Rejecting applications on the basis of criteria that disproportionately affect minorities but do not affect profitability
Product steering	Explicit policy of advising minorities to use government-insured loans (with higher interest rates)	Implicit policy of steering by giving different advice to whites and minority applicants	Recommending a loan product on the basis of criteria that disproportionately affect minorities

Source: Adapted from Carr and Megbolugbe (1993), Table 1.

An important underlying question is whether policies that seem racially discriminatory actually come about due to a characteristic, unobserved by the economist doing the analysis, that both affects the likelihood of default *and* is correlated with race. If there is discrimination, then presumably black applicants are held to a higher standard of loan approval than are white applicants. The default rate for black mortgage holders, then, should be lower than that for whites if racial discrimination is occurring. Berkovec et al. (1994) investigate this possibility and find no evidence that the default rate for black mortgage debtors is lower than the default rate for comparable whites. This result is consistent with an absence of racial discrimination in the mortgage market.

There is a problem with interpreting the default rates in the way that Berkovec et al. do, though. The decision to accept or reject is made on the basis of individual loan applications, not averages. Imagine ranking all of the applications for mortgages by whites from least risky to most risky and then doing the same thing for blacks. Even if the cutoff for riskiness were the same, it the average riskiness of the groups of people might still be different. Consider the following example. Suppose the bank knows the probability that an applicant will default on the loan. A low probability is a less-risky loan. There are three white applicants, with probabilities equal to 0 percent, 2 percent, and 4 percent. There are three black applicants, with probabilities equal to 1 percent, 3 percent, and 4 percent. If the bank rejects anyone with a probability over 2 percent, then one of the white applications and two of the black applications will be rejected. The average white loan recipient will have a default rate of 1 percent, while the average black loan recipient will have a default rate of 1 percent. The average white rejected application has a default rate of 4 percent, while the average black rejected application has a default rate of 3.5 percent. The observed difference among the rejected applications occurs despite the fact that the bank is using the same rule to evaluate both groups of applications. Note that the pattern of a black default rate among accepted applications equal to the white default rate is consistent with the findings by Berkovec et al. Suppose the bank discriminates, accepting any white application of 4 percent or less but rejecting any black application over 3 percent. We would find no whites rejected, but one black would be rejected. The default rate among the whites would be 2 percent (average of 0, 2, and 4 percent), which would equal the default rate among the blacks (average of 1 and 3 percent). This finding too is consistent with that of Berkovec et al. So looking at the average default rate does not provide us with enough information to know whether or not there is discrimination. However, if we knew that the white loan with a 4-percent risk was approved while the equivalent black loan was denied, then we would have evidence of racial discrimination.

In order to purchase a house, one is usually required to obtain insurance. Recently, insurance companies have begun to remove restrictions on the types of houses they are willing to insure. These restrictions included a minimum house value ($40,000 for Allstate) that would qualify. Similarly, a house can be insured at replacement cost (the cost of rebuilding it). This cost can differ from the appraised value, especially in high-cost, low-value areas. Companies imposed a maximum percentage (150 percent for Allstate) of the appraised value that could be insured under a replacement-cost policy. These restrictions had the cumulative effect of making it very difficult for people to buy homes in low-income neighborhoods, a form of insurance redlining. In the summer of 1996, two of the largest insurers, State Farm and Allstate, announced that they were removing these restrictions (*Wall Street Journal*, 14 August 1996). Of course, the insurance policies may still be too expensive for people interested in purchasing such housing.

Racial Discrimination in Housing Markets: Steering, Price Discrimination, and Exclusion

In addition to differential treatment in the mortgage process, racial discrimination can take three other forms. The first of these is "steering," which is a practice in which real estate agents show different houses to otherwise comparable potential buyers of different races. Because most home buyers rely on their real estate agent to identify appropriate homes for them to purchase, this practice can lead to entrenched segregation as people buy houses in the neighborhoods in which they are shown houses. This practice is illegal, but there is evidence that it has not completely disappeared. Yinger (1986) reports the results from audits by the Federal Department of Housing and Urban Development in which comparable buyers of different races were sent out to test whether or not real estate agents were steering. The results indicated that the practice remained widespread, and so federal, state, and local governments continue to monitor the real estate market. A possible response to charges of steering is that the agents are merely reflecting the perceived preference of home buyers to live in segregated neighborhoods.

The second form of racial discrimination is charging buyers different prices on the basis of race. Yinger (1979, p. 457) points out that any theory of racial discrimination in housing implies that there should be racial differences in prices paid both across neighborhoods and within any given neighborhood for comparable housing. The approach used to measure these differences is the hedonic price model introduced earlier in this chapter. If the prices of two houses in the same neighborhood with the same set of characteristics differ depending on whether the buyer is white or black, then this is evidence of racial discrimination. Yinger (1979, p. 457) summarizes studies using data from the 1950s and 1960s and finds that there is evidence that blacks pay a premium for housing. Cromwell (1990) summarizes studies using data from the 1970s and 1980s and finds that the more recent measured premium is lower. This could reflect a reduction in discrimination, or it could reflect "white flight" from integrated neighborhoods and the associated reduction in housing demand (and, therefore, in housing price). An alternative approach is to predict the racial composition of an area based on the match between the characteristics of the houses and the characteristics of the population. If a systematic difference is noted between the predicted racial composition and the actual racial composition, it may be the result of racial discrimination. Kain and Quigley (1975) use this approach to show that blacks in the St. Louis metropolitan area were much more concentrated in the central city than would be expected on the basis of characteristics other than race, such as household income.

The third, and most drastic, form of discrimination is to exclude blacks or other minority groups entirely. Of course, this could be viewed as just an extreme form of price discrimination, but the legal implications of exclusionary policies warrant their treatment separately. Until 1948, when they were found unconstitutional by the U.S. Supreme Court, a widespread practice in the United States was the writing of covenants (contracts) forbidding the sale of property to members of certain races or religions. The FHA had actually encouraged developers to include racial covenants in newly constructed neighborhoods as a way of maintaining stability. In fact, the FHA stopped insuring mortgages on property subject to racial covenants only in 1950, two years after the Supreme Court ruling.

Racial Prejudice in Housing Markets: Neighborhood Tipping

When you choose a house, you also choose a neighborhood and, therefore, neighbors. One of the characteristics of your neighbors that you might care about is their race. To take an extreme case, maybe you would live only in a neighborhood in which there is no one of another race. If everyone felt that way, then there would be complete segregation (and everyone would be happy). Racial prejudice, then, can lead to racial segregation.

Thomas Schelling (1978, ch. 4) provides a cautionary analysis of the power of prejudice. Consider the following model. There are two races, black and white. Everyone prefers to live in an integrated neighborhood, thus obviating the extreme case described above. However, no one wishes to be a minority in the neighborhood. The only stable equilibrium in this setting is complete racial segregation. There is an unstable equilibrium of 50 percent white and 50 percent black, but any small change in the balance leads to an immediate segregation of the neighborhood. This sudden change from a mixed racial composition to segregation is known as *neighborhood tipping*. This is clearly a strong result, and it depends heavily on the extent to which people are willing to be in the minority. For example, if people are willing to live in a neighborhood as long as the racial composition is no more than 65 percent of the other race, then integrated neighborhoods of between 35 and 65 percent of a given race can be sustained (although these are stable only in the interior of this region).

Although the theoretical result of neighborhood tipping is interesting, it would not be worth the extensive investigation it has received had not tipping been observed in practice. Alfred and Marcoux (1970) conclude that "integration is no more than the brief span of time between the arrival of the first black and the departure of the last white." An example of how quickly tipping can occur is the Cleveland suburb of Warrensville Heights, which went from all white in 1960 to 21 percent black in 1970, 75 percent black in 1980, and 89 percent black in 1990 (Keating 1994, p. 72). Keating (1994, p. 80) cites the even more extreme case of a census tract in East Cleveland (a suburb of Cleveland) that went from 0.3 percent black in 1950 to 91 percent black in 1960. In contrast, some Cleveland suburbs, such as Shaker Heights and Cleveland Heights, have maintained a fairly stable integrated racial composition over a long period of time. As we will see below, it can be argued that the success of these suburbs is, at least in part, attributable to targeted policies of local governments and nonprofit organizations intended to promote and maintain integration and is not purely the result of happy coincidence.

Call the percentage of the other race you are willing to tolerate in your neighborhood your *tipping point*. Suppose there is a distribution of tipping points among the white population, as drawn in Figure 14.2. (For simplicity of exposition, I am assuming that the black population is indifferent to racial composition; in reality, there would be a corresponding distribution of tipping points, which would complicate the analysis.) For example, 80 percent of the whites have a tipping point that is greater than 15 percent black. The dashed line represents feasible racial compositions of the community; in other words, percentages of white and black would sum to 100 percent.

Suppose the current community composition is 85 percent white and 15 percent black. This is not an equilibrium, since only 80 percent of whites have a tipping point of at least 15 percent. Therefore, whites would sell to blacks, and the racial composition of the neighborhood will change, with the percentage of white decreasing and the percentage of black increasing.

As drawn, there are four equilibrium racial compositions. Two are unstable equilibria, one with 100 percent white and the other with 20 percent white. Two are stable equilibria, one with 65 percent white and the other with 0 percent white. To verify that these are stable or unstable, consider a small perturbation from each of the equilibria. If the perturbation leads to a return to the equilibrium, then it is a stable equilibrium.

Galster (1990a, 1990b) uses data on the racial composition of census tracts in the city of Cleveland and some of its suburbs to estimate tipping points. He finds that integration can be maintained if the nonwhite percentage of the population is less than 35 percent but that tipping occurs at a higher nonwhite percentage. He also finds that affirmative marketing programs in the suburbs of Cleveland Heights and Shaker Heights aimed at encouraging and maintaining racial integration have been somewhat successful in their goals.

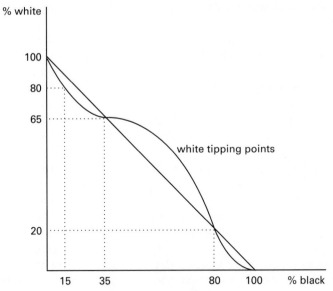

FIGURE 14.2 Tipping Points and Equilibrium

It is possible that people will have different tipping points for making their decisions about buying and selling their houses. Because the decision to buy or sell a house involves not only the current characteristics of the house but also future characteristics, a racially prejudiced person will base that decision at least in part on a prediction of the neighborhood's future composition. It is possible that the predictions of buyers and sellers are systematically different; for example sellers may have better information about the likely future of the neighborhood. It is also possible that the preferences of buyers and sellers in integrated neighborhoods are systematically different; the tipping point of a white buyer, for example, might be at a higher percentage of nonwhite than the tipping point of a white seller. Both tipping points are important in determining the equilibrium racial composition of a neighborhood. In the short run, the tipping points of the sellers are vital, as they determine which houses are available. In the long run, tipping points of buyers determine whether sellers who sell for nonracial reasons (life cycle, job relocation, etc.) have a chance of being replaced by someone of the same race or not. For a racial composition to be a long-run, steady-state equilibrium, it must be the case that the fraction of sellers and buyers from each racial group reflects the current neighborhood composition.

Suppose the equilibrium racial composition is an unstable one. In that case, government policy might be required to maintain a given racial composition. Prior to civil rights laws, one possible unstable composition the government promoted was complete segregation. In fact, exclusionary covenants and zoning are a way of maintaining an unstable segregated outcome. An early practice to encourage tipping was known as "blockbusting," in which one house in a segregated white neighborhood would be sold to a black family, generating a flight of white families from the neighborhood, encouraged by unscrupulous real estate agents who would call and solicit them to consider moving. One response to this practice by some suburbs was to ban "For Sale" signs and phone solicitation by real estate agents, so that people would not feel panic that the neighborhood was turning over rapidly. More recently, governments and nonprofit organizations have endeavored to maintain unstable integrated neighborhoods. We will consider several cases here, as well as some evidence on tipping points estimated from actual housing choices.

One example of an anti-tipping strategy was that pursued by the Starrett City housing project in Brooklyn. For 15 years, the management of Starrett City followed a practice of maintaining a racial composition of 55 percent white and 45 percent non-white in each of 46 buildings. This was challenged by the federal government, and in 1988 this policy was ruled to be illegal by the Second Circuit Court of Appeals. As the general manager of Starrett City pointed out (*New York Times*, 20 February 1988), this ruling came despite the agreement by the civil rights division that racial segregation would be the likely outcome in the absence of quotas.

Another example of an anti-tipping strategy is described and analyzed by Cromwell (1990). He describes the creation of a low-interest loan program by the city of Shaker Heights that targeted people buying homes in integrated neighborhoods. This program, known as the Fund for the Future of Shaker Heights, was developed especially because people were worried that the Lomond neighborhood, which bordered the city of Cleveland, was tipping towards resegregation. Between 1982 and 1986, the percentage of nonwhite residents in the western half of Lomond increased from 40 percent to 65 percent, while sales to whites declined from 81 percent of the sales in 1981 to 47 percent in 1985. After the introduction of the Fund for the Future of Shaker Heights in 1986, the racial composition of the Lomond neighborhood stabilized. Cromwell used detailed data on housing characteristics to estimate a hedonic price regression. He found that the small loan (between $3,000 and $5,000) that the Fund offered did not affect price, but it did affect the perception of whether the neighborhood was tipping. He estimated white tipping points before and after the introduction of the program and found that under the program a stable racial composition could be maintained because of an increase in the willingness of whites to buy. These findings support the idea that the tipping points of buyers determine the long-run equilibrium racial composition; they also emphasize the idea that the willingness to buy a house depends not only on current conditions but on the expectations of future conditions, including neighborhood racial composition. Whites were more willing to buy into an area that they perceived as integrated and likely to remain so than they were to buy into an area that they perceived as integrated but tipping.

The Fund for the Future of Shaker Heights was only the latest of a number of policies pursued by the suburb to maintain and increase racial integration. Keating (1994) describes the various approaches used in Shaker Heights over time and recounts the experiences of several other Cleveland suburbs.

CHAPTER SUMMARY

- The federal government has been directly involved in housing markets since the 1930s. The intervention takes several forms. First, the government is involved in assisting homeowners with receiving mortgages. Second, the government constructs and operates rental housing and subsidizes private construction and operation of rental housing (supply-side policies). Third, the government subsidizes rent payments for people (demand-side policies).

- Local governments intervene in housing markets indirectly through zoning policy and directly through rent-control programs. Rent control acts as a price ceiling and as such has been criticized for leading to shortages of housing in the short run and reductions in the supply of housing in the long run. However, if rental housing is a monopolistically competitive market, then rent control can cause price to be equal to marginal cost rather than greater than marginal cost.

- Racial prejudice is defined as an attitude toward members of a racial group. Racial discrimination is defined as differential behavior toward members of different racial groups. Racial segregation is defined as an outcome in which people of different races live in separate areas.

- There is a great deal of racial segregation in the United States. This can be the result of discrimination or the result of prejudice. A strong legal argument exists for government intervention if segregation is the result of discrimination. If segregation is the result of prejudice, an argument exists for government intervention if segregation itself is viewed to be a problem. One approach that has been tried is to subsidize people whose purchase of a home in a neighborhood increases the racial integration of the neighborhood. Another approach that has been tried is to enforce racial quotas, but this approach has faced legal challenges.

- One form of racial discrimination is the differential treatment of people who are in the process of applying for a mortgage. Another form of racial discrimination is for real estate agents to show different houses to different people on the basis of their race. Another form of racial discrimination is to charge one price for members of one race and a different price for members of another race. There is some evidence that all three of these forms of discrimination persist today.

EXCERPT: *THE TIME MACHINE* (H. G. WELLS)

The following excerpt from H. G. Wells's classic book *The Time Machine* (1895, pp. 59–61) illustrates what thousands of years of enforced segregation can lead to. The time traveler, in this excerpt, describes his thoughts after his first discovery that the underground-dwelling Morlocks share the world of the future with the pastoral Eloi he had previously met.

Here was the new view. Plainly, this second species of Man was subterranean. . . . Beneath my feet, then, the earth must be tunneled enormously, and these tunnelings were the habitat of the new race. The presence of ventilating shafts and wells along the hill slopes—everywhere, in fact, except along the river valley—showed how universal were its ramifications. What so natural, then, as to assume that it was in this artificial Under-world that such work as was necessary to the comfort of the daylight race was done? The notion was so plausible that I at once accepted it, and went on to assume the how of this splitting of the human species. I dare say you will anticipate the shape of my theory; though, for myself, I very soon felt that it fell far short of the truth.

At first, proceeding from the problems of our own age, it seemed clear as daylight to me that the gradual widening of the present merely temporary and social difference between the Capitalist and the Labourer, was the key to the whole position. No doubt it will seem grotesque enough to you—and wildly incredible!—and yet even now there are existing circumstances to point that way. There is a tendency to utilize underground space for the less ornamental purposes of civilization; there is the Metropolitan Railway in London, for instance, there are new electric railways, there are subways, there are underground workrooms and restaurants, and they increase and multiply. Evidently, I thought, this tendency had increased till Industry had gradually lost its birthright in the sky. I mean that it had gone deeper and deeper into larger and ever larger underground factories, spending a still-increasing amount of its time therein, till, in the end—! Even now, does not an East-end worker live in such artificial conditions as practically to be cut off from the natural surface of the earth?

Again, the exclusive tendency of richer people—due, no doubt, to the increasing refinement of their education, and the widening gulf between them and the rude violence of the poor—is already leading to the closing, in their interest, of considerable portions of the surface of the land. About London, for instance, perhaps half the prettier country is shut in against intrusion. And this same widening gulf—which is due to the length and expense of the higher educational process and the increased facilities for and temptations towards refined habits on the part of the rich—will make that exchange between class and class, that promotion by intermarriage which at present retards the splitting of our species along lines of social stratification, less and less frequent. So, in the end, above ground you must have the Haves, pursuing pleasure and comfort and beauty, and below ground the Have-nots, the Workers getting continually adapted to the conditions of their labour. Once they were there, they would no doubt have to pay rent, and not a little of it, for the ventilation of their caverns; and if they refused, they would starve or be suffocated for arrears. Such of them as were so constituted as to be miserable and rebellious would die; and, in the end, the balance being permanent, the survivors would become as well adapted to the conditions of underground life, and as happy in their way, as the Upper-world people were to theirs.

The great triumph of Humanity I had dreamed of took a different shape in my mind. It had been no such triumph of moral education and general cooperation as I had imagined. Instead, I saw a real aristocracy, armed with a perfected science and working to a logical conclusion the industrial system of today.

Source: The Time Machine by H. G. Wells. This material is in the public domain in the United States.

Questions for Review and Discussion

1. Do you agree with Wells that residential segregation will eventually lead to a splitting of the human species? How long would such a process take?

2. "A large number of people do not live in decent housing. Therefore, government housing policy in the United States has failed." Do you agree or disagree? Explain.

3. "Rent control is clearly undesirable in perfectly competitive markets, but it can work well in monopolistically competitive markets. The rental housing market where I live is monopolistically competitive, and it would be a good thing for my local government to impose rent control." Do you agree or disagree? Explain.

4. "Mortgage discrimination can't exist, because a nondiscriminating bank could take over a part of the market and make a profit." Do you agree or disagree? Explain.

5. "Racial prejudice will disappear only when people get to know people of different races, which will occur only after racial segregation disappears. Local governments should therefore require neighborhood racial integration in both owner-occupied housing and rental housing." Do you agree or disagree? Explain.

6. Calculate the exposure index and the dissimilarity index for the central city and the suburbs in your metropolitan area. How do you interpret the results?

CHAPTER

Transportation

15

In order for trade to occur, a nexus for each transaction must be created. Either goods and services must be taken to the consumer, or the consumer must travel to obtain the goods and services. Factors of production need to be combined in order for production to occur. The common factor in all these transactions is the need for transportation. In this chapter we will analyze transportation of people and products within a metropolitan area. We will focus on commuting decisions and their implications.

COMMUTING AND CARS

Travel from home to work and back again accounts for about 25 percent of all personal trips, easily the largest portion of total trips in U.S. metropolitan areas. Therefore, understanding the commuting decision is vital to understanding urban transportation. Even more important, commuting is not evenly distributed throughout the day but instead is concentrated into peak periods known colloquially as "rush hours." Approximately 40 percent of all trips occur during the morning and evening rush hours (6 to 9 a.m. and 4 to 7 p.m.), according to Downs (1992, p. 14). Trips to and from work are, of course, the most concentrated during these times, but even nonwork trips cluster during these periods. For example, during the morning rush hour some people are driving their children to school or day care, while during the evening rush hour some people are driving to the grocery store or dry cleaner. On a recurring basis, the greatest stress on a transportation system is placed during these peak periods. This is especially true of mass-transit systems; as much as 80 percent of their total ridership is concentrated into 20 hours of the week (Dyckman in Davis, ed., 1973, p. 198). It has been said that a transport system that can deal with rush hour can deal with anything. So analyzing commuting behavior is also a vital component of designing an efficient transportation system.

An important preliminary to analyzing rush-hour transportation problems is to ask why there should be a peak period at all. Why not, for example, evenly stagger arrival and departure times to and from work throughout the day? This would not only reduce traffic but could also improve efficiency by recognizing individual preferences for different work schedules. The presumed reason for the absence of staggered work schedules is that workers' efficiency increases when they interact with one another during the working day. This gain in efficiency has to offset the efficiency loss of traffic congestion and the loss of individual choice, however, in order for universal adherence to "normal working hours" to be socially optimal (Downs 1992, p. 15).

Modal Choice

The commute, like Gaul, is divided into three parts. (This follows the analysis in the classic book, *The Urban Transportation Problem,* by John Meyer, John Kain, and Martin Wohl.) Consider a person who travels from a house in the suburbs to an office downtown. The first phase of the trip, *suburban collection*, involves getting from the house to the main mode of commuting. The second phase of the trip, *line haul*, involves traveling using the main mode of commuting. The third phase of the trip, *downtown distribution*, involves getting from the line-haul vehicle to the office.

Some examples will help to clarify this idea of the commute. First, consider the case of a person who drives a car from home to the office. The suburban collection portion of the commute is the walk from the door to the car (and maybe the short drive to a main street). The line haul is the drive to the office. The downtown distribution is parking the car and walking to the office.

Second, consider the case of a person who walks to a bus stop, rides the bus to a train station, rides the train downtown, and then walks to the office. In this case, the suburban collection is the walk to the bus stop and the bus trip to the train station. The train ride constitutes the line haul, and the walk from the train station to the office is the downtown distribution.

In the United States, the dominant line-haul vehicle is the private automobile. Downs (1992, p. 34) reports that almost 90 percent of the commuters in 1983 used private automobiles, either as drivers or as passengers. Less than 5 percent of the commuters used public transportation. Although these figures are somewhat dated, there is no reason to believe that they have substantially changed during the intervening time period. Why does "everyone" choose to drive to work?

The choice of the line-haul vehicle is known as "modal choice," although the choice of collection and distribution modes is clearly related and important. How will a commuter choose a line-haul vehicle? According to consumer theory, the choice will maximize utility. Factors to consider are the cost in time and money of the commute, the "quality" of the mode, and the characteristics of the user.

Table 15.1 illustrates an example of the modal choice decision. The person is assumed to have a line-haul commute of 10 miles to the CBD. If he or she drives, there are no collection costs (the person just gets in the car). The collection costs for transit involve a walk to a bus stop or rail station and a wait for the bus or train. The bus stop is assumed to be closer to the person's house than the rail station. Similarly, the distribution costs for the bus system are lower than for the rail system. An important question for this comparison is the monetary value that people place on their time. A standard finding is that people value their line-haul time at about one-half their hourly wage, while they value the collection and distribution time at about one and one-half times their hourly wage. Suppose that the person earns $42,000 per year. At 2,000 work hours per year, this is equivalent to a wage of $21 per hour.

The results in the table illustrate that the automobile is the clear choice for this person. The key point is that the costs of time—especially time spent waiting—play a dominant role in the choice of commuting mode. Cars have a huge advantage in exactly these costs, in addition to being more comfortable, safer (barring carjackings), and readily available. If the person has to ride a bus to the rail station, collection costs increase and make rail even less attractive. Similarly, if there is no bus stop within walking distance and a person must pay for parking, both collection costs and monetary costs increase. That's why everybody drives to work. Of course, the numbers used in Table 15.1 are illustrative only, but they do give you an idea of the magnitude of the problem facing people who advocate a large-scale shift from cars to public transit. The numbers also give you an idea of why most economists do not find it plausible that mass transit is a competitive alternative for most commuters.

Congestion

Consider a stretch of road connecting point A and point B. Define the traffic volume on this stretch of road as the number of cars passing point A each hour. If the speed limit is 35 miles per hour (and everyone observes the speed limit!), then for traffic below a certain critical volume the average speed of cars along the stretch of road will be 35 miles per hour. At some critical volume, though, the cars will start to interfere with each other, forcing traffic to slow. As volume increases, the average speed decreases. A typical relation between volume and speed is shown as Figure 15.1. (Small 1992, provides a general survey, and much of the following discussion is based on his work.) The volume T_0 is known as the "design capacity" of the road.

TABLE 15.1 Example of Modal Choice

Cost Components	Automobile	Bus	Rail
Collection time			
Collection time (minutes)	0	10	15
Cost per minute	$0.525	$0.525	$0.525
Collection time cost	$0.00	$5.25	$7.875
Line-haul time			
Line-haul time (minutes)	40	50	30
Cost per minute	$0.175	$0.175	$0.175
Line-haul cost	$7.00	$8.75	$5.25
Distribution time			
Distribution time (minutes)	0	5	10
Cost per minute	$0.525	$0.525	$0.525
Distribution cost	$0.00	$2.63	$5.25
Money			
Operating cost / fare	$3.00	$1.50	$2.00
Parking cost	$2.00	$0.00	$0.00
Total money cost	$5.00	$1.50	$2.00
Total time cost	$7.00	$16.63	$18.38
Total cost	$12.00	$18.13	$20.38

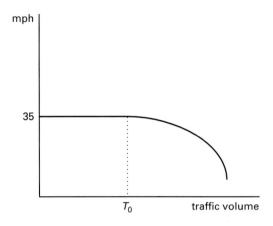

FIGURE 15.1 Traffic Volume and Speed

The average speed at which traffic travels obviously has implications for the total cost of travel. The time costs, for example, are inversely related to speed, since the faster you drive, the sooner you arrive. Suppose that operating costs depend only upon distance traveled, not speed. (This is not completely accurate, since you get better gas mileage at certain speeds, for example.) Small (1992, p. 76) cites evidence that costs are higher on arterial roads than on expressways, and higher when congestion forces the average speed below 30 miles per hour. But the assumption of constant operating costs is not too bad an approximation for a wide range of speeds. Further, suppose that "aggravation" from traffic does not depend on volume. (This is totally unrealistic, as anyone who has been in a traffic jam can testify.) Then, given a value for travel time, we can transform Figure 15.1 into a relation between traffic volume and average variable cost (the driver is *both* supplier and demander; the variable input is time), as shown in Figure 15.2. The average variable costs are the sum of the time costs (which vary with volume) and the operating costs (which are assumed not to

FIGURE 15.2 Traffic Volume and Cost

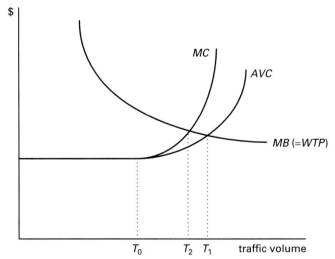

vary with volume). The marginal cost of adding another car to the road is simply the addition to total variable cost ($TVC(T) - TVC(T–1)$, where $TVC = AVC * T$), and this is also graphed in Figure 15.2. The MC and AVC are constant up to the design capacity of the road (T_0) because the speed of traffic is the same at all these volumes; therefore, the travel time per car does not vary for these volumes. The demand for travel reflects the marginal benefit (MB) to the traveler, as expressed in the traveler's willingness to pay (WTP). The MB curve is downward sloping because I assume that some people value the ability to travel on the road more than others do. For example, one person might have few alternative travel routes, while another has more choices. Or maybe people's preferences just differ. In equilibrium, the marginal benefit to the last traveler will equal the price of travel.

The situation pictured in Figure 15.2 illustrates a negative externality. Each traveler perceives (and pays) the AVC but imposes an addition to total cost of MC. The difference between the private cost and total social cost arises because each driver does not take into account the delay he imposes on all the other drivers by reducing the average speed. In equilibrium, the travel volume will be T_1, where the marginal benefit to the last driver just equals the average variable cost (the price the driver must pay). However, this exceeds the optimum volume of T_2. If the driver took into account the congestion externality, then the equilibrium volume would be T_2.

If aggravation is also increasing with volume, as seems likely, there is another external cost. (You know about all those idiots out on the road—but have you ever considered the fact that *you* are someone else's idiot?) Pollution adds yet another external cost, not only to other drivers but even to people not on the road. Including aggravation and pollution in the analysis would increase the difference between the cost faced by the driver and the true social cost of driving. In Figure 15.2, this would mean an increase in MC holding AVC constant, which would reduce the optimal traffic volume to an amount even lower than T_2.

The next question is the relative amount in dollars of each of the components of cost. Small (1992, p. 76) estimates vehicle operating costs of approximately $0.068 per mile, varying between $0.057 on expressways and $0.079 on arterial roads. He also estimates capital costs of about $0.188 per mile, reflecting the approximate lifetime usage and sales price of a typical car. Of course, these capital costs are to a large extent fixed costs and so should not be influential in determining the efficient operation of a car once a person decides to own one. Economists have estimated time costs equal to approximately 50 percent of the hourly wage. The average hourly wage in 1989 was $9.66, implying an average time cost of about $4.80. In a car traveling 40 miles per hour, this results in a time cost of $0.120 per mile, and so on. The time costs are almost double the operating costs, and so they are the dominant consideration in the operating decision. There is one other privately borne cost to consider. If the road is congested, people either depart earlier than they would otherwise, arrive later than they would otherwise, or alter their travel plans altogether. This "schedule-delay" cost is estimated by Small to be about $0.066 per mile, or about the level of operating costs.

In addition to the privately borne costs, several social costs are imposed by drivers. The first is clearly the time cost they impose on other drivers. The second is the external cost of automobile accidents. This cost has several components, including the traffic delay resulting from an accident, lost production due to death and injury, property damage, and insurance administration. Small estimates these costs to total about $0.179 per mile, a figure even greater than the time cost. A third social cost is the necessity to provide parking at the car's destination. Depending on the type of parking and the type of location (especially the land value), the cost per mile will vary. Small estimates that a figure of $0.136 per mile is a conservative one. There are also costs in the necessity for municipal government services such as traffic control and courts. Some of these costs are included in the accident estimate, so they will not be added separately. Negative externalities of air pollution and noise pollution result from operating cars and trucks, and environmental degradation results from road construction. The total pollution externality is approximately $0.007 per mile for cars and is on the order of $0.05 for trucks. While pollution is nonnegligible, stricter emissions standards have reduced the impact per mile.

The negative externality of traffic accidents has recently received renewed attention with the decision by Congress in 1995 to remove the federal mandate of a 55-mile-per-hour speed limit. The speed limit, originally imposed in 1974, was credited with a large reduction in the number of deaths from automobile accidents, down to a historic low rate of 1.8 deaths per million miles traveled in 1992. However, some of this reduction is due to better seat belts, air bags, motorcycle helmets, and drunk driving enforcement, so that identifying the effect of the reduced speed alone is difficult. Even the lower death rate represents a large number of deaths; the total highway death toll has been over 3 million since 1904—four times the total combat deaths in every war the United States has been in (*Plain Dealer,* 17 December 1995a). The use of public policy to control speeding and thus prevent accidents, is not new. A *Plain Dealer* newspaper article (17 December 1995b) cites a Paris ordinance of 1487 that warned that anyone galloping his horse on city streets would be punished with a flogging. In New York in 1899, a speed limit of 8 miles per hour was imposed for bicyclists. Speed limits for cars in the United States date to 1901, when Connecticut established a limit of 15 miles per hour on rural roads and a limit of 12 miles per hour in cities.

Congestion Tolls

Road congestion imposes very high costs, as can be seen by looking at historic figures. The cost of traffic congestion in New York City was estimated to be $365 million per year—in 1924! By 1953, congestion was estimated to cost local businesses in New York almost $1.1 billion per year. Those are large numbers even by today's standards, and the figures have not been adjusted to account for inflation (Lampard 1955, p. 124).

More recently, the Texas Transportation Institute released its findings on the cost of congestion in 50 urban areas between 1982 and 1993 (press release on World-WideWeb site http://tti.tamu.edu). The researchers there found a total of $51 billion in congestion costs in 1993, with schedule delays representing about 90 percent of the total costs. They also found that 32 of the 50 areas had seen at least a 100-percent increase in the amount of "wasted" gasoline, with the extreme cases being New York and Los Angeles. Each of these cities uses over 598 million gallons per year of gasoline more than it would in the absence of congestion.

In the appendix to chapter 1, we considered the various mechanisms for alleviating negative externalities. Let us see how we could apply these remedies to the problem of road congestion. The generic term for the remedies is a *congestion toll*. Implementing such a toll, though, is not without cost. If the costs of collecting the toll exceed the benefits from imposing the toll, it should not be done. The legal remedies of injunction and liability both seem difficult to implement. An injunction would stop someone from driving if he or she would cause congestion for others; a liability rule would require compensation ex post facto for congestion costs imposed on others. Direct regulation would involve mandating which cars were allowed to use the road at various times of day. A Pigouvian tax could be calculated on the basis of some assumptions about marginal benefits and marginal costs of travel. How large would the appropriate Pigouvian tax be? The data on external costs of automobile operation presented earlier make it possible to estimate the appropriate tax. However, the assumptions needed to generate those cost figures also illustrate the difficulty of implementing a Pigouvian tax. Recall that all the costs were averages over a variety of cars and a variety of times. Imposing a Pigouvian tax equal to the average level of the externalities would impose too high a cost during nonpeak hours and too low a cost during peak hours. Assigning property rights to travel on an uncongested road would be the "Coase Theorem" solution. However, this solution would require other drivers to negotiate with the owners of the right to travel uncongested on the road. Of these four general solutions, the one that is most promising is to force drivers to face the full social costs of their choices by imposing a toll equal to the congestion costs being imposed on others.

One class of solutions to the problem of congestion that does not rely on imposing congestion tolls should be mentioned before considering tolls in detail. Suppose that roads and cars can be technologically improved so that people are able to travel without worrying about congestion. For example, synchronizing traffic lights can reduce waiting time and increase the flow of traffic along a road. A variety of technological improvements are also being proposed as solutions to congestion. An article in *Fortune* (20 February 1995) lists satellite navigation, roadside traffic computers, collision-avoidance radar, infrared blind-spot sensors, infrared night-vision screen, radar-enhanced cruise control, programmable traffic signs, and vision-enhancement radar with heads-up display—all technologies that are currently available or will soon be available. All these technologies reduce congestion by making it possible to operate cars more efficiently, with improved routing, increased speeds, and reduced accidents. However, even if these technologies reduce congestion, they do so at a cost. And it is unlikely that even all of them in concert will completely eliminate traffic congestion in the foreseeable future.

Before analyzing the mechanics of collecting a congestion toll, it is important to emphasize that its basic purpose is to ensure that roads are used efficiently. A congestion toll is not necessarily intended to raise large amounts of revenue or even to reduce the number of trips people make by car. Rather, it is intended to make a person considering a trip by car include all the costs associated with the trip in his or her private cost-benefit calculation. If we impose the optimal congestion toll and still find roads crowded, we can conclude that the benefits of driving truly exceed the cost for the drivers. It should be noted that some roads are almost certain to be crowded if they are well designed and optimally used. Roads in and near centers of business activity represent a low-density use of very valuable land. A way of increasing the effective density of use is to have a large amount of traffic over the road.

A congestion toll could be collected in several possible ways. Direct methods include the familiar toll booths as well as electronic monitors that record the presence of a transponder in a car in a particular place at a given time (AVI, for automatic vehicle identification). With AVI, it might be possible to receive a monthly congestion toll bill akin to the phone bill, itemizing the times and places at which the car had been in dense traffic. One advantage of AVI is that it allows quick adjustemnt of the tolls for actual traffic conditions. If it is not possible or cost effective to implement these direct policies, there are also indirect methods of making people face the full cost of the commute. These methods include gasoline taxes, parking taxes, and subsidies to public transportation. Downs (1992) is a recent book that thoroughly explores the problem of congestion and its possible solutions.

How does a congestion toll help? There are four ways that people can change their behavior in response to a congestion toll. The first behavioral response is modal substitution. Rather than driving their own cars, people might walk, ride public transportation, or carpool. The second response is to alter their time of travel to avoid the peak hours if the congestion toll varies according to the time of travel. The third response is to alter the travel route away from the route where the toll is levied. The fourth response is to alter location choices—in particular, to live closer to work.

Each method of collecting a congestion toll has weaknesses. The problem with toll booths is that they cause additional congestion as people slow down to pay the toll. This implies that toll booths will be worth installing on only a few roads, and travelers may be able to avoid the tolls at the expense of increasing congestion on alternate routes. The main concern that people have about AVI is the potential invasion of privacy, should the records of a person's whereabouts be disclosed. One possible solution to this concern is to operate the monitors like a cash toll booth; a driver would replenish the transponder when necessary, and the toll would be deducted without recording the actual car involved in the transaction.

The indirect methods also suffer from some disadvantages. The main problem with all of them is that they are not necessarily related to the operation of the automobile in congested situations. Gasoline taxes, for example, provide an incentive to reduce the use of the car at all times. This might, perversely, lead to an increase in the percentage of the time that the car is operated in congested situations if commuting trips have a lower price elasticity than leisure trips. Further, gasoline taxes might just encourage a shift to cars with better fuel efficiency rather than lead to a shift in driving habits. The level of gasoline taxes needed to make a significant reduction in driving is estimated to be very large. Downs (1992, p. 69) reports that a doubling of gasoline prices would lead to a short-run decrease of only 35 percent in gasoline consumption, while even a 10-percent decrease in consumption would require a 25-percent increase in gasoline prices. Meyer and Gomez-Ibañez (1981, p. 145) estimate a price elasticity of gasoline to equal about –0.2, so they agree that gasoline is inelastically demanded. Of course, the level of congestion tolls suggested by economic analysis are fairly substantial. Suppose that total external costs are about $0.25 per mile, surely a conservative figure given the data we saw earlier. If a typical car gets 25 miles per gallon, the gasoline tax should be $6.25! This is about five times the current level of gasoline prices in the United States.

Parking taxes affect only those drivers who actually stop at a particular location. Thus, they completely miss drivers who are "just passing through." Parking taxes have the advantage of being extremely easy to collect, in that parking fees can be increased by the amount of the tax without interfering with the flow of traffic. However, parking taxes do not distinguish between drivers who travel on congested routes and those who travel on uncongested routes.

Subsidies to public transportation are a second-best type of solution to the problem of congestion. Rather than increase the price of a car trip to cause drivers to pay for congestion, they follow the principle of reducing the cost of alternatives in order to encourage people to switch modes of transportation. However, the size of the subsidy required to have a large effect is huge, as we will see in more detail later in this chapter. Private automobiles are not only more convenient than public transportation but are also more comfortable. Further, public transit is a relevant travel option only if a person is traveling to places served by the transit system. In a monocentric city, almost all the commercial and industrial destinations were in the central business district, accessible by streetcar from the suburbs along the route. In this age of decentralized edge cities, it is less certain that all the destinations will be accessible via public transportation in a timely and efficient manner. One option that combines the efficiency advantages of public transportation with the comfort of the private car is ride sharing or carpooling. Meyer and Gomez-Ibañez (1981) present evidence that suggests policies that encourage carpooling are the only ones likely to have a significant impact on automobile use.

Parking

Anyone parking a chariot so as to obstruct the royal road should be put to death with his head impaled on a pole in front of his house.*

They paved Paradise, and put up a parking lot.**

To a first approximation, every person in the United States makes every trip by car. This implies, of course, that upon arrival they must do something with the car before continuing about their business. Joel Garreau (1991) argues that much of modern urban land use can be understood by the imperative to accommodate all these automobiles. He estimates that the typical office worker requires 250 square feet of space, while the typical parking space requires 400 square feet of space. In other words, the major use of land in an edge city is for car parks. The quote from the Assyrian king Sennacherib that heads this section suggests that parking has been an important issue since the seventh century B.C.

Developers looking to provide parking places have several different options. (The cost figures in this paragraph are taken from Garreau, 1991, p. 119.) The first option is to designate a vacant area of land next to the office or mall as a parking lot. This has the advantage of being inexpensive, costing about $2,000 per parking space (not including the cost of the land). It is a wasteful use of land, though, if the land is at all valuable. The second option is to use the land for parking more intensively by building a parking garage. A parking garage allows you to park more than one car on the same piece of land, improving the efficiency of land use. However, it is more ex-

---

*Sennacherib, King of Assyria (quoted in Garreau 1991, p. 119).
**From a song by Joni Mitchell.

pensive to provide; the cost, not including land, is about $5,000 per parking space. The third option is to tunnel underground to provide parking. This is even more efficient because land is being used both for parking and for commercial, office, or residential purposes as well. It is also the most expensive alternative, costing about $20,000 per parking space.

When is it worthwhile to build a parking garage? The short answer is when the land is too valuable to be left idle or in low-intensity use. In other words, once the density of economic activity reaches a certain level, the same imperative that leads to capital-land substitution in building also leads to capital-land substitution in parking. However, large fixed costs are involved in constructing a parking garage. This implies some measure of increasing returns to scale in the number of stories in a parking garage because the fixed costs of having a garage can be spread out over a number of stories. Thus, when it is worthwhile to build a parking garage, it is cost-effective to build a large parking garage relative to the surface parking that is being replaced. But in order to justify that many parking spaces, it is vital to have a valuable land use that generates enough traffic to fill the parking garage. This in turn implies a discontinuity in the density of land use around the point where parking garages become economically viable. You can imagine density increasing gradually over time to the point where parking garages become necessary. At that point, we would expect to see a large increase in the density of land use in a fairly short time. If the land is truly valuable, then access to the land is worth something. One way of charging for access is to collect parking fees. You might expect to find that parking is free in places where the land is less expensive and that parking becomes increasingly expensive as the land becomes more expensive. We have already discussed one example (in chapter 9), the case of increasing parking lot fees as you move closer to a stadium hosting a professional sporting event.

As an example of how to use the parking problem as a way to think about land use, one can consider multiplex cinemas in shopping malls. These can be thought of as drive-in movie theaters where the cars are left in the parking spaces that were expensively constructed for the use of mall shoppers. The peak times for movies do not coincide with the peak times for shopping, allowing the developer to let the large investment in parking serve double duty in generating revenues for mall tenants, hence rent to the mall owner (Jackson 1985, p. 256). The conclusion: If you want to know how valuable the land is in an area, there are two quick rules of thumb—first, look at how tall the buildings are; second, look at how parking is managed.

Although parking problems are a common complaint in the United States, the abundant land surrounding most metropolitan areas make it less pressing than in a country such as Japan that is very short on undeveloped land. In 1991, a rule was imposed in Japan that every car owner must have proof of a parking space at home or near the office in order to register the car. These parking spaces can be expensive, costing up to $1,700 per month in residential areas. So some of the car makers in Japan began selling machines that allow people to "stack" cars on top of each other in a double tier, essentially doubling the number of parking spaces in a spot without the necessity of constructing a garage (*The Economist*, 14 September 1991). More recently, the lull in the construction industry in Japan has led to businesses' paving their (future) construction sites and using parking fees to help defray the interest costs on the property. Technological advances continue with the advent of unmanned parking machines, including parking meters that automatically clamp on tires when they expire and forklifts that can place up to eight cars in stacks and retrieve them in just one minute (*The Economist*, 13 April 1996).

The idea of using parking prices as a substitute for congestion tolls was discussed earlier in this chapter. However, casual observation suggests that most U.S. firms have policies that provide a subsidy to parking rather than the opposite. Free parking, or parking at less than market rates, is an employee perquisite that is taken for granted at most places. Let me give one example. The parking garage where I park charges visitors $7 per day to park. Let this represent the market price of parking, so it is an underestimate of what a parking price that included a congestion toll would be. Multiplying that daily figure by an estimated 250 working days per year yields an annual parking fee of $1,750 if employees were charged a market price. My actual annual payment is about $550, less than one-third of the market price. This is further incentive to drive to work. I will note in passing that the daily parking prices in downtown Cleveland range from $6 to $10, suggesting that the density of economic activity in the neighborhood of the university is comparable to that in downtown Cleveland. And the increasing density of land use in the neighborhood of the university has led to the construction of several parking garages during the past five years, illustrating the principle that parking and land use are inseparable.

Highway Capacity

The discussion above focused on the average variable cost of travel, ignoring any fixed costs. The most important fixed cost is clearly the amount of highway that exists. One possible reaction to highway congestion is to alleviate it by building more highway, thus increasing T_0, the design volume of the highway. An example of this is shown in Figure 15.3 below, where the original design volume is denoted T_0 and the new design volume T_0'. The consumer surplus available to drivers increases as a result of the expansion. However, the expansion comes at some cost. If the cost exceeds the

FIGURE 15.3 Highway Widening and Consumer Surplus

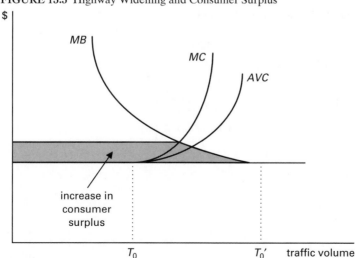

increase in consumer surplus, it is not socially efficient to expand the highway. If the cost is less than the increased consumer surplus, it may be socially efficient to expand the highway. Of course, if there is a Pareto-improving expansion available, you might think it would automatically be adopted by policy makers. However, the actual criterion for reaching a decision may not be Pareto efficiency; instead, it might weight one group's welfare more than that of another. Further, there may be several alternative ways of financing even a socially desirable expansion, and some ways could result in larger benefits to some groups than to other groups.

The question of the long-run capacity of a road brings up the issue of the long-run cost curve for highways. It should be noted that not all highways are alike—an expressway with limited access and elevated right-of-way has very different cost and operating volumes than a surface-level downtown boulevard. Small (1992, p. 100) describes the available information about the relation between road type and cost per mile, and these findings are summarized in Figure 15.4. There is a range of decreasing returns to scale where various arterial roads are the lowest-cost alternatives, and there is a range of increasing returns to scale where the volume becomes sufficient to justify expressways. In general, there are three aspects to costs. The first is the construction cost of the road, which will vary depending on the design of the road and the nature of the terrain. The second is the cost of acquiring the land on which to build the road. This cost, too, will vary depending on the location of the road. The third cost is the operating cost, including painting, traffic enforcement, and repair. Although the examples in Figure 15.4 are discrete, in practice there is considerable flexibility in design, so that almost any configuration of highway can be created.

Most roads in the United States are funded and provided by the government. Private toll roads are an alternative, however. In September, 1995, a 14-mile, privately owned and operated toll road opened in northern Virginia between Dulles Airport and Leesburg. This was the first such road in over a century. Other roads have been proposed near cities in California, Arizona, and Oregon. Privatization is not a panacea, though. In some places, a company would have to acquire too much expen-

FIGURE 15.4 Long-run Average Cost of Highways

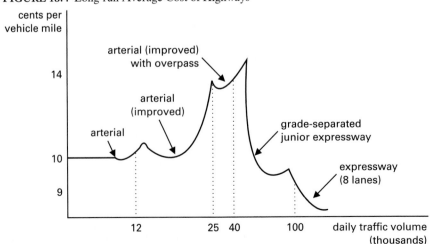

sive land in order to enable it to earn a profit in the short run. The political problems caused by collecting tolls are also exacerbated when the tolls are being paid to private firms rather than a government agency (*The Economist*, 18 November 1995).

Automobiles are a private means of transport that rely on travel along public rights-of-way. Governments could have responded to their development in two possible ways. First, high tolls could have been levied to regulate their use, and that revenue would have financed road construction. Second, general government revenue could have been used to subsidize automotive travel. The latter solution to the problem of funding highway construction in the United States dates to the early 1900s, when the widespread use of automobiles began. There were two reasons for this approach. The first, naturally, was private pressure in the form of automobile drivers and manufacturers. The second was a belief that automobiles would reduce pollution in the city and promote public health. As Jackson (1985, p. 164) puts it, the automobile represented "a clean and efficient alternative to the old-fashioned, manure-befouled, odoriferous, space-intensive horse."

In order to generate the revenues needed for major road construction, every state enacted a tax on gasoline between 1919 and 1929. Another innovation was the expressway, a right-of-way reserved exclusively for use by automobiles. This made possible higher speeds and, therefore, increased the accessibility of land near entrances and exits. The higher-speed roads, of course, were completely unsuited for pedestrians. As expressways were built to connect outlying areas with downtowns, they often bisected older neighborhoods, either demolishing them or changing their ambiance completely. These changes in turn hastened the movement of people along the expressways to the newly accessible land. Caro (1974, ch 37, 38) describes in detail the way that the construction of the Cross-Bronx Expressway destroyed the East Tremont neighborhood.

Pollution, Climate Change, and Alternative Fuels

Although congestion is the largest negative externality in dollar terms that results from automobile use, a long-term concern that has been the focus of public policy is the relation between automobile use and climate change, especially global warming. (The discussion in this section follows that in the International Energy Agency 1993.) Cars emit a variety of chemicals as the result of combustion of gasoline; among the chemicals are carbon monoxide (CO), carbon dioxide (CO_2), nitrogen oxides (NO_x) and nitrous oxide (NO_2). Catalytic converters, required in the United States since the 1970s, reduce emissions of CO and NO_x but increase the emission of CO_2, the gas believed most important in causing the so-called greenhouse effect that leads to a gradual warming of the earth's climate.

If awareness has increased of the relationship between automobile use and climate change, a natural question is, Why don't automobile manufacturers and consumers switch to an alternative to gasoline power? First, consider the problem from the manufacturer's point of view. Risk is involved in developing an alternatively fueled vehicle. The new technology may not work, or may be too expensive. Worse, a competitor might successfully develop—and patent—a new technology first, leaving the firm that much worse off. The large fixed costs associated with new-car development require large production runs to make the new cars competitive, and manufacturers are uncertain whether consumers would purchase the new technology. (Recall the discussion in chapter 8 about the effect of sunk costs and uncertainty on investment. This is an application of those ideas.) Governments have responded to this problem by offering incentives to firms that develop alternatives to gasoline-powered cars. Governments, most notably the state of California, have also guaranteed a market for the cars by imposing severe emissions restrictions that will take effect in the near future.

Now consider the question of alternatively fueled vehicles from the consumer's point of view. Most cars are sold to individual households for private use. A car, like a house, can be considered as a combination of attributes; among them are performance, fuel availability, expected reliability, and perceived safety. All the alternative fuels suffer by comparison with gasoline in some or all of these dimensions. For example, the electric cars currently in use have an extremely limited range. Compressed natural gas (CNG) and liquified petroleum gas (LPG), two fairly close substitutes for gasoline in performance terms, do not have the ubiquitous distribution network that assures motorists that they can fill up almost anywhere. It is interesting to note that in the United States government fleets have been some of the principle customers for CNG and LPG cars. Because these cars often have a limited work radius (especially in the case of municipal governments) and because the requirement of refueling at a central location is possible to impose and not very onerous (if the refueling point is close to work), local governments have been able to overcome some of the difficulties facing private owners.

The purchase of a car with a new technology represents more of a sunk cost than the purchase of a conventional new car. After all, if a new gasoline-powered car doesn't meet the buyer's needs, then there is an active market for used cars. In the case of a new technology, though, this secondary market does not yet exist; and if the new technology is unsuccessful, the secondary market will never exist. (When was the last time you saw a used car dealer who sold steam-driven cars?) This sunk investment combined with the greater uncertainty about the performance and reliability of a new technology also reduces the willingness of households to invest in alternatively fueled cars.

Wasteful Commuting

The ubiquity of freeways and auto travel have implications for household location decisions. If it is fairly easy to travel from home to work regardless of where you live, then people might be driving "too far" relative to a situation where they were forced to consider the external costs of their commute. In an ingenious study, Bruce Hamilton (1982) analyzed the difference between actual commuting distances and an estimated minimum commute, calling the difference "wasteful commuting."

The clever part of Hamilton's approach was estimating the minimum commute. Consider a monocentric city model. Given a set of housing locations, the total distance commuted is the same regardless of how people are assigned to houses, because they all must drive to the CBD. This is too simplistic, though. A simple generalization of the monocentric city model would be one in which employment density, like residential density, declined exponentially with distance from the CBD. This is illustrated in Figure 15.5.

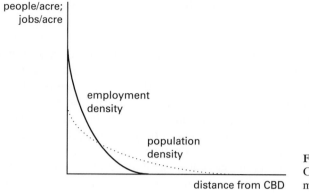

FIGURE 15.5 Monocentric City with Ubiquitous Employment and Housing

Now, the total distance everyone commutes will depend on how people are allocated to jobs and houses. If the density of jobs and population were identical, in the minimum commute each person would live next to his or her job, essentially having a commute of zero. But because there are more jobs than people close to the CBD, some people have to commute a distance greater than zero. You should check for yourself that the allocation of people to houses that minimizes the total commute has each person commuting towards the CBD to their jobs along rays from the CBD to their houses. Given that fact along with empirical estimates of employment and population density, Hamilton calculated the minimum commute for 14 U.S. cities. He found that the average commute in the sample was 8.7 miles, compared with an average optimal commute of 1.1 miles. This led to the conclusion that 7.6/8.7, or almost 90 percent, of the commuting distance in the United States was wasteful. Hamilton calculated the average commuting distance if households and firms chose their locations randomly, and he found it to be 12.1 miles. Thus, the actual average commute was only a 30-percent (12.1–8.7 divided by 12.1) improvement over a random distribution of households and jobs. Hamilton also calculated similar statistics for a set of Japanese cities and found that about 50 percent of the commuting there was wasteful.

The conclusion that almost 90 percent of the commuting in the United States was wasteful was a stunning and controversial one. In the most detailed rebuttal, White (1986) illustrates how two of Hamilton's assumptions led him to overestimate the "wastefulness" of commuting. First, the fact that employment is not evenly distributed throughout the city but is instead concentrated at the suburban employment centers and the CBD implies that the actual minimum commute is greater than that estimated by Hamilton. Second, the actual road network is not ubiquitous, again implying that the actual minimum commute is greater than that estimated by Hamilton, who implicitly assumed that all trips consisted of straight lines from home to work.

White also argues that Hamilton uses the wrong measure of the length of the commute by focusing on distance. She presents results based on commuting time, arguing that it is commuting time rather than commuting distance that a household considers when deciding on work and residence location. Using a sample of U.S. cities, she estimates that the average minimum commuting time is 20.0 minutes. However, the actual average commuting time is 22.5 minutes. Thus, about 11 percent of the commuting is wasteful in the sense that it exceeds the minimum possible. While even this set of results implies some waste, it is far less serious than Hamilton's results indicate.

Hamilton (1989) agrees with White that his original results have some bias toward finding greater amounts of wasted time. He argues that White's estimates, though, are biased towards finding too little. Because the data that White used do not allow her to calculate waste within each suburb but only when people travel from suburb to suburb (or downtown), her optimum is not as low as it would be if within-suburb trips could be examined. In other words, White did not account for the fact that suburbs are not single points in space; they *cover* space, too. He also argues that part of the discrepancy in the findings is because he measured distance while White measured time. When Hamilton replicates White's approach using commuting distance rather than time, he finds that the minimum commute is only 53 percent of the actual commute. Half the difference between their results, then, is caused by using different measures of commuting length. Small and Song (1992) find evidence of the bias in White's estimates caused by intrasuburb commutes using detailed data for the Los Angeles area. They do not find, though, that using time instead of distance significantly affects the results.

Hamilton (1989) points out that the findings have strong negative implications for the monocentric city model. If the fixed cost of commuting ("residential collection" and "downtown distribution" from the analysis of the commute above) is, say, 10 minutes out of the total commute of 20 minutes, then the variable costs of commuting are very small with respect to household location. Thus, unlike the monocentric city model, accessibility is not scarce, and households are free to locate anywhere within the metropolitan area while maintaining comparable accessibility. This criticism does not apply to the approach we have taken to analyzing household location, though. Even if a household is able to travel anywhere within a metropolitan area, it might still care about where it lives, as long as suburbs vary in their local public services, zoning laws, recreational amenities, and other characteristics.

MASS TRANSIT

In previous sections, we have seen in passing the difficulties that mass transit (buses and subways) has in competing with the private automobile. In this section we consider the question of the cost of constructing and operating a transit system and evaluate its role in a well-designed urban transportation network. We also consider an important policy question: To what extent do fixed-rail transit systems contribute to the economic development of a city?

Intermodal Cost Comparisons

In comparing modes, it is useful to first recall the division of a commute into three parts: collection, line haul, and distribution. Advocates of mass transit often point out the speed of subways, for example. Their line-haul advantage, though, is usually outweighed by the collection and distribution costs at either end. If the subway reduces the line haul by 3 minutes but increases collection time by 10 minutes, then it is not much of a bargain for commuters! Recall that collection and distribution costs were precisely those that commuters were most responsive to, and these costs are precisely those that are minimal for private automobiles.

Let us begin our cost comparison with the already familiar automobile and highway system. These entail private costs—the driver's time and the operating costs of the car—as well as public costs—road construction, accidents, and pollution. Figure 15.4 illustrates the long-run average cost for a variety of car systems. For consistency, we will use arterial improved (downtown) streets as the relevant comparison. There are roughly constant returns to scale over a large range of volumes, so that the marginal cost of increasing the size of a highway system is approximately equal to the average cost.

Next, consider a bus system. Clearly, buses can operate on highways just as cars can. Therefore, there is no necessity to construct special rights-of-way for buses, although reserved lanes and other additions can add to the system's attraction. Mohring (in Mieszkowski and Straszheim, eds., 1979) demonstrates that reserved bus lanes can increase system efficiency by a significant amount and suggests that allocating rights-of-way for buses is a strong second-best alternative to congestion tolls. Like cars, buses emit pollution and require road construction and maintenance costs, but they impose some additional costs as well. The bus system requires both administrative oversight and operating expenses (drivers, mechanics, etc.). Since each bus requires only one driver but can carry many passengers, the operating cost per passenger will decrease with the number of passengers riding a bus. Administrative expenses are also subject to increasing returns to scale. Thus, the system as a whole has some amount of increasing returns to scale. Small (1992, p. 105) summarizes the research to say that buses have average costs that decrease up to about 20,000 riders per hour (measured along one commuting corridor, such as a main road into the CBD), and that the total social costs of buses are lower than those for cars once a volume of about 5,000 people per hour has been reached. Of course, this only considers providing service during peak hours, and so it overstates the advantage of the bus system.

Finally, consider an integrated rail system. Unlike a bus system, rail transport is limited to a fixed path, making the residential collection and downtown distribution problems even more crucial than they were in the case of buses. An "integrated" rail system is one that relies on buses to gather people at the station and then distribute them upon arrival in the CBD. An alternative would be to provide parking at the station and let people drive there, but there is ample evidence that once people get in their cars, they do not like to get out again. Another alternative would be to have people dropped off at the station by a family member, and in fact this is the origin of the term "station wagon." The increasing prevalence of two-worker families makes this solution less feasible than it might have been during an earlier era. The costs of acquiring rights-of-way and laying track are substantial fixed capital costs; therefore, the rail system is also subject to increasing returns to scale. Small (1992, p. 105) finds that the familiar subway systems are the low-cost alternative only for extremely high corridor volumes (over 50,000 per hour, a figure seen only in Manhattan). According to some studies, some forms of light rail (trolleys, for example) can be competitive with buses at volumes as low as 10,000 per hour. Studies provide ample evidence that government subsidies for rail transit have led to its introduction in cities where buses would be more appropriate; evidence also shows that subsidies led to the introduction of bus service in low-density areas where private cars would be socially optimal (Meyer and Gomez-Ibañez 1981).

Subsidizing Transit

In 1985, fares covered 39 percent of operating costs for transit, leaving 61 percent of operating costs and 100 percent of capital costs to be paid for in some other way. In practice, that other way has consisted of revenue from general- and special-purpose taxes levied for the purpose of subsidizing transit. Of course, an immediate question is raised by this practice: Why should transit be subsidized?

There are two reasons. First, mass transit is produced under conditions of increasing returns to scale; in fact, it could even be a natural monopoly. Thus, if the price of transit is set equal to marginal cost, then a deficit remains because marginal cost is less than average cost. This standard theoretical problem has two well-known resolutions. The first is to set the price equal to average cost, allowing the operation to earn a normal rate of return but zero economic profits. This solution, though, results in ridership that is "too low" from a social welfare point of view. The second resolution is the so-called *two-part tariff*, a tax imposed to cover the deficit remaining when marginal cost pricing is used. (If transit is a natural monopoly, so that average cost falls over the range of demand, then marginal cost is less than average cost at the point where marginal cost crosses the demand curve. Setting the price at this level would thus leave price less than average cost, so that profits would be less than zero.) A two-part tariff leaves the benefits of marginal cost pricing in place while making it possible for the transit operation to break even. The pure theory of a two-part tariff would say that the taxes should be collected from those who obtain a great deal of consumer surplus from the presence of the transit line—for example, automobile drivers who value less-congested highways. In practice, general taxes such as sales taxes or broad-based excise taxes (especially on gasoline) are used to subsidize transit. Of course, none of these arguments justify pricing transit below its marginal cost.

The second reason for subsidizing mass transit is that unpriced congestion and pollution externalities mean that auto travel is essentially subsidized. Ideally (for Pareto efficiency), the marginal cost of auto travel equals the price, as is also the case for transit. Given the subsidy to auto travel, one could argue for subsidizing transit. This would underprice all forms of transportation relative to all other goods and services, introducing yet another distortion into the economy. The problem then is one of choosing which among several imperfect situations is the best. The general theory of the second-best deals with this situation (Baumol and Bradford, 1970). How big would the subsidy have to be? The conservative estimate of external costs imposed by an automobile driver is $0.25 per mile. If a typical commute is about eight miles in each direction, then a subsidy of about $2.00 per transit trip can be argued for. Who benefits from the subsidy? Not necessarily the same people who pay for the subsidy. If the subsidy is paid for by general taxes, then all consumers are paying. The people who benefit, though, are those who place a high value on their travel time, because the main external costs from automobile use are congestion costs. These people are likely to continue to drive even if a transit system is subsidized; further, they are likely to be higher-income people. The implication is that a transit subsidy involves a transfer from the general population to higher-income automobile drivers. The most common tax used to finance transit is the general sales tax, considered to be regressive or, at best, proportional. Its use to finance a regressive form of expenditure makes the tax, or at least the portion financing transit, unquestionably regressive. Landowners near transit stations also benefit from the improved accessibility of their property. Unless these landowners are disproportionately poor, the conclusion that the tax is regressive is unchanged by accounting for their benefits.

Another problem with the way mass transit is financed in the United States is that perverse incentives are provided for the relatively desirable maintenance of existing equipment and the aquisition of new equipment. The federal government provides a large matching grant, on the order of 80 percent, for the acquisition of new equipment but provides almost nothing for operation and maintenance costs. Cromwell (1991) uses data on public and private bus operations to conclude that the subsidy to purchase new equipment may lead to underinvestment in maintaining existing equipment. However, he is unable to distinguish between the subsidy effect and the potentially different incentives brought about by public versus private ownership.

Charles Lave, in an opinion piece published in the *Plain Dealer* (24 August 1992), presents evidence from Europe suggesting that even large incentives against use of private automobiles in the form of high gasoline prices, expensive parking, and inadequate roads have been insufficient to prevent a dramatic increase in the use of automobiles relative to the use of mass transit. This is even more striking given the higher population densities found in Europe than in much of the United States. Not only are Europeans increasing their ownership of cars, they are also using them almost as much as Americans. The average European car is driven 9,000 miles per year, compared with about 9,900 miles per year for a U.S. car. Lave attributes the growth in private automobile use to an increase in personal income, and he argues that mass transit is an inadequate substitute for the car. Thus, rather than continue with ineffective policies aimed at curbing automobiles, governments should instead focus on reducing the adverse environmental impact of cars.

Some states, though, continue to make large efforts to reduce automobile use and increase mass-transit ridership. The *Wall Street Journal* (8 April 1992) reported that New Jersey is not only subsidizing public transit but actually canceled $1.2 billion in new highway projects. The state transportation officials cite the experiences of Portland, Oregon, and of San Francisco, California, as evidence that people can adjust their life styles to reduce automobile use. In San Francisco, for example, commuters line up to share rides in order to use high-occupancy-vehicle lanes. Although the state is hoping to increase public transit ridership, officials there say that the top goal in much of the state is to encourage carpooling. This is consistent with the argument of Meyer and Gomez-Ibañez (1981) that carpooling and ride sharing were the only policies likely to enjoy widespread success in the United States.

Transit Construction as Economic Development Policy

A popular justification for developing mass-transit systems is that they promote economic development by focusing traffic in a particular area. For example, the *Wall Street Journal* (8 April 1992) cites a figure of $800 million of office, retail, and residential development near train stations in Portland, Oregon, since a light rail line there opened in 1986. This argument is made most strongly by those concerned with the "flight to the suburbs" of commercial and industrial activity. Of course, if the only effect of a mass-transit system is to move business around within a metropolitan area, then the city's gain is exactly balanced by the suburbs' loss, and there is no net improvement in the region. Proponents of mass-transit systems argue that an increase in ridership will reduce automobile use, implying a reduction in the negative externalities from cars. Some planners even advocate designing residential areas centered on transit stations in order to take full advantage of the possibilities for mass transit.

Boarnet and Crane (forthcoming) carefully examine the possibility of residential areas centered on transit stations using detailed zoning information on Southern California. They find that the preponderance of the land near stations is zoned for use as commercial and industrial property, so that the transit system is best understood as a way of transporting people among various business centers rather than as a direct link between residential and business areas. We have already seen the high costs involved in changing modes during the line-haul, so that these transit lines are not likely candidates for transport of a large volume of commuters. Hence, if there is to be a benefit from transit, it must come entirely from economic development resulting from the greater ease of transport among places linked by the rail system. The preference for commercial and industrial zoning near transit stations reflects the belief by local governments that residential land use requires more spending on local government services than the additional taxes yield, while business land use adds taxes in excess of the additional local government services required. If a strategy of using transit to connect residential and business areas is to succeed, it must overcome this incentive for each community to try to capture the business land use. Even if transit is optimal for the region as a whole, and thus some stations need to be in the midst of residential areas, each town has an incentive to try to not be the one with the residents. This is analogous to the "mayor's dilemma" that we analyzed in chapter 11.

The evidence that mass transit is an effective economic development device is not encouraging, though. A study of a light rail system in Calgary (Taylor and Wright 1983) identified five benefits from the system. These included reduced travel time for the commuters that chose rail, reduced congestion on the roads for those who continued to drive, reduced automobile operating costs because of higher efficiency associated with less congestion, reduced social costs from parking, and reduced bus operating costs. These benefits were calculated to have a discounted present value of about $138 million; the discounted present value of the costs of the system amounted to $224 million.

A study of a light rail system built in Buffalo during the late 1970s (Berechman and Paaswell 1983) found that service employment in the central business district was expected to increase by about 5,370 as a result of the $750-million-dollar investment. The study also found that private investment in the central business district would increase. However, the authors emphasize that transit alone is insufficient to increase downtown activity without the help of a range of other policies that promote economic development.

The Greater Cleveland Regional Transit Authority (RTA) recently proposed a major expansion and renovation of the light rail system in the city of Cleveland (Greater Cleveland Regional Transit Authority 1995). The proposal was intended to better link the "dual hub" of the city—the central business district and the University Circle area about four miles away along Euclid Avenue—with high-speed rapid transit. The proposal included constructing a subway from the central business district to Playhouse Square and Cleveland State University, and then adding an above-ground trolley from Cleveland State to University Circle. Reserved bus lanes would also be constructed on Euclid Avenue, and existing above-ground trolley stations would be relocated, closer to current centers of economic activity. This proposal was projected to increase system ridership by 4.7 percent, including a doubling of rail ridership. This extra ridership would increase the share of *operating* costs covered by fares to 30 percent from its current (1994) level of 27 percent. Increases in private development of 6.2 million square feet of commercial office space, 1,700 housing units, and 25,000 jobs (implying $15 million in city payroll taxes per year) were also projected. The RTA also claimed that the proposal would prevent the existing investment in transit from being wasted and would lay the foundation for further extension of service to the suburbs. The proposal was rejected, and a scaled-down version of the project, whose main feature is reserved bus lanes along Euclid Avenue, is currently in progress.

CHAPTER SUMMARY

- The private automobile is the dominant form of transportation in metropolitan areas in the United States today. People choose to drive cars because of their convenience relative to the alternatives, especially public transportation. The main advantage of the car over public transportation is its ready availability; a person does not have to wait to use a car but does have to wait to take a bus or a train.

- Private automobile use generates several negative externalities, including congestion and pollution. The most important externality is congestion; drivers are delayed by the addition of more and more cars to the road. One way to correct this externality is to force drivers to face the full costs of their driving by charging a congestion toll. The optimal toll would vary by time of day and by travel route. There are no real examples of an ideal congestion toll. Some alternatives include tolls on a few roads or bridges, taxes on gasoline, taxes on parking, and subsidies to public transit. Congestion tolls affect car use in four ways: people alter their mode of transportation, people alter their travel routes, people alter their times of travel, and people alter their location choices.

- One way of reducing congestion is to construct additional highways. If people are not paying congestion tolls, though, the true costs and benefits of new road construction are not straightforward to determine. A crowded road is not itself justification for new construction.

- In all but a few cities, rail-transit systems fail a cost-benefit test. If mass transportation is desired, then a bus system is the low-cost alternative for nearly all urban conditions.

- One justification for constructing rail transit lines is the economic development that will be generated near the stations. Some urban planners even advocate stations linking dense residential areas to business and commercial areas. There is little evidence, though, that station construction has a large net impact on the economy.

EXCERPT: *CITY* (CLIFFORD SIMAK)

We come now to the end of our exploration of the economics of cities. It is appropriate to conclude with a final fictional look at the urban future, this time through the eyes of Clifford Simak (1952, pp. 18, 24–26). Simak recognizes the strong connection between transportation and urban form, and the future he predicts is one that you might already recognize.

The years had moved too fast. Years that had brought the family plane and helicopter, leaving the auto to rust in some forgotten place, the unused roads to fall into disrepair. Years that had virtually wiped out the tilling of the soil with the rise of hydroponics. Years that had brought cheap land with the disappearance of the farm as an economic unit, had sent city people scurrying out into the country where each man, for less than the price of a city lot, might own broad acres. Years that had revolutionized the construction of homes to a point where families simply walked away from their old homes to the new ones that could be bought, custom-made, for less than half the price of a prewar structure and could be changed at small cost, to accommodate need of additional space or just a passing whim.

"I have something to say," said Webster. "Something that should have been said long ago. Something all of you should hear."

"Alderman Griffin said the city is dying on its feet and his statement is correct. There is but one fault I would find with it and that is its understatement. The city . . . this city, any city . . . is already dead."

"The city is an anachronism. It has outlived its usefulness. Hydroponics and the helicopter spelled its downfall. In the first instance the city was a tribal place, an area where the tribe banded together for mutual protection. In later years a wall was thrown around it for additional protection. Then the wall finally disappeared but the city lived on because of the conveniences which it offered trade and commerce. It continued into modern times because people were compelled to live close to their jobs and the jobs were in the city."

"But today that is no longer true. With the family plane, one hundred miles today is a shorter distance than five miles back in 1930. Men can fly several hundred miles to work and fly home when the day is done. There is no longer any need for them to live cooped up in a city."

"The automobile started the trend and the family plane finished it. Even in the first part of the century the trend was noticeable—a movement away from the city with its taxes and its stuffiness, a move toward the suburb and close-in acreages. Lack of adequate transportation, lack of finances held many to the city. But now, with tank farming destroying the value of land, a man can buy a huge acreage in the country for less than he could a city lot forty years ago. With planes powered by atomics there is no longer any transportation problem."

"So what have we?" asked Webster. "I'll tell you what we have. Street after street, block after block, of deserted houses, houses that the people just up and walked away from. Why should they have stayed? What could the city offer them? None of the things that it offered the generations before them, for progress had wiped out the need of the city's benefits. They lost something, some monetary consideration, of course, when they left the houses. But the fact that they could buy a house twice as good for half as much, the fact that they could live as they wished to live, that they could develop what amounts to family estates after the best tradition set them by the wealthy of a generation ago—all these things outweighed the leaving of their homes."

"And what have we left? A few blocks of business houses. A few acres of industrial plants. A city government geared to take care of a million people without the million people. A budget that has run the taxes so high that eventually even business houses will move to escape those taxes. Tax forfeitures that have left us loaded with worthless property. That's what we have left."

"If you think any Chamber of Commerce, any bally-hoo, any hare-brained scheme will give you the answers, you're crazy. There is only one answer and that is simple. The city as a human institution is dead. It may struggle on a few more years, but that is all."

Source: City by Clifford Simak. Copyright © 1952 by Clifford Simak, renewed 1980. Reprinted by permission of the estate of Clifford Simak.

Questions for Review and Discussion

1. What would be the effect on urban land use of the invention of a relatively safe airplane for household use? Do you agree with Simak's verdict in the excerpt from *City*?
2. "The invention of the car guaranteed the decline of the city." Do you agree or disagree? Explain.
3. "Given a choice, a city is better off building a subway system than a baseball stadium." Do you agree or disagree? Explain.
4. "If a highway is congested, it is too small for the existing demand and should be expanded." Do you agree or disagree? Explain.
5. "Highway congestion is a good thing because it forces people to live closer to work, reducing urban sprawl." Do you agree or disagree? Explain.
6. "It is inefficient for roads in the CBD not to be crowded." Do you agree or disagree? Explain.
7. Does your college or university charge you a market price to park your car? Does the university charge a higher price to students (considering the relative remoteness of the parking lots) than to faculty and staff?
8. It could be argued that firms are unwilling to develop alternatively fueled cars and that consumers are unwilling to purchase these cars because of the presence of sunk costs and uncertainty. Can you think of government policies that could serve to reduce either the sunk costs or the uncertainties? Are such policies currently being advocated or implemented in your area?

References

Adams, Charles, Howard B. Fleeter, Yul Kim, Mark Freeman, and Imgon Cho (1996). "Flight from Blight and Metropolitan Suburbanization Revisited." *Urban Affairs Review* 31:529–543.

Alfred, Stephen, and Charles Marcoux (1970). "Impact of a Community Association on Integrated Suburban Housing Patterns." *Cleveland State Law Review* 19:90–99.

Alonso, William (1964). *Location and Land Use*. Cambridge, MA: Harvard University Press.

Ardrey, Robert (1970). *The Social Contract: A Personal Inquiry into the Evolutionary Sources of Order and Disorder*. New York: Atheneum.

Arnott, Richard (1995). "Time for Revisionism on Rent Control?" *Journal of Economic Perspectives* 9:99–120.

Asimov, Isaac (1954). *The Caves of Steel*. New York: Ballantine Books (1983).

Austrian, Ziona, and Susan Helper (1990). "Trade and Education." *REI Review* Fall 1990:20–21.

Baer, William (1986). "The Shadow Market in Housing." *Scientific American* 255:29–35.

Baim, Dean (1994). *The Sports Stadium as a Municipal Investment*. Westport, CT: Greenwood Press.

Bairoch, Paul (1988). *Cities and Economic Development: From the Dawn of History to the Present*. Chicago: University of Chicago Press.

Bartik, Timothy (1991). *Who Benefits from State and Local Economic Development Policies?* Kalamazoo, MI: W.E. Upjohn Institute for Employment Research.

Bartik, Timothy (1994a). "What Should the Federal Government Be Doing About Urban Economic Development?" Staff Working Paper 94-25. Kalamazoo, MI: W.E. Upjohn Institute for Employment Research.

Bartik, Timothy (1994b). "Jobs, Productivity, and Local Economic Development: What Implications Does Economic Research Have for the Role of Government?" *National Tax Journal* 47:847–861.

Barzel, Yoram, and Tim Sass (1990). "The Allocation of Resources by Voting." *Quarterly Journal of Economics* 105:745–771.

Baumol, William (1967). "Macroeconomics of Unbalanced Growth: The Anatomy of Urban Crisis." *American Economic Review* 62:415–426.

Baumol, William, and David Bradford (1970). "Optimal Departures from Marginal Cost Pricing." *American Economic Review* 60:265–283.

Berechman, Joseph, and Robert Paaswell (1983). "Rail Rapid Transit and CBD Revitalisation: Methodology and Results." *Urban Studies* 20:471–486.

Berkovec, James, Glenn Canner, Stuart Gabriel, and Timothy Hannan (1994). "Race, Redlining, and Residential Mortgage Loan Performance." Unpublished paper presented at the Conference on Information and Screening in Real Estate, Federal Reserve Bank of Philadelphia, March 1994.

Berliant, Marcus, and Hideo Konishi (1994). "The Endogenous Formation of a City: Population Agglomeration and Marketplaces in a Location-Specific Production Economy." Working paper. Department of Economics, University of Rochester.

Berry, Brian, and William Garrison (1958a). "The Functional Bases of the Central Place Hierarchy." *Economic Geography* 34:145–154.

Berry, Brian, and William Garrison (1958b). "A Note on Central Place Theory and the Range of a Good." *Economic Geography* 34:304–311.

Bingham, Richard D., and Deborah Kimble (1995). "The Industrial Composition of Edge Cities and Downtowns: The New Urban Reality." *Economic Development Quarterly* 9:259–272.

Black, Dan A., and William H. Hoyt (1989). "Bidding for Firms." *American Economic Review* 79:1249–1256.

Boal, William (1995). "Testing For Employer Monopsony in Turn-of-the-Century Coal Mining." *RAND Journal of Economics* 26:519–536.

Boarnet, Marlon (1995). "The Economic Effects of Highway Congestion." Working Paper 1995-34. University of California, Irvine.

Boarnet, Marlon (1996). "Geography and Public Infrastructure." Working Paper. University of California, Irvine.

Boarnet, Marlon, and William T. Bogart (1996). "Enterprise Zones and Employment: Evidence from New Jersey." *Journal of Urban Economics* 40:198–215.

Boarnet, Marlon, and Randall Crane (forthcoming). "L.A. Story: A Reality Check for Transit-Based Housing." *Journal of the American Planning Association.*

Bogart, William T. (1993). "What Big Teeth You Have! Identifying the Motivations for Exclusionary Zoning." *Urban Studies* 30:1669–1681.

Bogart, William T. (1995). "Environmental Contamination As a Local Tax." In *Papers and Proceedings of the Eighty-Sixth Annual Conference of the National Tax Association.* Columbus, OH: National Tax Association-Tax Institute of America. 153–159.

Bogart, William T., and David Bradford (1990). "Incidence and Allocation Effects of the Property Tax and a Proposal for Reform." In M. Hughes and T. McGuire (eds.) *Research in Urban Economics* 8. Greenwich, CT: JAI Press. 59–82.

Boulding, Kenneth E. (1963). "The Death of the City." In Handlin and Burchard (eds.) op. cit. 133–145.

Bradford, David (1978). "Factor Prices May Be Constant But Factor Returns Are Not." *Economics Letters* 1:199–203.

Bradford, David, and Wallace Oates (1974). "Suburban Exploitation of Central Cities and Governmental Structure." In H. Hochman and G. Peterson (eds.) *Redistribution Through Public Choice*. New York: Columbia University Press. 43–90.

Brezis, Elise, and Paul Krugman (1993). "Technology and The Life Cycle of Cities." NBER Working Paper #4561. Cambridge, MA: National Bureau of Economic Research.

Brueckner, Jan, and David Fansler (1983). "The Economics of Urban Sprawl: Theory and Evidence on the Spatial Sizes of Cities." *Review of Economics and Statistics* 65:479–482.

Business Week. 13 July, 1992. "The grass is looking greener for landowners." p. 31.

Capozza, Dennis, and Robert Helsley (1989). "The Fundamentals of Land Prices and Urban Growth." *Journal of Urban Economics* 26:295–306.

Carlino, Gerald, and Edwin Mills (1987). "The Determinants of County Growth." *Journal of Regional Science* 27:39–54.

Caro, Robert (1974). *The Power Broker: Robert Moses and the Fall of New York*. New York: Vintage Books.

Carr, James, and Isaac Megbolugbe (1993). "The Federal Reserve Bank of Boston Study on Mortgage Lending Revisited." *Journal of Housing Research* 4:277–313.

Case, Anne, and Lawrence Katz (1991). "The Company You Keep: The Effects of Family and Neighborhood on Disadvantaged Youth." NBER Working Paper #3705. Cambridge, MA: National Bureau of Economic Research.

Center for Regional Economic Issues (1991). "Manufacturing and Cleveland Neighborhoods: A Databook." Cleveland: Center for Regional Economic Issues.

Ciccone, Antonio, and Robert E. Hall (1996). "Productivity and the Density of Economic Activity." *American Economic Review* 86:54–70.

Citizens League of Greater Cleveland (1994). "Rating the Region: Closing the Gap." *Citizen Participation* June 1994.

Coase, Ronald (1960). "The Problem of Social Cost." *Journal of Law and Economics* 3:1–44.

Colten, Craig, and Peter Skinner (1996). *The Road to Love Canal: Managing Industrial Waste Before EPA*. Austin, TX: University of Texas Press.

Courant, Paul (1994). "How Would You Know a Good Economic Development Policy If You Tripped Over One? Hint: Don't Just Count Jobs." *National Tax Journal* 47:863–881.

Courant, Paul, and Alan Deardorff (1992). "International Trade with Lumpy Countries." *Journal of Political Economy* 100:198–210.

Courant, Paul, and Alan Deardorff (1993). "Amenities, Nontraded Goods, and the Trade of Lumpy Countries." *Journal of Urban Economics* 34:299–317.

Crain's Cleveland Business. 3 July 1995. "Most traveled intersections in Cuyahoga County." p. M-12.

Crain's Cleveland Business. 4 December 1995. "Ace of the aviation industry." p. B-47.

Crane, Randall (1996). "The Influence of Uncertain Job Location on Urban Form and the Journey to Work." *Journal of Urban Economics* 39:342–356.

Cromwell, Brian (1990). "Pro-Integrative Subsidies and Housing Markets: Do Race-Based Loans Work?" Working Paper #9018. Cleveland, OH: Federal Reserve Bank of Cleveland.

Cromwell, Brian (1991). "Public Sector Maintenance: The Case of Local Mass-Transit." *National Tax Journal* 44:199–212.

Crone, Theodore, and Richard Voith (1992). "Estimating House Price Appreciation: A Comparison of Methods." *Journal of Housing Economics* 2:324–338.

Curran, Christopher, and Joel Schrag (1996). "Trust No Agent: An Analysis of Real Estate Agency Relationships." Working Paper. Department of Economics, Emory University.

Davis, Kingsley, ed. (1973). *Cities: Their Origin, Growth, and Human Impact*. San Francisco: W. H. Freeman and Company.

DeCoster, Gregory, and William Strange (1993). "Spurious Agglomeration." *Journal of Urban Economics* 33:273–304.

de Tocqueville, Alexis (1840). *Democracy In America, Volume II*. Translated by Henry Reeve, edited by Phillips Bradley. New York: Random House (1945).

Dickens, Charles (1854). *Hard Times*. New York: Bantam Books (1981).

DiPasquale, Denise, and William Wheaton (1996). *Urban Economics and Real Estate Markets*. Englewood Cliffs, NJ: Prentice-Hall.

Dixit, Avinash, and Robert Pindyck (1994). *Investment Under Uncertainty*. Princeton, NJ: Princeton University Press.

Dowall, David (1996). "An Evaluation of California's Enterprise Zone Programs." *Economic Development Quarterly* 10:352–368.

Downs, Anthony (1992). *Stuck in Traffic: Coping with Peak-Hour Traffic Congestion*. Washington: Brookings Institution / Lincoln Institute of Land Policy.

Downs, Anthony (1994). *New Visions for Metropolitan America*. Washington: Brookings Institution / Lincoln Institute of Land Policy.

Dunphy, Robert (1993). "Houston Takes a Businesslike Approach to Regaining Mobility." *Urban Land* 52:31–34.

Eaton, B. Curtis, and Richard Lipsey (1976). "The Non-Uniqueness of Equilibrium in the Löschian Location Model." *American Economic Review* 66:77–93.

Eaton, Jonathan, and Zvi Eckstein (1994). "Cities and Growth: Theory and Evidence from France and Japan." NBER Working Paper #4612. Cambridge, MA: National Bureau of Economic Research.

Eberts, Randall (1995). "Urban Labor Markets." Staff Working Paper #95-32. Kalamazoo, MI: W.E. Upjohn Institute for Employment Research.

Eberts, Randall, and Michael Fogarty (1987). "Estimating the Relationship Between Local Public and Private Investment." Working Paper #8703. Cleveland, OH: Federal Reserve Bank of Cleveland.

Eberts, Randall, and Joe Stone (1992). *Wage and Employment Adjustment in Local Labor Markets*. Kalamazoo, MI: W.E. Upjohn Institute for Employment Research.

EcoCity Cleveland (1996). *Moving to Cornfields*. Cleveland Heights, OH: EcoCity Cleveland.

The Economist, 14 September 1991. "Running out of road." p. 80.

The Economist, 16 July 1994. "The tyranny of triangles." p. 65.

The Economist, 8 April 1995. "Surely not rent controls?" p. 70.

The Economist, 29 July 1995. "Turn up the lights: A survey of cities."

The Economist, 30 September 1995. "The revolution begins, at last." pp. 15–16.

The Economist, 18 November 1995. "From highway to my way." pp. 29–31.

The Economist, 25 November 1995. "It's a small town, after all." pp. 27–28.

The Economist, 23 December 1995. "The strange death of corporationville." pp. 73–75.

The Economist, 13 April, 1996. "Yes, parking." p. 63.

The Economist, 4 May 1996. "Single market, single minded." pp. 63–64.

The Economist, 20 July 1996. "Has Cleveland mortgaged its tomorrows?" pp. 22–23.

Ellickson, Robert (1982). "Cities and Homeowners Associations." *University of Pennsylvania Law Review* 130:1519–1588.

Engels, Friedrich (1844). *The Condition of the Working Class in England*. Edited with an introduction by David McLellan. New York: Oxford University Press. (1993).

Evans, Michael, and Barry Barovick (1994). *The Ernst & Young Almanac and Guide to U.S. Business Cities*. New York: John Wiley & Sons, Inc.

Feldstein, Martin, and Charles Horioka (1980). "Domestic Saving and International Capital Flows." *Economic Journal* 90:314–329.

Fernandez, Roberto (1994). "Race, Space, and Job Accessibility: Evidence from a Plant Relocation." *Economic Geography* 70:390–416.

Fischel, William (1985). *The Economics of Zoning Laws: A Property-Rights Approach to American Land Use Controls*. Baltimore: Johns Hopkins University Press.

Fischel, William (1992). "Property Taxation and the Tiebout Model: Evidence for the Benefit View from Zoning and Voting." *Journal of Economic Literature* 30:163–169.

Fischel, William (1994). "Zoning, Nonconvexities, and T. Jack Foster's City." *Journal of Urban Economics* 35:175–181.

Fisher, Ronald (1996). *State and Local Public Finance, 2nd Edition*. Homewood, IL: Irwin.

Fishman, Robert (1987). *Bourgeois Utopia: The Rise and Fall of Suburbia*. New York: Basic Books.

Florida, Richard, and Donald F. Smith, Jr. (1993). "Venture Capital Formation, Investment, and Regional Industrialization." *Annals of the Association of American Geographers* 83:434–451.

Fortune, 26 July, 1993. "How jobs die—and are born." p. 26.

Fortune, 20 February, 1995. "Cars that beat traffic." pp. 64–72.

Freeman, Richard (1992). "Crime and the Employment of Disadvantaged Youths." In George Peterson and Wayne Vroman (eds.) *Urban Labor Markets and Job Opportunity*. Washington, DC: Urban Institute.

Freeman, Richard, and Brian Hall (1987). "Permanent Homelessness in America?" *Population Research and Policy Review* 6:3–27.

Frieden, Bernard, and Lynne Sagalyn (1989). *Downtown, Inc.: How America Rebuilds Cities*. Cambridge, MA: MIT Press.

Galster, George (1990a). "Neighborhood Racial Change, Segregationist Sentiments, and Affirmative Marketing Policies." *Journal of Urban Economics* 27:344–361.

Galster, George (1990b). "White Flight from Racially Integrated Neighborhoods in the 1970s: The Cleveland Experience." *Urban Studies* 27:385–399.

Garber, Carter (1990). "Saturn: Tomorrow's Jobs, Yesterday's Myths." In John Gaventa, Barbara Ellen Smith, and Alex Willingham (eds.) *Communities in Economic Crisis: Appalachia and the South*. Philadelphia: Temple University Press. 175–189.

Garreau, Joel (1991). *Edge City: Life on the New Frontier*. New York: Doubleday.

Garreau, Joel (1994). "Edge Cities in Profile." *American Demographics* 16:24–33.

Garrett, Randall, and Lin Carter (1957). "Masters of the Metropolis." In *Takeoff!* Norfolk / Virginia Beach, VA: The Donning Company (1986).

George, Henry (1880). *Progress and Poverty*. New York: Robert Schalkenbach Foundation (1955).

Giuliano, Genevieve, and Kenneth Small (1991). "Subcenters in the Los Angeles Region." *Regional Science and Urban Economics* 21:163–182.

Glaeser, Edward, Hedi Kallal, José Scheinkman, and Andrei Schleifer (1992). "Growth in Cities." *Journal of Political Economy* 100:1126–1152.

Gottlieb, Paul (1994). "Amenities as an Economic Development Tool: Is There Enough Evidence?" *Economic Development Quarterly* 8:270–285.

Gould, John, and Joel Segall (1969). "The Substitution Effects of Transportation Costs." *Journal of Political Economy* 77:130–137.

Gramlich, Edward, Deborah Laren, and Naomi Sealand (1992). "Moving into and out of Poor Urban Areas." *Journal of Policy Analysis and Management* 11:273–287.

Greater Cleveland Regional Transit Authority (1995). "Dual Hub Corridor Improvement Plan: A Project of Transit 2010." Cleveland, OH: Greater Cleveland Regional Transit Authority.

Hamilton, Bruce (1975). "Zoning and Property Taxation in a System of Local Governments." *Urban Studies* 12:205–211.

Hamilton, Bruce (1976). "Capitalization of Intrajurisdictional Differences in Local Tax Prices." *American Economic Review* 66:743–753.

Hamilton, Bruce (1982). "Wasteful Commuting." *Journal of Political Economy* 90:1035–1053.

Hamilton, Bruce (1989). "Wasteful Commuting Again." *Journal of Political Economy* 97:1497–1504.

Handlin, Oscar, and John Burchard, eds. (1963). *The Historian and the City*. Cambridge, MA: Harvard University Press and MIT Press.

Hansmann, Henry (1991). "Condominium and Cooperative Housing: Transactional Efficiency, Tax Subsidies, and Tenure Choice." *Journal of Legal Studies* 20:25–71.

Harris, Chauncy D. (1954). "The Market as a Factor in the Localization of Industry in the United States." *Annals of the Association of American Geographers* 64:315–348.

ed Suburbs: Toronto's American Tragedy, 1900 to 1950.
versity Press.

ral Government and Urban Housing: Ideology and Change
y, NY: State University of New York Press.

rugman (1985). *Market Structure and Foreign Trade.* Cam-

Urban Development: Theory, Fact, and Illusion. New York:

"Some Favorable Impacts of a U.S.-Mexico Free Trade
Employment." In Peter Garber (ed.) *The Mexico-U.S. Free*
e, MA: MIT Press. 129–161.

ncoro, and Matt Turner (1995). "Industrial Development in
Economy 103:1067-1090.

nd Gateway." *Urban Land* 52:34–37.

. "Correspondence: Public Investment in Infrastructure."
ectives 7:231–233.

Spatial Mismatch Hypothesis: What Has the Evidence
105–122.

k Employment Problems: New Evidence, Old Questions."
and Management 13:699–722.

ll Filer (1993). "Causes of Intercity Variation in Homeless-
Review. 83:248–255.

iles: The Building of the Subways and How They Transformed
non & Schuster.

tability in Competition." *Economic Journal* 39:41–57.

Hoyle, Fred (1987). me to Slippage City." In *Element 79.* New York: Signet (New American Library).

Hubert, Franz (1993). "The Impact of Rent Control on Rents in the Free Sector." *Urban Studies* 30:51–61.

Hughes, Mark (1989). "Concentrated Deviance and the 'Underclass' Hypothesis." *Journal of Policy Analysis and Management* 8:274–282.

Hughes, Mark, and Therese McGuire (1991). "A Market for Exclusion: Trading Low-Income Housing Obligations under Mount Laurel III." *Journal of Urban Economics* 29:207–217.

Ihlanfeldt, Keith, and Madelyn Young (1994). "Intrametropolitan Variation in Wage Rates: The Case of Atlanta Fast-Food Workers." *Review of Economics and Statistics* 76:425–433.

International Energy Agency (1993). *Cars and Climate Change.* Paris: Organization for Economic Cooperation and Development / International Energy Agency.

Isserman, Andrew M. (1980). "Estimating Export Activity in a Regional Economy: A Theoretical and Empirical Analysis of Alternative Methods." *International Regional Science Review* 5:155–184.

Jackson, Jerry (1979). "Intraurban Variation in the Price of Housing." *Journal of Urban Economics* 6:464–479.

Jackson, Kenneth T. (1985). *Crabgrass Frontier: The Suburbanization of the United States*. New York: Oxford University Press.

Jacobs, Jane (1969). *The Economy of Cities*. New York: Random House.

Jaffe, Adam (1986). "Technological Opportunity and the Spillovers of R&D: Evidence from Firms' Patents Profits and Market Value." *American Economic Review* 76:984–1001.

Jaffe, Adam (1989). "Real Effects of Academic Research." *American Economic Review* 79:957–970.

Jencks, Christopher (1994). *The Homeless*. Cambridge, MA: Harvard University Press.

Johnson, Arthur (1993). *Minor League Baseball and Local Economic Development*. Urbana and Chicago: University of Illinois Press.

Jordan, Robert (1984). *Conan the Victorious*. New York: Tom Doherty Asssociates.

Justman, Moshe (1994). "The Effect of Local Demand on Industry Location." *Review of Economics and Statistics* 77:742–753.

Kain, John (1968). "Housing Segregation, Negro Employment, and Metropolitan Decentralization." *Quarterly Journal of Economics* 82:175–197.

Kain, John, and John Quigley (1975). *Housing Markets and Racial Discrimination: A Microeconomic Analysis*. New York: National Bureau of Economic Research.

Keating, W. Dennis (1994). *The Suburban Racial Dilemma: Housing and Neighborhoods*. Philadelphia: Temple University Press.

Kelly, Barbara M. (1993). *Expanding the American Dream: Building and Rebuilding Levittown*. Albany, NY: SUNY Press.

Kenen, Peter (1985). *The International Economy*. Englewood Cliffs, NJ: Prentice-Hall.

Khadduri, Jill, and Kathryn Nelson (1992). "Targeting Housing Assistance." *Journal of Policy Analysis and Management* 11:21–41.

Kilgore, James (1971). "The White Man Pressed the Locks." In *A Time of Black Devotion*. Ashland, OH: Ashland Poetry Press.

Kim, Sukkoo (1995). "Expansion of Markets and the Geographic Distribution of Economic Activities: The Trends in U.S. Regional Manufacturing Structure, 1860–1987." *Quarterly Journal of Economics* 110:881–908.

Kingsbury, George W. (1915). *History of Dakota Territory*. Chicago: The S. J. Clarke Publishing Company.

Kirman, Alan (1992). "Whom or What Does the Representative Individual Represent?" *Journal of Economic Perspectives* 6:117–136.

Knight, Richard V. (1973). *Employment Expansion and Metropolitan Trade*. NY: Praeger Publishers.

Krugman, Paul (1991a). *Geography and Trade*. Cambridge, MA: MIT Press.

Krugman, Paul (1991b). "Cities in Space: Three Simple Models." NBER Working Paper #3607. Cambridge, MA: National Bureau of Economic Research.

Krugman, Paul (1995). *Development, Geography, and Economic Theory*. Cambridge, MA: MIT Press.

Krugman, Paul, and Gordon Hanson (1993). "Mexico-U.S. Free Trade and the Location of Production." In Peter Garber (ed.) *The Mexico-U.S. Free Trade Agreement*. Cambridge, MA: MIT Press. 163–186.

Krugman, Paul, and Raul Livas Elizondo (1996). "Trade Policy and the Third World Metropolis." *Journal of Development Economics* 49:137–150.

Ladd, Helen, and John Yinger (1989). *America's Ailing Cities: Fiscal Health and the Design of Urban Policy*. Baltimore: Johns Hopkins University Press.

Lampard, Eric E. (1955). "The History of Cities in the Economically Advanced Areas." *Economic Development and Cultural Change* 3:81–136.

Lancaster, Kelvin (1980). "Intra-Industry Trade under Perfect Monopolistic Competition," *Journal of International Economics* 10:151–175.

Lawrence, Robert, and Robert Litan (1987). "The Protectionist Prescription: Errors in Diagnosis and Cure." *Brookings Papers on Economic Activity* 1:289–310.

Leamer, Edward (1984). *Sources of International Comparative Advantage: Theory and Evidence*. Cambridge, MA: MIT Press.

Leamer, Edward (1987). "Paths of Development in the Three-Factor, *n*-Good General Equilibrium Model." *Journal of Political Economy* 95:961–999.

Leamer, Edward (1993). "Wage Effects of a U.S.-Mexican Free Trade Agreement." In Peter Garber (ed.) *The Mexico-U.S. Free Trade Agreement*. Cambridge, MA: MIT Press. 57–125.

Le Guin, Ursula K. (1974). *The Dispossessed*. New York: Harper & Row.

Levine, Lawrence (1988). *Highbrow/Lowbrow: The Emergence of Cultural Hierarchy in America*. Cambridge, MA: Harvard University Press.

Lewis, Sinclair (1922). *Babbitt*. New York: New American Library (1961).

Liu, Ben-Chieh (1976). *Quality of Life Indicators in U.S. Metropolitan Areas: A Statistical Analysis*. New York: Praeger.

Lund, Leonard (1986). *Locating Corporate R&D Facilities*. New York: Conference Board.

Macdonald-Taylor, Loma (1992). "Metropolitan Tax-Base Sharing: An Alternative to Tax Abatement for CALE?" Unpublished research paper. Department of Economics, Case Western Reserve University.

Manson, Robert (1987). "*Ball* in Play: The Effect of *Ball v. James* on Special District Voting Scheme Decisions." *Columbia Journal of Law and Social Problems* 21:87–136.

Marshall, Alfred (1920). *Principles of Economics,* 8th ed. New York: Macmillan (1952).

Marshall, John U. (1989). *The Structure of Urban Systems*. Toronto: University of Toronto Press.

McCallum, John (1995). "National Borders Matter: Canada-U.S. Regional Trade Patterns." *American Economic Review* 85:615–623.

McDonald, John (1992). "Assessing the Development Status of Metropolitan Areas." In Mills and McDonald (eds.) op. cit. 86–121.

McMillen, Daniel (1993). "Can Blacks Earn More in the Suburbs? Racial Differences in Intra-metropolitan Earnings Variation." *Journal of Urban Economics* 33:135–150.

McMillen, Daniel, and John McDonald (1993). "Could Zoning Have Increased Land Values in Chicago?" *Journal of Urban Economics* 33:167–188.

McMillen, Daniel, and Larry Singell, Jr. (1992). "Work Location, Residence Location, and the Intraurban Wage Gradient." *Journal of Urban Economics* 32:195–213.

McNeill, William (1976). *Plagues and Peoples*. Garden City, New York: Doubleday.

Meyer, John, and José Gomez-Ibañez (1981). *Autos, Transit, and Cities*. Cambridge, MA: Harvard University Press.

Meyer, John, John Kain, and Martin Wohl (1965). *The Urban Transportation Problem*. Cambridge, MA: Harvard University Press.

Mieszkowski, Peter, and Edwin Mills (1993). "The Causes of Metropolitan Suburbanization." *Journal of Economic Perspectives* 7:135–147.

Mieszkowski, Peter, and Mahlon Straszheim, eds. (1979). *Current Issues in Urban Economics*. Baltimore: Johns Hopkins University Press.

Mieszkowski, Peter, and George Zodrow (1989). "Taxation and the Tiebout Model: The Differential Effects of Head Taxes, Taxes on Land Rents, and Property Taxes." *Journal of Economic Literature* 27:1098–1146.

Mills, David (1989). "Is Zoning a Negative-Sum Game?" *Land Economics* 65:1–12.

Mills, Edwin (1967). "An Aggregative Model of Resource Allocation in a Metropolitan Area." *American Economic Review (Papers and Proceedings)* 57:197–210.

Mills, Edwin (1972). *Studies in the Structure of the Urban Economy*. Baltimore: Johns Hopkins University Press.

Mills, Edwin, and Bruce Hamilton (1989). *Urban Economics,* 4th ed. Glenview, IL: Scott, Foresman, and Company.

Mills, Edwin, and John McDonald, eds. (1992). *Sources of Metropolitan Growth*. New Brunswick, NJ: Center for Urban Policy Research.

Mills, Edwin, and Ronald Simenauer (1996). "New Hedonic Estimates of Regional Constant Quality House Prices." *Journal of Urban Economics* 39:209–215.

Mojtabai, A. G. (1986). *Blessed Assurance: At Home with the Bomb in Amarillo, Texas*. Boston: Houghton Mifflin Company.

Money magazine web site (http://pathfinder.com)

More, Thomas (1515). *Utopia*. Translated by Paul Turner. New York: Penguin Books (1965).

Moroney, John, and James Walker (1966). "A Regional Test of the Hecksher-Ohlin Hypothesis." *Journal of Political Economy* 74:573–586.

Morse, George, and Michael Farmer (1986). "Location and Investment Effects of a Tax Abatement Program." *National Tax Journal* 39:229–236.

Moses, Leon, and Harold F. Williamson, Jr. (1967). "The Location of Economic Activity in Cities." *American Economic Review (Papers and Proceedings)* 57:211–222.

Mumford, Lewis. (1961). *The City in History: Its Origins, Its Transformations, and Its Prospects*. New York: Harcourt, Brace, & World.

Munnell, Alicia (1992). "Policy Watch: Infrastructure Investment and Economic Growth." *Journal of Economic Perspectives* 6:189–198.

Munnell, Alicia, Geoffrey Tootell, Lynn Browne, and James McEneaney (1996). "Mortgage Lending in Boston: Interpreting HMDA Data." *American Economic Review* 86:25–53.

Muth, Richard (1969). *Cities and Housing: The Spatial Pattern of Urban Residential Land Use*. Chicago: University of Chicago Press.

Newsweek, 15 May 1995. "Bye-bye, suburban dream." pp. 40–53.

New York Times, 20 February 1988. "Starrett City's sound racial policy."

New York Times, 19 October 1988. "Jersey tells town to plan housing despite lack of open land." p. B1.

New York Times, 26 May 1996. "Sprawling Phoenix getting a downtown." p. Y26.

Norman, Victor, and Anthony Venables (1995). "International Trade, Factor Mobility, and Trade Costs." *Economic Journal* 105:1488-1504.

Noyelle, Thierry, and Thomas Stanback, Jr. (1984). *The Economic Transformation of American Cities*. Totowa, NJ: Rowman & Allanheld.

Oates, Wallace, E. Phillip Howrey, and William Baumol (1971). "The Analysis of Public Policy in Dynamic Urban Models." *Journal of Political Economy* 79:142–153.

Oates, Wallace, and Robert Schwab (1995). "The Impact of Urban Land Taxation: The Pittsburgh Experience." Working Paper. Cambridge, MA: Lincoln Institute of Land Policy.

Ohlin, Bertil (1933). *Interregional and International Trade*. Cambridge, MA: Harvard University Press.

Okner, Benjamin (1974). "Subsidies of Stadiums and Arenas." In *Government and the Sports Business*, Roger Noll (ed.). Washington: Brookings Institution.

Ottensmann, John R. (1996). "The New Central Cities: Implications of the New Definition of the Metropolitan Area." *Urban Affairs Review* 31:681–691.

Papke, Leslie (1993). "What Do We Know About Enterprise Zones?" In *Tax Policy and the Economy*, James Poterba (ed.). Cambridge, MA: MIT Press.

Papke, Leslie (1994). "Tax Policy and Urban Development: Evidence from the Indiana Enterprise Zone Program." *Journal of Public Economics* 54:37–49.

Pellechio, Anthony (1988). "Taxation, Rental Income, and Optimal Holding Periods for Real Property." *National Tax Journal* 41:97–107.

Plain Dealer, 24 August 1992. "Cars will crash every stop sign." p. 3-C.

Plain Dealer, 5 March 1993. "Zoning plan riles some Avon residents." p. 1-C.

Plain Dealer, 1 August 1994. "Opening soon at a site near you." p. 1-A, 8-A.

Plain Dealer, 12 December 1995. "Old couch on porch is no longer welcome." p. 8-A.

Plain Dealer, 17 December 1995a. "Experts rush to reconsider highway safety." p. 27-A.

Plain Dealer, 17 December 1995b. "Speeding was concern way back when." p. 27-A.

Plain Dealer, 21 December 1995. "National City loan policies questioned." p. 1-C.

Pogodzinski, J. M., and Tim Sass (1990). "The Economic Theory of Zoning: A Critical Review." *Land Economics* 66:294–314.

Pogodzinski, J. M., and Tim Sass (1991). "Measuring the Effects of Municipal Zoning Regulations: A Survey." *Urban Studies* 28:597–621.

Pohl, Frederik, and C. M. Kornbluth (1955). *Gladiator-At-Law*. New York: Ballantine Books.

Porter, Michael (1994). "The Competitive Advantage of the Inner City." Discussion paper, Harvard Business School.

Pred, Allan (1966). *The Spatial Dynamics of U.S. Urban-Industrial Growth, 1800–1914: Interpretive and Theoretical Essays*. Cambridge, MA: MIT Press.

Price, Richard, and Edwin Mills (1985). "Race and Residence in Earnings Determination." *Journal of Urban Economics* 17:1–18.

Rabelais, François (1546). *The Histories of Gargantua and Pantagruel, Book III*. Translated and with an introduction by J. M. Cohen. New York: Penguin Books (1955).

Rauch, James (1993a). "Does History Matter Only When It Matters Little? The Case of City-Industry Location." *Quarterly Journal of Economics* 108:843–867.

Rauch, James (1993b). "Productivity Gains from Geographic Concentration of Human Capital." *Journal of Urban Economics* 34:380–400.

Reschovsky, Andrew (1980). "An Evaluation of Metropolitan Area Tax Base Sharing." *National Tax Journal* 33:55–66.

Ricketts, Erol, and Isabel Sawhill (1988). "Defining and Measuring the Underclass." *Journal of Policy Analysis and Management* 7:316–325.

Roback, Jennifer (1982). "Wages, Rents, and the Quality of Life." *Journal of Political Economy* 90:1257–1278.

Rolleston, Barbara (1987). "Determinants of Restrictive Suburban Zoning: An Empirical Analysis." *Journal of Urban Economics* 21:1–21.

Romer, Paul (1994). "New Goods, Old Theory, and the Welfare Costs of Trade Restrictions." *Journal of Development Economics* 43:5–38.

Rossi, Peter H. (1955). *Why Families Move: A Study in the Social Psychology of Urban Residential Mobility*. Glencoe, IL: The Free Press.

Rossi, Peter H. (1989). *Down and Out in America: The Origin of Homelessness*. Chicago: University of Chicago Press.

Rothenberg, Jerome, George Galster, Richard Butler, and John Pitkin (1991). *The Maze of Urban Housing Markets: Theory, Evidence, and Policy*. Chicago: University of Chicago Press.

Rubin, Marilyn (1990). "Urban Enterprise Zones: Do They Work? Evidence from New Jersey." *Public Budgeting and Finance* 10:3–17.

Rusk, David (1995). *Cities Without Suburbs,* 2nd ed. Washington, DC: Woodrow Wilson Press.

Samuelson, Paul (1954). "The Pure Theory of Public Expenditure." *Review of Economics and Statistics* 36:387–389.

Schelling, Thomas (1978). *Micromotives and Macrobehavior*. New York: W. W. Norton and Co.

Schwab, Robert, and Wallace Oates (1991). "Community Composition and the Provision of Local Public Goods: A Normative Analysis." *Journal of Public Economics* 44:217–237.

Schworm, Lisa (1995). "Property Value Differences in Similar Communities: A Comparison of Brecksville and Broadview Heights." Unpublished senior honors thesis. Department of Economics, Case Western Reserve University.

pact Studies: A Fashionable Excess." In *Economic Impact* enver, CO and Washington, D.C.: National Conference of

nage to Earth." In *The Wonderful World of Robert Sheck-* (1979).

Without Zoning. Lexington, MA: D.C. Heath & Co.

York: Ace Fantasy Books (1983).

Vheaton (1992). "Wage and Rent Capitalization in the ." *Journal of Urban Economics* 31:206–229.

ansportation Economics. Philadelphia: Harwood Aca-

(1992). "'Wasteful' Commuting: A Resolution." *Jour-* -898.

Nations. Chicago: University of Chicago Press (1976).

hussen (1980). "Neighborhood Stability in Changing w 70:415–419.

Economics of Adam Smith." *Journal of Urban Eco-*

ldings on Cheap Land: Building Heights and Intra-*Irban Economics* 29:310–328.

Luce (1987). *Economic Development Within the* adelphia: University of Pennsylvania Press.

3). "An Economic Evaluation of Calgary's North-*istics and Transportation Review* 19:351–365.

in the Woods. New York: Penguin Books (1980).

). A Pure Theory of Local Expenditures." *Journal of Political* Economy 64:416–424.

Toledo Blade, 24 November 1996. "Modern stadium can create a winning image." p. A10.

USA Today, 23 September 1996. "Widening income gap divides USA." p. 1B and continuing.

Veblen, Thorstein (1899). *The Theory of the Leisure Class*. New York: New American Library (1953).

Voith, Richard (1994). "Do Suburbs Need Cities?" Working Paper #93-27. Philadelphia: Federal Reserve Bank of Philadelphia.

Wallace, Nancy (1988). "The Market Effects of Zoning Undeveloped Land: Does Zoning Follow the Market?" *Journal of Urban Economics* 23:307–326.

Warner, Sam Bass, Jr. (1962). *Streetcar Suburbs: The Process of Growth in Boston, 1870–1900*. Cambridge, MA: Harvard University Press / MIT Press.

Wall Street Journal, 8 April 1992. "Different road." p. A1.

Wall Street Journal, 14 August 1996. "Allstate relaxes standards on selling homeowners' policies in poor areas." p. A3.

Wassmer, Robert (1993). "The Use and Abuse of Economic Development Incentives in a Metropolitan Area." *Proceedings of the Eighty-Sixth Annual Conference, National Tax Association*. 146–157.

Weiss, Leonard (1972). "The Geographic Size of Markets in Manufacturing." *Review of Economics and Statistics* 54:245–257.

Weitzman, Martin (1974). "Prices *vs.* Quantities." *Review of Economic Studies* 41:477–491.

Wells, H.G. (1895). *The Time Machine*. New York: Bantam Books (1968).

Wheaton, William (1977). "Income and Urban Residence: An Analysis of Consumer Demand." *American Economic Review* 67:620–631.

White, Michelle (1986). "Property Taxes and Urban Housing Abandonment." *Journal of Urban Economics* 20:312–330.

White, Michelle (1988). "Urban Commuting Journeys Are Not 'Wasteful.'" *Journal of Political Economy* 96:1097–1110.

Wilson, J. D. (1987). "Trade in a Tiebout Economy." *American Economic Review* 77:431–441.

Wolkoff, Michael (1985). "Chasing a Dream: The Use of Tax Abatements to Spur Urban Economic Development." *Urban Studies* 22:305–315.

Yinger, John (1979). "Prejudice and Discrimination in the Urban Housing Market." In P. Mieszkowski and M. Straszheim (eds.) op. cit. 430–468.

Yinger, John (1986). "Caught in the Act: Measuring Racial Discrimination with Fair Housing Audits." *American Economic Review* 76:881–893.

Yount, Kristen, and Peter Meyer (1994). "Bankers, Developers, and New Investment in Brownfield Sites: Environmental Concerns and the Social Psychology of Risk." *Economic Development Quarterly* 8:338–344.

Index

Abrams, Charles, 208–209
accelerated depreciation, 287
actual expenditure needs, 247
actual fiscal health, 247
Adams, Charles, 181, 248
adjustment costs, housing, 278–279
adverse impact, 310. *See also* discrimination
agglomeration economies of scale, 11–14
  false, 124–126, 146–147
  localization, 12–13, 127–136
  metropolitan growth and, 122–143
  nontradables and, 110
  urbanization, 12–13, 122–127
agriculture, 10–11
  innovation in, 25
  land available for, 226–227
  origins of, 227
Alfred, Stephen, 314
Alonso, William, 178
anonymity, 26
Ardrey, Robert, 296–297
area probability design, 269. *See also* homelessness
Arnott, Richard, 306
Asimov, Isaac, 36–38
athletic teams, and economic development, 167–171
attraction, economic development and, 158–160
Austrian, Ziona, 92–93
autarky
  definition of, 74
  economies of scale and, 114
  production/consumption under, 82–84
automatic vehicle identification (AVI), 326
automobiles
  alternative fuels and, 332
  commuting and, 320–334
  highways and, 331
  household mobility and, 196
  mass transit and, 336–337
  pollution and, 331–332
  subsidization of, 336–337
  suburban development and, 208

Babbitt (Lewis), 172–173
Baer, William, 291
Baim, Dean, 167, 168–169, 170–171
Bairoch, Paul, 26, 27, 31, 35–36
Baltimore, MD, 169, 170–171

barriers
  effects of removing, 138–140
  effects of trade, 108–109
  entry, monopolistic competition and, 40–41
  nontradables as, 109–110
  trade, and factor mobility, 108–109
  zoning as, 212–216
Bartik, Tim, 152, 157, 158–159, 233, 238, 239
Barzel, Yoram, 228
Baumol, William, 111–112, 164–165, 336
Berechman, Joseph, 338
Berkovec, James, 311–312
Berliant, Marcus, 39, 62
Berry, Brian, 42–43
Bible, 116–117
bid-rent curve, 185–186
  factor substitution and, 187–189
  in household location decisions, 191–193
Bingham, Richard, 200
blatant discrimination, 310. *See also* discrimination
blockbusting, 315–316
Boal, William, 132–133
Boarnet, Marlon, 159–160, 161, 162, 338
Bogart, William T., 159–160, 236–237, 242
Boston, MA, 194
Boulding, Kenneth, 141–143
Bradford, David, 155–156, 236–237, 244–245, 336
Brecksville, OH, 283–284
Brezis, Elise, 136
Broadview Heights, OH, 283–284
Brogan, Denis, 125
Browne, Lynn, 310
brownfields problem, 240–241
Brueckner, Jan, 227
budget constraints, 99–100
  and household location decisions, 190–193
building height
  and land value at city edges, 189–190
  and residential density, 184
bus systems, 335
Butler, Richard, 283
buyers' agents, 293–294

Calgary, Canada, 338
Canada, trade with United States, 136–137
Canner, Glenn, 311–312

capital
  effects of tax on, 156–158
  public sector, 160–163
capital gains, housing and, 285–286
capital-land ratios
  distance from CBD and, 178
  effects of taxes on, 156–158
Capozza, Dennis, 189–190
Carlino, Gerald, 52
Caro, Robert, 331
Carr, James, 310, 311
Carter, Lin, 19–21
Case, Anne, 259
Caves of Steel, The (Asimov), 36–38
Celebration, FL, 229
census blocks, 308–309
census tracts, 308–309
Center for Regional Economic Issues, 197–199
central business districts (CBDs)
  demolition costs of transforming, 245–246
  household income and distance from, 194–195
  in monocentric cities, 177–178
  wage differences and, 254–259
central cities, definition of, 9
central place theory, 48–51
  application of in location decision, 58–59
  firm orientation and, 58–69
Chicago, IL, 208, 209, 216
China, urban structure in, 138
Cho, Imgon, 181, 248
Ciccone, Antonio, 14, 62
cities. *See also* suburbs
  ability of to annex surroundings, 34–35, 179–181, 248
  benefits of growth of, 147–153
  central, as developing countries, 248–250
  communication and, 202–203
  competition between, 232–253
  costs of growth of, 152–155
  definitions of, 3–24
  in developing countries, 125, 166
  economic definitions of, 7–10
  forms/models of, 177–206
  future of, 200–202
  growth patterns of and principle of median location, 59–61
  hierarchies of, 49–51
  historical patterns of productivity and, 62
  history of, 25–38

cities (*continued*)
  international trade policy and
    growth of, 165–167
  largest, 5–6
  limits to growth of, 11
  lumpiness and, 104–108
  measuring economic size of, 13–14
  measuring/relieving fiscal distress of,
    246–248
  optimally sized, 18–19
  political definitions of, 10
  quality of life rankings of, 63–67
  reasons for growth/nongrowth of,
    10–11
  size distribution of, 17–19, 32–36
  as small open economies, 4–6
City (Simak), 339–341
Cleveland, OH
  busiest intersections in, 182
  clustered manufacturing in,
    197–199
  CMSA in relation to Ohio, 7, 8, 9, 10
  dissimilarity index for, 308
  economy of, 4
  intergovernment competition and,
    238–239
  light rail system in, 338–339
  neighborhood tipping in, 314
  professional sports in, 169–171
  quality of life ranking of, 63–65
  suburbs and, 179–180
climate improvement, economic development and, 158–159
clustering
  in Europe, 137–138
  intermediate inputs and, 133–134
  and investment decisions, 146–147
  and negative externalities, 13
  technology/inventiveness and,
    134–136
  and worker education/skill level,
    162–163
Coase, Ronald, 23–24
Coase point, 219
Coase Theorem
  congestion taxes and, 325
  and zoning as collective property
    right, 218–220
cocaine, 270
Colten, Craig, 24
communication
  clustering and, 12
  technology and urbanization, 27
  and urban structure, 202–203
commuting, 319–334
  alternative fuels and, 332
  congestion and, 321–324
  congestion tolls and, 324–327
  costs, monocentric model and,
    193–195

  costs of, 322–323
  estimating minimum, 332–333
  highway capacity and, 329–331
  intermodal cost comparisons,
    334–335
  mass transit and, 334–339
  modal choice in, 320–321
  negative externalities of, 324
  pollution and, 331–332
  public transportation in, 320
  social costs of, 323–324
  three parts of, 320
  wasteful, 332–334
company towns, 132–133
comparative advantage, 73–80
  of central cities, 249–250
  definition of, 11
  preferences, relative size, transport
    costs, trading patterns and,
    76–78
  spurious agglomeration and false,
    124–126
  trade, wages and, 78–80
compensating differentials, 110, 111
compensation rule, 220
competition, intrametropolitan,
  232–253
complements, location decisions and,
  52
Comprehensive Environmental
  Response, Compensation,
  and Liability Act (CERCLA),
  240–241
compressed natural gas (CNG), 332
Conan the Victorious (Jordan), 44–45
*Condition of the Working Class in Eng-
  land, The* (Engels), 186–187,
  272–274
condominiums
  associations, 228–229
  conversion of low-income housing
    to, 304–305
congestion tolls, 324–327
  collection methods for, 326
consolidated metropolitan statistical
  areas (CMSAs), definition of, 7
conspicuous consumption, 26
conspicuous leisure, 26
constitutional issues, in zoning,
  211–212
consumption
  determining, 77–78
  location quotients and, 148–150
  possibilities, budget constraint,
    99–100
consumption effect, 80
consumption zoning, 242
contagion effects, 259
core-periphery model, 122–124
  intermediate inputs and, 133–134

  investment decisions in, 145–147
  reduction of trade barriers and,
    138–139
  services in, 140–141
  and size distribution, 17–18
cost minimization, 96–100
  factor substitution and, 98–100
cost-minimizing scales of production,
  35–36
costs. *See also* transport costs
  adjustment, in housing, 278–279
  communication, 202–203
  commuting, 193–195, 322–324
  of converting land use, 190
  demolition, 245–246
  distribution, 56, 58–59
  of growth of cities, 152–155
  housing maintenance, 285,
    288–290
  procurement, 56
  production, 43, 122–124, 155–165
  sunk, 144–147
  transaction, 220–221, 295
coterminous jurisdictions, 235–236
countries
  central cities as developing,
    248–250
  as collections of cities, 136–140
  defining, 136
  developing, cities in, 125, 166
  lumpy, trade and, 104–108
Courant, Paul, 107–108, 152, 154–155,
  196
covenants, exclusionary, 313,
  315–316
covenants not to sue, 241
Crane, Randall, 279, 338
Cranston-Gonzalez National Affordable Housing Act of 1990,
  304–305
crime, as income, 258–259
Cromwell, Brian, 313, 316, 337
Crone, Theodore, 281
cross-hauling, 148
cultural opportunities, 22
Curran, Christopher, 293
Current System, 244–245

Davis's Law, 17–19
Dayton, OH, 239
deadweight losses, 81
  of taxation, 245
Deardorff, Alan, 107–108, 196
"Death of the City, The" (Boulding),
  141–143
DeCoster, Gregory, 125
demand, change in, 100
demolition costs, 245–246
density
  of economic activity, 3

and location decisions, 47, 48
population, 3–4
and productivity advantages, 14
residential, 184, 192–193
depreciation, accelerated, 287
"Description of a City Shower, A"
   (Swift), 28
deterioration
   of housing, 288–290
   model of, 164–165
   neighborhood, 289
Detroit, MI, 235
deviant behavior, poverty as,
   262–267
Dickens, Charles, 21–22
differential factor endowments, 11
differentials, compensating, 110, 111
DiPasquale, Denise, 46–47
discounted present value, 290–291
discrimination. *See also* segregation
   definition of, 307
   household mobility and, 266–267
   housing markets and, 306–316
   spatial mismatch hypothesis and,
      259–262
   types of, 310–311
disease, cities and, 27–29
disparate treatment, 310. *See also* discrimination
Dispossessed, The (Le Guin), 53–54
dissimilarity index, 307–308
distribution costs, 56, 58–59. *See also*
   transport costs
diversification
   triangles of, 119–120
diversification, *vs.* labor pooling,
   129–130
Dixit, Avinash, 144–147
Dowall, David, 160
Downs, Anthony, 200–201, 319, 320,
   326
downtown distribution phase, 320
due process, 211

Eaton, B. Curtis, 42
Eaton, Jonathan, 34
Eberts, Randall, 66, 152, 153, 160–162,
   257
Eckstein, Zvi, 34
economic activity
   and definition of edge city, 8–9
   density of, 3
   location of, 55–70
   measuring, 181–184
economic development
   and central cities as developing
      countries, 248–250
   central city *vs.* suburbs in, 240–246
   factor mobility in, 111–112
   infrastructure and, 160–163

job costs under, 233
mass-transit construction as,
   337–339
policies, intrametropolitan competi-
   tionand, 232–253
policies, taxonomy of, 158–160
stadium construction and, 167–171
three-factor case of, 117–121
two-factor case of, 111–112
economic development policies
   measuring/alleviating fiscal distress
      in, 246–248
   race for ratables in, 236
   social benefits from, 239
economies of scale, 11. *See also* comparative advantage
   agglomeration, 11–14
   external, 12
   internal, 11–12, 61
   localization, 12–13, 127–136
   residential density and, 184
   transportation, 57
   urbanization, 12–13, 122–127
Economist, The, 132, 202
Economy of Cities, The (Jacobs),
   251–252
edge cities. *See also* polycentric city
   model
   as centers, 181–184
   definition of, 8–9, 184
   demolition costs and, 245–246
   future of, 200–202
   parking in, 327
   specialization in, 199–200
Edgeworth, Francis Ysidro, 75
Edgeworth Box
   factor price equalization in,
      102–103
   flexible factor proportions for,
      90–91
   nontradables factor price equaliza-
      tion in, 110
   potential gains and, 75–76
education
   level and income, 260
   and worker productivity, 162–163
elastic cities, 248
Ellickson, Robert, 228
emissions retrictions, 332
employment
   centers of in U.S., 9
   decentralization of, 240–241
   density in suburban centers,
      182–184
   effects of taxes on, 157
   enterprise zones and, 159–160
   and homelessness, 270
   job-creation policies and, 152
   multipliers and, 147–151
   race and access to, 259–262

urban growth and, 152–153
U.S. distribution of, 15–16
variations in composition of, 246,
   247
worker skill/education level and,
   162–163, 257
empowerment zones, 159–160
endowment effect, 221, 222
endowment triangles, 119–121
Engels, Friedrich, 186–187, 289–290
   *The Condition of the Working Class in
      England,* 272–274
England, Industrial Revolution in,
   29–30
enterprise zones, 159–160
   spatial mismatch and, 262
entitlements diagrams, 219–220
entry barriers, monopolistic competition and, 40–41. *See also*
   barriers
Environmental Protection Agency
   (EPA), 166
equal protection, 211–212
equilibrium
   flexible factor proportions and,
      91–93
   housing markets, 291–293
   integrated, 102–103, 133–134
   knife-edge/unstable, 129
   location with endogenous price,
      46–47
   location with given price, 45–46
   monopolistic competition and,
      41–42
   partial, 80–81
   real wages in, 86
   taxes and, 155–158
   trade, wages in, 78–80
Euclid v. Ambler, 211, 220
Europe
   automobile use in, 337
   capital cities in, 125
   city size in, 34–36
   population density in, 13
   specialization in, 137–138
European Union (EU), 138
exclusion, in housing, 313
exponential specification, 282
export base theory, 147–148. *See also*
   multipliers
exports
   base theory of, 147–151
   central city development and,
      249–250
   central place theory and, 49–51
   definition of, 147
   location quotients and, 93
   net *vs.* total, 148
   tourism as, 250
exposure index, 308

expressways, 331. *See also* highways; transportation
external economies of scale. *See* agglomeration economies of scale
externalities, 21–24
  from better housing, 302–303
  definition of, 3–4
  housing maintenance and, 289
  internalizing, 23
  model for, 22–24
  negative, 13, 22
  positive, 22
  property rights and, 23–24
  responses to, 23–24
  zoning as response to, 216–218
Ezekiel (book of Bible), 116–117

factor abundance theory. *See* Hecksher-Ohlin model
factor intensity reversal, 88
factor price equalization, 101–104
  with nontradables, 109–110
  region, 103–104, 108
factors
  cost-minimizing combinations of, 88–90
  economic development and mobility of, 111–112
  endowments of, 117–119
  flexible proportions of, 88–93
  input-output analysis and, 150–151
  lumpiness in, 104–108
  mobility of and trade barriers, 108–109
  monopolistic competition and, 114
  output effect and, 98
  price equalization in, 101–104
  prices and product prices, 79–80
  of production, 85–88
  regional allocation of and international trade, 107–108
  relative prices of, 88–89
  Rybczynski Theorem and, 90–91
  substitution and cost minimization, 98–99
factor substitution, 56, 98
  and rent gradients, 187–189
false agglomeration, 124–126, 146–147
Fannie Mae, 301
Fansler, David, 227
Farmer, Michael, 235–236
Federal Housing Administration (FHA), 300–301
  racial covenants and, 313
  redlining by, 309–310
Federal National Mortgage Association (FNMA), 301
Federal Reserve Bank of Boson, 310
Feldstein, Martin, 163
Fernandez, Roberto, 259–260

fertility rates, 28
Filer, Randall, 271
filtering model, 294–295
  public housing and, 302–303
firms
  cost minimization by, 96–98
  definition of, 96
  economic impact of, 147–155
  inframarginal, 39–40
  input-oriented, 56, 113
  investment decision by, 144–147
  marginal, 39–40
  strategic interaction among, 45–48
  targeting, 236
first nature, of sites, 62
fiscal burden, 217
fiscal health
  actual, 247
  standardized, 246–248
fiscal zoning, 241–242
Fischel, William, 211, 220, 225, 227, 228–229
Fisher's law, 286
Fishman, Robert, 187, 208
Fleeter, Howard B., 181, 248
flight from blight, 181. *See also* suburbs
Florida, Richard, 135
Fogarty, Michael, 160–162
food surplus, 10–11, 25
footloose firms, 61–62
Foster City, CA, 228–229
Freeman, Mark, 181, 248
Freeman, Richard, 258, 268
free-rider problem, 216, 223. *See also* public goods
Fund for the Future of Shaker Heights, 316

Gabriel, Stuart, 311–312
gains from exchange, 84
gains from specialization, 84
Galster, George, 283, 314
game theory, 45–48
Gargantua and Pantagruel (Rabelais), 24
Garreau, Joel, 6–7, 8–9, 17, 177, 184, 199–200, 229, 327–328
Garrett, Randall, 19–21
Garrison, William, 42–43
gasoline taxes, 326, 331
General Motors, 149–150, 238
gentrification, 295
George, Henry, 190
Giuliano, Genevieve, 182, 183, 200
Gladiator-at-Law (Pohl, Kornbluth), 204–205
Glaeser, Edward, 13
Gomez-Ibañez, Josè, 326, 327, 335, 337
Gottlieb, Paul, 167
Gould, John, 44

government. *See also* zoning
  approaches to economic development policy, 158–160
  and business investment decisions, 145–147
  centralized, and size distribution, 17–19
  competition among as prisoner's dilemma, 237–239
  cooperation between, 238–239
  costs/benefits of urban growth for, 147–155
  determining economic policy spending for, 232–237
  factor mobility, trade barriers and, 108–109
  housing maintenance/deterioration and, 289–290
  housing policies, 271
  housing policy, federal, 299–305
  income accounting/constraints and, 163–164
  Industrial Revolution and, 30
  infrastructure and, 160–163
  international trade policy and urban growth, 165–167
  pollution regulation, 166
  productivity changes and, 111–112
  and public goods, 223–225
  responses to externalities, 23–24
  shadow, 229
  short-/long-run effects of policy, 164–165
  subsidies, 154–155
  takings, 212, 220
  taxes and business location, 155–165
  urban growth and, 144–173
Gramlich, Edward, 266–267
gravity models, 51–52
Greater Cleveland Committee for Co-operative Economic Development, 238–239
gross price, 40–41
  for equilibrium location with endogenous price, 46–47

Hall, Brian, 268
Hall, Robert E., 14, 62
Hamilton, Bruce, 224–225, 246, 332, 334
Hannan, Timothy, 311–312
Hansmann, Henry, 288
Hanson, Gordon, 139
Hard Times (Dickens), 21–22
Harris, Chauncy D., 52
Harrisburg, PA, 170
Hays, R. Allen, 300
Hecksher-Ohlin model, 92–93
  economic development patterns and, 111–112
  economies of scale in, 127

factor price equalization and, 101–104
monopolistic competition and, 114
natural resources in, 117–121
public goods and, 115
reduction of trade barriers and, 139–140
transport costs and, 113
hedonic price analysis, 279–284
example of, 283–284
price calculation in, 281–283
hedonic price indices, 281–283
Helper, Susan, 92–93
Helpman, Elhanan, 103, 114, 133–134
Helsley, Robert, 189–190
Henderson, J. Vernon, 13, 15, 17–18, 111, 138, 140, 165
heroic extrapolation, 268. *See also* homelessness
highways
capacity of, 329–331
design capacity of, 321–322
and labor markets, 161–162
and movement of manufacturing, 257
type of and cost per mile, 330
Hirzel, David, 167, 169
Holtz-Eakin, Douglas, 160
Holzer, Harry, 260
homelessness, 267–272
causes of, 269–271
definition of, 268
measuring, 268–269
shelters and, 271–272
Home Mortgage Disclosure Act (HMDA), 310
homeowners' associations, 228–229
Home Owners Loan Corporation (HOLC), 309–310
Honig, Marjorie, 271
Horioka, Charles, 163
Hotelling, Harold, 45–46
households
female-headed, 263–264
income level and suburbanization of, 181
location decisions of, 190–193, 241–243, 332–334
mobility of poor, 266–267
utility maximization by, 98–100
housing
abandonment of, 289
adjustment costs of, 278–279
affordable, zoning and, 241–243
as commodity, 275–279
conversion of nonhousing property to, 291
demand/supply in, 284–293
durability of, 278
expense/income relationship in, 278

federal policy on, 299–305
filtering model of, 294–295
hedonic price analysis of, 279–284
heterogeneity of, 276–277
immobility of, 278
land use by, 275
maintenance of, 285, 288–290
market equilibrium, 291–293
markets, 275–298
ownership rates of, 299–300
personal preferences in, 276–277
price indices, 280–281
public, 301–303
quality of, 217, 249, 300
race and, 306–316
real estate agents and, 293–294
rent control and, 305–306
renting *vs.* purchasing, 276, 285–288
single room occupancy, 270–271
strategy, 261 (*See also* spatial mismatch)
submarkets in, 282–283
subsidies/allowances, 303–305
supply, 290–291
Housing Act of 1974, 304–305
Howrey, E. Phillip, 164–165
Hoyle, Fred, 68–69
Hubert, Franz, 306
Hughes, Mark, 243, 263–266

iceberg transportation costs, 74
Ihlanfeldt, Keith, 256
illegal activities, 258–259
imports
central place theory and, 49–51
computing, 4–5
location quotients and, 93
substitution and, 151, 166
incentives, 236
income
and access to job information, 257
city-suburban inequality in, 224
and education level, 260
effects of taxes on, 164–165
filtering model of housing and, 294–295
firm concentration and, 52
household, and surburbanization, 181
housing demand and, 290
housing expense relative to, 278
from illegal activities, 258–259
increase in household, and location decisions, 194–195
intrametropolitan differences in, 254–259
segregation by, 241–243
and urban fiscal health, 246–248

income accounting, 163–164
income effect, 100, 191
index of compatibility, 277
index of effectiveness, 276–277
indifference curves
community, 82–85
household, 98–100
income/amenities, 111
increasing returns to scale and, 84–85
labor market pooling and, 128–129
industrial complexes, 133–134
Industrial Revolution, 29–31
factor mobility and, 112
urbanization and, 26–27
industry, exodus of, 257. *See also* firms
inelastic cities, 248
information transfer, 135–136
ambiguous, 135
inframarginal firms, 39–40
infrastructure, economic development and, 160–163
injunctions, 23
innovation, cycle of, 135
input-oriented firms, 56
Hecksher-Ohlin model and, 113
input-output analysis, 150–151. *See also* multipliers
inputs
intermediate, 133–134
monetary weight of, 56
multiple, location theory and, 59–61
nontradable, location theory and, 61–62
single, location theory and, 55–57
substitutability of, 96–98
integer problems, 42–43
integrated rail systems, 335
International Energy Agency, 331–332
international trade policies, 165–167
interstate commerce, 108–109
intrasectoral trade, 114
investment decisions, 144–147
sunk costs in, 144
timing in, 144, 145–146
uncertainty in, 144–145
isocosts
bid-rent curves and, 187–188
cost minimization and, 96–98
curve of, 97
flexible factor proportions and, 88–90
isoquants
bid-rent curves and, 187–188
cost minimization and, 96–98
definition of, 96
deriving slope of, 97
flexible factor proportions and, 88–93
Isserman, Andrew M., 147

Jackson, Jerry, 178
Jackson, Kenneth T., 179, 181, 295, 331
Jacobs, Jane, 151, 227
   The Economy of Cities, 251–252
Jaffe, Adam, 134–135
Japan, parking in, 328–329
Jencks, Christopher, 269–270, 271
job-creation policies, 152
jobs strategy, 261, 262. *See also* spatial
   mismatch
Johnson, Arthur, 170
Jordan, Robert, 44–45
Justman, Moshe, 61–62

Kain, John, 260, 313, 320
Kallal, Hedi, 13
Katz, Lawrence, 259
Keating, W. Dennis, 316
Kelly, Barbara, 291
key person surveys, 268. *See also*
   homelessness
Khaddurri, Jill, 304
Kim, Sukkoo, 138
Kim, Yul, 181, 248
Kirman, Alan, 82
knife-edge equilibrium, 129
Knight, Richard V., 16
Konishi, Hideo, 39, 62
Kornbluth, C. M., 204–205
Krugman, Paul, 48, 58–59, 103, 114,
   124, 133–134, 136, 139, 166
Kuncoro, Ari, 13, 111

labor
   allocation of, 85–88
   division of and market size, 27
   impact of crime on markets, 258–259
   in location quotients, 148
   markets and highways, 161–162
   markets and poverty, 254–274
   markets and race, 259–262
   percentage of required to produce
      local services, 14–15
   pools, 12, 128–133
   skill differences in, 121
   supply and quality of life, 66
   unskilled, 270
Ladd, Helen, 246–248
Lancaster, Kelvin, 125–126
land development patterns, 225–227
landlords
   costs of, 285–287
   property abandonment by, 289
land rent
   at city edges, 189–190
   classical in monocentric model,
      185–195
   and distance from CBD, 178
   factor substitution and, 187–189
   housing density and, 192–193

and quality of life rankings, 66, 67
and wage differences, 254–256
land use
   and conflict resolution, 211–212
   controls, 207–231
   controls, and public goods, 223–225
   controls, and urban sprawl, 225–227
   controls, history of, 207–212
   controls, restrictiveness of, 220–223
   controls as collective property right,
      218–220
   controls as response to externalities,
      216–218
   controls as trade restrictions,
      212–216
   costs of converting, 190
   externalities associated with,
      216–218
   housing and, 208–209, 275
   percentage of rural in U.S., 8,
      209–210, 226–227
   private zoning and, 227–229
   and urban sprawl, 225–227
land value taxes, 236
Laren, Deborah, 266–267
Lave, Charles, 337
Lawrence, Robert, 163–164
Leamer, Edward, 117, 121, 140
leapfrog development, 225–226
Le Guin, Ursula K., 53–54
Leontief, Wassily, 150
Levine, Lawrence, 207–208
Levittown, NY, 291
Lewis, Sinclair, 172–173
liability rules, 23
life expectancy, 28, 29
linear specification, 282
line haul phase, 320. *See also*
   commuting
Lipsey, Richard, 42
Litan, Robert, 163–164
Liu, Ben-Chieh, 66, 67
Livas Elizondo, Raul, 166
localization economies of scale, 12–13,
   127–136
   intermediate inputs in, 133–134
   labor market pooling in, 128–133
   sources of, 12
   technological spillovers in in,
      134–136
locational orientation, 61–62
location decisions, firm, 55–70
   amenities and, 63–67
   brownfield sites and, 240–241
   communications costs and, 202–203
   economic development policies and,
      232–253
   equilibrium with endogenous price,
      46–47
   equilibrium with given price, 45–46

industrial parks and, 146–147
interdependent products and, 52
market potential and, 51–52
multiple markets/multiple inputs
   and, 59–61
nontradable inputs and, 61–62
with one input source/one market,
   55–57
relocation and, 146–147
service industries, 140–141
strategic interaction and, 45–48
tax abatements and, 232–237
taxes effects on, 155–165
location decisions, household, 190–193
   constraints on, 256
   inclusionary zoning and, 241–243
   and income increases, 194–195
   market potential and, 52
   wasteful commuting and, 332–334
location quotients, 93, 148–150. *See
   also* multipliers
   calculating, 149–150
Los Angeles, CA
   employment density in, 182–184
   suburbanization in, 179
lot-size restrictions, 215–216
low-income housing, 301–303
   negative externalities associated
      with, 217, 242
   stigma of, 302–303
   zoning and, 241–243
*Lucas v. South Carolina Coastal
   Commission,* 211, 220
Luce, Thomas F., 180–181
lumpy factor allocation, 104–108
   public goods and, 115
Lund, Leonard, 63

maintenance
   costs, housing, 285, 288–290
   mass transit equipment, 337
Manchester, England, 186–187,
   290–291
Manson, Robert, 228
manufacturing wages *vs.* service wages,
   256–257
Marcoux, Charles, 314
marginal benefit (MB) curves, 22–24
marginal cost curves, 22
marginal firms, 39–40
marginal rate of substitution, 98–99
marginal revenue product, 85–86
market areas, 39–54
   and central place theory, 48–51
   definition of, 40
   gravity models and, 51–52
   monopolistic competition *vs.* perfect
      competition in, 40
   space implications of, 30–40
   and strategic interaction, 45–48

market failures, 152, 154
market-oriented firms, 56
market potential, 51–52
markets for exclusion, 243
Marshall, Alfred, 31, 127–128
Marshall, John U., 34–35
mass transit, 334–339
   construction as development policy,
      337–339
   subsidizing, 336–337
"Masters of the Metropolis" (Garrett,
      Carter), 19–21
McCallum, John, 136–137
McDonald, John, 184, 216
McDonald's restaurants, 217
McEneaney, James, 310
McGuire, Therese, 243
McMillen, Daniel, 216, 255–256, 261
McNeill, William, 28
median location, principle of, 59–61
Megbolugbe, Isaac, 310
Memphis, TN, 179–180
mental hospitals, 269–270
metropolitan statistical areas
      (MSAs), 7
Meyer, John, 320, 326, 327, 335, 337
Meyer, Peter, 241
Mieszkowski, Peter, 181, 225
migration
   factor mobility and, 113
   inter- and intrametropolitan, 66,
      181, 248
Mills, David, 221
Mills, Edwin, 52, 135, 178, 181, 184,
      246, 260, 281
Minneapolis, MN, 239
mobility strategy, 261, 262. *See also*
      spatial mismatch
model of deterioration, 164–165
monetary weight of inputs, 56
Money magazine, 64–66
monocentric city model, 6–7, 177–178
   building height/city edges and,
      189–190
   classical land rent and, 185–195
   economic environment changes and,
      193–195
   household location decisions and,
      190–193
   wasteful commuting and, 332–334
monopolistic competition
   Hecksher-Ohlin model and, 114
   market areas and, 40–43
monopsonies, 132–133
Moore, Michael, 150
More, Thomas, 230–231
Moroney, John, 93
Morriss, Andrew, 233
Morse, George, 235–236
mortality rates, 28–29, 249

mortgages
   default rates, 311–312
   discrimination in, 309–312
   interest on, 285, 287, 299–300
   market for, 300–301
multipliers, 147–151
   definition of, 147
Mumford, Lewis, 25, 31, 125, 207
municipalities, 10
Munnell, Alicia, 160, 310
Muth, Richard, 178
mutually beneficial trade. *See* Pareto
      improvements

Nashville, TN
   growth of, 34
National Association of Realtors
      (NAR), 280
national boundaries, 136–137
National Housing Act of 1934, 300–301
natural evolution theory, 181
negative externalities. *See also* exter-
      nalities
   clustering and, 13
   definition of, 22
neighborhoods
   anti-tipping strategies for, 316
   definition of, 308–309
   deterioration of, 289
   housing revitalization and, 291
   life cycles of, 295
   tipping, 313–316
Nelson, Kathryn, 304
New Jersey
   mass transit in, 337
   zoning in, 242–243
New Orleans, LA, 34, 35
New York, NY
   cost of traffic congestion in, 324
   homelessness in, 268
   suburbs and, 179
   zoning in, 208
nonexcludable goods, 223
nonrival goods, 223
nontradables, 109–110
   factor price equalization and, 110
   inputs as, 61–62
   in polycentric model, 195–196
   public goods as, 115
Norfolk, VA, 170
Norman, Victor, 113
North American Free Trade Agree-
      ment (NAFTA), 121, 138–140
Noyelle, Thierry, 15–17
nuisance laws, 216. *See also* zoning

Oates, Wallace, 164–165, 236, 242,
      244–245
Olmsted, Frederick Law, 22
"one-story climb law, " 184

Ottensmann, John R., 9
outliers, 264
output effect, 98, 99
overlying jurisdictions, 235–236

Paaswell, Robert, 338
Panel Study of Income Dynamics
      (PSID), 266–267
Papke, Leslie, 159–160
Pareto, Vilfredo, 74
Pareto improvements
   in the absence of trade, 82–84
   definition of, 74
   transport costs and, 76–77
parking, 327–329
   taxes, 326–327
partial counts, 268. *See also* home-
      lessness
Perot, H. Ross, 138
Philadelphia, PA, 180–181
Phoenix, AZ, 169–170
Pigou, Arthur, 23
Pigouvian taxes
   congestian toll as, 325
   definition of, 23
"Pilgrimage to Earth" (Sheckley),
      93–95
Pindyck, Robert, 144–147
Pitkin, John, 283
Pittsburgh, PA, 236
Pogodzinski, J. M., 218
Pohl, Frederik, 204–205
political definitions of cities, 10
political economic zoning, 242–243
pollution
   commuting and, 331–332
   and decentralization, 240–241
   regulation, 166
polycentric city model, 6–7, 177, 178,
      179
   edge cities and services in, 199–200
   intrametropolitan trade and,
      195–200
   suburban specialization/trade in,
      196–197
   tradables/nontradables in, 195–196
population
   definition of urban, 7
   density, European *vs.* U.S., 3–5
   factor mobility and migration of,
      113
   intercity migration of, 66, 149, 181
   size distribution and, 17–19
   suburbs and, 180–181
   urbanization of, 26–27
Porter, Michael, 249–250
Portland, OR, 337
positive externalities, 22. *See also*
      externalities
potential gains, 75–76

poverty
    effect on children of, 267
    homelessness as, 267–272
    mobility and, 266–267
    underclass and, 262–267
    urban labor markets and, 254–274
Pred, Allan, 30, 32, 135
preferences
    comparative advantage and, 76
    household, 98–100
    increasing returns to scale and,
        84–85
prejudice. *See also* discrimination;
        segregation
    definition of, 307
    segregation due to, 313–316
Price, Richard, 260
price controls, 212–216
price discrimination, 313
price indices, housing, 280–283
primary metropolitan statistical areas
        (PMSAs), 7
principle of median location, 59–61
Principles of Economics (Marshall),
        127–128
prisoner's dilemma
    definition of, 237
    government competition as,
        237–239
    inclusionary zoning as, 243
    tax abatements and, 236
private covenants, 228–229
procurement costs, 56. *See also* trans-
        port costs
production
    complementarities in, 11
    costs, core-periphery model and,
        122–124
    costs and taxes, 155–165
    effect, 80
    factor lumpiness and, 104–108
    specific factors of, 85–88
    zoning as restriction on, 215–218
production possibility frontier (PPF),
        74, 79
    allocation of factors and, 90–91
    with increasing opportunity cost,
        82–83
    linear, 104–106
    nonlinear, 106–108
productivity
    changes in and governments,
        111–112
    private, and public capital, 160–162
    and worker education/skill level,
        162–163
products, linkages among, 133–134
profits, monopolistic competition and,
        40–43
Progress and Poverty (George), 190

property rights
    externalities and, 23–24
    zoning and, 211, 218–220
property rule, 220
public goods
    definition of, 223
    Hecksher-Ohlin model and, 115
    shadow governments for, 229
    Tiebout model and, 223–225
    zoning and, 223–225, 241–243
public health, 27–29
public housing, 301–303
public sector capital, 160–163
Public Use Micro Sample (PUMS),
        255–256

quality of life rankings, 63–67
Quigley, John, 313
quotas, 214
    factor mobility and, 108

Rabelais, François, 24
race for ratables, 236
railroads, 62
    intrametropolitan competition
        for, 233
rail systems, integrated, 335, 338–339
rank-size rule, 17–19
    central place theory and, 49–51
Rasmussen, David, 289
Rauch, James, 146–147, 162–163
real estate agents, 293–294
    discrimination by, 312–313
redlining, 309–312
    insurance, 312
regional contribution agreements
        (RCAs), 243
relative size, and comparative advan-
        tage, 76–77
rental price, 290
rent-control, 288, 305–306
rent gradient, 278–279
renting *vs.* purchasing housing, 276,
        285–288
repeat sales price indices, 280–281
Research Triangle, 134
reservation wage, 258
residential density, 184
resources, depletion of, 11
returns to scale, constant, 115
returns to scale, increasing, 84–85,
        126–127
revenue-raising capacity, 246–248
Ricardo, David, 185
Ricketts, Erol, 263–265
Roback, Jennifer, 66, 67
"Roger and Me" (Moore), 150
Rolleston, Barbara, 242
Romer, Paul, 84–85
Rossi, Peter H., 268–269, 271, 276–277

Rothenberg, Jerome, 283
Route 128, 134
Rubin, Marilyn, 159
rural areas
    central place theory and, 49
    as foundation of city growth, 10–11
    U.S. percentage of land used by, 8,
        226–227
rush hours, 319–320. *See also*
        commuting
Rusk, David, 34, 248
Rybczynski line, 106, 107
Rybczynski Theorem, 90–91

San Francisco, CA, 337
Sass, Tim, 218, 228
Sawhill, Isabel, 263–265
Scheinkman, Josè, 13
Schelling, Thomas, 313–314
Schleifer, Andrei, 13
Schrag, Joel, 293
Schwab, Robert, 236, 242
Schworm, Lisa, 283–284
Sealand, Naomi, 266–267
Seaman, Bruce, 151
second nature, of sites, 62
Section 8, 304–305
Section 235, 303
Section 236, 303
Section 221 (d)(3), 303–304
sector, definition of, 114
Segall, Joel, 44
segregation
    definition of, 307
    inclusionary zoning and, 241–243
    and job access, 309
    measuring, 307–309
    neighborhood tipping and, 313–316
    racial, in housing markets, 307–309
    spatial mismatch and, 259–262
services
    edge cities and, 199–200
    Industrial Revolution and, 31
    shift toward, 15–17
    specialization in, 15–17
    suburban use of central city, 243–245
    technological progress and, 26
    tradability of, 16–17
    vs. manufacturing, 140–141
    wages, *vs.* manufacturing, 256–257
Shaker Heights, OH, 316
Sheckley, Robert, 93–95
shelters, homeless, 271–272
Siegan, Barnard, 208
Silicon Valley, 134
Simak, Clifford, 339–341
Simenauer, Ronald, 281
Singell, Larry, Jr., 255–256
single-room occupancy (SRO) hous-
        ing, 270–271

sites
  first nature/second nature of, 62
  selection factors in, 63–67
Sivitanidou, Rena, 214, 255
Skinner, Peter, 24
slums, destruction of, 270
Small, Kenneth, 182, 183, 200, 322,
    323–324, 330, 335
small open economies
  cities as, 4–6
  suburbs as, 6–7
Smith, Adam, 27, 49
  city hierarchy of, 50
Smith, Donald F., Jr., 135
Snohomish County, WA, 49–50
social benefits, from economic devel-
    opment policies, 239
Social Contract, The (Ardrey), 296–297
social norms
  definition of, 263
  the underclass and, 262–267
society, fragmentation of, 207–208
*Southern Burlington County NAACP v.
    Mount Laurel,* 212
spatial mismatch, 259–262, 309
  approaches to alleviating, 261–262
  choosing, 261
  measuring, 260
specialization
  in cities *vs.* manufacturing, 15–18
  city size and, 35–36
  comparative advantage and, 74–76
  early history of, 25
  economic development and, 111–112
  and economies of scale, 11–13 (*See
    also* comparative advantage)
  in edge cities, 199–200
  in Europe, 137–138
  factor abundance and, 101–121
  factor endowments and, 119–121
  factor price equalization and,
    101–104
  fixed costs and, 85
  gains from, 84
  Industrial Revolution and, 30–31
  international trade and, 165–166
  suburban, in polycentric model,
    196–197
  in U.S. cities, 14–17
specific factors of production, 85–88
speed limits, 324
spurious agglomeration, 124–126
stadiums, 167–171
  benefits/costs of, 168–169
Stanback, Thomas, Jr., 15–17
standardized expenditure needs,
    246–248
standardized fiscal health, 246–248
Standard Zoning Enabling Act of
    1926, 211

Starrett City project, 316
steering, 312–313
Stegman, Michael, 289
Stone, Joe, 66, 152, 153
St. Paul, MN, 239
Strange, Will, 125
strategic interaction, 45–48
subsidies
  housing, 303–305
  mass transit, 336–337
  parking, 329
  public transportation, 327
  reduction in local economic welfare
    by, 154–155
  stadiums, and 167, 170–171
  and trade composition/balance,
    163–164
substitution
  import, 151
  location decisions and, 52
substitution effects
  of transportation costs, 44–45
  utility maximization and, 100, 191
suburban collection phase, 320
suburban downtown, definition of,
    184
suburbs
  as centers, 181–184
  competition of with central city,
    240–246
  education level and income in, 260
  and estimates of city size, 34
  exploitation of central cities by,
    243–245
  future of, 203
  history of, 178–181
  as small open economies, 6–7
  three-factor model of development
    of, 206
  zoning restrictiveness in, 220–223
subways, 335
Sullivan, Arthur, 189
Summers, Anita A., 180–181
Sun City, AZ, 229
sunk costs, in investment decisions,
    144–147
Superfund act, 240–241
Supreme Court
  exclusionary policies and, 313
  segregation and, 309
  zoning and, 210–212
Swift, Jonathan, 28

takings, 212, 220
targeting, 236
tariffs
  factor mobility and, 108
  and trade composition/balance, 164
  two-part, 336
  and urban growth, 165–167

zoning as, 212–216
tax abatements, 232–237
  alternatives to, 236–237
  costs/benefits of, 233–236
tax arbitrage, 287
taxes
  -base sharing, 239
  deadweight loss of, 245
  housing and, 285, 287, 299–301
  and location decisions, 155–165
  property, and housing abandon-
    ment, 289–290
  property, and zoning, 224–225
  property, housing and, 285
  true burden of, 240–241
technology
  congestion solutions and, 325
  effects on urban growth of, 136
  knowledge spillovers, 12, 134–136
  localization *vs.* urbanization
    economies of scale and, 31
  monocentric city model and, 185
  proximity and adoption of, 111
  specialization and, 26–27
  urbanization and, 26–27
terminal costs, 57. *See also* transport
    costs
Texas Transportation Institute, 324
Tiebout, Charles, 223–224, 244
Tiebout model, 223–225
  private zoning and, 228–229
Time Machine, The (Wells), 317–318
tipping, neighborhood, 313–316
tipping points, 314–315
toll roads, private, 330–331
Tootell, Geoffrey, 310
tourism, 250
townhouse associations, 228–229
townhouse developments, 203
toxic waste sites, 240–241
trade
  among suburbs in polycentric model,
    196–197
  barriers and factor mobility, 108–109
  definition of, 4–5, 77
  effects of on wages, 78–80
  factor lumpiness and, 104–108
  general equilibrium and, 82–84
  gravity models/market potential and,
    51–52
  Hecksher-Ohlin model of, 92–93
  increasing returns to scale and,
    84–85
  intermetropolitan, 73–100
  international policies on, 165–167
  intrasectoral, 114
  mutually beneficial, 74
  Pareto improvements in, 74
  partial equilibrium and, 80–81
  restrictions, zoning as, 212–216

training programs, 152
transaction costs, 113
  of housing conversion, 295
  of zoning, 220–221
transition matrix, 266–267
transportation, 319–341
  commuting/cars in, 319–334
  congestion in, 321–324
  congestion tolls, 324–327
  economies of scale in, 11
  efficient system design for, 319–320
  highway capacity and, 329–331
  mass transit, 334–339
  mass transit and, 334–339
  parking and, 327–329
  pollution and, 331–332
  rush hours and, 319–320
  separation of residential/commercial areas and, 207–208
  as site advantage, 62
  suburbanization and, 181
  technology and urbanization, 27
  wasteful commuting and, 332–334
transport costs
  building height and, 189–190
  comparative advantage and, 76–78
  distribution, 56
  Hecksher-Ohlin model and, 113
  iceberg, 74
  market areas and, 39–43
  partial equilibrium effects of, 80–81
  procurement, 56
  scale economies in, 57
  service industries and, 141
  substitution effects of, 44–45
triangles of diversification, 119–120
Turner, Matt, 13, 111
two-part tariffs, 336

uncertainty, investment decisions and, 144–147
underclass, the, 262–267
  defining/measuring, 263–266
  definition of, 263
  mobility of, 266–267
unemployment. See also employment
  and the production possibility frontier, 82
  rates and quality of life rankings, 66
Unified System, 244–245
United States
  Census Bureau, 7, 9, 254

as collection of small open economies, 4–6
Constitution, 108
Department of Commerce, 211
Dept. of Housing and Urban Development, 268, 304–305
differential growth in cities in, 33–36
Environmental Protection Agency, 166
Hecksher-Ohlin model and, 92–93
homelessness in, 269
home ownership in, 299–300
job centers in, 9
manufacturing belt emergence in, 124
percentage of urban population in, 7–8, 32
Supreme Court, 210–212, 309, 313
trade with Canada, 136–137
unjust relationships, 243–245
urbanization, preindustrial levels of, 27
urbanization economies of scale, 12–13, 122–127
  increasing returns to scale and, 126–127
  sources of, 12
  spurious agglomeration/false comparative advantage and, 124–126
urbanized areas, definition of, 7
urban places, definition of, 7
urban sprawl, 225–227. See also land use
utility maximization, 98–100
Utopia (More), 230–231

Veblen, Thorstein, 26
Venables, Anthony, 113
Voith, Richard, 281
von Thünen, Johann Heinrich, 48
voting, efficiency of, 228

wages. See also income
  crime as supplemental, 258–259
  and education level, 260
  effects of trade on, 78–80
  in equilibrium, 86
  and household location decisions, 256
  intrametropolitan differences in, 254–259
  labor pooling and, 130–132
  manufacturing vs. services, 256–257
  and quality of life rankings, 66, 67
  real, 79
  reservation, 258

Walker, James, 93
Wall Street Journal, 337
Walt Disney Company, 229
Warner, Sam Bass, Jr., 194, 208
Wassmer, Rob, 237
wealth effect of endowment, 221, 222
weight-gaining firms, 56
weight-losing firms, 56
  Hecksher-Ohlin model and, 113
Weiss, Leonard, 47, 48
Weitzman, Martin, 214–215
"Welcome to Slippage City" (Hoyle), 68–69
Wells, H. G., 317–318
Wheaton, William, 46–47, 194–195, 214, 255
White, Michelle, 289, 333–334
Wilson, J. D., 115
windshield street surveys/censuses, 268–269. See also homelessness
Wohl, Martin, 320
Wolkoff, Michael, 234–236
worker exploitation, 132–133

Yinger, John, 246–248, 307, 312–313
Young, Madelyn, 256
Yount, Kristen, 241

zero-sum games, 239
Zipf's Law, 17–19
  central place theory and, 49–51
Zodrow, George, 225
zoning, 207–231
  as collective property right, 218–220
  comprehensive, 210–211
  conflict resolution and, 211–212
  cumulative, 208
  definition of, 208
  excessive restrictiveness of, 220–223
  fiscal, 241–242
  and housing value, 278
  illegitimate preferences in, 221–222
  inclusionary, 241–243
  monopoly control of development by, 222–223
  prescriptive, 208
  private, 227–229
  and provision of local public goods, 223–225
  as response to externalities, 216–218
  segregation by, 241–243
  taxonomy of, 210–211
  as trade restriction, 212–216
  transactions costs, 220–221
  transit stations and, 337–338
  and urban sprawl, 225–227